Impoliteness in Language

Language, Power and
Social Process   21

Editors

Monica Heller
Richard J. Watts

Mouton de Gruyter
Berlin   ·   New York

Impoliteness in Language

Studies on its Interplay
with Power in Theory and Practice

edited by

Derek Bousfield
Miriam A. Locher

Mouton de Gruyter
Berlin · New York

Mouton de Gruyter (formerly Mouton, The Hague)
is a Division of Walter de Gruyter GmbH & Co. KG, Berlin.

Library of Congress Cataloging-in-Publication Data

Impoliteness in language : studies on its interplay with power in theory
and practice / edited by Derek Bousfield and Miriam A. Locher.
   p. cm. − (Language, power, and social process ; 21)
   Includes bibliographical references and index.
   ISBN 978-3-11-020266-3 (hardcover : alk. paper)
   ISBN 978-3-11-020267-0 (pbk. : alk. paper)
   1. Politeness (Linguistics)   2. Power (Social sciences)   3. Interpersonal relations. I. Bousfield, Derek.   II. Locher, Miriam A., 1972−
   P299.H66I47   2008
   306.44−dc22
                                2008001064

♾ Printed on acid-free paper which falls within the guidelines
of the ANSI to ensure permanence and durability.

ISBN 978-3-11-020266-3 hb
ISBN 978-3-11-020267-0 pb

Bibliographic information published by the Deutsche Nationalbibliothek

The Deutsche Nationalbibliothek lists this publication in the Deutsche
Nationalbibliografie; detailed bibliographic data are available in the Internet
at http://dnb.d-nb.de.

Cover design: Christopher Schneider.
Printed in Germany.

Acknowledgements

The idea for this collection of papers on impoliteness emerged in a discussion of the editors after the conference *Politeness: Multidisciplinary Perspectives on Language and Culture* in Nottingham in March 2005. We realised that there was neither a monograph nor an edited work on impoliteness available to researchers interested in the phenomenon and decided, rather grandly, to mend this. The result is what you hold in your hands. We would like to thank the general editors of the series *Language, Power, and Social Processes,* Richard J. Watts and Monica Heller, as well as Anke Beck, Rebecca Walter and Marcia Schwartz from Mouton for supporting this project and making it possible.

Our heartfelt thanks further go to the authors of the individual chapters of this edition. Not only were they exemplary in keeping to deadlines and in making revisions, they also participated extensively in the reviewing process and provided valuable feedback to their peers. Every chapter in this collection therefore received comments from at least three different authors, in addition to the critiques made by the external Mouton reviewers. To the latter, we also wish to express our thanks.

While this collection has been edited by 'Bousfield and Locher', and our introduction has been written by 'Locher and Bousfield', we would, however, prefer to be viewed as having shared equally both the editorial load for this project and the writing of the introduction. In this sense, we also share equally the responsibility for any editorial or authorial shortcomings that remain.

Last, but by no means least, the editors would like to thank their families for their patience, good humour and support.

We dedicate this work to them.

Miriam Locher
Derek Bousfield

Contents

Part 4. Workplace interaction

Part 5. Further empirical studies

Chapter 1
Introduction: Impoliteness and power in language

Miriam A. Locher and Derek Bousfield

1. Introduction

This collection of papers on impoliteness and power in language seeks to address the enormous imbalance that exists between academic interest in politeness phenomena as opposed to impoliteness phenomena. In 1990 Fraser presented a paper detailing the then four approaches to politeness.[1] Things have moved on somewhat since then. DuFon et al. (1994) identified an extensive bibliography of publications on politeness which runs to 51 pages. Eelen (1999, 2001) and Watts (2003) identified at least nine separate approaches to politeness and, indeed, Fraser (1999) notes that there are well over 1,000 books, papers and articles published on the concept of politeness. At this time little had been written or researched on impoliteness. The notable exceptions being Lachenicht (1980), Culpeper (1996, 1998) and Kienpointner (1997). In addition to Fraser's observation of the profligate nature of research in this area, Chen (2001: 87) has noted the "mammoth-like", and Xie (2003: 811) the "nearly geometric", increase in the number of texts dealing with, critiquing, 'correcting' or commenting upon politeness since Lakoff's seminal article introduced the concept to academic scrutiny in 1973 (Bousfield 2006: 9–10).

Since Fraser's original comments in December 1999 work on politeness has burgeoned yet further with well over a dozen research monographs and collections (cf. Beeching 2002; Bayraktaroğlu and Sifianou 2001; Eelen 2001; Fukushima 2000; Hickey and Stewart 2005; Holmes and Stubbe 2003b; Kumar 2001; Lakoff and Ide 2006; Lee-Wong 2000; Locher 2004; Marquez-Reiter 2000; Mills 2003; Mühleisen and Migge 2005; Pan 2000; Watts 2003; Youmans 2006) and at least 75 individual journal papers in production or in press on the phenomenon; circa 50 of these papers in-press are within the *Journal of Pragmatics* alone. Fraser (2006: 65) notes that the number of publications on politeness (since 1999) has increased "by several hundred." And Watts (2003: xi) mentions that his bibliographic collection of work on politeness "contains roughly 1,200 titles and is growing steadily week by week." Indeed, given Chen's and Xie's observations above, this growth may well be on the path to becoming virtually exponential, especially when we consider that 2005 witnessed the launching of *The Journal of Politeness Research* which must surely be testimony to the growing academic interest in the phenomenon. This has wide-reaching implications for such areas as cross-cultural communication, TEFL, TESOL and conflict resolution to name but four.

In the face of this continual rise in interest for politeness phenomena, our understanding of impoliteness, by contrast, has merely crawled forward. For example, at the time of writing this introduction, the *Journal of Pragmatics* lists just five papers dealing with impoliteness since its inception in 1977 (Hickey 1991; Culpeper 1996; Culpeper, Bousfield and Wichmann 2003; Rudanko 2006; Bousfield 2007b). There are, of course, some few other articles dealing with related phenomena that have been published in different journals (cf. Austin 1990; Beebe 1995; Bousfield 2007a; Culpeper 2005; Harris 2001; Kienpointner 1997; Lachenicht 1980; Mills 2005, to identify a few). However, a little more than a dozen articles on the phenomenon cannot hope to compete with the embarrassment of research riches which the concept of politeness enjoys. The paucity of research into impoliteness is telling, especially when we consider that several researchers (e.g. Craig, Tracey and Spisak 1986; Culpeper, Bousfield and Wichmann 2003; Tracy 1990) have argued that any adequate account of the dynamics of interpersonal communication (e.g. a model of politeness) should consider hostile as well as cooperative communication. Indeed, in response to claims made by researchers such as Leech (1983: 105), in that "conflictive illocutions tend, thankfully, to be rather marginal to human linguistic behaviour in normal circumstances", Culpeper, Bousfield and Wichmann (2003) make their case for the necessity of an impoliteness framework by noting (amongst other things) that:

> Conflictive talk has been found to play a role – and often a central one – in, for example, army training discourse (Culpeper 1996), courtroom discourse (Lakoff 1989; Penman 1990), family discourse (Vuchinich 1990), adolescent discourse (Labov 1972; Goodwin and Goodwin 1990), doctor-patient discourse (Mehan 1990), therapeutic discourse (Labov and Fanshel 1977), 'everyday conversation' (Beebe 1995) and fictional texts (Culpeper 1998; Liu 1986; Tannen 1990).
>
> (Culpeper, Bousfield and Wichmann 2003: 1545–1546)

In connection with the need to address conflictive interaction in linguistic studies in general, we argue that it is also time to systematically look at impoliteness, the long neglected 'poor cousin' of politeness. In what follows, we will address the issues that this collection has raised by discussing the different theoretical stances towards the study of impoliteness, the connection between the exercise of power and impoliteness, and the outline of the book.

2.   What is 'impoliteness'?

After decades of work inspired by Brown and Levinson's ([1978] 1987) seminal work on politeness, politeness research is on the move again with both revisions to the classic model being suggested and alternative conceptions of politeness, which have been in existence for over a decade, being further tested, applied and developed. As the chapters in this collection show, research on impoliteness is inextricably linked to these developments. All contributors have previously worked in the field of politeness studies and have now decided to answer the call and extend their frameworks in such a way that a meaningful discussion of impoliteness becomes possible. For readers familiar with politeness research, it will also be immediately clear from a quick glance over the list of contributors that they will not find one single methodological approach to impoliteness phenomena in this collection. It was indeed the editors' aim to invite researchers from rather different theoretical camps to contribute their ideas to this endeavour in order to encourage a critical exchange. Since none of the chapters pursue a purely 'classical' Brown and Levinson line of argumentation, it is hoped that this collection can also contribute to broadening the horizons of research into im/politeness by making new paths of research more visible.

Coming from different theoretical camps means that the actual subject of study is already hotly contested. While there is a fair amount of agreement that politeness and impoliteness issues can (some would say should) be discussed together, and that impolite utterances have an impact on the ties between social actors, there is no solid agreement in the chapters as to what 'impoliteness' actually is. The lowest common denominator, however, can be summarised like this: *Impoliteness is behaviour that is face-aggravating in a particular context.* Most researchers would propose that this is ultimately insufficient and have indeed proposed more elaborate definitions. One of the main differences that emerges when comparing some of these is the role assigned to the recognition of intentions in the understanding of impoliteness:

(1)   I take impoliteness as constituting the issuing of intentionally gratuitous and conflictive face-threatening acts (FTAs) that are purposefully performed. (Bousfield, this volume: 132)

(2)   Impoliteness, as I would define it, involves communicative behaviour intending to cause the "face loss" of a target or perceived by the target to be so. (Culpeper, this volume: 36)

(3)   *impoliteness* occurs when the expression used is not conventionalised relative to the context of occurrence; it threatens the addressee's face (and, through that, the

speaker's face) but no face-threatening intention is attributed to the speaker by the hearer. (Terkourafi, this volume: 70)

As we can see, Bousfield and Culpeper make the hearer's understanding of the speaker's intentions the key for impoliteness. In contrast, Terkourafi maintains that the recognition of intentions constitutes 'rudeness' rather than impoliteness (for an elaboration of these points, see Chapters 2, 3 and 6). It is apparent that more research is needed here to establish whether the recognition of intentions by the interactants involved is indeed the key to define impoliteness and rudeness and to distinguish the terms from each other.

What is clear currently is that the two terms would appear to occupy a very similar conceptual space. This is a point explicitly explored by Locher and Watts, who in fact state that the conceptual space of impoliteness is also shared by other negatively evaluated terms within face-aggravating linguistic behaviour. They note that:

(4)   Negatively marked behaviour, i.e. behaviour that has breached a social norm . . ., evokes negative evaluations such as *impolite* or *over-polite* (or any alternative lexeme such as *rude, aggressive, insulting, sarcastic*, etc. depending upon the degree of the violation and the type of conceptualisation the inappropriate behaviour is profiled against). (Locher and Watts, this volume: 79)

This is only part of a much larger argument made by Locher and Watts that ultimately we need to adopt the terms that members themselves use in order to explain the concepts discussed throughout this collection. We will revisit this issue later in this introduction.

In what follows, some of the lines of reasoning that emerged in our reading of the chapters will be commented on. In section 2.1, we deal with impoliteness as a means to negotiate relationships. In Section 2.2, we comment on an important difference that can be found with respect to the general methodological approach taken to study impoliteness phenomena, i.e. whether researchers pursue a first order or a second order approach. In Section 2.3, the aspect of contextualisation and the importance of the norms of discursive practices in judging impoliteness are introduced.

2.1.   *Impoliteness as a means to negotiate relationships*

In all chapters of this collection, the feeling that we are not dealing with an easy to grasp or one-dimensional concept is all pervasive. Several researchers in fact point out that we are only at the beginning of our understanding of the phenomenon (e.g. Bousfield; Culpeper; Terkourafi). Impoliteness, even if most generally seen as face-aggravating behaviour in a specific context, clearly involves the relational aspect of communication in that social actors negotiate their positions vis-à-vis each other. Locher and Watts (this volume and elsewhere; see also Bousfield, this volume) maintain that impolite behaviour and face-aggravating behaviour more generally is as much part of this negotiation as polite versions of behaviour. Locher and Watts thus claim that "[r]elational work refers to all aspects of the work invested by individuals in the construction, maintenance, reproduction and transformation of interpersonal relationships among those engaged in social practice" (Locher and Watts, this volume: 96). This general statement basically sets the stage for claiming that all aspects of relational work should be studied, and indeed that it is time to also focus on impoliteness. At the same time, however, the complex nature of relational work is recognised.

Many of the researchers in this collection make use of the term 'relational work' and understand impoliteness as being one aspect of this concept (e.g. Locher and Watts; Schnurr, Marra and Holmes).[2] Culpeper discusses the term and its usefulness for research in his chapter. As soon as the most general definition of impoliteness as behaviour that is face-aggravating in a particular context is deemed to be not entirely sufficient, the question arises as to what part of relational work is covered by the term *impolite*. Before we can outline how different approaches have dealt with this question, we need to introduce the terms 'first order impoliteness' (impoliteness$_1$) and 'second order impoliteness' (impoliteness$_2$).

2.2. *First order and second order investigations*

The distinction between first order and second order approaches in politeness research stems from work which goes back to Watts, Ehlich and Ide (1992) and Eelen (2001). First order concepts are judgements about behaviour, such as *impolite, rude, polite, polished*, made by the social actors themselves. They arrive at these judgements according to the norms of their particular discursive practice. We are, in other words, dealing with a lay-person's understanding of the concepts italicised above. Second order approaches use the concepts and consider them on a theoretical level. These theories do not disregard first order notions as, in fact, it is argued that the second order theories are necessarily informed by first order notions in the first place (see, e.g. Bousfield, this volume).

To give a concrete example of the most prominent second order theory: Brown and Levinson ([1978] 1987) treat 'politeness' as a universal concept and as a technical term to describe relational work that is carried out to mitigate

face-threatening acts. Whether or not a particular member of a discursive practice is in agreement that a particular utterance is also perceived as *polite* is no
longer of relevance (for a discussion of this point, see also Locher 2006a). The
way in which Brown and Levinson's theory has been understood and used in
the past means that relational work has been split into only two components,
namely polite and impolite behaviour. A second order researcher who uncriti-
cally follows Brown and Levinson might thus answer the question of what part
of interactive behaviour or relational work constitutes impoliteness (raised in the
previous section) simply by saying that impoliteness equals non-politeness, i.e.
non-adherence to the politeness strategies proposed in Brown and Levinson's
framework. After all, Brown and Levinson ([1978] 1987) themselves note that:

> ... politeness has to be communicated, and the absence of communicated polite-
> ness may, *ceteris paribus*, be taken as the absence of a polite attitude. (Brown and
> Levinson [1978] 1987: 5)

Whilst far from being uncritical of Brown and Levinson's approach, a number of
authors (e.g. Bousfield, García-Pastor) who have contributed to this collection
are nevertheless at least partially sympathetic[3] to the notion of a dichotomous aspect to politeness and impoliteness in certain circumstances. Such circumstances
are those explained by Culpeper (1996: 357), who notes that impoliteness may be
realised through "... the absence of politeness work *where it would be expected*"
(our emphasis), and further gives the example that "failing to thank someone
for a present may be taken as deliberate impoliteness" (Culpeper 2005: 42).

In contrast, researchers pursuing a first order approach explicitly leave open
the option that there is more in relational work than just impolite or polite
behaviour. They claim that judgements with respect to appropriateness of relational work by interactants may lead to a more diverse labelling of behaviour
than simply *polite* and *impolite* (e.g. Locher and Watts; Schnurr, Marra and
Holmes). While this may be expected from approaches that do not use the italicised lexemes as theoretical concepts, we note that some of the theoretically
oriented researchers also break up the dichotomy between politeness and impoliteness. Bousfield, for example, while clearly stating that he pursues a second
order approach, still maintains that the aspect of relational work which can most
generally be described as face-aggravating is not necessarily synonymous with
impoliteness. Archer, too, working with a second order approach, suggests refining the definition of *impoliteness* yet further as she sees the concept as a
sub-variety of "linguistic aggression". The approaches that have evolved out of
second order conceptualisations (e.g. Archer; Bousfield; Cashman; Culpeper;
García-Pastor; Terkourafi) are therefore no longer using a clear dichotomy of
theoretical concepts à la Brown and Levinson. It is indeed the case in Bousfield's,

Culpeper's and Terkourafi's contributions that their definitions of impoliteness all contain elements of speaker and/or hearer interpretation and explicitly stress context sensitivity – points on which Archer, Cashman and García-Pastor implicitly agree. Such points have always been at the heart of first order approaches. In addition, Bousfield, Culpeper, and Terkourafi also discuss *rude* behaviour and how it might be distinguished from *impolite* behaviour. All this effectively narrows the scope of the term 'impoliteness' within relational work and shifts the discussion in the direction of a first order approach. What we therefore see in this collection is a rapprochement of the two fields.

Since much of what the researchers sympathetic to a first order approach (Graham; Limberg; Locher and Watts; Mullany; Schnurr, Marra and Holmes) put forward for discussion is connected to an understanding of relational work in a particular discursive context, the notions of Community of Practice and discursiveness have to be introduced next.

2.3. *The negotiation of norms in discursive practices*

In no chapter can we find any claims for a simple form and function correlation with respect to language usage and its impact as impoliteness on a more global level. This might sound like a truism nowadays, but we believe that it is worth repeating it here. What this boils down to, then, is that we wish to highlight the importance of locally made judgements on the relational aspects of language usage, i.e. 'relational work'. In Brown and Levinson's ([1978] 1987) framework an attempt was made to capture these contextual influences on relational work by introducing the variables of power, distance and the ranking of the social imposition. To claim that context matters is therefore no new insight. What has changed is our awareness that judgements about the relational aspect of an utterance may differ from discursive practice to discursive practice.

A number of researchers explicitly argue with a Community of Practice (see Eckert and McConnell-Ginet 1992), Activity Type (see Levinson 1992) or, more generally, a discursive practice approach when interpreting data (Graham; Locher and Watts; Mullany; Schnurr, Marra and Holmes). This means that the researchers do not link the observation of a linguistic strategy, for example indirectness, directly with a judgement as to whether this strategy is to be interpreted as *impolite* or *polite*. Instead, they claim that this judgement has to be made with the norms of the particular discursive community in mind. In addition, judgements about relational work (be it *polished, polite, impolite, rude,* or *uncouth,* etc.) are said to be points of reference, placed along a continuum with fuzzy borders between the concepts.

It is hypothesised that members of a discursive practice negotiate and rene-gotiate the norms of the community and thus share expectations about relational work. This means that what is perceived as impolite behaviour in one group may be shared by its members to a large degree. What is highlighted, however, is that the norms themselves are in flux, since they are shaped by the individuals who make up the discursive practice. This discursiveness is one of the reasons pro-posed for preferring a first order rather than a second order approach by some researchers in this collection (cf. Locher and Watts). At the same time, it needs to be highlighted that the second order researchers are well aware of the fact that expectations about a particular practice influence the participants' judgements about impoliteness. See, for example, Culpeper's and Bousfield's chapters in which they discuss the impact of aggressive verbal behaviour on TV shows and army training camps with respect to whether or not the linguistic behaviour is still interpreted as hurtful and impolite by the participants, despite the fact that this behaviour may have been expected ('sanctioned') from the beginning.

3.   Power and impoliteness

In the same way that impoliteness is not a concept upon which all are agreed in this collection, neither can we give a definitive account of power, nor how it operates in impolite, or otherwise face-damaging interactions after our reading of the chapters. A number of different sources have been used by the differ-ent researchers contributing to this collection. These include accounts of power adapted or adopted from Foucault (1980), van Dijk (1989, 1996, 1997), Warten-berg (1990), Watts (1991), Thornborrow (2002) and Locher (2004), to name just a few. Culpeper cautions with respect to attempting a single definition of power by saying "I will not, however, attempt a comprehensive overview or critique of the notion of power, as it looms like the many-headed Hydra in a volumi-nous literature" (this volume: 17–18). This is, perhaps, a wise move, but should not be taken to mean that we can neglect the aspect of power when analyzing impoliteness.

On the contrary, the discussion of power within each chapter is critically rel-evant to the phenomena under scrutiny: firstly, there is and can be no interaction without power; secondly, and more pertinently, impoliteness is an exercise of power as it has arguably always in some way *an effect* on one's addressees in that it alters the future action-environment of one's interlocutors. Impoliteness – whether understood as intentional face-aggravation (Bousfield; Culpeper) or not (Terkourafi) – is inextricably tied up with the very concept of power because an interlocutor whose face is damaged by an utterance suddenly finds his or her response options to be sharply restricted. The notion of the restriction of an "action-environment" is taken from Wartenberg's (1990) definition of power:

> A social agent *A* has *power over* another social agent *B* if and only if *A* strategically constrains *B*'s action-environment. (Wartenberg 1990: 85, emphasis in original)[4]

Such restrictions of interactants' action-environments through the use of face-aggravating behaviour in its 'impolite' form can be observed within many of the situations, settings, activity types or communities of practice here discussed. Whilst definitions of power differ throughout the collection, the *lowest common denominator* here centres therefore around this effect of impoliteness in restricting the actions of the target.

Restricting the action environment of an individual, as is apparent from virtually all of the chapters here, is not a sacrosanct, concrete aspect of any one individual, in any one role, in any one setting. In short, there is agreement in this collection that power is not static; rather, power is highly dynamic, fluid and negotiable. Even interactants with a hierarchically lower status can and do exercise power through impoliteness, as many examples demonstrate.

Having outlined the general theoretical tendencies that we perceive to be under discussion in this collection, we will move to an explanation of what is in store in the chapters on impoliteness in language.

4. The organisation of the book

We originally expected a more clear-cut methodological division between the contributors' texts. This would have allowed us to clearly attribute the chapters to first or second order approaches to the study of impoliteness. As we noted above, however, the approaches the researchers have taken are in many cases based on a fusion of methodologies and/or are elaborated explorations of their own methodological paths.

The sequence of chapters as it presents itself to the reader, then, is along thematic lines. The two chapters by Culpeper and by Terkourafi in Part 1 are predominantly theory-oriented. (Culpeper, however, also discusses empirical data.) While the remaining chapters also have strong theory sections, they are nevertheless ordered according to the type of data that was used for their empirical analyses: Part 2 entails data from political interaction (Locher and Watts; García-Pastor), Part 3 interaction with legally constituted authorities (Bousfield; Limberg; Archer), Part 4 workplace interaction in the factory and offices (Schnurr, Marra and Holmes; Mullany) and Part 5 presents data on code-switching (Cashman) and from the Internet (Graham). By choosing to present theory focused papers first, it is hoped that the readers can make a comparison of the theoretical ideas at the beginning of this collection, and then see the different approaches in use on similar data sets.

Part 1 of this collection thus contains chapters that have a predominantly theoretical focus. Jonathan Culpeper's work merges a discussion of impoliteness, relational work and power. Coming from a second order approach to impoliteness, Culpeper discusses both the advantages and the drawbacks of the terminology employed in primarily first order approaches, and also engages critically with his own previous work. By offering a discussion of the use of the lexemes *over-polite* on the Internet, Culpeper tests his line of argumentation empirically. His lucid discussion of the connection between impoliteness and power sets the stage for the other chapters in this collection.

Marina Terkourafi's chapter is an attempt to unify a theory of politeness, impoliteness, and rudeness. In her theoretical considerations, she reviews both first order and second order approaches to politeness and impoliteness and merges them in a compelling synthesis of her own. In particular, she discusses the concept of 'face' in detail. Terkourafi also proposes that interactants might make first order distinctions between behaviour that is deemed *impolite* and behaviour that is deemed *rude*. According to her, the perception/construction of 'intention' by the receiver is the key to this distinction (see her definition of *impoliteness* in Section 2 of this introduction). While there is much overlap of Terkourafi's approach with, for example, Culpeper (2005) but also Locher and Watts (2005), the author also distinctly goes her own way in theorizing politeness and impoliteness.

In Part 2 the common denominator is interaction in the political sphere of life. Miriam Locher and Richard Watts' chapter, however, first of all explains the point of view of researchers who favour a first order approach over a second order approach to the study of impoliteness, as outlined in section 2.2 above. They then move to an illustration of the discursive nature of concepts such as *polite* or *impolite* by using meta-comments found on an Internet discussion board. The main empirical analysis offered in this chapter is one that looks at a political interview broadcast in 1984. It is argued that a sequence of social practice needs to be studied within its wider socio-political and socio-historical context. Locher and Watts also call for a close analysis of non-linguistic evidence, such as facial expressions or body posture, to arrive at an understanding of what interactants might have perceived or constructed as *impolite* (negatively marked, and inappropriate) behaviour when judging this behaviour against their particular Community of Practice norms.

María Dolores García-Pastor, on the other hand, takes a clearly second order theoretical stance (based on Lachenicht 1980; Kienpointer 1997; Culpeper

1996, 2005; Culpeper, Bousfield and Wichmann 2003; Blas Arroyo 2001). She studies impoliteness and power in U.S. electoral debates, collected in 2000, and argues that the notion of 'negativity cycles' is helpful to describe how interactants constrain and influence each other's action-environments. In her analysis, García-Pastor uses second order strategies for impoliteness to describe how "[p]oliticians discredit the opponent, and coerce him/her into a specific course of action in their interchanges. This gives place to a discursive struggle which 1) evinces the interrelation between impoliteness and power in debates, and 2) underscores the relational, dynamic and contestable features of this concept".

Interaction with legally constituted authorities, as can be found in court or police contexts, is at the heart of Part 3. Derek Bousfield's chapter adds further points to the theoretical discussion of the concept of impoliteness. He develops the second order models proposed by Culpeper (1996, 2005) and Culpeper, Bousfield and Wichmann (2003) by especially subsuming the five 'super-strategies' (Bald on record; positive impoliteness; negative Impoliteness; off-record impoliteness; withhold politeness) within two: *On-record impoliteness* and *Off-record impoliteness*. By doing this, Bousfield stresses that face-considerations are always at the heart of relational work, irrespective of the form a particular utterance may take. Further, he acknowledges that off-record strategies can be as damaging as on-record strategies in terms of impoliteness. Finally, whilst adaptable to the Brown and Levinson notion of face, Bousfield's approach presupposes no positive/negative aspect. In his discussions of examples, Bousfield focuses especially on the power relations of the interactants and points out that power is dynamic and contestable even in institutional discourses with rigid hierarchies.

Holger Limberg works on threats in conflict talk, derived from police patrolling interaction (as shown on TV). He defines threats as face-damaging and as having pragmatic as well as symbolic power, and discusses their potential to serve manipulation. Limberg's discussion of power, based largely on Wartenberg's (1990) distinction between *force, coercion* and *influence*, is especially illuminating when he analyses threats uttered both by the police (the institutionally more powerful) and by the offenders (the institutionally less powerful). Limberg maintains that he did not find any meta-comments on whether or not the interactants involved perceived first order impoliteness to have taken place and concludes that "[a]ssessments about impoliteness and the use of threats can only be made on the grounds of the situational usage of this strategy and whether it has been implemented appropriately".

Dawn Archer is the only researcher in this collection to use historical data that is taken from English courtroom interaction in the 17th and 18th centuries. Archer discusses and adds to the second order theories proposed by Culpeper,

Bousfield and Wichmann, but also calls for more contextualisation. She claims that much of the verbal aggression witnessed in a courtroom, which can be described by super-strategies proposed by second order researchers, should nevertheless not be taken as synonymous to impoliteness. This is, she argues, because the courtroom is a context in which verbal aggression is tolerated (*sanctioned*) to a large degree. In this sense, Archer is one of the researchers in this collection who stress a combination of both first and second order methods.

Part 4 of this collection contains two further studies that discuss data derived from a work context. In both Schnurr, Marra and Holmes' as well as in Mullany's chapter, the focus is on office or factory work, rather than on interaction that is characterised by legally constituted authorities as discussed in Part 3. Stephanie Schnurr, Meredith Marra and Janet Holmes emphasise the importance of a Community of Practice approach and are sympathetic towards a first order approach to the study of impoliteness. The authors investigate the ways in which impoliteness is employed by subordinates as a means to challenge and subvert existing power relations in the workplace. They maintain that behaviour that might be perceived as impolite from the perspective of the researcher should in fact be investigated with the norms of the respective discursive practice in mind, since these norms are negotiated by its members.

Louise Mullany investigates interactions within corporate business meetings. She takes a context-based, Community of Practice perspective to conceptualise impoliteness, and utilises an approach that is influenced by both conversation analysis and critical discourse analysis. In this way, Mullany uses a first order approach to impoliteness that is based on knowledge about the norms negotiated in the discursive practices that she studies by using recordings and questionnaire data. The author adds the aspect of gender to the discussion of impoliteness and power and claims that both concepts have to be seen as possessing a fluid and dynamic nature.

In part 5, one article on code-switching and one on Internet communication can be found. Holly Cashman investigates the function of code-switching with respect to relational work. Cashman proposes that a methodological mixture – a combination of interviews, questionnaire data and role play – can yield fruitful results when zooming in on the function of code-switching in interaction. She uses a second order approach, but combines it with a discussion of the interactants' perception of what was or was not perceived as impolite in real interaction. Code-switching, it turns out, can be used to create polite as well as impolite interpretations.

Sage Lambert Graham offers a study of exchanges on an Internet mailing list. In particular, she investigates the norms of this discursive practice as outlined by the FAQs of the Internet mailing list. This list reflects the expectations that the members of this community have put into writing with respect to appropriate interaction. The list, however, is also contradictory in its messages and puts new members in a difficult position if they want to follow the guidelines. Graham discusses reactions to violations of these rules and shows how the communities' norms are in a process of being discussed and shaped by its members.

Finally, two points bear making here. First, as this collection is in many ways a joint enterprise in that we are all drawing on and building on existing politeness research and are expanding *im*politeness research, we are also referring the reader to the same literature in many cases. For this reason and to avoid unnecessary repetition, we have compiled one single reference section for all chapters. This can be found at the end of this collection. Second, while it would be presumptuous to expect that this collection will spark off an equally large interest in impoliteness such as that which already exists for politeness, we do hope that it can serve as a starting point for future, much needed, studies on the phenomenon, and that it will be as well-received as its sister *Politeness in Language* (1992, 2005), also published by Mouton.

Notes

1. The four approaches identified by Fraser are: (1) the social-norm view, (2) the conversational-maxim view, (3) the face-saving view and (4) the conversational-contract view. For a discussion, see Locher (2004: 60–62).
2. However, rather than working with the notion of face outlined in Locher and Watts, some researchers prefer to work with Spencer-Oatey's (2000a/b, 2002, 2005) ideas on 'rapport management' (e.g. Cashman; Culpeper; Graham).
3. As the distinctions between first and second order approaches to the study of impoliteness are not as clear-cut as could have been expected, we have opted for using the adjective 'sympathetic to' to describe a researcher's position. In most cases this is a simplification of the researcher's theoretical stance, and the readers are encouraged to read the chapters to learn more about the different approaches of the contributors.
4. For a discussion of this definition and Wartenberg's ideas on power in general, see Locher (2004: Chapter 2) and Limberg (this volume).

Part 1. Theoretical focus on research on impoliteness

Chapter 2
Reflections on impoliteness, relational work and power

Jonathan Culpeper

1. Introduction[1]

As Christie (2005: 4) points out, three of the five articles constituting the very first edition of the *Journal of Politeness Research: Language, Behaviour, Culture* stress that politeness is some form of "relational work". Whether one uses the term "relational work" (Locher and Watts 2005), "relational practice" (Holmes and Schnurr 2005) or "rapport management" (Spencer-Oatey 2000b, 2005), they have in common a central focus on interpersonal relations rather than a central focus on the individual performing "politeness", which is then correlated with interpersonal relations as variables. Spencer-Oatey's (e.g. 2000b, 2005) approach and that of Locher and Watts (e.g. Locher 2004; Locher and Watts 2005) explicitly accommodate impoliteness, although Locher and Watts provide rather more detail on this specifically, for which reason the bulk of this chapter examines their conception of relational work and uses that examination as a springboard for issues relating to impoliteness. I begin by briefly reviewing the backdrop provided by classic politeness studies. I then discuss "over-politeness", "impoliteness" and "rudeness", all of which are claimed by Locher and Watts to be "negative" and generally "marked" and "inappropriate" behaviour. I do not disagree with this claim in its broad outline; my aims are to show that there are various ways in which one's behaviours might be considered negative, and also to investigate behaviours that might be considered both negative and appropriate in some sense. The final and longest single section of this chapter addresses one specific relational aspect, namely, power. The momentum for this section derives from an off-the-cuff comment made to me by Miriam Locher: "Isn't all impoliteness a matter of power?" Of course, power, just like social distance, is involved in any social interaction. The point of interest here is whether there is some special relationship between impoliteness and power, and a key aim of this section is to assess the extent to which this might be true, as well as the ways in which it might be true. In order to pursue this aim, it will first be necessary to get a handle on what is meant by power. I will not, however, attempt a comprehensive overview or critique of the notion of power, as it looms like the many-headed Hydra in a voluminous literature – well beyond the scope of this chapter (readers will find additional discussions of power in the other chapters of this volume). Finally, I concentrate on the ways in which impoliteness and power might interact in communication, and as well as situations characterised by both impoliteness and power.

2. The backdrop of studies on politeness

On the face of it, impoliteness *appears* to be the opposite of politeness, and so discussions of politeness might represent an obvious first port of call. However, the notion of politeness does not constitute a generally accepted, stable point of departure. For example, is it opposite politeness as the lay person would conceive it or is it opposite politeness as academics would conceive it? And in what sense is it opposite? These questions are being hotly debated in the literature. An alternative tack is to consider whether the conceptual apparatus used to describe politeness can be used to describe impoliteness. After all, the politeness apparatus is designed to analyse social interaction and so would seem a good bet as a starting point in the treatment of impoliteness. However, there are reasons why the concepts, dimensions and interrelations of a model of politeness cannot straightforwardly be used in a model of impoliteness (see Eelen 2001: 98–100, who elaborates the issues). For example, classic politeness theories (e.g. Brown and Levinson [1978] 1987; Lakoff 1973; Leech 1983) give the impression that impoliteness as the result of doing nothing (i.e. the result of not taking redressive action or not undertaking communicative work in order to abide by politeness maxims). This, then, would not accommodate the rich array of purposeful communicative action undertaken to achieve impoliteness (see, e.g. Beebe 1995; Culpeper 1996; Lachenicht 1980). Furthermore, if the source of the conceptual apparatus were classic politeness theories, then such a move would result in the transference of problems associated with those theories into the new impoliteness model. For example, with respect to Brown and Levinson's ([1978] 1987) politeness theory, the theory which has had most impact on research, those problems include:

(1)   Ignoring the lay person's conception of politeness, as revealed through their use of the terms *polite* and *politeness*;

(2)   Postulating a facework-based theory of politeness but with an inadequate conception of "face", particularly across diverse cultures;

(3)   Basing the politeness model on an inadequate model of communication, and one which is biased towards the speaker and the production of language;

(4) Focussing almost entirely on lexical and grammatical realisations of the outputs of politeness strategies, to the near-exclusion of prosody and non-verbal aspects;

(5) Failing to articulate an adequate conception of context, despite the key importance of context in judgements of politeness.

It should be noted here that some of these problems, specifically (3)–(4), are not exclusive to classic politeness theories but reflect the fact that thinking about how communication works has moved on since the 1970s, when the seeds of, for example, Brown and Levinson ([1978] 1987) and Leech (1983) were sown.[2] Classic politeness theories are built on classic speech act theory and Grice, which, separately or together, do not offer an adequate account of communication, not least because they treat communication as rationalist and objectifiable. They tend to focus on speaker intentions as reconstructed "faithfully" by hearers (ignoring the co-construction of meanings in the interaction between speaker and hearer), utterances with single functions, single speakers and single addressees (ignoring multi-functionality and the complexity of discourse situations), short utterances or exchanges (ignoring the wider discourse), and lexis and grammar (ignoring, for example, prosody and non-verbal aspects of communication).[3] Moreover, neither speech act theory nor Grice's Cooperative Principle offer an adequate theory of context, leading to politeness theorists bolstering their models with a few sociological variables. This approach ignores the sheer complexity of context, which encompasses not only aspects of the world relevant to communication, but also their cognitive representation, their emergence in dynamic discourse, different participant perspectives on them and their negotiation in discourse, and so on. Although the best way forward is still hotly disputed, these problems have been addressed in various books and papers. For example, a development beyond speech act theory can be seen in Herbert Clark's (e.g. 1996) useful notion of "joint projects"; "Post-Gricean" work has been led by Sperber and Wilson's Relevance Theory (1995) and "Neo-Gricean" work has relatively recently seen a substantial monograph by Stephen Levinson (2000); and work on context was given a notable boost by Duranti and Goodwin (1992).

More recent views of politeness have addressed the above problems. We might note Arundale's (e.g. 1999, 2006) Face Constituting Theory, Spencer-Oatey's (e.g. 2000b, 2005) work on Rapport Management, or Terkourafi's (e.g. 2001, 2005a) frame-based view of politeness. A particularly noteworthy line of work, sometimes referred to as "post-modern" or "discursive", emphasises that the very definitions of politeness itself are subject to discursive struggle (e.g. Eelen 2001; Locher 2004, 2006a; Locher and Watts 2005; Mills 2003; Watts 2003, 2005; Watts, Ide and Ehlich [1992] 2005[4]). In this approach, classic politeness theories are criticised for articulating a pseudo-scientific theory of particular social behaviours and labelling it politeness (so-called politeness$_2$), whilst ignoring the lay person's conception of politeness as revealed through their use of the terms *polite* and *politeness* to refer to particular social behaviours (so-called politeness$_1$) (these were the different conceptions of politeness alluded to at the beginning of section 2). They are also criticised for treating the notion of face as a matter of the psychological "wants" of individuals, rather than a matter of "the social self and its relationship to others" (Bargiela-Chiappini 2003: 1463; see also Arundale 2006). Furthermore, the classic approach to face has not easily accommodated a diverse range of cultures, because it has a Western bias (see, for example, Matsumoto 1988; Gu 1990). The focus of the post-modern approach is on the micro – on participants' situated evaluations of politeness, not shared conventionalised politeness strategies or shared notions of politeness. Not surprisingly, the communicative theories employed here, notably Relevance Theory (see, for example, Watts 2003), emphasise the hearer and do not have norms as a starting point.

As an antidote to classic politeness theories, post-modern politeness work has been effective. In particular, they have drawn attention to the fact that (im)politeness is not inherent in particular forms of language, and argued that it is a matter of the participants' evaluations of particular forms as (im)polite in context. They have also been influential in broadening the scope of the field, as I will discuss in the following section. However, there are problems here too. Despite criticising earlier studies for labelling certain behaviours as polite without particular regard for what the lay person might do, the post-modern scholars do not offer an authoritative account of the lay person's use of politeness terms. One might have expected, for example, a corpus-based exploration of the terms. This would be an interesting exercise in lexical semantics, and one that could feed in to a theory of politeness. The fact that this does not happen is partly a consequence of the fact that the stability of meanings of politeness is repeatedly denied:

> ... politeness will always be a slippery, ultimately indefinable quality of interaction which is subject to change through time and across cultural space. There is, in other words, no stable referent indexed by the lexeme *polite* ... (Watts 2005: xiii)

It is also a result of the fact that a "theory" seems not to be the objective here (cf. Watts 2005: xlii). A consequence of focusing on the dynamic and situated characteristics of politeness is that politeness is declared not to be a predictive theory (Watts 2003: 25), or, apparently, even a post-hoc descriptive one (Watts 2003: 142). This does not match, then, the sociopragmatic agenda I have, namely, to explain a particular area of communicative behaviour (see

Leech 2003: 104). As Terkourafi comments (2005a: 245): "What we are then left with are minute descriptions of individual encounters, but these do not in any way add up to an explanatory theory of the phenomena under study". In fact, it is not always entirely clear whether post-modern studies always pursue (or can always pursue) their own agenda to the full. In the absence of participants deploying and debating explicit evaluations of (im)politeness in the discourse that has taken place, some data analyses that appear in post-modern studies are selected on the basis of claims *by the researcher*, pointing to implicit evidence, that they involve politeness (or a weaker claim of "potential politeness"), much in the same way, though with a different focus, as data analyses of naturally occurring conversation in studies of politeness$_2$.

3.   Impoliteness in a relational perspective

3.1.   *Relational work: An overview*

This overview relates specifically to the view of relational work espoused by Locher and Watts (e.g. Locher 2004, 2006a; Locher and Watts 2005, this volume; Watts 2003). Locher and Watts state that "relational work can be understood as equivalent to Halliday's (1978) interpersonal level of communication" (2005: 11), and further that "[r]elational work is defined as the work people invest in negotiating their relationships in interaction" (this volume: 78). Relational work is not switched off and on in communication but is always involved. Locher (2004: 51) writes that "[t]he process of defining relationships in interaction is called *face-work or relational work*", and states a preference for the term "relational work" because "it highlights the involvement of at least two interactants". The concept of face is central to relational work, though not as defined by Brown and Levinson ([1978] 1987) but by Goffman (1967: 5), thus: "the positive social value a person effectively claims for [her/him self] by the line others assume [s/he] has taken during a particular contact"; "an image of self delineated in terms of approved social attributes". Face is treated as discursively constructed within situated interactions. Relational work covers "the entire continuum from polite and appropriate to impolite and inappropriate behaviour" (Locher 2004: 51; see also Locher and Watts 2005: 11). In this perspective, Brown and Levinson's work is not a theory of politeness but "a theory of facework, dealing only with the mitigation of face-threatening acts", and fails to "account for those situations in which face-threat mitigation is not a priority, e.g., aggressive, abusive or rude behaviour" (Locher and Watts 2005: 10).[5] Watts (2005: xliii; see

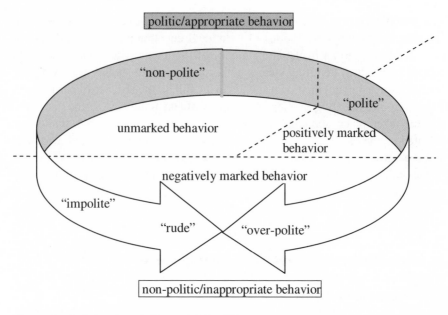

Figure 1.   Relational work (Watts 2005: xliii)

also Locher and Watts 2005: 12; Locher 2004: 90) offers a diagram which use-
fully attempts to map the total spectrum of relational work, reproduced above
as Figure 1.

Importantly, relational work in this perspective incorporates the issue of
whether behaviour is marked or not. Markedness here relates to appropriateness: if the behaviour is inappropriate, it will be marked and more likely to be
noticed. Unmarked behaviour is what Watts (1989, 2003) refers to in his earlier work as "politic behaviour"[6]: "[l]inguistic behaviour which is perceived to
be appropriate to the social constraints of the ongoing interaction, i.e. as non-
salient, should be called *politic behaviour*" (Watts 2003: 19), and is illustrated
by the following examples:

A: Would you like some more coffee?
B: Yes, *please.*

M: *Hello*, Mr. Smith. *How are you?*
S: *Hello* David. Fine *thanks. How are you?*
(Watts 2003: 186, emphasis as original)

Politeness, on the other hand, is positively marked behaviour. Watts (2003: 19)
writes that "[l]inguistic behaviour perceived to go beyond what is expectable,

i.e. salient behaviour, should be called *polite* or *impolite* depending on whether the behaviour itself tends towards the negative or positive end of the spectrum of politeness". By way of illustration, we can re-work Watts's examples accordingly:

A: Would you like some more coffee?
B: Yes, *please, that's very kind, coffee would be wonderful.*

M: *Hello*, Mr. Smith. *It's great to see you. We missed you. How are you?*
S: *Hello* David. *I'm fine thanks. It's great to see you too. How are you?*

Some researchers (e.g. Meier 1995) see politeness as a matter of doing what is appropriate, but Watts is clearly right in allowing for the fact that people frequently do more than what is called for. Note here, and as can be seen in Figure 1, that marked behaviour is not co-extensive with politic/appropriate behaviour. Positively marked behaviour, which is likely to be evaluated as "polite", is *also* politic/appropriate. This raises the issue of how "markedness" differs from "appropriacy", as both seem to be related to situational norms. Perhaps the distinguishing characteristic of markedness is its relationship with affect. Note that in Figure 1 "unmarked" is contrasted with "positively/negatively marked"; it involves neutral versus positive/negative emotion. This is clearly an area that needs clarification. Locher and Watts's writings indicate that the distinction between "appropriate" or "unmarked" and "inappropriate" or "marked" is not absolute but fuzzy-edged, as is indicated by the dotted lines in Figure 1. I would argue that it is important to see these as scales, capturing degrees of difference between relatively "normal" behaviours and situations, such as greetings and leave-takings in expected contexts, and those which are more creative. One particular problem with the appropriacy distinctions is identifying what is "perceived to be appropriate to the social constraints of the ongoing interaction" and "what is expectable". In this chapter, and particularly in sections 3.3 and 4.2, I will argue that expectations about appropriacy are based on two very different kinds of norm, "experiential" norms and "social" norms, and this can lead to different evaluations of behaviour.

It should be stressed that there is no claim in Watts's and Locher's relational approach that merely being marked is a guarantee that a particular behaviour will be considered polite or impolite. Instead, the authors argue that behaviours which are appropriate, or otherwise, "to the social context of interactional situation only warrant *potential* evaluation by the participants (or others) as polite or impolite" (Locher and Watts 2005: 17; see also Watts 2005: xliv). Nevertheless, Figure 1 captures at least some hypotheses about factors that underlie (im)politeness, and specifically two hypotheses about impoliteness: (1) it is negatively marked/non-politic/inappropriate behaviour, and (2) it can be related to "over-politeness". I shall comment on these in reverse order.

3.2.   Over-politeness

Watts (2005), in reference to the diagram in Figure 1, writes that marked behaviour:

> [m]ay be perceived as negative either if it is open to an interpretation as impolite (or as downright rude), or if it is perceived as over-polite, i.e. those kinds of negatively marked non-politic behaviour tend towards similar kinds of affective reaction on the part of co-participants. Certain speakers consistently evaluate polite behaviour as unnecessary and offensive. The figure is thus meant to represent situations in which the communicative effects of over-polite behaviour may seem remarkably similar to those of downright rude behaviour, which is why the two ends of the spectrum are shown as turning in upon themselves. (Watts 2005: xliv)

Similarly, Locher (2004: 90) remarks: "[o]ver-politeness is often perceived as negative exactly because it exceeds the boundary between appropriateness and inappropriateness", also adding the usual caution that the "the final decision as to whether something is perceived as polite or impolite lies in H's interpretation, who judges the relational aspect of the utterance with respect to H's own norms (frames, appropriateness, expectations, personal style, etc.)". However, no data are presented or research cited in support of these claims, something which partly reflects the fact that there is no obvious research on the perceptions of over-politeness to cite – this is relatively unexplored territory. One might note here that Watts's claim *appears* to fly in the face of that made by Leech (1983):

> [t]here will naturally be a preference for overstating polite beliefs, and for understating impolite ones: while an exaggeration such as *That was a delicious meal!* is favoured in praising others, an uninformative denial – a typical device of understatement – is frequently used in criticism: *I wasn't over impressed by her speech.*[7] (Leech 1983: 146)

However, Watts is referring to over-politeness, whereas Leech is discussing overstatement, i.e. hyperbole, treating politeness as one possible motivating factor. Thus, *That was a delicious meal!* could well be taken as an appropriate amount of politeness in the context, yet still be hyperbole from a Gricean point of view (a departure from the Maxim of Quality). Note here that departures from Gricean cooperation in no way imply departure from polite, social cooperation; in fact, in the classic politeness theory perspective, departures from Gricean cooperation can be motivated by the wish to maintain polite, social cooperation.

The question as to whether over-politeness is taken positively or negatively by interactants can be explored empirically. I investigated people's usage of the expressions *over-polite* and *too polite*, using WebCorp available at www.webcorp.org.uk. WebCorp treats the language on the World Wide Web as a (non-prototypical) corpus.[8] It has two advantages for my purposes: (1) the vast size of the language sources it draws upon (much more than all the corpora created by linguists put together), and (2) the fact that its language sources are relatively "unstandardised" and colloquial (compared with extant corpora which tend to include relatively "standardised" material drawn from printed publications). Of course, it has disadvantages too: 80% of the language on the World Wide Web is in English, and the bulk of that emanates from North America.[9] It is thus linguistically and culturally biased. Nevertheless, it provides a starting point.

Examples (1) and (2) suggest that over-politeness need not be taken negatively:[10]

(1)   Strolling along the streets you are bound to discover something, friendly invited by over polite personnel willing to see you as a respected guest.

(2)   i ve been in that place last friday and last saturday. atmosphere was amazing each night, bartenders are super cool, music is very eclectic, food is fine, dor staff over polite .. i loved the place and i ll be there next week end

However, such potentially positive usages are in a very small minority. The strongest pattern consisted of examples like the following:

(3)   I agree that over polite messages are not really helpfull – and also agree that they are written by people who are less comfortable with confrontation. I always write mesages like that first, then go over them and force myself to make them more direct.

(4)   As a website author it is easier for me to get feedback because I have provided the means to contact me on my website. When I am performing however, I find people are too polite to say anything which they think might offend. Usually people are complimentry about a performance to your face regardless how they actually feel. This does not help you as a performer to get a true measure of your performance.

(5)   Some people are just too polite. You come away from a meeting thinking you may have a deal on the table. When the truth is the person has no intention of ever purchasing from you, they are just too polite to say no.

Generally, these usages seem to be reactions to cases where, in Leech's (1983) terms, the speaker maintains the Politeness Principle at the expense of the Cooperative Principle; or, in Brown and Levinson's ([1978] 1987) terms, the speaker performs the strategy "Don't do the FTA". But there is more than this: they are reactions to what might be called relational mismanagement; in this case, a speaker's assessment that the interlocutor's need to maintain face would be in excess of the interlocutor's need for truth in the pursuit of a particular interactional goal turned out to be incorrect. There is no implication here that all cases of relational mismanagement involve the speaker "slipping up"; it is simply a matter of participants having differential perceptions resulting in the communicative behaviour chosen being negatively evaluated from at least one perspective.[11] Note that the negative evaluation here is not solely driven by facework alone but by facework in relation to somebody's "interactional wants", something which Spencer-Oatey (2005) very explicitly incorporates into her Rapport Management scheme. The situations reflected in examples (3) to (5) can be viewed as maintaining face at the expense of the hearer's interactional wants, whilst examples (6) and (7) maintain it at the expense of the speaker's presumed interactional wants:

(6)   Nigel on the other hand is still an innocent, protected by the discipline of English middle-class manners, a man who is too polite to tell a cripple to go to hell, too polite to be in any other role than that of the masochist.

(7)   There's nothing wrong with vigorous invective. The left doesn't get places often because it's way TOO polite, too reluctant to air differences, too polite about people like Tom Hayden when they are selling a pwog Democrat line.[12]

And examples (8) to (10) maintain face at the expense of a particular social group's presumed interactional wants:

(8)   We are approaching the thousandth death in the Iraq war. John Kerry is too polite to mention it.

(9)   the difference between a couple of blue haired nannies from pasadena yapping it up in the car and talking on a cell phone is that the person on the cell phone has NO IDEA about your current road conditions. a kid may run out in front of you to chase a ball and the person on the phone keeps yapping away. and most people are too polite (or stupid) to just say "hold on a minute" to the person on the phone.

(10)   Today I turn your attention to the underbelly of the matter to reveal the detriment that occurs when a society is so over-polite that it loses touch with itself.

Such usages are indeed negative in the general sense of attracting a negative evaluation, at least as far as North American culture is concerned. More specifically, they are negative in the sense of "misjudged" (hence attributions such as "stupid"). However, they do not suggest the kind of negative behaviour by which over-politeness can be equated with "downright rude behaviour".

There is yet, however, a further pattern, though much weaker than that above, which does support a version of negativity that is somewhat closer to "downright rude behaviour". Consider examples (11) to (13):

(11)   Come to the Emirates Palace Homer – you won't be able to walk 10 feet without someone calling you sir. In fact, they make a scene of it. From the second we stepped out of the taxi to the moment we arrived at the restaurant (a walk of 60 seconds) nine people came forward to welcome me. There appeared to be a gaggle of people employed solely to stand around – like Hare Krishners at an airport – chanting a mantra of 'evening sir'. This is all part of the hyperbolic service of a hotel that's the dictionary definition of over the top. ... And when one of the waiters rushed over, mid-meal, to correct the way we were eating – informing us that the sauce should have been poured onto the rice rather than left in the dish on the plate, it was very tempting to say, 'well, why wasn't it served over the rice in the first place?' But we were too polite for that. And they were too polite as well. Polite in an irritatingly fussy and obsequious way. As we've said in these pages before, if there's one thing that's guaranteed to ensure the meal isn't OK, it's being asked every five minutes if the meal is OK.

(12)   Job interview. * DO act polite but not over polite. "Yes Sir," "No Sir," and "Thank You" can appear to [sic] insincere if used too frequently.

(13)   The skeptics range from the oily, over-polite professionals who discreetly drop hints of the heresy of universalism, to the Bible thumper who sees only the dusty, robust war God of the Pentateuch, and who insists on restating the cold demands of rule-ridden perfectionism.

Interestingly, a strong characteristic of negatively marked over-politeness, as illustrated by the first two examples, is that being over-polite is a matter – at least in this cultural context – of doing politeness too *frequently*, or, more precisely, doing politeness too frequently with respect to what is appropriate in the situation, i.e. politic. Leech (1983: 147) comments: "hyperbole suffers from diminishing returns because of incredulity". Similarly, I would argue that a negatively marked perception (cf. "fussy and obsequious", "insincere", "oily") can come about through overuse of otherwise politic items, because overuse makes salient the fact that those items are merely politic, a situational norm, and not a sincere personal expression (cf. example (12): "'Yes Sir,' 'No Sir,' and 'Thank You' can appear to [sic] insincere if used too frequently").

In sum, we need to: consider what *over*-politeness might mean (e.g. is it the use of language that is too polite for the situation? the overly-frequent use of otherwise politic language?), accommodate a range of evaluations (positive to negative), and also pay attention to communicative dynamics (e.g. the (mis)management of interpersonal relationships and interactional goals). Locher and Watts (2005: 30) acknowledge in a footnote that their hypothesis that over-politeness and rudeness/impoliteness will have similar effects needs to be investigated empirically, but predict that "it is almost certain that they will both be negative". They do indeed both have negative effects, but those effects are very different in type. The strongest pattern for over-politeness consists of cases which are negative because they reflect relational mismanagement. This has more to do with "failed politeness" than impoliteness, as I would define it. It is difficult to construe any of the examples in this section as intentionally produced to create a negative effect (I return to the issue of intentionality in the following section). Thus, I would argue that none of them are likely to be considered impolite (indeed, that term was never used in the examples I analysed). However, it is worth noting that over-politeness (in whatever way "over" is defined) *can* be intentionally used and/or can be perceived to be intentionally used to create a negative effect. In this case it is not referred to as "over-politeness" but as "sarcasm"; over-politeness is one strategy by which the super-strategy of sarcasm (or "mock-politeness") can be realised (for my understanding of sarcasm, see Culpeper 1996 and 2005, and also my main source of inspiration, Leech 1983).

3.3.   Impoliteness and rudeness

In this section I focus on the bottom left quarter of Figure 1, and consider first the characteristics of that quarter with respect to appropriateness and norms, and then, more briefly, a possible distinction between impoliteness and rudeness.

Is it always the case that impoliteness is non-politic/inappropriate and marked? Are these defining features? Locher and Watts (2005: 12) do not clarify this point (although they are clear about the converse situation, "polite behaviour is always politic"). There seems to be some support in Locher's (2004: 83) comments: "If S's goal is to hurt H's feelings, he or she can still choose to do so via language. I believe that considerations of acceptability will not be of primary importance then." Watts argues on a number of occasions that if politic behaviour is "missing", it "tend[s] to lead to an evaluation of a participant's behaviour as 'impolite', 'brash', 'inconsiderate', 'abrupt', 'rude', etc." (Watts 2003: 169, see also 131, 182). Furthermore, Locher and Watts (this volume: 81) write that they understand impoliteness as "breaches of norms that are negatively evaluated by interactants according to their expectation frames". In general, then, impoliteness and politic/appropriate behaviour seem to be mutually exclusive. However, one particularly problematic area relates to contexts, such as army recruit training, in which face-attacking discourse of some kind plays a central role, and thus might be said to be "normal". Such discourses are accommodated by Watts, who refers to them as "sanctioned aggressive facework" (2003: 260). So, is it the case that we should place these discourses above the horizontal line in Figure 1 and treat them as politic/appropriate and unmarked, and thus unlikely to be evaluated as impolite? To do so, would gloss over some complicating factors, not least of which are that such discourses may involve one individual or more for whom such face-work is not normal, and that they may be differently categorised according to one's understanding of what a "norm" is. In this section, I will concentrate on frequency-based or "experiential norms", which have their basis in each individual's total experiences, whilst later I will concentrate on "social norms", which have their basis in the structures of society (this distinction in norm type is pointed out by Haugh 2003: 398–400; the label 'experiential norms' is mine). Essential to the latter is social power, which is why I discuss them in section 4.2, where I deal with impoliteness and power.

Part of the difficulty with Figure 1, and indeed the relational approach as a whole, is that the notion of contextual norm and how it might be applied in practice is not fully worked out. This is partly because, hitherto, the postmodernist approach has been particularly focused on the *in situ* emergence of politic behaviour and its evaluation by participants (e.g. Watts 2003: 164), as opposed to more abstract and general norms (see Terkourafi's 2005a: 243–4 critique of norms in the postmodernist perspective). Being politic/appropriate is a matter of being "normal" with respect to a particular social situation. Having said that, Locher and Watts have a cognitive view of the basis of participants' expectations, and the basis of those expectations is more abstract and general than a particular event. An individual's on-going accumulation of experiences and the cognitive representation of those experiences leads to the creation of more abstract and continually up-dated cognitive structures, and it is these cognitive structures that are an individual's norms, providing a basis for expectations and salience (for the importance of expectations and salience in relation to politic/polite behaviour, see the wording of Watts's definitions given in section 3.1). In their work, both Locher and Watts treat such cognitive structures as "frames", referring to, for example, Tannen (1993).[13] Obviously, no individual experiences an event in exactly the same way as others and no accumulation of experiences is exactly the same, and so we can assume that everybody has a different set of norms. However, many experiences are shared; in fact, all social interactions are shared in some way. Thus, although all individuals have different norms, we can expect considerable overlap with the norms of those with whom we interact. Indeed, it is those shared norms that facilitate understanding and communication. And lack of norm "sharedness" may cause communicative difficulty: some cross-cultural misunderstandings, for example, are a result of norms not being shared. Similarly, face-attack in a particular context could be a shared norm for some participants but not others. This is not the only difficulty. Every individual has many norms in their head – even if we share to some extent the norms of other participants in an event, we can only assume but not guarantee that they will apply the same set of norms (i.e. access the same cognitive structures). And this can have the consequence of different perceptions as to what is normal. For example, what might be normal in a specific context might not be normal at a more general level. An analogous point is made by Christie (2005: 6), who points out that without the understanding that Brown and Levinson's ([1978] 1987) model gives us of more general norms "the significance of the community in generating localised meanings would not come into view". Similarly, if some individuals apply local norms to the understanding of face-attack whilst others apply general norms, we are likely to end up with very different perceptions as to whether it counts as "real" impoliteness.

Locher and Watts do explicitly and repeatedly acknowledge the variability and relativity of an individual's frames (and hence norms) concerning the situational appropriacy of behaviours (see this volume, for example). The thrust of my argument is more a counter-balance to their general emphasis on the social and the local. In practice, normality is relative to an individual's experiences. What might be more relevant to an individual in a particular situation are more general, abstract norms. In order to illustrate this point, let me start by hypothesising that there are four types of 'norm' relevant to an individual engaged in a particular interaction:

- *Personal norms* based on the totality of X's social experiences.
- *Cultural norms* based on the totality of X's experiences of a particular culture.
- *Situational norms* based on the totality of X's experiences of a particular situation in a particular culture.
- *Co-textual norms* based on the totality of X's experience of a particular interaction in a particular situation in a particular culture.

These norms are based on particular types of context, and become less abstract and more situated (i.e. located in time and space) as one moves down the list. They are also hierarchical in the sense that an individual's cultural norms are embedded in their personal norms, their situational norms are embedded in their cultural norms, and their co-textual norms are embedded in their situational norms. One might visualise all this as a set of concentric rings, with personal norms as the outer-ring and co-textual norms at the ring surrounding the centre, which is made up of linguistic norms.

Now let us consider this with reference to army recruit training. The recruit's experiences of army training will be by definition minimal; it is more likely that the face-attack they experience will be seen as abnormal against the accumulation of other socialising experiences they have had, i.e. against their cultural and personal norms. Note that what I am saying here is that they are likely to *experience* it as abnormal, even though they may know that it is socially acceptable in that context and may even expect it to occur. In contrast, the recruit trainer's experiences of army training are likely to be substantial, as they are usually seasoned non-commissioned officers. For them, such face-attack could well be experienced as politic/appropriate against the situational norms of military training. It is also possible, given the norms of military life and the frequency of their own experiences in military training, that such face-attack is experienced as relatively politic/appropriate against their cultural and personal norms. Of course, what norms are brought into play in the process of understanding an interaction partly depends on the nature of that interaction itself, as language can prime its own context. The argument I made in Culpeper (2005: 63–67), drawing support from attribution theory, is that the salience of face-attacking linguistic and non-linguistic behaviours against personal and cultural norms can engulf local norms which might otherwise "neutralise" a judgement that it is impolite.

My arguments above support the idea that rudeness/impoliteness should be located in the bottom left quarter of Figure 1, characterised by inappropriate and negatively marked behaviours. The possible exceptions discussed here turn out to be less than water-tight, but we will need to return to them in section 4.2.[14] Before concluding this section, I want briefly to return to the issue of what is meant by "negative", and more particularly whether "rudeness" is negative in the same way as "impoliteness". No comments are made by Locher and Watts (2005) or Watts (2005) as to whether they consider rudeness and impoliteness to be different or just a couple of examples of terms for "situations in which face-threat mitigation is not a priority" (Locher and Watts 2005: 10), although the term *impolite* seems to be more frequent in their writing, as indeed that of other scholars, and is described as "relatively neutral" (this volume: 96) compared with *rude* and other terms. In Culpeper (2005: 63), I suggested that the term *rudeness* could be reserved for cases where the offence is unintentionally caused (a matter of relational mismanagement), whilst the term *impoliteness* could be used for cases where the offence was intentionally caused (a matter of negatively-oriented relational management). Intentionality is associated with (im)politeness2 approaches (the so-called pseudo-scientific approaches) and resisted by (im)politeness1 approaches:

In a first order approach to impoliteness, it is the interactants' *perceptions* of communicators' intentions rather than the intentions themselves that determine whether a communicative act is taken to be impolite or not. (Locher and Watts, this volume: 80, emphasis in original)

This seems to assume a traditional view of intentions as the private mental acts of speakers that precede and determine language use. Contrary to this, I follow Gibbs (1999: 17) in viewing intentions as "dynamic, emergent properties of interactive social/cultural/historical moments within which people create and make sense of different human artifacts". Thus, I would argue that "interactants' judgements" are not mutually exclusive with intentions: people make use of understandings of intentions in their judgements. Moreover, the perception of intention is a crucial factor in an evaluation of potentially face-attacking behaviour. By way of illustration, consider these quotations from WebCorp:

(14)   Will, a lesson I learned when I was a little kid was that if you think someone's saying something that's offensive, shocking, or out of character, have the decency and respect to ask him if he meant it.

(15)   "Yes, my best friend. . . anyway, he kept talking about her when I was there with him. It was kind of rude."
       "Perhaps he didn't mean it that way."

Furthermore, research in social psychology has repeatedly shown that hostile or aggressive behaviours are considered more severe (particularly, more marked for negative emotion), and are more likely to receive a strong response if they are considered intentional (see Gibbs 1999: 76–78 and the references therein).

My decision to use *impoliteness* to label cases of intentional face-attack and *rudeness* to label cases of unintentional face-attack was done because *I* as the researcher thought it a useful distinction to make; in other words, I did this in the spirit of defining impoliteness$_2$, without consideration of the lay-person's usage of these terms. I also intended my usage to have an inter-textual dimension as a counterpart to classic studies of politeness. Given that it is those classic studies of politeness that highlight the role of intention and are generally geared towards politeness$_2$, then impoliteness, as opposed to rudeness, would seem to be a better term for "intentional face-attack" with respect to the academic field. With regard to the lay person's usage of the terms *impoliteness* and *rudeness*, whilst their usages overlap, my preliminary investigation of the terms in the 100–million word British National Corpus suggests that they are not used in the same way or in the same contexts.[15] But it is not clear at this stage as to whether the difference is a matter of intention. *The Collins Cobuild English Language Dictionary* (Sinclair 1987) (a corpus-based dictionary and hence one more likely to reflect "real" usage and meanings), would seem to support my usage of the terms. Its definition of *impolite* is that "someone who is impolite is rather rude and offends people". For *rude* it is that "if someone is rude, they are not polite in their behaviour towards other people", and (the second listed meaning) that "rude is used to describe words or behaviour that are likely to embarrass or offend other people, usually words or behaviour relating to sex or other bodily functions". Here, it is "someone who is impolite" who "offends people", whereas with rudeness it is "behaviour towards other people" that is "not polite"; in other words, it is the term *impoliteness* that better allows for the attribution of intention to a person and not *rudeness*. However, as I said above, in my own corpus investigations I could not find a clear distinction based on intention. The resolution of this issue awaits future research. In concluding this paragraph and section, it is intriguing to note that the positioning of the terms *impolite* and *rudeness* in Figure 1 happens to match – perhaps coincidentally – my definitions. The label *rude* is much closer to *over-polite*, which, as I established in section 3.2, is most often negative in the sense of unintentional relational mismanagement, just as is the case with *rude*, whereas *impolite* as intentional negatively-oriented relational management is much further away. Readers may wish to note that Terkourafi (this volume) presents a case for using the labels *rude* and *impolite* conversely, with respect to intention, from that which I have just described.

4. Impoliteness and power

4.1. Power

Power seems to have a close relationship with politeness, given its treatment in the literature. Power figures in classic approaches to politeness (e.g. Brown and Levinson [1978] 1987; Leech 1983) and postmodern approaches (e.g. Watts 2003; Mills 2003). Power and politeness are the focal points of two recent monographs, Holmes and Stubbe (2003b) and Locher (2004), and various articles (e.g. Harris 2003; Mullany 2004; Tiisala 2004). In Brown and Levinson ([1978] 1987: 77), power is seen as an "asymmetric social dimension of relative power, roughly in Weber's sense. That is ... the degree to which H can impose his own plans and self-evaluation (face) at the expense of it S's plans and self-evaluation." Power in the sense of the ability to control someone else is also reflected in Brown and Gilman's (1972: 255) definition. It needs to be stressed here that power is defined as "relative" and not "absolute". Also, note that a connection with "face" is alluded to, such that the exercise of power is involved in trade-offs between the speaker's and the hearer's faces. Moreover, Brown and Levinson ([1978] 1987: 74–76) state that:

> We are interested in D[istance], P[ower], and R[anking of imposition] only to the extent that the actors think it is mutual knowledge between them that these variables have some particular values. Thus these are not intended as *sociologists'* ratings of *actual* power, distance, etc, but only as *actors'* assumptions of such ratings, assumed to be mutually assumed, at least within certain limits. (original emphasis)

All this should bode well for integrating such a model into relational work. However, Brown and Levinson ([1978] 1987) do not show how to realise the promise of their definition, and the practice demonstrated by the huge literature following the publication of Brown and Levinson's work certainly did not. The notion of power is reduced to static, given values on a variable that provides input to a formula for calculating the weightiness of a face-threatening act. This research has supported Brown and Levinson's predictions for the power variable: the more the relative power of the speaker, the more politeness they tend to receive (e.g. Baxter 1984; Brown and Gilman 1989; Holtgraves 1986; Holtgraves and Yang 1990; Lim and Bowers 1991; Leichty and Applegate 1991).

However, concerns have been raised about the way in which different studies tend to emphasise different aspects of the notion of power (see, for example, Spencer-Oatey 1996), and about the fact that the power variable does not reflect the complexity of how power works in interaction (see, for example, Turner 2003). A further point we might note is that Brown and Levinson ([1978] 1987) say little about the type of power that might be involved in interaction. For example, French and Raven (1959) distinguish amongst "coercive", "reward", "legitimate", "referent" and "expert" power (see also the types of power listed in Emmet 1953–54). In order to get a sense of the state of the art with respect to thinking about power, I will cite Locher's (2004: 39, 100) checklist, derived from a review of the literature:

- Power is (often) expressed through language.
- Power cannot be explained without contextualisation.
- Power is relational, dynamic and contestable.
- The interconnectedness of language and society can be seen in the display of power.
- Freedom of action is needed to exercise power.
- The restriction of an interactant's action-environment often leads to the exercise of power.
- The exercise of power involves a latent conflict and clash of interests, which can be obscured because of a society's ideologies.

- The exercise of power is often accompanied by displays of unmarked or positively marked relational work in order to maintain the social equilibrium and to negotiate identities.

This checklist attempts to account for power in terms of relational work. Note also that this list accommodates the *exercise* of power in language. Fairclough (e.g. 1989: 43) makes a distinction between power *in* and power *behind* discourse. Power in discourse refers to the exercise of power in the language, whilst power behind discourse concerns the constitution of social institutions and societies through power relations.

Brown and Levinson ([1978] 1987) and subsequent researchers in that tradition have been generally more concerned with aspects of the power behind the interaction, for example, the participant's status. However, Locher points out on a number of occasions that "people with higher status can refrain from exercising power", whilst "interactants with low status can decide to exercise power over people with relatively greater status" (2004: 31, see also 208, 218; Watts 1991 and Berger 1994 are cited as making a similar point). In other words, there is no simple match between power in language and power behind it. Moreover, Watts (1991: 56) argues that a notion of power based on status (a person's position in the structure of social relationships) is not very helpful for the analysis of the exercise of power in "face-to-face verbal interaction, particularly in the absence of overt institutionalised status differences". Consequently, Watts (1991: 60) deploys the idea of restriction of "freedom of action" to complement status (which is more oriented to power behind), and Locher (2004) adopts this too, as can be seen from the checklist above. This notion of the restriction of freedom of action, as Locher (2004: Chapter 2) observes, is common to several definitions of power (e.g. van Dijk 1989: 20; Wartenberg 1990: 85, 88), and indeed successfully deployed by Locher in her own analyses. Note that the restriction of a person's action-environment is not in itself enough to warrant the label "power". Locher's definition of power also involves a "latent conflict and clash of interests". This would seem to rule out more positively oriented types of power (e.g. a teacher exercising power over a pupil in order to ensure that pupil's examination success). However, such types of power are more marginal. As Watts (1991: 58) states: "[t]he central meaning of power surely involves a conflict of interests rather than a consensus".

4.2. *Impoliteness and power*

Is there a fundamental connection between impoliteness and power? Let us start with remarks made by Locher (2004). Locher (2004) does not discuss impoliteness. However, she touches on "serious FTAs" and "serious conflict" and the issue of power in the context of disagreements:[16]

> Committing serious FTAs is thus a powerful linguistic strategy to exercise power in order to engage an opponent in interaction. (Locher 2004: 201)

> Power and disagreement are connected through conflict and clashes of interest. Disagreement restricts an interactant's action-environment insofar as the recipient of disagreement will feel that some kind of answer or retort is expected, or necessary in order to prevent loss of face. In the case of a clear challenge this is even more pronounced. However despite the fact that action-restriction and conflict can be found in disagreement I argued that not every occurrence of disagreement is to be interpreted as an exercise of power. To qualify as an exercise of power, a qualitative analysis is needed in order to establish whether there has indeed been a serious conflict and clash of interests. (Locher 2004: 323, see also 328).

What I would like to do is consider whether her argument here can be applied to cases of behaviour that might be evaluated as impolite.

Impoliteness, as I would define it, involves communicative behaviour intending to cause the "face loss" of a target or perceived by the target to be so. And face loss in the context of impoliteness involves a "conflict and clash of interests", as the producer wishes (or is perceived to wish) to devalue "the positive social value" (Goffman 1967: 5) a target wants to claim for themselves or to deny some of their entitlements to freedom from imposition or freedom of association.[17] Thus, impoliteness can restrict an interactant's action-environment insofar as the producer pressures the interactant into a reaction, whether that means taking self-preservatory action or deciding not to react. To help illustrate the point, let me draw a possible analogy with a bank robbery (the money in the bank being your face). Consider this scenario:

> An assailant brandishes a gun (produces some communicative behaviour), symbolic of their power, with the intention, as you understand it, of getting money from you the bank clerk (to damage your face). Assuming the gun is real and loaded (you evaluate the face-attack as impoliteness and not, for example, banter or failed politeness), your actions are restricted.

Thus, insofar as one's action-environment is perceived to be restricted and there is a clash of interests, it can be argued that impoliteness always involves power.

From an interactional point of view, however, my scenario above is rather limited: it is only part of the story – we do not yet know how the clerk reacted. Let me pursue the scenario of the gun-wielding assailant confronting the clerk in a bank:

> You thus choose amongst: (1) doing nothing (risk loss of face), (2) handing over the money (accept the face loss), (3) trying to negotiate (defend your face, e.g.

abrogate responsibility), or (4) getting your own gun out from underneath the counter (counter with face-attack).

My aim here is not to challenge the argument in the previous paragraph: the fact that the clerk is forced into a reaction is a consequence of power in language restricting the clerk's action-environment. Rather, it is to broaden the perspective so that we can see how impoliteness and power might be managed in interaction and the implications thereof. In Culpeper, Bousfield and Wichmann (2003), one general aim was to consider impoliteness management across longer stretches of discourse than typically appear in classic politeness face-related works. In fact, the four options in the extended scenario above are the response strategies discussed in Culpeper, Bousfield and Wichmann (2003: 1562–1568) (see also Bousfield 2007b, for more detail and further development). For example, if the target counters with face attack (the fourth option above), the target not only in turn restricts the action-environment of the first speaker by forcing a reaction, but also challenges the power sustaining an asymmetrical relationship which allows the first speaker to be impolite in the first place (i.e. it challenges the power behind the first speaker's discourse). For example, if an army sergeant is impolite to a recruit and then that recruit responds with impoliteness, that recruit's impoliteness not only restricts the sergeant's action-environment (just as the sergeant had done to the recruit), but also challenges the (largely institutional) power sustaining an asymmetrical relationship, which allows the sergeant to be impolite to the recruit but not vice versa (hence such impoliteness from a recruit could result in a charge of insubordination).[18] In contrast, if the target accepts the face loss (the second option above) and neither restricts the first speaker's action-environment nor attempts to cause face loss in return, the target accedes to the power imbalance. A striking case of this is interactions between traffic wardens and car owners. We noted in Culpeper, Bousfield and Wichmann (2003) that:

> whilst a clamper has the power to ticket, clamp or even tow away an owner's illegally parked vehicle, they do not in their particular socio-discoursal role have the legitimate power to respond to the impoliteness of car owners with clear, unambiguous impoliteness. (Culpeper, Bousfield and Wichmann 2003: 1563)

There, as here, the social context (of which, of course, power is a part) constrains the response options used by a participant in an interaction, though that social context can be negotiated or challenged. Power – indeed, meanings – are co-constituted in interaction. If (im)politeness and power are relational, it matters *how* the target responds to that discourse, as that has implications for the kind of relationship that pertains between the interlocutors. We need to consider whether power is acceded or challenged (with the possible consequence of a power struggle) or otherwise managed in interaction.

Impoliteness and power need not only be conceived of in the fundamental reaction-to-face-attack sense discussed at the beginning of this section. Impoliteness can potentially restrict broader spheres of action; indeed, this is precisely the kind of issue I was referring to in the previous paragraph and will develop below. Beebe (1995), having analysed approximately 600 examples of perceived rudeness, argued that there were two main functions of "instrumental rudeness" (which roughly corresponds to what I consider to be impoliteness): (1) to get power, and (2) to vent negative feelings. "Getting power" here can be understood as the exercise of power. Beebe (1995) argues that rudeness to get power has the following purposes (summarised from pages 159–163):

> (1) To appear superior. Includes "insults" and "putdowns".
> (2) To get power over actions (to get someone else to do something or avoid doing something yourself). Includes "sarcasm" and "pushy politeness" used to get people to do something, as well as attempts to get people to "go away or leave us alone or finish their business more quickly".
> (3) To get power in conversation (i.e. to do conversational management) (to make the interlocutor talk, stop talking, shape what they tell you, or to get the floor). Includes saying "shush!" and rude interruptions.

A striking feature of this list is that each purpose relates to Brown and Levinson's ([1978] 1987) negative face or what Spencer-Oatey (e.g. 2000b, 2002) would call "equity rights".[19] Thus, I would generally describe these as "negative impoliteness", using the terms of my 1996 paper, or "equity rights impoliteness", using the terms of my 2005 paper. It is clear from Brown and Levinson (e.g. [1978] 1987: 130, 178–179, 209) that power is closely related to negative face, as they define it, particularly with regard to deferential behaviour (see also Holmes 1995: 17). The purpose "to appear superior" in the above list is obviously related to deference. The close relationship between power and negative face is not surprising, given Brown and Levinson's ([1978] 1987: 61) definition of negative face as "freedom of action and freedom from imposition", words which echo part of the definition of power drawn from Locher (2004) and discussed above. Note that the broader spheres of action referred to in this paragraph interact closely with the power behind discourses. Thus, for example, the unequal distribution of conversation could reflect an unequal distribution of power behind the conversation. Social structures (e.g. status, roles, institutions), of course, shape and are shaped by discourses. In the remainder of this section, I will look more closely at power in those social structures shaping power in discourses.

In Culpeper (1996), I argued that:

A powerful participant has more freedom to be impolite, because he or she can
(a) reduce the ability of the less powerful participant to retaliate with impoliteness (e.g. through the denial of speaking rights), and (b) threaten more severe
retaliation should the less powerful participant be impolite. (Culpeper 1996: 354)

This led to a prediction that impoliteness is "more likely" to occur in situations
where there is an imbalance of social structural power. This seems to be confirmed by research on the courtroom (e.g. Lakoff 1989; Penman 1990), army
recruits training (e.g., Culpeper 1996; Bousfield 2004, this volume) and ex-
ploitative TV shows (e.g. Culpeper 2005). However, there are difficulties. Why
does impoliteness occur in some situations characterised by symmetric social
structures, as is the case with much children's discourse (see Cashman's 2006
analyses of strategic impoliteness in child discourse, and also the references
she cites on pages 219–220)? And why does impoliteness, as I have defined it,
not occur more frequently in some situations characterised by markedly asymmetric social structures, such as doctor–patient interactions? Nevertheless, it
is safe to make the weaker prediction that situations characterised by asymmetric social structures are predisposed to impoliteness, and, more specifically,
unidirectional impoliteness produced by the more powerful targeting the less
powerful. An explanation as to why this is so relates to the legitimisation of
that impolite discourse. In situations such as the courtroom, as Kasper (1990:
210) points out, the institutional constraints do not licence the target to retaliate,
reflecting "an asymmetric distribution of rights to communicative practice that
reflects the unequal power relationship between prosecutor and defendant". In
all three of the asymmetric situations mentioned above, the powerful participants not only do impoliteness but are supported by the social structure in doing
so (e.g. the speaking rights afforded to a judge); in contrast, the less powerful participants are restricted by the social structure from meeting impoliteness
with impoliteness – they are more likely to suffer face loss without the ability to counter it. Of course, this does not mean that impoliteness will never be
done by the less powerful participants to the more powerful. Indeed, one possible motivation for doing so may be to gain status within a less powerful group
by vigorously challenging somebody with markedly more social institutional
power using techniques such as impoliteness (e.g. being impolite to a school
teacher, in order to gain status within a particular student peer group).

I have just described situations in which impoliteness is legitimised. Such situations contain what Watts (2003: 260) calls "sanctioned aggressive facework".
The sanctioning of impoliteness within particular situated discourses can be related to social norms as opposed to experiential norms. Coleman (1990) states

that a social norm is a rule of behaviour enforced by social sanctions. For example, throwing litter on the floor breaks a social norm in many cities. That social norm is driven by a social rule, "do not litter", and breaking that rule incurs sanctions. Those sanctions are underpinned by social institutions and structures (e.g. a legal system) and enforced by those in power. Also, if social norms become internalised by members of society, sanctions can take the form of disapproval from others or guilt emanating from oneself. Thus, they take on a moral dimension. Sanctioned behaviour also relates to social norms: it is their flip side, as it is unrestricted, legitimate and free from social sanctions. Sanctioned aggressive facework involves the unrestricted and legitimated occurrence of potentially impolite communicative behaviour. However, it is worth noting here that not all sanctioned aggressive facework situations involve the sanctioning of impoliteness produced by those with relatively great power targeting those with relatively little power. Harris (2001), for example, describes the sanctioned impoliteness that takes place in the UK's House of Commons, giving the Opposition MPs opportunities to attack the Government that they might not have had in other contexts.

We need a complex vision of norms if we are to explain cases like that reported in Mills (2002: 86) in which a conference participant stated that in his year's army training "he found the level of impoliteness personally threatening and offensive", but that nevertheless he "recognized that it was appropriate to the context and did not in fact complain to the authorities about it". The first quotation seems to orient to experiential norms, whereas as the second seems to orient to social norms. And just because something is sanctioned does not mean impoliteness is neutralised for all participants (e.g. Culpeper 2005: 66–67; see also Bousfield 2007b, who provides more evidence and extends the argument with regard to norms). Importantly, note that relatively powerless participants in the situations I have been discussing (the army recruits, defendants in the courtroom and gameshow participants) tend to be much less familiar with those situations than the relatively powerful participants (the officers, judges/prosecutors and hosts) – they are at an experiential disadvantage. This is not to say that impoliteness in such situations is unexpected by such participants, but having "theoretical" knowledge about what is likely to happen in such situations (e.g. being told about them or making predictions based on situations presumed to be analogous) is different from having personally experienced what happens in them.

5. Conclusion

One advantage of relational work, as Holmes and Schnurr (2005: 124) point out in their discussion of "relational practice", is that it avoids "the definitional traps, referential slipperiness, and emotional baggage of the term 'politeness'". Moreover, relational work offers an all-embracing framework. *Politeness, impoliteness* and other such terms are labels of contextual evaluations of particular manifestations of relational work. However, these are early days: some aspects of relational work are underspecified and/or lacking in empirical support. The label *negative* is insufficient to capture the very different kinds of relational work that can be classified by it. For example, I demonstrated that people's negative evaluations of "over-politeness" are largely an assessment that the speaker is guilty of relational misjudgement, not attempting to cause damage to face. In terms of both how the researcher might classify orientation to face and how the lay person evaluates such different types of facework such a distinction is crucial. Of course, one reason why that distinction might be absent from relational work in its current form is that it involves "interactional wants", something which is closely related to intentions (note that my above wording "attempting to cause damage face" assumes intention). Unlike Locher and Watts, I argued for the importance of intention, and specifically the importance of intention in identifying a type of facework that is likely to be evaluated as *impolite*, as distinct from, say, *rude* or *over-polite*.

I also pointed out that the notion of "norms" is underspecified in relational work. The distinction between appropriacy and markedness is not yet clear. Both appropriacy and markedness are related to norms, but they are clearly not co-extensive in Locher and Watts's framework, and so must have a different or somewhat different basis (markedness seems to be more closely associated with affect, but it is not clear how). Regarding appropriacy norms, impoliteness/rudeness is generally considered inappropriate, and intuitively this seems right. Of particular interest are specific contexts – often asymmetrical and institutional – in which face-attacking behaviour might be considered "normal". These are discussed by Watts (2003) and Mills (2002), but largely from the perspective of social norms. From this perspective, face-attacking behaviour could indeed be normal. However, I stressed that there are different ways of defining norms, and dwelt on a distinction between experiential norms and social norms. I argued that different participants may have different experiential norms and/or evoke different experiential norms. In fact, in the kinds of asymmetric "face-attack as normal" contexts discussed by Watts (2003) and Mills (2002), I would argue that the less powerful participants may well have and evoke different experiential norms – for them, face-attack could well be abnormal and taken as impoliteness.

It can be argued that power merits even more attention in the study of impoliteness compared with politeness (see Bousfield, this volume, for a somewhat different view). If power in discourse is defined as the restriction of somebody's action-environment and a clash or conflict of interests, then it can be argued that impoliteness always involves power as it forces (or at least pressurises) the target to react. However, an act of action-environment restriction can be challenged: we must consider the full relational implications of the kind of reaction/response that the target makes to that act. Thus the notion of action-environment restriction must be applied reiteratively as the discourse progresses, encompassing both what the speaker does and the hearer does. For example, by meeting impoliteness with impoliteness, one not only restricts the first speaker's action-environment in turn, but also challenges the power relationship sustaining that first speaker's impoliteness act, and a power struggle ensues. Note in this example that the notion of action-environment restriction is applied to power in discourse but simultaneously has implications for power behind discourse.

In my discussion, I noted how impoliteness generally relates to power behind discourse. Referring to Beebe's (1995) three purposes of impoliteness in relation to power (i.e. to appear superior, to get power over actions and to get power over conversation), I highlighted overlap with what Brown and Levinson ([1978] 1987) would think of as negative face, a concept which has a particularly close association with power. Then, looking more closely at the social structures underpinning particular asymmetric situations, I argued that such situations were predisposed to impoliteness, specifically, unidirectional impoliteness from the relatively powerful to the relatively powerless. Finally, I considered particular situations where sanctioned aggressive face-attack is said to occur, bringing the discussion back to the notion of norms. I argued that neutralisation and sanctioning are very different. In *some* asymmetric situations where sanctioned aggressive facework takes place, for the relatively powerless the salience of face-attack against (possibly stronger) experiential norms acquired outside that specific context could mean that that face-attacking behaviour is more likely to engulf the immediate situational context, with the consequence that the "impoliteness" is not discounted by the context but taken as very "real". In contrast, the expectancies of the relatively powerful are very different: for them attacking-facework may well be relatively normal. Moreover, for the relatively powerful it is also sanctioned. That is to say, against social norms impoliteness in such situations is "normal", and as such it is unrestricted, legitimate and free from sanctions – it is sustained by social structures.

Much of what I have written here is the tip of the iceberg. There are huge conceptual and methodological problems to tackle. Relational work points towards a promising way forward on the conceptual front, but the proof of the pudding is in the data and its analysis, both qualitative and quantitative. With regard to a methodology for helping to move research forward, I have given a glimpse of one corpus-related methodology that can be used to enhance our understanding of people's conceptions of (im)politeness-related terms (interestingly, Locher and Watts in this volume, also deploy meta-linguistic data from the web).

Notes

1. The project of which this publication is a part is funded by the U.K.'s Economic and Social Research Council (ESRC) (RES-063-27-0015). I would also like to acknowledge the challenging and helpful comments made by the reviewer and the editors. Needless to say, remaining errors and infelicities are mine.
2. The problem of the limitations of classic communicative theory, particularly with respect to how it copes with interaction, is in fact acknowledged by Brown and Levinson ([1978] 1987: 48), although critics usually ignore this acknowledgement, as Arundale (2006: 194–195) points out.
3. To be fair, Grice did at least accommodate the full range of linguistic "behaviour" in his scheme, and even includes non-linguistic examples. However, subsequent generations of Griceans have mostly had a much narrower focus, ignoring prosody and non-verbal aspects.
4. Whilst it is clear that this volume did much to set the agenda for the new discursive approach to politeness, it should be noted that not every paper within it could be described as discursive.
5. The fact that face attack or aggravation should be included in a theory of facework has been acknowledged for some time (see the clear statement in Craig, Tracy and Spisak 1986: 457–458).
6. Later work tends to include the synonym "appropriate" along with "politic". Because the term "politic" can be considered as loaded as the term "politeness", the use of the more neutral (though still discursively constructed) and also more transparent term "appropriate" is preferable.
7. Bear in mind that Leech's generalisations here reflect British culture.
8. If we take a corpus to be a "large and principled collection of natural text" (Biber, Conrad and Reppen 1998: 12), then all the texts of the web certainly constitute a large body of natural language data, but it can hardly be described as principled. Here, principled means designed to represent a language or part of a language, which then involves issues of sampling and representativeness. However, John Sinclair (e.g. 2004: 188–190), possibly the leading figure in British corpus linguistics, would strongly argue that it is size that matters, and uses huge unstructured (unprincipled) corpora, notably, the Bank of English, in his own research.

9. Of course, giving precise figures for the share of particular languages of the whole internet is impossible. The figure of 80% English is given in the Humanising Language Teaching journal at: http://www.hltmag.co.uk/may00/idea.htm.

10. The typos, grammatical errors, and other infelicities that appear in the examples quoted from the Web in this chapter are as per the original.

11. Of course, many examples could be given here from the cross-cultural pragmatics literature.

12. "Pwog" seems to be an acronym for "people who own gold", used to imply hypocrisy.

13. I prefer to treat them in terms of schema theory (see references in Eysenck and Keane 2000, especially pp. 252–257 and pp. 345–362), though there is some overlap with frame theory (depending on which version of frame theory one considers).

14. There may be other kinds of exception that are more viable. Banter, for example, may involve a stronger sharedness of norms amongst the relatively equal participants.

15. *Rude/rudeness* are vastly more frequent than *impolite/impoliteness* (raw figures for the adjectival and nominal forms of the respective terms are: 55/2 versus 950/101). They distribute across genres differently (for example, *rude* = 19.5 per million in spoken data versus 2.3 in academic writing; *impolite* = 0.2 per million in spoken data versus 0.6 in academic writing). They have completely different collocates (for example, the top five collocates within a five-word span for *rude*, calculated on the basis of Mutual Information scores, are *awakening, downright, arrogant, jokes, aggressive*, whereas for *impolite* they are *would, been, be, have, it*).

16. Of course, "disagreement" is not at all synonymous with "impoliteness", and is often discussed within politeness frameworks and analyses.

17. The conception of "face" I articulate here both goes beyond that of Goffman (1967) and subsumes the positive and negative faces of Brown and Levinson ([1978] 1987). I follow Spencer-Oatey's (e.g. 2002: 540–542) components of Rapport Management, which consist of Face (Quality face and Social identity face) and Sociality rights (Equity rights and Association rights) (see Culpeper 2005 and Cashman 2006, for how these components might be utilised in the description of impoliteness).

18. As might be guessed, this is rare in army recruit training discourse. In approximately a dozen hours of video recording, I know of only two cases where this happened.

19. Of course, just because I use the term "negative face" here should not be taken to imply that I accept the concept without question. Note that I also supply the very approximate equivalent for Spencer-Oatey's (e.g. 2000b) scheme, which I prefer. Also, I would be the first to acknowledge that that face is context-sensitive: I am not suggesting, for example, that all cultures have the same conception of negative face and link it in the same way to power.

Chapter 3
Toward a unified theory of politeness, impoliteness, and rudeness

Marina Terkourafi

1. Introduction

Some of the earliest suggestions that politeness in language deserves to be studied in its own right are found in the works of H.P. Grice and John Searle. Both scholars acknowledged that treating conversation simply as an information-exchanging process is something of an oversimplification, and that to do justice to the complexities of real conversational exchanges, social factors – indeed, politeness – should be factored in (Grice 1989a: 28; Searle [1975] 1996: 177). Similar remarks provided the impetus for generations of scholars to seek out the ways in which politeness is realised in language.

One thing that quickly became evident in the course of those investigations was that, if explicitly expressed politeness was on occasion incongruous with the context, or even missing, the result was not merely neutral or puzzling but rather impoliteness/rudeness.[1] This is not to say that participants may not on occasion suspend judgement until they have more evidence to decide whether politeness or impoliteness/rudeness is intended. Respondents' replies to a survey of intuitions about politeness suggest just such an ability to suspend judgement: asked how they would understand an utterance of "I was wondering if you could help me and I'm not trying to be polite," 22 native English speakers responded that despite explicitly denying a polite intention, such an utterance is not necessarily impolite; rather, they would seek further clues (body language, subsequent turns) to understand how it was meant (Terkourafi 2001: 142). What respondents' replies suggest is that judgements about politeness or impoliteness/rudeness are not always automatic but may be reached after some deliberation about the speaker's intention. Crucially, information from all channels (verbal and nonverbal) will be taken into account during this process. At the same time, their replies highlight the fact that participants can generally suspend judgement about politeness or impoliteness/rudeness only temporarily. Settling how Self stands in relation to Other in conversation (i.e. whether Self's face is being constituted or threatened)[2] is important – indeed, I will argue in section 2.2, it is a *sine qua non* of human communication – and that is why respondents in the survey reported above would be willing to expend the extra effort needed to decide whether their interlocutor was polite or not by paying attention to his/her subsequent behaviour.

Interlocutors' preparedness to engage in potentially costly inference to settle how they stand in relation to each other suggests that the choice between politeness and impoliteness/rudeness is not only important, but may in fact be a dichotomous one. In other words, there may not be an interactional 'middle ground' one can safely straddle between the two.[3] Early works on politeness show some awareness of this. Lakoff (1973) discusses a situation where two friends who would normally exchange "Shut the window"-type requests switch to "Please shut the window":

> [i]n this case, if [the] A[ddressee] is at all acute, he will note from the use of <u>please</u> alone that [the] Sp[eaker] is not kindly disposed toward him; that there has been a change for the worse in the relationship (Lakoff 1973: 295, 302).

Similarly, Brown and Levinson ([1978] 1987) acknowledge that when an FTA is of low R[anking], off-record indirectness may seem "inappropriately devious" (1987: 17), and discuss several politeness strategies which can easily be tipped over into rudeness and vice versa, including indexical switches (1987: 122), tense and location markers (1987: 174–176), use of emphatic particles (1987: 211), metaphors (1987: 222–223), and ritualised insults (1987: 229). Finally, Leech (1983) points out that increased indirectness does not necessarily lead to increased politeness, but may also lead to the contrary effect: in a situation where an airport official asks a passenger going through customs whether s/he has something to declare, "the more indirect kinds of question are progressively more impolite, more threatening, than the ordinary *yes-no* question" (1983: 171).

Despite the above observations suggesting an understanding of politeness and impoliteness/rudeness as two sides of the same coin, these authors still write of "face redress felt to be irrelevant" because "the focus of interaction is task-oriented" or the speaker does "not care about maintaining face" (Brown and Levinson [1978] 1987: 97), and of "politeness [being] waived" in "desperation" (Lakoff 1973: 305). Lakoff even proposes a category of "non-politeness" defined as "behaviour that does not conform to politeness rules, used where the latter are *not expected*" (1989: 103, emphasis added). These latter comments suggest an understanding of face considerations as an optional add-on, (almost) a luxury attended to time permitting, but otherwise easily and quickly dispensed with in the interests of urgency, clarity, and generally efficient information exchange, or when the speaker is powerful enough to "not care."

The view that face considerations may be dispensed with is categorically denied in Scollon and Scollon's dictum *"there is no faceless communication"* (1995: 38, original emphasis; cf. Arundale and Ashton 1992). Developing that line of thought, I have argued that face considerations along with rationality lie at the basis of the Cooperative Principle (henceforth CP), producing the whole gamut of behaviours from 'altruistic,' 'going-out-of-one's-way' cooperation to outright conflict (Terkourafi 2007a).[4] The guiding principle is now reformulated as "co-operate as much as necessary to constitute your own face (which may involve constituting or threatening your interlocutor's face in the process)" (Terkourafi 2007a: 317). Rather than re-iterating that argument here, I will use an example to illustrate how use of language can never be innocent with respect to face considerations, and how, in effect, interactants always come out of an exchange feeling that their faces have been constituted or threatened to a greater or lesser extent.

Consider potential answers to an information-seeking question such as "Where do you live?" Answers to this question can be ranked on a scale of informativeness, from less to more informative. So long as A finds B's reply appropriate given the situation, both A's and B's faces will have been constituted – that is, they will walk away from the exchange and probably not think about it again, since there was nothing memorable about it. But if A receives the answer "At the centre" when A had been expecting a more informative one, A may feel that B does not wish to associate with A, and experience that as a threat to A's positive face (by the very same token, of course, B is thereby constituting B's negative face). On the other hand, if B replies "I live at 10, Church Street, apartment 302" – a totally appropriate, hence face-constituting, answer if giving testimony at a police station, but perhaps not during casual conversation – A may feel that his/her negative face is being imposed upon this time (in one possible scenario, B may be 'coming on' to A by inviting A to come home with B).

According to this line of argument, one would be hard pressed to find an expression whose use on an occasion is inconsequential to face. This includes expressions associated with informativeness *par excellence* such as numerals and scalar terms, along the lines outlined above. The upshot of this discussion is that even speaking according to the Gricean maxims (informatively, truthfully, relevantly) is not uninformed by face considerations, but is regulated by face (e.g. with respect to the maxim of Quantity, face considerations regulate how much is "as much as one can say" and how much is "more than one must say"). But if there is 'no escape from face,' so to speak, then it is not possible to single out a set of expressions that 'do facework' as opposed to those that do not: all linguistic expressions do 'information work' *and* 'facework' at the same time all the time.[5] Nonetheless, although it is impossible to engage in one without simultaneously engaging in the other, some linguistic expressions (conventionalised ones; see section 4) do facework more frequently (and therefore, more economically) than others (cf. Terkourafi 2002, 2003).[6] Furthermore, if face considerations pervade the fabric of conversation in the ways just suggested, and if politeness shares with impoliteness/rudeness the same interactional space such that one may easily tip over into the other, then face provides a common basis on which to build a unified theory of politeness, impoliteness and rudeness.

The purpose of this chapter is precisely to suggest some of the defining lines of such a theory without claiming to be offering anything approximating to a complete sketch. Specifically, I will address three questions in turn:

- How is face to be defined to serve as the common basis of politeness, impoliteness and rudeness? (section 2)
- Is recognition of the speaker's intention required to determine whether politeness, impoliteness, or rudeness is taking place? (section 3)
- If recognition of the speaker's intention is not (always) required, what can the speaker do to ensure his/her behaviour is interpreted by the hearer as it was intended? (section 4)

Before setting off, two provisos are in order. First, the present chapter is programmatic. Its aim is to offer theoretical support to a set of hypotheses that remain to be tested empirically. It is not grounded in the analysis of a corpus of data, although it draws on real-life examples and others' analyses of pertinent data from different languages. Since studies of impoliteness are still in their infancy, I believe that using our existing theoretical battery to carve out an area of investigation and to suggest hypotheses that may guide the collection and analysis of data within that area can be a worthwhile enterprise.

Second, the reader may have noticed above the nearly interchangeable use of the terms politeness/impoliteness/rudeness and face. Ever since Brown and Levinson ([1978] 1987) drew an explicit link between Goffman's notion of face and linguistic politeness, they opened the way for a wholly new definition of politeness as a technical term (i.e. following recent practice, as Politeness$_2$) referring to all face-constituting linguistic behaviour. And since all linguistic behaviour impacts on face along the lines suggested above, a theory of politeness will be interested in all linguistic behaviour seen through the lens of its potential impact on face, in much the same way as speech act theory takes in all linguistic behaviour seen through the lens of its illocutionary-force-expressing potential. Objections to using the term 'politeness' to designate such a theory are then well founded, if what is understood by politeness is Politeness$_1$. For Politeness$_2$ as just defined is a much broader notion, *not* co-extensive with intuitive definitions of Politeness$_1$. A more appropriate name for such a broader theory of Politeness$_2$

would include 'face' in the title, as in Arundale's "Face Constituting Theory" (e.g. 1999). Preserving the name 'politeness theory' or 'politeness studies' is then only justifiable on historical grounds, safeguarding continuity across the field over time. But while preserving 'politeness' in the title(s) of our theor(ies), we should not lose sight of the fact that, ultimately, it is *not* definitions of Politeness₁ that are the topic of investigation – after all, a lexeme 'politeness' as such is not attested in all languages (cf. Terkourafi 2005a: 242–243) – but how face is continuously and unavoidably brought into existence, constituted, and threatened through language.

2.   Face and the roots of politeness, impoliteness and rudeness

2.1.   Face in Brown and Levinson's work

Given the central place awarded to the notion of face in a unified theory of politeness, impoliteness and rudeness, an opportune place to begin is by defining the applicable notion of face. As already mentioned, the notion of face was introduced into linguistic theorising by Brown and Levinson ([1978] 1987), inspired by Goffman's (1971) distinction between supportive and remedial interchanges. Brown and Levinson ([1978] 1987) define face as:

> the public self-image that every member wants to claim for himself consisting in two related aspects: (a) negative face: the basic claim to ... freedom of action and freedom from imposition (b) positive face: the positive consistent self-image or 'personality' claimed by interactants, crucially including the desire that this self-image be appreciated and approved of. (Brown and Levinson [1978] 1987: 61)

Prior to providing the basis for a theory of linguistic politeness, the term 'face' had been in common use in English and in other languages in such expressions as 'saving face' and 'losing face' (Ervin Tripp, Nakamura and Guo 1995), and Brown and Levinson ([1978] 1987: 61) explicitly acknowledge drawing on the English folk-term when formulating their definition of face. This intimate relationship between the scientific and folk terms in English is perhaps to blame for several of the shortcomings researchers noted over the years in their efforts to apply the theory to different cultural settings. In particular, other cultures seem to emphasise the possibilities of enhancing face as well as threatening it (Matsumoto 1988; Bayraktaroğlu 1992; Mao 1994), of positive face being more important than negative face (Rhodes 1989; Sifianou 1992b), and of group considerations taking priority over individual wants (Nwoye 1992; Mao 1994), all of which are absent from Brown and Levinson's discussion of face. To remedy these shortcomings, further distinctions have been proposed (see Nwoye 1992; Mao 1994, among others).

2.2.   Toward a notion of Face$_2$

Paralleling the distinction between Politeness$_1$ and Politeness$_2$ mentioned earlier, O'Driscoll (1996: 8) proposes that "[w]hat we need is a theoretical construct, not a notion which various societies invest with varying connotations", in other words, a second-order notion of face, or Face$_2$. Taking his proposal as a starting point, I investigate what may be the defining properties of such a universalising notion of Face$_2$. I focus on two such properties (see also Terkourafi 2007a): (a) the biological grounding of face in the dimension of approach versus withdrawal, and (b) the intentionality of face, i.e. its directedness, or aboutness. These two properties are all that is universal about face. Its culture- and situation-specific contents are then filled in under particular socio-historical circumstances, yielding distinct, but motivated, conceptualisations of Face$_1$.

The biological grounding of Face$_2$ refers to its grounding in the dimension of approach versus withdrawal (or avoidance), a dimension that goes well beyond the realm of the human:

> Organisms approach and withdraw at every level of phylogeny where behaviour itself is present. To approach or to withdraw is the fundamental adaptive decision in situations or conditions that have recurred during our evolutionary past .... In very primitive organisms with simple nervous systems, rudimentary forms of approach and withdrawal behaviour occur .... Over the course of evolution, approach and withdrawal action emerged prior to the appearance of emotions to solve adaptive problems in simple species. (Davidson 1992: 259)

According to neuroscientific evidence, incoming stimuli are simultaneously sent to two types of brain mechanisms (LeDoux 1998: 67–71, reported in Theodoropoulou 2004: 110–111). Evaluation mechanisms assess whether a stimulus is good or bad, prompting a suitable response from a finite and fixed suite of actions. Such mechanisms are fast and coarse because the organism's survival depends on them. Identification mechanisms, on the other hand, are slower and more flexible. They classify incoming stimuli as particular kinds of stimuli, opening up a range of possible reactions to them. Approach or withdrawal result when a stimulus is evaluated as friendly or hostile respectively, before it is further identified as this or that type of stimulus.

Variously referred to as positive versus negative 'valence' or 'affect,' the dimension of approach/withdrawal has been proposed as the common substratum of all human emotions, and associated with the pre-cognitive reactive level (Ortony, Norman, and Revelle 2005: 179–182). Indeed, there may be little beyond it that is universal about human emotions (Davidson 1992: 259). Its importance has been recognised at least since Aristotle (*On Rhetoric*, Book II, § 6), and underlies Gibson's distinction between affordances of benefit and injury (1982), and Damasio's views on the duality of pleasure and pain:

> Pain and pleasure are thus part of two different genealogies of life regulation. Pain is aligned with punishment and is associated with behaviours such as withdrawal or freezing. Pleasure, on the other hand, is aligned with reward and is associated with behaviours such as seeking and approaching. . . . . This fundamental duality is apparent in a creature as simple and presumably as nonconscious as a sea anemone. (Damasio 1999: 78)

The literature on human emotions is interspersed with similar observations highlighting the phylogenetically primary, universal, and pre-conscious nature of approach/withdrawal. These properties make approach/withdrawal a natural candidate to provide the basis for a universalising notion of Face$_2$ "divorc[ed] from any ties to folk notions" (O'Driscoll 1996: 8). The biological grounding of Face$_2$ in approach/withdrawal affords us with an explanation for its universality and its dualism between positive (approach) and negative (withdrawal) aspects, without for that matter introducing an otherwise unmotivated ordering between these two aspects.

However, if Face$_2$ is universal and encompasses both positive and negative aspects, it does not necessarily follow that it is uniquely human. The property making Face$_2$ uniquely human is its *intentionality*.[7] In the philosophical tradition of phenomenology (Brentano [1874] 1981); Husserl [1900] 1970), intentionality refers to the distinguishing property of mental (as opposed to physical) phenomena of being *about* something, i.e. directed at an object. Beliefs, hopes, judgements, intentions, love and hatred all exhibit intentionality, inasmuch as they presuppose that which is being believed, hoped, judged, intended, loved or hated. Similarly, face is intentional inasmuch as it presupposes an Other toward whom it is directed.[8]

Awareness of the Other, in turn, presupposes an awareness of the Self, which is known to emerge from 9 months onwards through joint attentional behaviours involving the primary caretaker (usually the mother; Tomasello 1999: 61–77; Brinck 2001). At the heart of these behaviours is the infant's newly found ability to make a distinction between "others not just as sources of animate power but as individuals who have goals and make choices among various behavioural and perceptual strategies that lead toward those goals" (Tomasello 1999: 74). Understanding others as intentional agents in turn prompts the infant's understanding of *him/herself* as an intentional agent, and is neurophysiologically mediated by the experience-dependent maturation of a "dual process frontolimbic system" around the middle of the second year (Schore 1994). Interestingly, children with autism and some non-human primates including chimpanzees also exhibit a basic understanding of the efficacy of their own actions on the environment. This understanding, nevertheless, does not reach full-blown intentionality, inasmuch as it is not supported by "the uniquely human biological predisposition for identifying with others in a human-like manner" (Tomasello 1999: 76–77). This uniquely human predisposition, sometimes referred to as "empathy," appears to be favoured by a combination of factors that include "an extended life history, altricial [sic] development, and the increase in prefrontal functions" (Preston and de Waal 2002: 20).[9] And while cross-disciplinary evidence concurs on the fact that empathy is *phylogenetically continuous* (Preston and de Waal 2002: 2), these factors are co-instantiated to a high degree only in normally developing humans, creating the semblance of a predisposition that is "uniquely human."

2.3.   The interactional dyad as the locus of Face$_2$

The intentionality of Face$_2$ guarantees that face is characteristically human and irreducibly relational. Because it is intentional, Face$_2$ cannot be an attribute of individuals in isolation. Individuals alone do not 'have' face and cannot 'gain' or 'lose' face. Rather, Face$_2$ is grounded in the interactional dyad.[10] Without an Other to whom they may be directed, face concerns cannot arise. The moment an Other enters the Self's visual field creating the possibility to approach or to withdraw, that is the moment when face concerns prototypically arise. To adapt a well-known expression, face is 'in the eye of the beholder.'

At the same time, the intentionality (or directedness) of Face$_2$ toward an Other means that Self will have several faces concurrently, as many as there are Others involved in a situation. Putting this somewhat schematically, if I am interacting with an interlocutor in front of an audience, I make (and am aware of making) a bid for face not only in the eyes of my interlocutor, but also in the eyes of each of the members of that audience taken separately and as a group (for an example, see section 3.2). And the same applies to each of them. Since face is relational, bids for face are always bi-directional. As Self makes a bid for face in the eyes of Other, by the very same token Other too makes a bid for face in the eyes of Self.

Speaking about Self and Other does not mean they are to be understood as monolithic entities co-extensive with the physical body. Rather, Self and Other are sociopsychological constructs. In the physical presence of one participant,

I may be simultaneously apprehending several Others, some of whom I may be approaching while withdrawing from others. There is nothing preventing the same instance of behaviour achieving approach on one level and withdrawal on another – what Arundale calls connection and separation face being "co-instantiated" (2004: 16–17) – so long as these are directed at different Others (for an example, see Terkourafi 2007a, section 6.1).

As interlocutors constitute their own faces in conversation, this multiplicity of faces may lead to interesting permutations of face-constituting and face-threatening behaviours directed at different Others, what may be termed 'instrumental' uses of face constituting/threatening (see also the reformulation of the CP in Terkourafi 2007a: 317, cited in section 1). For instance, Self may be constituting Self's face in the eyes of Other by threatening Self's face in the eyes of Other – self-humbling honorifics work in this way. Or, Self may be constituting Self's face in the eyes of some Other by threatening the face of yet a different Other, who may or may not be the addressee, in an instance of 'instrumental rudeness.' Ultimately, I would like to claim that all rudeness (though not all impoliteness; see section 3.3) is instrumental in this way. When Self threatens Other's (or even Self's) face, it is in order to constitute Self's face in the eyes of Self,[11] Other, or yet a different Other or Others. Clearly, considerations of power permeate this interactional game, in that they determine whose face may be threatened and whose face may be constituted. That is, power is acted out in the hierarchical ranking of the multiple faces that arise in interaction.

2.4. *Face$_2$ and power as emergent from the interaction*

Pinning down the notion of power in any coherent way is famously difficult, not least because what counts as 'power' seems to depend on context. Institutional power, sexual power, consumer power are different kinds of power, but one would be hard pressed to make explicit a set of constitutive properties they all share. Moreover, 'powerful' is not just a characteristic of persons, but also of impersonal organisations, and even particular behaviours. Particular ways of speaking, standing, walking, dressing, and eating, to mention but a few, may be invested with (symbolic) power – symbolic because it is presumably a matter of collective practice reproduced over time – but such power is no less real, as is quickly seen when it is in turn 'passed on' to persons enacting these behaviours, such that in the end it is difficult to tell whether the person or the behaviour is the source of power: sometimes, the clothes, apparently, do "maketh the man!"

On the other hand, while in a Marxist framework economic power would be the ultimate source of all power, recent approaches have challenged the "monist base-superstructure determination of classical Marxism" (Chouliaraki and Fair-clough 1999: 24), pointing to "the primacy of the symbolic sphere with respect to political economy, and against the autonomy of the symbolic sphere with re-spect to power" (Leezenberg 2002: 905). According to Leezenberg, a conception of power as an "intentional, but not subjective relation, conceived of as a set of strategies rather than rules, to which resistance and struggle are internal" is found in the work of Michel Foucault and offers a promising way forward, inasmuch as it does not take for granted (as does Bourdieu's notion of symbolic power, for instance) the conceptual priority of the sphere of political economy over the sphere of meaning and significance (Leezenberg 2002: 905–906). Leezenberg argues convincingly against a conception of power as solely negative or repres-sive, and grounded in consent, and makes a case for power as a necessary force for the attainment of meaning, and therefore productive of meaning. Meaning may thus be seen as the hallmark of a successful bid for power. Finally, he lists four relevant features of such a notion of power: it is a relation between two or more actors; it is intentional in that it cannot be characterised in isolation from the beliefs, aims and goals involved in social action; it is pervasive in all social action (economic, cultural, linguistic); and, it may well be productive, indeed constitutive, of institutional facts (Leezeberg 2002: 906–907).

Although Leezenberg does not put it in those terms, his analysis suggests that power may be *emergent* from practices, such that we shouldn't be surprised to find that it has no single essence, nor can it be reduced to another sphere from which it inherits its significance. One way to approach power as emergent from practices is to start from recent suggestions in the evolutionary linguistics lit-erature that the use of language to "manipulate others into physical, emotional, and perceptual reactions" is phylogenetically as well as ontogenetically prior to its descriptive/referential use (Wray 2002: 114). The manipulative function of language may be seen as a natural concomitant of Face$_2$: any organism suscep-tible to approach or withdraw and capable of intentional thought would also be naturally inclined to manipulate others. Once manipulation is possible, strate-gies to secure its effectiveness also become pertinent. Power may then emerge over time as a cumulative effect of several successful acts of manipulation. That would make power an emergent property of interaction, without tying it down to particular attributes of the participants or the situation. Rather, it would be "power from below" as proposed by Foucault (1976: 124) and explicated by Leezenberg, that is, power which "is not imposed from above in the force of domination by a sovereign, but arises from the collective action, or interac-tion, of the different social actors involved" (2002: 899). Moreover, such power would not be reducible to purely deontic power, or "status valued for its own sake" (Searle 1995, reported in Leezenberg 2002: 899), since, in agreement with Bourdieuan notions of symbolic power, it would serve ulterior practical goals.

The potential multiplicity of faces introduced in section 2.3 as a consequence of the intentionality of $Face_2$ suggests a way to integrate a further aspect of Leezenberg's proposal, namely the fact that power does not presuppose consensus but may be "conceived of as a set of strategies ... to which *resistance and struggle are internal*" (2002: 905, emphasis added). Since Self is not co-extensive with the physical body such that when two interlocutors are conversing several Selves and several Others may be construed in parallel, it is possible to claim power by 'switching' between these different Selves, and construing the situation as one regulated by a different set of practices from which a different balance of power may emerge. Such switching need not necessarily be co-opted by one's interlocutor: so long as what one is doing remains intelligible to one's interlocutor (i.e. remains within a recognisable space of possibilities), the Other appealed to by the Self under which one is currently acting is irrevocably brought into existence.[12] In this way, institutional facts may be created "through the struggle for, or even the arrogation of, powers" (Leezenberg 2002: 902). *Contra* Searle (1995: 118–119 cited in Leezenberg 2002: 902), the relevant speech acts are not pretended and parasitic, since the multiple faces at stake are not *a priori* hierarchically ordered, which would make some acts more canonical than others. The impression of canonicity, that is, emerges only as a concomitant of power that is itself emergent from practices and remains open to challenge. Taking on board the proposed notion of $Face_2$ with the resulting multiplicity of faces may thus offer new ways of accounting for the emergent nature of power, as well as its dynamicity.

3. The role of intention in constituting – and threatening – face

3.1. Face constituting/threatening and recognising the speaker's intention[13]

Following Grice,

> U meant something by uttering x' is true iff, for some audience A, U uttered x intending:
> (1) A to produce a particular response r
> (2) A to think (recognise) that U intends (1)
> (3) A to fulfil (1) on the basis of his fulfilment of (2).
> (Grice 1989b: 92)

As this quotation makes clear, not just any type of intention is involved in communication but characteristically r-intentions, where 'r' stands for 'reflexive.' R-intentions are special in two ways. First, they are *intended to be recognised* by the hearer as being intended by the speaker. Second, their *fulfilment consists in such recognition*. To give an example, if I say to you "Paris is the most beautiful city in the world," I am communicating to you that I want you to believe that *I* believe that Paris is the most beautiful city in the world. If you recognise that *I want you to believe that I believe this*, then my intention in uttering "Paris is the most beautiful city in the world" will have been fulfilled. The content of your relevant belief may be spelled out as "MT wants me to believe that MT believes that Paris is the most beautiful city in the world." You do not have *actually to believe* that I believe this,[14] much less *share my (purported) belief* that Paris is the most beautiful city in the world. If you were to come to hold any of these further beliefs, they would be *perlocutionary effects* of my utterance. Although my purpose in communicating may be to bring about these effects, ultimately I have absolutely no control over whether they are achieved or not.

According to Brown and Levinson ([1978] 1987: 5), politeness is just such a matter of r-intention. Brown (1995), in particular, notes:

> Politeness inheres not in forms, but in the attribution of polite intentions, and linguistic forms are only part of the evidence interlocutors use to assess utterances and infer polite intentions. . . . [Interlocutors] must continuously work at inferring each other's intentions, including whether or not politeness is intended. (Brown 1995: 169)

On this view, the speaker's intention to be polite by uttering expression x is fulfilled if the hearer, upon hearing x, recognises this intention along the lines outlined above. Notice that, if politeness is a matter of intention recognition, it is not necessary that the hearer actually comes to believe that the speaker *is* polite as a result of the speaker's uttering x. That would be a perlocutionary effect of the speaker's utterance. It is perfectly imaginable that the hearer may recognise the speaker's polite intention, yet not be convinced that the speaker is polite as a result. Utterances such as "I was only trying to be nice," or "I know she was trying to be polite, but she came across as rude" illustrate the gap between the speaker's (polite) intention and the perlocutionary effect achieved.

Having distinguished between recognition of the speaker's intention and perlocutionary effect achieved, the question facing us is: which is required to say that face has been constituted/threatened? Must the hearer recognise the speaker's intention, that is, must the hearer believe *that the speaker wants the hearer to believe* that the speaker is constituting/threatening face? Or must the hearer ac-

tually believe that the speaker is constituting/threatening face? There are a few indications that the latter is the case.

Consider the two cases of 'failed politeness' mentioned above. In the first case ("I was only trying to be nice"), the speaker's polite intention in making some previous utterance has not been recognised, and that is why the speaker needs to make this intention explicit in a subsequent turn. Not only was the speaker's polite intention not recognised, what is more, it is likely that an *im*polite/rude effect has been achieved.[15] The speaker's subsequent turn then has the dual purpose of counteracting this negative effect by re-instating the speaker's original polite intention. Conversely, in the second case, the first conjunct shows that the speaker's polite intention *has* been recognised ("I know she was trying to be polite"), yet this is not enough to convince the hearer that the speaker is polite ("but she came across as rude"). Additional facework is then likely to be needed on behalf of the 'rude' speaker to dispel the impression of rudeness. This should not be the case if constituting face consisted of recognising the speaker's intention.

Another piece of evidence that constituting/threatening face does not amount to recognising the speaker's intention lies in the fact that politeness/impoliteness/ rudeness cannot be part of 'what is said' by an utterance of a sentence. If face constituting/threatening were tantamount to recognising the speaker's intention, the shortest way to achieve this should be to state that intention explicitly, e.g. by uttering something like "I am (being) polite/rude." However, rather than being the prototypical way of being polite, "I am (being) polite" sounds nonsensical at worst, and has a corrective flavour to it at best ("I am (being) rude" cannot have this corrective flavour, of course). Like "I was only trying to be nice," claims that one is polite can only be used to make up for a previous utterance that went wrong. But why is it that politeness/impoliteness/rudeness cannot be stated directly, when so many other beliefs and desires can?

The reason why they cannot be stated directly lies with the fact that politeness/ impoliteness/rudeness *evaluate* behaviour but they do not *constitute* behaviour in and of themselves. A request or a complaint, on the other hand, constitute particular behaviours, and as such they can be realised more or less directly, and evaluated for their politeness/impoliteness/rudeness. In other words, politeness/ impoliteness/rudeness are second-order notions ranging over behaviours.[16] Like other second-order notions (e.g. modifiers such as 'fast'), they must be fleshed out in the shape of a particular behaviour ('fast turtle') to come into being. An utterance such as "I am (being) polite/rude" is unlikely to constitute/threaten face even if the hearer recognises the speaker's intention, because such an utterance fails to provide behavioural evidence that the hearer can evaluate it as polite (or rude).

3.2.   *Face constituting/threatening as perlocutionary effects*

While recognition of the speaker's intention may not in and of itself consti-
tute/threaten face, since face constituting/threatening are perlocutionary effects
beyond the control of the speaker, it is still possible that achieving these perlocutionary effects necessitates prior recognition of the speaker's intention. That is,
face constituting/threatening may rely on recognition of the speaker's intention,
such that they cannot be achieved in the absence of such an intention. Alternatively, face constituting/threatening may not rely on recognition of the speaker's
polite intention. In the latter case, face constituting/threatening are, as Fraser
and Nolen (1981: 96) put it, "totally in the hands (or ears) of the hearer", and
are achieved (or not) independently of whether a face-constituting/threatening
intention was even there to begin with. Real life provides many examples supporting the latter possibility.

Take a situation where a female shopper is browsing items in a shop and
is interpreted by other shoppers as making way for them to pass. She had no
intention to be polite to anyone, yet her behaviour was positively evaluated by
them, as evidenced by their thanking her for it. Her concurring with their interpretation, as evidenced by her smiling, meant that her behaviour went down on
the conversational record not as she had originally intended it – browsing mer-
chandise – but as others interpreted it – an 'after you' gesture. Had this shopper
not been the author, it would have been impossible to know that a discrepancy
ever existed between her intention and the perlocutionary effect achieved by
it. Similar examples where face is constituted/threatened in the absence of a
corresponding intention by the speaker may be multiplied. The point is that
they remain unaccounted for if face constituting/threatening as perlocutionary
effects are made contingent upon recognising the speaker's intention.

Two further types of evidence support this claim. The first comes from instances when one is polite to one's addressee not so much to constitute that
addressee's face (as a means of constituting one's own face), but rather to constitute one's own face in the eyes of some audience (on the multiplicity of one's
faces, see section 2.3). Take the Cypriot Greek exchange below:

(1)   [On TV; Speaker: male, 31–50, middle-class. Addressee: female, over 51, middle-
       class. Relationship: interviewer to interviewee)
       *na **se** ðiakopso? ixa ðjavasi akrivos afto pu **lete** ...*
       to **you-sg.** interrupt? I-had read exactly that which **you.pl-are-saying**
       'May I interrupt {you}? I read exactly what YOU are saying' ...

The interviewer's fluctuation between the 2nd person singular ('you') and the 2nd
person plural ('YOU') can hardly be attributed to a change in his relationship

with the addressee within the space of a few words. Their relationship is perfectly compatible with using the 2sg.: using it constitutes the addressee's face, since contrary to what happens in Standard Greek, the 2sg. in Cypriot Greek does not carry connotations of familiarity/equality that may have been inappropriate in this context (Terkourafi 2005b).

However, the speaker is not simply interested in constituting his face in the eyes of his interlocutor, but also in the eyes of each of the members of the audience. By using the 2pl., he displays familiarity with the linguistic norms of the current interview setting, establishing his professional competence, and thereby constituting his positive face. Crucially, the speaker's second desire cannot in principle be directed to any well-circumscribed, identifiable audience, as is required by Grice's definition of r-intention cited earlier. The perlocutionary effect of constituting his face is achieved so long as anyone and everyone who might ever watch this broadcast, including those present in the studio (including the hearer), thinks he is familiar with the operative linguistic norms, in virtue of his addressing the hearer in the 2pl. Therefore, the second desire of the speaker in (1) cannot be modelled as an r-intention, since membership of the audience responsible for producing the response r is open-ended. Still, the perlocutionary effect of constituting his face is achieved. Consequently, face-constituting must be construed as a perlocutionary effect, which can be achieved irrespective of the recognition of the speaker's polite intention by any particular audience.

The final supporting piece of evidence builds on the observation that, more often than not, face is constituted over several conversational turns rather than in single utterances. Building on Goffman's concept of interactional imbalance, Bayraktaroğlu (1992) shows that certain kinds of acts may be required in order to ensure face-constituting given the kinds of acts that preceded them. In such cases, face-constituting is distributed over all of these acts rather than being associated with any one of them in isolation. This possibility remains unaccounted for if constituting face is tied up with recognising the speaker's r-intention. Following Grice (1989b: 92, cited above), each time a speaker utters an utterance, s/he does so with a particular r-intention, and each time this r-intention is recognised by the hearer, some further perlocutionary effects may or may not be achieved. Consequently, a perlocutionary effect which is contingent on recognising the speaker's intention is either achieved or not following the understanding of this utterance alone: achieving it cannot be distributed over several utterances occurring sequentially in discourse, since a distinct r-intention corresponds to each of these. This is not to deny that a distinct perlocutionary effect can in principle follow the recognition of each of these r-intentions. However, this perlocutionary effect alone does not amount to face-constituting: only when taken jointly do these perlocutionary effects – what Bayraktaroğlu (1992: 15) terms "changes in face-values" – constitute face. Once more, we conclude that face-constituting must be construed as a perlocutionary effect achieved independently of the recognition of the particular r-intention with which the speaker uttered any one particular utterance.

3.3. Impoliteness, rudeness and the speaker's intention

Much like politeness, impoliteness/rudeness are also types of perlocutionary effect. These consist of the hearer thinking that the speaker is approaching/ withdrawing *in*appropriately – given cultural norms – whether this involves omitting an appropriate move or adding an inappropriate one.[17] Rather than constituting face, the effect now is a threat to face.

Speaking of a threat to face does not entail that interlocutors enter a conversation already having face which is then threatened. Rather, interlocutors take for granted that Other is interested in constituting Other's face through conversation (see also the reformulation of the CP in Terkourafi 2007a: 317, cited in section 1), and interpret Other's behaviour accordingly. What they are trying to determine, of course, is whether Self's face is constituted or threatened in this process.

I argued in section 1 that every behavioural (including linguistic) move necessarily effectuates approach/withdrawal. However, not all moves are equivalent in this respect: some approach/withdraw appropriately, while others approach/ withdraw inappropriately. Approaching/withdrawing inappropriately results in face-threat for the addressee, and potentially also for the speaker. Approaching/ withdrawing appropriately can also threaten the addressee's face, as we shall see in section 4.3. That happens when face-threat is *expected*, resulting in 'unmarked' rudeness. The difference between unmarked rudeness and rudeness proper (or marked rudeness) lies in their effect on the speaker's face: the former regularly (i.e. directly) constitutes the speaker's face in the eyes of Other, while the latter does so contingent on Other's assessment of the situation. In sum, three types of face-threatening behaviour may be distinguished: impoliteness, rudeness proper, and unmarked rudeness. Of these, impoliteness and rudeness proper are *marked*. That is, these behaviours are noticed because they involve a departure from the expected course of events.

Some support for classifying impoliteness and rudeness (whether proper or unmarked) together under face-threatening behaviour comes from etymological and cross-linguistic evidence. Cross-linguistically, distinguishing between them seems to be the exception rather than the rule. Although French too lexicalises a distinction between *impolitesse* and *rudesse*, other European languages, including Spanish (*grosería*), Italian (*scortesia*) and Greek (αγένεια), do not. Lack of a distinction between *impoliteness* and *rudeness* in this very small sample of languages, as well as the definition of one with recourse to the other in those languages (English, French) that do distinguish between them, suggest that impoliteness and rudeness share the same interactional space: that of face-threatening behaviour.[18]

Moreover, etymological evidence suggests that face-threatening behaviour is generally marked. According to the Oxford English Dictionary (OED), of the three terms, *politeness*, *impoliteness*, and *rudeness*, *rudeness* is the oldest. The adjective *rude* ultimately descends from Latin *rudis* meaning 'unwrought, crude, uncultivated,' much as *polite* descends from Latin *politus* meaning 'polished.' However, the temporal discrepancy between the two regarding when they entered the English language is worth noticing. *Rude* is first attested meaning 'ignorant, uneducated' in 1366 (1380 for *rudeness* in the corresponding sense), while it is used to characterise human relationships as early as 1590 (*rudeness* in this sense is attested even earlier, in 1532). *Polite*, on the other hand, meaning 'smoothed, polished' enters the language at about the same time (1398), but does not develop a sense meaning 'courteous' until 1751. Furthermore, the corresponding noun, *politeness*, does not appear before 1627, and then directly with a figurative meaning ('intellectual refinement, elegance, taste'), developing the sense of 'courtesy' soon thereafter (1655). In sum, over a century separates the interactional sense of *rudeness* from the interactional sense of *politeness*. Moreover, this temporal discrepancy cannot be put down to the origins of the two lexemes, since both were borrowed into English from (Old) French.[19] Needless to say, *impolite/impoliteness* is the youngest pair of the three, attested figuratively as 'wanting polite manners/want of politeness' in 1739 and 1773 respectively. Clearly, much deeper cross-linguistic investigation is required to substantiate a claim based on etymological evidence as to the cognitive importance of the corresponding categories in human experience. Nevertheless, the English evidence does suggest a tentative hypothesis for further research, namely that the reason why the lexemes *rude/rudeness* appear earlier in the language is because the corresponding behaviours are more salient. Face-threatening behaviour that departs from what is appropriate in the situation is noticed, and therefore easier to point out and circumscribe (see also the analysis of rudeness proper in section 4.3).

If impoliteness and rudeness are characterised by a face-threatening perlocutionary effect, that doesn't mean that a distinction between them cannot be drawn. In languages like English that do draw this distinction, attribution of intention seems to be the basis for it. I would like to suggest (*pace* Culpeper 2005: 39, 63, 69; this volume) that in impoliteness the face-threat is taken to be accidental, i.e. attributed to the speaker's ignorance or incompetence – as may occur, for instance, in cross-cultural communication – whereas in rudeness the face-threat is taken to be intentional. Support for dividing the pie in this way comes, once more, from lexicographical evidence. Several dictionaries of English use terms relating to the speaker's intention when defining *rude* (e.g. '*offensively* or *deliberately* discourteous'; OED, 1989, 2nd edition, emphasis added), but not so when defining *impolite* (e.g. 'not having or showing good manners'; OED, 1989, 2nd edition).[20] Diachronic data confirm their different semantic shading. Senses of *rude* have included 'uncivilised, barbarous' and 'violent, harsh,' whereas *impolite* merely refers to 'wanting polite or courteous manners,' i.e. behaviour that is less than, or imperfectly, polite. The temporal precedence of *rude* by a few centuries as outlined above adds a further piece of evidence: early lexicalisation can be explained if *rude(ness)* is more salient, noticed, and commented upon, because it is thought to provide an insight into a person's character, i.e. to be linked to intention, contrary to *impolite(ness)* which refers to an accidental slight, not a stable character trait, and therefore constitutes a lighter offence.

Rudeness, then, contrary to impoliteness, is generally characterised by attribution of a face-threatening intention. In addition, impoliteness and rudeness proper are both marked, i.e. noticed. Consequently, they both trigger an inferential process of recognition of the speaker's intention. The difference between them is that, in impoliteness, actively inferring the speaker's intention leads to the conclusion that the speaker had *no* face-threatening intention, while in rudeness proper it leads to the conclusion that the speaker *did* have a face-threatening intention. Pinning down the speaker's intention plays a decisive role for charting one's subsequent course of action (i.e. how to bring it about that one's face, having been threatened, is now constituted). For this reason, resolving the speaker's intention cannot be dispensed with but always takes place in the case of unexpected face-threatening behaviour.[21]

3.4. An undecided example

The following real-life incident pushes to its limits the distinction between intentions and perlocutionary effects as it applies to impoliteness/rudeness.[22] A man apprehended by a policeman whom the man found to be obnoxious 'got his own back' on him by singing in a foreign language a song about the evils of police brutality. The question is: has rudeness occurred? What is interesting about this incident is that the man chose to be rude *in another language*. In terms of face, switching to a language the speaker knows the hearer does not understand signals disassociation and is common in cases of communication breakdown (for instance, a similar incident occurred between the bus-conductor and a ticket-less passenger on the Oxford–Cambridge coach line on March 19, 2006).[23] By the same token, it also ensures that the speaker's intention behind the switch remains obscure. *Singing a song* in the other language further obscured this intention, since singing can be an otherwise innocent, non-communicative (in the sense that it does not necessarily involve an r-intention) activity, comparable, for instance, to whistling. The man's face-threatening intention, then, dressed up in a song sung in an unintelligible language, was simply not designed to be recognised (was not an r-intention). The policeman may well have been at a loss as to how to evaluate the speaker's action beyond noticing it, unexpected and hence marked as it was. Unable to resolve whether a face-threat was intended or not, the policeman could not accuse the man of rudeness. The man, then, had the best of both worlds: as far as he was concerned, he was rude, but as far as the policeman was concerned, he could not be accused of rudeness. Observation suggests that rudeness designed not to be recognised is often chosen as an optimal solution to threaten the face of an Other who has power over Self.

However, although the man thought he was constituting his face by means of attacking the policeman's face, strictly speaking, his actions had no such effect. He was not communicating anything, but merely venting his feelings.[24] On the other hand, had there been a bystander able to decipher the lyrics of the song, then the man's face could have been constituted *in that bystander's eyes*, as a result of that bystander's recognition of the man's intention (and subject to the bystander's sharing the man's attitude towards policemen). Indeed, constituting his own face is what the man would be trying to achieve later by recounting his exploits.

What all this points to is that rudeness, no matter how strongly intended by the speaker, cannot go down on the conversational record, i.e. influence the subsequent course of events, unless the speaker's rude intention is somehow recognised by the addressee. In the case of rudeness proper, a face-threatening perlocutionary effect *must* be accompanied by Other's recognition of the speaker's face-threatening intention. Another term for rudeness thus understood would be *face-attack*. In the case of impoliteness, however, a face-threatening perlocutionary effect is achieved but Other does not attribute a face-threatening intention to the speaker.

4. Unmarked politeness and unmarked rudeness

4.1. *Marked and unmarked politeness*

Now, it may appear as if defining face-constituting/threatening as a perlocutionary effect and divorcing this from the speaker's intention leaves the speaker totally helpless: if face-constituting/threatening are "totally in the hands (or ears) of the hearer" (Fraser and Nolen 1981: 96), is there anything the speaker can do to increase the chances that his/her face will be constituted? Before answering this question, a couple of clarifications are in order. First, much as in cases of rudeness discussed earlier, it is not the case that recognising the speaker's intention *never* plays a part in reaching the perlocutionary effect of constituting face. Sometimes, reaching this effect may *depend* on recognising the speaker's polite intention first. That will be the case, for instance, in situations of cross-cultural communication, when we are prepared to make allowances for different ways of saying things, and seek other clues (intonational, facial, gestural; subsequent turns) to help us decide what our interlocutor's intention was. In fact, 'cross-cultural' need not imply speaking different languages. Speaking the same language but not adhering to the same, recognisable conventions is enough to cause the impression that different 'cultures' are at play, as suggested by the results of the native speaker survey reported in section 1. Whether we ultimately come to believe that the speaker is polite (i.e. reach the perlocutionary effect of constituting face) is then based on our prior recognition of the speaker's intention.

Another class of cases when recognising the speaker's intention plays a part in constituting face is strategic politeness, that is, politeness used as a social "accelerator" or "break" (Brown and Levinson [1978] 1987: 93, 228). In such cases, the speaker is manipulating the situational context (i.e. the values of D, P and R in Brown and Levinson's theory) in which his/her utterance is to be interpreted, rather than taking it to be as both participants perceived it to be so far. Furthermore, the speaker seeks to secure the hearer's concurrence with his/her manipulation of the situational context. But the hearer's concurring with whatever the speaker is trying to do depends on the hearer's first recognising *what* it is the speaker is trying to do. That is, it depends on the hearer's recognition of the speaker's intention. Significantly, the perlocutionary effect now sought is manipulation of the situational context, in addition to face-constituting.

A final class of cases where reaching the perlocutionary effect of constituting face depends on first recognising that the speaker's polite intention are instances of what has been called 'over-politeness' (Locher 2004; Locher and Watts 2005; Culpeper, this volume). Instances of over-politeness (e.g. "Thanks ever so much indeed" uttered in response to a customer picking up her clothes at the dry-cleaner's) may of course also constitute instances of strategic politeness, in that the speaker may additionally be manipulating how the situational context is to be construed. Over-politeness, however, need not serve a particular strategic, self-serving goal. It may also be motivated by liking (without for that matter implying that rapprochement/acceleration, i.e. lowering of D values, is to occur), a good mood, or their opposites, dislike and anger. Which of these the hearer thinks is intended by the speaker will determine whether the hearer ends up believing that the speaker is approaching/withdrawing appropriately or inappropriately, i.e. whether face will be constituted or threatened.

If the above instances (of cross-cultural communication, strategic politeness, and over-politeness) require taking into account the speaker's intention before reaching the perlocutionary effect that itself constitutes face, they also have a *marked* flavour about them. Trivially, none are referred to by a simple term; they are all modified by an adjective/adverb: *cross-cultural* communication, *strategic* politeness, *over*-politeness. Intuitively, they represent instances when we may need to take a step back and think about what the speaker is trying to do before we decide whether to go along with it. This marked flavour suggests that there must also be another set of *unmarked* instances when we feel safe jumping to conclusions about what is going on and behave accordingly. Such by-passing of the speaker's intention and reaching face-constituting directly occurs when politeness passes unnoticed, which is, admittedly, most of the time (how many times did you say 'please' or 'thank you' today?). Reaching face-constituting directly, rather than via scrutinising the speaker's intention, underlies 'unmarked' politeness (Terkourafi 2001, 2003). In unmarked politeness, the speaker's intention is presumed rather than actively inferred: we do not stop to think about it. We take it for granted.[25] This brings us back to our original question: when the speaker's intention is not involved in constituting the hearer's (and through that, the speaker's) face, is there anything the speaker can do to increase the chances that his/her face will be constituted in the ears of the hearer? Or is s/he totally helpless with the hearer holding all the cards?

4.2.   *Unmarked politeness and short-circuiting of the speaker's intention*

To increase the chances that his/her face will be constituted, there is something the speaker can do. The speaker can provide samples of behaviour that *the speaker thinks* will constitute his/her face in the ears of the hearer. Clearly, the felicitousness of this move is contingent upon the speaker's making accurate assumptions about the hearer's value system or *habitus* (Terkourafi 2001:

18–19, 182–184). Introducing this move at once shifts the onus of proof from the speaker's intention to the speaker's and hearer's *habitus*. Bourdieu (1990) defines *habitus* as:

> systems of durable, transposable dispositions, structured structures predisposed to function as structuring structures, that is, as principles which generate and organise practices and representations that can be objectively adapted to their outcomes *without presupposing a conscious aiming at ends or an express mastery of the operations necessary in order to attain them*. (Bourdieu 1990: 53, emphasis added)

Such dispositions include linguistic dispositions: knowledge of usage conventions (from lexemes to less or more abstract constructions) above and beyond the abstract rules of Universal Grammar. Acting out these linguistic dispositions is part and parcel of one's *habitus*. It is not something one has rational control over, although *habitus* are continuously formed and reformed through experience and extended socialisation within a community of practice. Linguistic dispositions, in other words, reflect one's experience of language use in particular situations.

Such experience will include correlations between linguistic expressions and the situations in which they are used. The use, in a particular situation, of an expression which is regularly used to achieve a certain perlocutionary effect in that situation – in other words, which is conventionalised relative to that context[26] – will, then, increase one's chances of achieving that perlocutionary effect *to the extent that* one's experience and one's interlocutor's experience are similar enough to have led to the development of similar linguistic dispositions, or overlapping *habitus*. In this way, conventionalised expressions emerge as one's safest bet *as long as* interlocutors' experiences are similar, and the expression is used in a context relative to which it is conventionalised. All else being equal, what the current speaker's actual intentions are does not matter. Lacking an indication to the contrary – an unusual intonation, creative modification of a conventionalised expression and so on, which may attract attention to the speaker's intention pushing the expression over into the 'marked' category and triggering explicit inferencing about the speaker's intention – simply uttering the expression in that context will achieve the perlocutionary effect conventionally associated with it *ipso facto*. To put this differently, face constituting/threatening will fall out as a by-product of speaking in the normal (most common, expected, unmarked) way for the situation one is in – or, of cooperating as redefined above (section 1). Conversely, should interlocutors' experiences diverge (as in instances of 'cross-cultural' communication mentioned above), or the expression be used in a context other than the one relative to which it is conventionalised (instances of strategic or over-politeness), face constituting cannot be automatically assumed.

Deciphering the speaker's intention will then be required to decide whether the speaker's and hearer's faces have been constituted.

To sum up so far, the speaker's face is constituted through language when, taking his/her linguistic behaviour as evidence, the hearer thinks the speaker is approaching/withdrawing appropriately. Reaching this evaluation is a perlocutionary effect of the speaker's linguistic behaviour. This perlocutionary effect is reached without recourse to the speaker's intention, as long as the expression uttered is conventionalised (in a broad sense, including intonation) relative to the surrounding context *in the experience of both interlocutors*. Discrepancies in interlocutors' experiences or mismatches between the context and the expression uttered mean that resolving whether approaching and/or withdrawing are taking place in an appropriate manner requires taking the speaker's intention into account (that is, it requires explicit inferencing, and, potentially, recursive application of the maxims; cf. Terkourafi 2001: 134–136, 2003, 2007a).

4.3.   Unmarked rudeness

In the preceding section, I suggested that perlocutionary effects such as face-constituting/threatening can be conventionally associated with the utterance of particular expressions in particular contexts, that may be construed as culturally recognisable scenes modelled as frames (Terkourafi 2001, forthcoming), or as activity types (Culpeper, Crawshaw and Harrison 2006). What this suggestion implies, on closer inspection, is that particular contexts may be invested with particular expectations about how face will be handled in them. Just as some situations call for face-constituting, other situations call for face-threatening by definition. The latter include police and other types of interrogations, army-training discourse, courtroom discourse, and the types of parliamentary discourse and confrontational encounters analysed by Harris (2001) and Culpeper, Bousfield and Wichmann (2003) respectively. In adversarial contexts in general, it is often – though not necessarily – the case that a transgression has occurred prior to the encounter. When conversing in such contexts, interlocutors constitute their own faces as always, but there is the added assumption that, in doing so, each will threaten the other's face. In other words, this time face-threat is expected.

Language provides for these situations too. In virtue of occurring most frequently in situations calling for face-threat, some expressions may be conventionalised to express face-threat. All languages have constructions used for swearing. An example of this is the cognate curse in Egyptian Arabic. Stewart defines this as "a single sentence with an optative verb, either explicit or understood, in which a keyword echoes the root-letters of a keyword [a verb or a noun; MT] in the initiator phrase to which it responds" (1997: 331). Cognate curses "are most often used by parents or superiors towards children and subordinates. They are used by women more than men, and typically by women of lower socio-economic status in traditional society" (1997: 344). In other words, the cognate curse is an elaborate construction with constraints on phonological form and meaning, as well as on its sequential placement in discourse, and situational contexts of occurrence.

Through particularly frequent association with face-threatening contexts, some expressions can go even further, acquiring face-threat as their encoded (or semantic) meaning, much as expressions such as 'please' or 'thank you' that can be argued to have face-constituting written in their semantics. It cannot be stressed enough that *this does not mean that these expressions will always achieve face-constituting (or, face-threatening) when uttered*, since face-constituting/threatening are perlocutionary effects beyond the speaker's control. Much as through metaphor or irony an expression can mean something different from, or even the opposite of, its encoded meaning, expressions encoding face-threat or face-constituting can be used to achieve the reverse effect. Banter (Leech 1983: 144–145) and ritualistic insults (Labov 1972) provide examples of such exploitations, when participants' face is constituted through what would have been conventionally a face-threat.

The existence of expressions conventionalised for face-threat to a greater or lesser extent[27] opens up the possibility that a face-threatening perlocutionary effect, much like a face-constituting one, can also be reached directly, without reference to the speaker's intention. As with 'unmarked politeness,' 'unmarked rudeness' is achieved when the expression is used in a context relative to which it is conventionalised, and the interlocutors' *habitus* are homologous. On the other hand, departures from these two conditions would render the speaker's utterance unexpected, and therefore marked, requiring a reference to the speaker's intention to determine whether face-constituting or threatening is occurring.

In sum, there are times when face-threat can be appropriate.[28] Threatening the face of the addressee on these occasions is the shortest and safest way for the speaker to constitute his/her own face, because by threatening the face of the addressee *when it is appropriate to do so* s/he displays familiarity with the operative norms and therefore claims to be a competent member of society. It is then up to the addressee to provide an appropriate response, one constituting his/her face in return, potentially leading up to the kinds of 'escalation' and 'conflict spirals' mentioned by Culpeper, Bousfield and Wichmann (2003: 1564).

Unmarked rudeness contrasts with rudeness proper (or marked rudeness). In rudeness proper, the speaker still threatens the face of the addressee in order to constitute his/her own face, but because face-threat is now unexpected, i.e.

inappropriate, the speaker is on much shakier ground. By being properly rude, the speaker is 'sticking his neck out', 'taking his chances,' so to speak. There is no convention supporting, or better, ratifying, his/her choice of words, as in 'unmarked' rudeness. Whether his/her face will ultimately be constituted, and in whose eyes, is totally up to the other participants: their value systems, their construal of the situation, their mood of the moment, their emotional predispositions toward the speaker. That is why properly rude encounters are always marked and stressful to deal with, and properly rude behaviour a risky business, normally avoided with addressees more powerful than oneself (for an ingenious compromise, see section 3.4). I believe we have no term at present to refer to instances of 'unmarked' rudeness as outlined above, *rudeness* having been traditionally identified with inappropriateness and negative feelings, i.e. with rudeness proper. I nevertheless am convinced that such instances exist, and deserve to be studied in their own right, for they can reveal to us a lot about the ways in which face influences, and is influenced by, the way we speak.

5. Conclusion

The criss-crossing of the notions of face, intention, perlocutionary effect, and conventionalisation discussed in the previous sections presents us with a rather complex picture of the interrelations between politeness, impoliteness, and rudeness. There is little reason to think that our social world is actually any simpler than that. In this concluding section, I attempt a preliminary synthesis of the various strands of politeness, impoliteness, and rudeness distinguished earlier, without harbouring any illusions as to its accuracy or completeness. Some of these categories may have to be collapsed, while others may have yet to be discovered. The full canvas of possibilities when it comes to face-constituting/ threatening linguistic behaviour remains to be drawn in detail. But for the moment, I would like to propose that it looks something like this:

- *unmarked politeness* occurs when an expression that is conventionalised relative to a context where face-constituting is expected is used in that context, and to the extent that the interlocutors' *habitus* are homologous; it constitutes the addressee's face (and, through that, the speaker's face) directly – that is, without first recognising the speaker's intention – because conventionalisation provides a shortcut from the ppropriate utterance of the expression to the face-constituting perlocutionary effect conventionally associated with it;

- *unmarked rudeness* occurs when an expression that is conventionalised relative to a context where face-threat is expected is used in that context, and
to the extent that the interlocutors' *habitus* are homologous; it threatens the
addressee's face (and thereby constitutes the speaker's face) directly – that is,
without first recognising the speaker's intention – because conventionalisation provides a shortcut from appropriate utterance of the expression to the
face-threatening perlocutionary effect conventionally associated with it;
- *marked politeness* occurs when the expression used is not conventionalised
relative to the context of occurrence; it constitutes the addressee's face (and,
through that, the speaker's face) following recognition of the speaker's face-
constituting intention by the hearer; over-politeness can lead to marked politeness, but it can also lead to impoliteness, or rudeness proper;
- *marked rudeness* or *rudeness proper* occurs when the expression used is not
conventionalised relative to the context of occurrence; following recognition
of the speaker's face-threatening intention by the hearer, marked rudeness
threatens the addressee's face (and, through that, the speaker's face in the
addressee's eyes – although it may also constitute it in the eyes of another
participant, including the speaker him/herself); when over-politeness leads to
rudeness proper it threatens the speaker's face;
- *impoliteness* occurs when the expression used is not conventionalised relative
to the context of occurrence; it threatens the addressee's face (and, through
that, the speaker's face) but no face-threatening intention is attributed to the
speaker by the hearer.

The set of hypotheses put forward in this chapter remain of course to be confirmed and further refined in the light of empirical data. Without sounding like
a pessimist, I would like to point out two added difficulties when it comes to
collecting data about face-threatening behaviour. The first follows from the fact
that face-threatening behaviour is sanctionable by definition. Face-loss is, then,
often associated with parts of our lives we would rather keep private, for pub-
licising them would only lead to further loss of face. Clever methods of data
collection are required in this case to counteract the worst effects of the observer's paradox while respecting subjects' privacy and anonymity. The second
problem cuts across the field of politeness studies, and concerns the changing
perceptions of politeness, impoliteness, and rudeness as well as of the public
and the private in today's multicultural societies and globalising world (cf. Truss
2005). All of these can easily create an impression of moving on quicksand when
trying to map this uncharted territory. I hope that being aware of the challenges
for data collecting and sharpening our definitional weapons will help us make
some progress in this new area of research.

Notes

1. On the distinction between impoliteness and rudeness see section 3.3.
2. Face, including its positive and negative aspects, is defined in section 2.2. The term 'constituting' face is preferred over 'enhancing' face, since the latter may create the false impression that face pre-exists interaction, while the view taken here is that face comes into being through interaction.
3. Denying the existence of a middle ground between politeness and impoliteness/ rudeness may create the false impression that I am refuting the existence of what I have called 'unmarked (or frame-based) politeness' (Terkourafi 2001, 2003, 2005a), and which has in other frameworks been called 'default politeness' (Usami 2002), or 'politic behaviour' (e.g. Watts 2003), when in fact I consider the recent focus on such behaviour as one of the major advances in politeness studies in recent years and have devoted a large part of my work to discovering its linguistic correlates (e.g. Terkourafi 2002, 2003, 2005c). However, I still see 'unmarked politeness' as a kind of 'politeness' inasmuch as it constitutes the addressee's face – this is the theoretical understanding of Politeness$_2$ as a technical term put forward in Terkourafi (2005a: 252–253) – in the same way as 'unmarked rudeness,' proposed in this chapter – is a kind of 'rudeness' because it threatens the addressee's face. In other words, rather than explicit tagging of particular behaviours as 'polite' or 'rude' by participants, I take face-constituting/threatening as the basis for my theoretical (second-order) definitions of politeness/rudeness. I am therefore not denying that there are types of behaviour (namely, unmarked politeness and unmarked rudeness) that participants may not explicitly tag as 'polite' or 'rude,' and which may thus seem to constitute a 'middle ground' between 'politeness' and 'rudeness.' However, although participants may experience it as such, and an approach based on Politeness$_1$, i.e. on participants' perceptions of politeness, would have to acknowledge it as such, the possibility of a middle ground between politeness and rudeness as second-order notions – i.e. as face-constituting and face-threatening behaviours respectively – is excluded. If one acknowledges that interlocutors do not 'have' face prior to entering particular encounters (section 2.3), and that all behaviour impacts on face whether it is so intended or not (sections 3 and 4), then it follows that it is impossible for interlocutors to come out of an encounter with their faces neither constituted nor threatened.
4. Contrary to Leech's proposal of the Politeness Principle as a first-order principle on a par with the CP (1983: 80), what I am proposing is that face considerations and rationality are *primary* notions from which the CP is *derived*. Consequently, the notion of cooperation I have in mind is much broader than what is traditionally understood by 'cooperative behaviour.'
5. Another term for facework is 'relational work' (Watts 2003; Locher 2004; Watts and Locher 2005).
6. Emphasis on conventionalised (or 'unmarked') aspects of politeness/rudeness and their theoretical underpinnings in Generalised Conversational Implicature theory (Levinson 2000) is one aspect where my work most clearly differs from recent pro-

posals concerned with 'relational' (Locher 2004) and 'discursive' (Watts 2003) aspects of politeness.

7. Not to be confused with 'intention' which is "a specific state of mind that ... plays a distinctive role in the etiology of actions" (Jacob 2003).

8. This analysis agrees with Goffman's conceptualisation of face as "located in the flow of events" (1967: 7) and "on loan from society" (1967: 10), while, as seen immediately below, also allowing us to explicate why face is uniquely human, something Goffman wasn't directly interested in.

9. Although "altricial" is a technical term in ornithology, the authors seem to be using it generically to refer to all species, including humans, whose young are born helpless and naked, increasing the period of parental dependence (Preston and de Waal 2003: 20).

10. Similar views have been most recently defended by Arundale (2004, 2005), and Locher and Watts (2005), and are ultimately descended from Goffman's view of face as "on loan from society" (1967: 10). The present analysis adds an explanation as to why face cannot be an attribute of individuals, by suggesting intentionality as one of its two defining properties. For a comparison of Face$_2$ as outlined above with the relational notion of face developed by Arundale (2004, 2005), see Terkourafi (2007a).

11. We also evaluate our own behaviour by treating Self as some kind of Other we can look at from the outside.

12. Kulick's (2003) analysis of 'no' in response to different types of sexual advances offers a parallel here. Kulick shows how 'no' in such cases reproduces established roles (woman–man, bottom–top) and patterns of power, such that both positive and negative replies automatically have the addressee playing the speaker's 'game.'

13. Sections 3.1 and 3.2 are based on Terkourafi (2001: 120–127).

14. Saving face by lying transparently should be impossible if understanding what the speaker meant entailed believing that the speaker meant it *sincerely*.

15. This is an opportune example of the impossibility of remaining neutral with respect to face (see section 1).

16. This can be formally stated by defining politeness as a function P that takes behaviours (B) and contexts (C) as inputs and produces politeness/ impoliteness/rudeness values as outputs. Given that P (B, C), P cannot appear in its own domain (if P were to appear in its own domain, the result would be what is known computationally as an 'infinite loop').

17. Although it is possible to distinguish empirically between omitting an appropriate move (e.g. not saying 'thank you' after being granted one's request) and adding an inappropriate one (e.g. shouting abuse; cf., among others, Culpeper 1996: 357; Watts 2003: 169), it is unclear to me at this stage what can be gained by drawing such a distinction theoretically. In fact, an important generalisation, namely that they both lead to comparable interactional consequences, would then be lost. Cases of deliberate omission (e.g. by native speakers) as opposed to cases of inadvertent

addition (e.g., by L2 learners) make the boundary between the two especially hard to draw.

18. That is not to say that the two lexemes are interchangeable in those languages that have them. As one reviewer points out, survey of the BNC reveals differences between 'rude/rudeness' and 'impolite/impoliteness' in terms of frequency, distribution across genres, and collocates. Such differences actually support the claim, developed below, that the relevant dimension for distinguishing between 'rude/rudeness' and 'impolite/impoliteness' in English is the speaker's intention. Similar emphasis on the speaker's intention is precisely what languages that do not lexicalise a distinction between 'rude/rudeness' and 'impolite/impoliteness' seem to lack.

19. Everyday terms in English tend to be inherited from Germanic, while intellectually/scientifically oriented terms tend to be borrowed from Romance and hence, as a rule, entered the language at a later stage.

20. The words 'offend/offensive' (9) and 'insulting' (1) occurred in definitions of 'rude' in all ten dictionaries consulted (Concise Oxford English Dictionary, Oxford Dictionary of English (2nd edition revised), New Oxford American Dictionary, Oxford American Dictionary of Current English, Australian Oxford Dictionary, New Zealand Oxford Dictionary, Canadian Oxford Dictionary, Longman Dictionary of Contemporary English, Cambridge Advanced Learner's Dictionary, Collins English Dictionary), but never in definitions of 'impolite.' 'Offend/offensive' are in turn defined with the help of such words as 'attacking', 'aggressing' and 'assailing,' definitions of which make explicit reference to 'hostile intent.' That would seem to suggest that the difference captured by presence/absence of the modifier 'offensive' in definitions of 'rude' and 'impolite' respectively is one of intention and not of degree. That said, the differences between the two lexemes are subtle (hence my earlier suggestion that they share the same interactional space), and one will probably always find uses of these lexemes that do not follow these general patterns.

21. Things are different with 'unmarked' rudeness; see section 4.3.

22. I am grateful to Eleanor Dickey who reported this incident to me, having heard it from its protagonist.

23. Although switching into a language the hearer does not understand signals disassociation, it is not necessarily always face-threatening. The speaker may, for example, be accommodating to the needs of another participant who did not understand the language used previously.

24. A reviewer suggests that the man has been successful in constituting his face in his own eyes. That is indeed possible, inasmuch as he may be acting as both Self and Other in this encounter, evaluating his own behaviour (see also note 11).

25. This may be pragmatically modelled by saying that on these occasions the perlocutionary effect of face-constituting relies on a Generalised Conversational Implicature (Levinson 2000; cf. Terkourafi 2001: 141–146, 2003).

26. Conventionalisation on this view includes intonation. Corpus studies of intonation are still very recent, but at first sight they confirm that a stereotyped intonational

pattern is part and parcel of conventionalisation (cf. Wichmann 2004; Terkourafi 2007b).

27. Paralleling what happens with face-constituting expressions that may be convention-alised to a higher or lower degree, swear words may semantically encode face-threat, but other constructions may simply pragmatically implicate face-threat in a gener-alised manner on a par with generalised conversational implicatures of politeness (Terkourafi 2003, 2005c).

28. As suggested by John Haviland at SS14 in Ghent in April 2002.

Part 2. Political interaction

Chapter 4
Relational work and impoliteness:
Negotiating norms of linguistic behaviour

Miriam A. Locher and Richard J. Watts

1. Introduction[1]

In this chapter we follow up the notion of relational work proposed in Locher and
Watts (2005), Watts (2005) and Locher (2006a). In Section 2 we will introduce
and explain our understanding of relational work in detail, which involves terms
such as appropriate social behaviour, and negatively and positively marked social
behaviour. Since we posit that interactants' judgements about the relational status of a message are based on norms of appropriateness in a given instance
of social practice, we will highlight the importance of frames of expectations
against which both the speaker and the hearer judge relational work. In addition,
it is important to stress that a term such as 'impoliteness' should be seen as a
first order concept, i.e. a judgement made by a participant in an interaction
with respect to the appropriateness or inappropriateness of the social behaviour
of co-participants, rather than a second order, technical term in a theory of
im/politeness. We therefore propose a discursive understanding of the norms of
appropriate social behaviour that underlie the interactants' judgements.

In Section 3 we will draw on a brief Internet discussion of behaviour in
a restaurant that was deemed impolite by some discussants but not by others
in order to illustrate the discursive nature of judgements on impoliteness. In
Section 4, we will present an analysis of a political interview on the BBC current
affairs programme *Panorama* between the moderator, Fred Emery, and the then
president of the National Union of Mineworkers, Arthur Scargill, recorded at
the time of the miners' strike in 1984. We will discuss how the two interactants
react to face attacks that can be understood as breaches of norms and how they
frame each other as violating expectations in front of the television audience. In
Section 5 we will present our conclusions and will offer implications for future
research.

2.   Relational work and frames of expectations

Relational work is defined as the work people invest in negotiating their relationships in interaction (Locher 2004; Locher and Watts 2005; Locher 2006a).
It is based on the idea that any communicative act has both an informational
as well as an interpersonal aspect (cf. Watzlawick et al. 1967; Halliday 1978).
In other words, communicative acts always embody some form of relational
work. Taking this approach means that we are not restricted to studying merely
the polite variant of the interpersonal aspect of a communication, as Brown
and Levinson ([1978] 1987) have predominantly done, but can equally focus on
impolite, or rude aspects of social behaviour. Relational work, in other words,
comprises the entire spectrum of the interpersonal side of social practice.

In our earlier work (e.g. Locher and Watts 2005), we argued that whether
interactants perceive or intend a message to be polite, impolite or merely appropriate (among many other labels) depends on *judgements* that they make at the
level of relational work *in situ*, i.e. during an ongoing interaction in a particular
setting. These judgements are made on the basis of norms and expectations that
individuals have constructed and acquired through categorising the experiences
of similar past situations, or conclusions that one draws from other people's
experiences. They are an individual's cognitive conceptualisations of those experiences. The notion of 'frame', as used, for example, by Tannen (1993) or
Escandell-Vidal (1996), is what we are evoking here. So the theoretical basis of
'frames' are cognitive conceptualisations of forms of appropriate and inappropriate behaviour that individuals have constructed through their own histories
of social practice. It is important to point out that these norms and expectations
are acquired over time and are constantly subject to change and variation.

Just as norms of appropriate behaviour within a community of practice
change over time, so do judgements about relational work. While individuals
of the same social group, interacting in the same situation may have developed
similar frames of expectations and may indeed judge the level of relational
work similarly, there can still be disagreement within any social group about
judgements on social behaviour. This is because the norms themselves are constantly renegotiated, and because the cognitive domains against which a lexeme
such as *polite* is profiled change conceptually over time as well (cf. Sell 1992;
Ehlich 1992; Watts 2006). We have called this flexibility the 'discursive' nature
of im/politeness (Watts 2003; Locher and Watts 2005). There is, in other words,
no linguistic behaviour that is inherently polite or impolite.

In Table 1, we present aspects of judgements that interactants might make
when confronted with relational work that might qualify as *polite*. The assumption is that they orient to the norms of behaviour that are evoked by the frames

Table 1. Aspects of the spectrum of relational work, exemplified with the lexeme 'polite', in a particular context Y

	LEXEME (first order)	Two of the cognitive domains against which the lexeme is profiled		
Judgement (a):	impolite	inappropriate/ non-politic	+	negatively marked
Judgement (b):	(non-polite)*	appropriate/politic	+	unmarked
Judgement (c):	polite	appropriate/politic	+	positively marked
Judgement (d):	over-polite	inappropriate/ non-politic	+	negatively marked

* The judgement 'non-polite' is unlikely to be uttered.

of expectations specific to the social situation, and that the notions of appropriateness and markedness are the domains against which the lexeme *polite* is profiled. An interactant might therefore think that a particular utterance represents socially appropriate behaviour of an unmarked kind (judgement b), i.e. it is not likely to evoke an evaluative comment. At a different moment in time or in a different instantiation of social practice, relational work might be judged as positively marked and at the same time as socially appropriate (judgement c). We argue that this positive aspect might trigger a judgement of behaviour with lexemes such as *polite* (and maybe also *courteous, well-mannered,* etc.). Negatively marked behaviour, i.e. behaviour that has breached a social norm (judgements a and d), evokes negative evaluations such as *impolite* or *over-polite* (or any alternative lexeme such as *rude, aggressive, insulting, sarcastic,* etc. depending upon the degree of the violation and the type of conceptualisation the inappropriate behaviour is profiled against).[2] A *negative* evaluation is to be understood quite literally as the emotional reaction of individual interactants (as are positive evaluations). People may respond quite forcefully when the level of relational work does not match their expectations.

The notions of 'impolite' or 'polite' should thus be understood as judgements by participants in the interaction in question. They are, in other words, first order concepts rather than second order, theoretical ones. In this way our approach differs considerably from that of other researchers who have worked on politeness and impoliteness. Kienpointner (1997: 252), for example, states quite clearly that his approach to rudeness (rather than impoliteness) is of a second order type. This is most manifest when he talks of linguistic strategies employed to achieve rudeness analogous to Brown and Levinson's ([1978] 1987) linguistic strategies for polite behaviour. The same can be said for Lachenicht (1980), Culpeper (1996), Culpeper, Bousfield and Wichmann (2003) and Culpeper (2005).

Another aspect of difference linked to the distinction between a first order and second order approach to impoliteness has to do with the notion of *intentionality*. Kienpointner (1997: 259) defines rudeness as "non-cooperative or competitive communicative behaviour". We certainly agree that non-cooperativeness may play a role in the definition of rudeness. On the other hand, if we interpret Kienpointner's 'or' as being an exclusive, logical operator (either P or Q, rather than P and/or Q), we wish to dispute that competitiveness is equal to rudeness. Competitive communicative behaviour may be cooperative and positively valued in certain contexts (cf. Tannen 1981; Schiffrin 1984; Watts 2003). Non-cooperativeness is important in behaviour that intentionally aims at hurting the addressee. Culpeper (2005: 37), Lachenicht (1980) and Bousfield (2007a/b, this volume) deal explicitly with intentional impoliteness/rudeness. Lachenicht (1980: 619), in mirroring Brown and Levinson's ([1978] 1987) politeness strategies, postulates the following:

> Aggravation strategies are also sensitive to social factors. A very powerful person will probably be attacked only by off record means. Friends and intimates would probably be attacked by means of positive aggravation whereas socially distant persons would be attacked by means of negative aggravation. (Lachenicht 1980: 619)

He goes on to say that "[i]f the purpose of aggravation is to hurt, then means must be chosen that *will* hurt" (1980: 619–620, emphasis in original). This comment points to the interlocutors' awareness of the norms of the interaction in question. If this were not the case, they could not play with the level of relational work and adjust it to their own ends. Taking a first order approach to impoliteness means that we are able to recognise this, whilst at the same time stressing the point that both the speaker's and the hearer's judgements have to be considered. A speaker may wish to be aggressive and hurtful, but still not come across as such to the hearer. Alternatively, a hearer may interpret the speaker's utterance as negatively marked with respect to appropriate behaviour, while the speaker did not intentionally wish to appear as such. In a first order approach to impoliteness, it is the interactants' *perceptions* of communicators' intentions rather than the intentions themselves that determine whether a communicative act is taken to be impolite or not. In other words, the uptake of a message is as important if not more important than the utterer's original intention.

There are also a number of important overlaps in our understanding of the phenomenon with previous work on impoliteness. Kienpointner (1997: 255), for example, also states that "rudeness could be termed inappropriateness of communicative behaviour *relative to* a particular context" (emphasis added) and is a matter of degree.[3] Mills (2005: 268) argues that "[i]mpoliteness can be considered as any type of linguistic behaviour which is *assessed as* intending to threaten the hearer's face or social identity, or as transgressing the hypothesized Community of Practice's norms of appropriacy" (emphasis added). Both Kienpointner's and Mills' perspective on rudeness here match our understanding of impoliteness as breaches of norms that are negatively evaluated by interactants according to their expectation frames.

Finally, the notion of power cannot be ignored when dealing with relational work in all its facets. Since relational work is defined as the work people invest in negotiating their relationships in interaction, power issues always play a crucial role in negotiating identities. In Watts (1991) and Locher (2004), we have dealt with the notion of power in interaction. Our understanding of power is that it is not a static concept, but is constantly renegotiated and exercised in social practice. All interlocutors enter social practice with an understanding of a differential distribution of social status amongst the co-participants, but the actual exercise of power is something that we can only witness in the interaction itself. We will return to the issue of power in the discussion of our examples, particularly in our analysis of the political interview in Section 4.

3. The dirty fork: Norms of behaviour discussed on an Internet forum

We have repeatedly argued in this chapter that norms of interaction are negotiable and in flux and that judgements about relational work are equally varied across social practices. In what follows we would briefly like to illustrate one instance of such a negotiation of norms that was found on a discussion board on a U.S. Internet site. This site deals with any issues that pertain to the topic of good eating (food, recipes, restaurants, etc.). One member describes the following scenario and ends with the question of whether or not the waiter's actions were "impolite":

(1)   Was this waiter's action impolite or not?
        So I was at a mid-priced restaurant (with tablecloths and cloth napkins) for lunch
        which was completely empty except for me and a dining companion at the window
        of the large dining room. After ordering, we were waiting for our food, when I

noticed that my fork was dirty. So, instead of bothering to call out to the waiter who was not in the room at the time, I decided to turn around and just grab the fork from the neighboring table. Just at that moment, the waiter walks in at the far end of the room who noticed me doing this. He promptly takes a fork from the service station and marches clear across the room, to place the missing fork on the neighboring table behind me. Not a word was spoken, and I thought nothing of it.

Question is, do you think this was rude of him to do this? Wouldn't a more discreet waiter have replaced the fork at another time than to 'correct' a diner's actions immediately after the fact?

The scenario described deals with a non-verbal example that evokes the question of appropriate behaviour in the frame of 'interaction in a restaurant'. It deals with the perceived rights and obligations of the waiter and the customer and reveals that the customer feels 'corrected' by the waiter. As a result, s/he is insecure about how to judge the situation with respect to whether the waiter's behaviour was impolite/rude or not.[4] It is interesting to see that the poster uses both the lexemes *impolite* and *rude* as first order terms and appears to equate the one with the other.[5]

By the time of the data collection, which took place 10 days after the original posting, this question had received 25 comments, but no further reaction from the original poster. The contents of these comments range from saying that there is no issue of impoliteness involved ([2] and [3]), to stating that the waiter may have breached a norm ([4] and [5]), and to postulating that it was in fact the customer who was *out of bounds/in the wrong* ([6] and [7]):

(2)   No. [in response to the question raised in (1)]

(3)   He replaced a fork so that the next table sat would have one. He did so "promptly" to make sure that when that table was sat the new customer would have a fork. You grabbed a fork from the next table; he replaced it. How is that rude?

(4)   Seems to me, the point is not what the waiter did, but how he did it. When it comes to customer service, it's about how you do your job, not just what you do. Since you remember the "incident" and enough to post it, it sounds like it was the way that waiter made a point of indiscretely replacing the fork. So just because he was doing his job, doesn't mean he wasn't also being rude about it.

(5)   maybe....depends on how he "marched," though. It sounds like the waiter did it to show that the customer transgressed. I see no mention of a mental inquiry of why the fork was taken off the table, and no mention of the waiter noticing the dirty fork. You can tell by the way someone goes about it – believe me, waiters can be pissy.

(6)   I think you were out of bounds by taking the fork. If you needed another napkin, would you've just jerked one off the neighboring table too? Why didn't you just ask the waiter for a new fork?

(7)   In my opinion, your actions were in the wrong. What if they had seated someone at that table not knowing that it was now short a fork?

What is interesting from our point of view is that there is no clear agreement among the contributors to the thread on how this brief episode should be classified with respect to the level of relational work. We can therefore witness the negotiability of norms and actually see them discussed by lay-people who evoke the first order lexemes of *impolite* and *rude* to describe their scenarios (see also Culpeper, this volume).

The thread actually becomes quite 'lively' with people adding to and disagreeing with each other's points of view. The contributors discuss different scenarios with respect to what would have been a (more) appropriate action on the part of the two interlocutors involved. They are thus comparing what would change with respect to relational work in alternative modes of behaviour. It also becomes clear that power issues are of importance here. They are evoked when the discussants define the roles of the customer and the waiter and talk about what is expected of them, i.e. they discuss their perceived rights and obligations. In example (8), a poster defends the waiter's actions:

(8)   I'm a waiter, I would have done exactly what the waiter did. I see something that needs to be taken care of, I will take care of it right at that very moment. If I don't, I'll forget and then someone will get sat at a table missing a fork.

This comment reveals that the poster perceives the waiter's behaviour to be within the bounds of appropriate behaviour. It also shows that s/he evokes his/her professional status as a waiter to give this comment more weight. Another contributor explicitly raises the issue of power in his/her contribution:

(9)   My question is why are you giving the waiter so much power to affect your lunch with a friend? Since the room was empty and your food hadn't arrived yet, maybe the best thing would have been to just wait until the waiter came back to your table and ask him for another fork but who really thinks about these things ahead of time? I probably would have done the same thing but since it was a 'tablecloth and cloth napkins' type of restaurant, the waiter probably should have replaced the fork for you. But hey – in the realm of things, nobody was hurt. I say let it go.

This contributor to the thread does not so much comment on the differential distribution of social status between the waiter and the customer, but on the fact that s/he believes that the customer let the waiter *exercise* power over him/her, which implies a reason why the customer has a negative feeling about the incident. The comment thus refers to the interactional emergence of power and shows quite nicely that the contributor sees its impact to be in the field of relational work.

4. Breaching norms in a political interview

Explicit metapragmatic comments on whether or not an individual's behaviour can be evaluated as *impolite*, *rude*, or any other of the extensive range of adjectives that may be used in English (and probably in any language) to refer to non-normative, inappropriate behaviour are almost invariably made after the event, which became evident from our discussion of the forum thread in the previous section. An immediate open evaluation of a co-participant's verbal behaviour as *rude* or *offensive* in the course of the interaction would constitute a face-threatening act and would endanger the efforts made to produce cooperative communication – although, as we pointed out in Section 2, by no means all instantiations of social practice *are* cooperative.

When we are confronted with openly competitive, conflictual social interaction, as is the case with the data we wish to analyse here, it is important to consider the kinds of institutional sanctions which constrain participants not to produce openly evaluative comments on inappropriate behaviour. This obviously makes our job as researchers more challenging. If impoliteness, like politeness, is a discursively disputable aspect of social practice (cf. the analysis in Section 3), we will need to use all our interpretative ingenuity in assessing co-participants' immediate reactions in order to arrive at our own evaluations of the non-normative and inappropriate nature of individuals' verbal behaviour. These will, of course, in turn be discursively produced first order constructs.

The stretch of social interaction we wish to analyse in more detail is a political interview on the BBC television current affairs programme *Panorama* which lasted for roughly ten minutes. Small sections of the interview have been used in previous research (cf. Watts 1991, 2003 and 2006). The programme was broadcast towards the end of the miner's strike in 1984 and the topic dealing with the miners' strike consists of a documentary film (purportedly giving evidence of violence on the picket lines, the hardship experienced by miners' families and the increasing number of miners trickling back to work) and the subsequent interview with Arthur Scargill, then president of the National Union of Mineworkers. The interviewer is the programme moderator, Fred Emery. In this chapter, we shall focus on selected passages from the interview and, from a digitalised version of the original videotape, will also present visual markers of exasperation and frustration on the part of Scargill.

4.1. Political interviews and the problem of power

The main purpose in analysing the interview is to show how our interpretation of inappropriate social behaviour – which could have been metapragmatically commented on by either of the two participants but wasn't – is intimately tied to issues of power and the exercise of power in the interview situation. Work on news interviews and political interviews (Beattie 1982; Jucker 1986, 2005; Greatbatch 1986; Clayman and Heritage 2002) gives evidence of an increased level of aggressiveness and a supposed concomitant loss of "respect" on the part of the interviewer towards political interviewees in the British media, although it is not entirely clear when this trend began. At all events, it was certainly in place at the beginning of the 1980s and was (and has remained) relatively prominent in the BBC's *Panorama* programme.

We define a "political interview" as a subgenre of the "news interview" as defined by Clayman and Heritage (2002: 7–8) since it is clear that not all news interviews involve politicians. The term "political interview" itself is used to define media interviews with politicians held with the intention of providing the wider audience with an idea of the interviewee's political views, policy statements and, obviously, media presence.

The development of a more conflictual, aggressive mode of conducting political interviews helps to counterbalance the status that politicians are institutionally endowed with when they appear as public figures in the media. In an extract from the BBC Editorial Guidelines[6] addressed to programme producers the following advice is given:

> **We should be clear when making requests for political interviews about the nature of the programme and context for which they are intended.** Our arrangements must stand up to public scrutiny and must not prevent the programme asking questions that our audiences would reasonably expect to hear. (emphasis in original)

The statement that the programme arrangements should not prevent questions "that our audiences would reasonably expect to hear" can be interpreted as a justification for these new interviewing techniques. Given the documentary shown at the beginning of the programme and the exasperation that the majority of *Panorama* viewers must have felt after almost eleven months of strike, interviewing Scargill certainly did "fit the nature of the programme". So most of

Emery's questions can be interpreted, without exaggeration, as those that the audience would have expected to hear.

Research work on interviewing assumes that the power relations between interviewer and interviewee are skewed in favour of the interviewer, since s/he has the right to choose which questions to ask, even though the interviewee is still at liberty to refuse to answer a question (e.g. Jucker 1986, 2005). However, what normally occurs in political interviews is that the interviewee hedges proper answers to questions or uses the question as a means to expatiate at length on other issues (cf. the analysis of the interview between David Dimbleby and Tony Blair in Watts 2003: chapter 9). We would prefer to consider power as playing a role in *all* social interaction, including any form of interviewing (Watts 1991; Locher 2004). Locher (2004: 38) uses both Watts' and Wartenberg's definitions of the exercise of power, which we present here as follows:

> A exercises power over B when A affects B in a manner contrary to B's initially perceived interests, regardless of whether B later comes to accept the desirability of A's actions. (Watts 1991: 62)

> A social agent A has *power over* another social agent B if and only if A strategically constrains B's action-environment. (Wartenberg 1990: 85, emphasis added)

The checklist Locher gives to summarise the nature and exercise of power contains the following propositions, which fit neatly into our way of viewing power in social practice:

- Power is (often) expressed through language.
- Power cannot be explained without contextualization.
- Power is relational, dynamic and contestable.
- The interconnectedness of language and society can also be seen in the display of power.
- Freedom of action is needed to exercise power.
- The restriction of an interactant's action-environment often leads to the exercise of power.
- The exercise of power involves a latent conflict and clash of interests, which can be obscured because of a society's ideologies.

(Locher 2004: 39–40)

Power, like impoliteness, is discursively negotiated and is always latently present in every instantiation of social practice. Indeed, power is intimately linked to individuals' perceptions of impolite behaviour, as we shall see in the analysis of the political interview.

4.2.   Contextualising the interview

Before proceeding to our analysis, we need to give some important background information in order to place the interview into its proper socio-historical context. The 1984 miners' strike began in the South Yorkshire coalfield as a protest against the National Coal Board's (NCB) decision to close five pits in the area. The National Union of Mineworkers (NUM), whose president at the time was Arthur Scargill, officially supported the strike action but omitted to hold a national ballot among the union's members as to whether the union as a whole wanted to continue the strike. When challenged on this issue by Emery, Scargill states the following (cf. the transcription conventions are given in the Appendix):

(10)   I carried out the wishes and instructions of my members\ and those instructions
       were\ that we should not have a (.) national ballot under rule 43\ (..) but that
       we should support the action that had already been taken by miners\ prior to me
       making any statement on the matter under national rule 41\ (..) if I had have
       ignored that instruction\ I would have been guilty (..) of defying the conference
       of my union\

The "conference" of the NUM, however, is not to be equated with a democratic, rank and file vote, as Emery suggests to Scargill at a later point in the interview. In the documentary film preceding the interview, one of the miners had commented on the fact that, had Scargill chosen to ballot the union members' views earlier in the strike, he would probably have won, thus implying that support of the rank and file of union members has now dwindled considerably.

   The strike openly played into the hands of the Conservative government of the time under Margaret Thatcher, who were determined not to give way. In fact, the NCB's closure plans went much further than the original five pits, as Scargill explicitly notes during the interview. Whether the Thatcher government *were* "guilty" of intervention with the Coal Board to prevent an agreement remains an allegation made by Scargill,[7] but close analysis of the interview appears to indicate the strength of Scargill's argument. The waste of large sums of taxpayers' money after 11 months of strike will not have disposed the television audience favourably to Scargill's attempted evasive tactics in answering Emery's first question: "Are you now willing to discuss uneconomic pits?"

   Another of the issues addressed by the documentary was the use of physical and verbal violence by NUM members manning the picket lines, although this is not particularly stressed during the interview. When it *is* mentioned by Emery (see stave 1 in example (14) below), Scargill counters with the accusation of police brutality in dealing with the picket lines ("I certainly condemn violence on the picket lines"). The main thrust of the film was to demonstrate the futility of the strike, given the fact that miners and their families were beginning to feel the pinch and were slowly giving up and trickling back to work. There are dramatic scenes towards the end of the film of miners searching for fuel on snow-bound slagheaps, and during the interview Scargill, but never Emery, refers to the miners being "starved back to work".

The physical set-up of the interview in the studio is that of an oval table with Emery at one end and Scargill at the other. The camera switches from one participant to the other.[8] The only time when we have a frontal view of the whole table showing both the interviewer and the interviewee is in example (12) below when they indulge in a veritable 20-second tirade of incomprehensible simultaneous speech, which took one of the authors of this chapter at least two hours to transcribe.

4.3.   Analysing the struggle for power

Given our comments on the conflictual nature of political interviews in the media and the BBC's own guidelines on the kinds of questions that audiences might reasonably be expected to hear, Emery's behaviour would appear to be sanctioned by a redefinition of the norms of appropriateness in this public form of social practice. The viewing audience are not likely to evaluate his utterances with adjectives such as *impolite, rude, insulting,* or *aggressive*, although the incomprehensible simultaneous speech in example (12) below might indeed be open to this kind of interpretation, as we shall argue later. Scargill, on the other hand, can frame[9] Emery's behaviour as having any of these qualities in order to present himself (and by extension the NUM) as the butt of unjustified criticism at the hands of the media. The problem is that Scargill, as a public figure, must be aware of the norms of appropriateness in operation during the interview, and for this reason could hardly allow himself to use any of the adjectives listed above. The analysts' question, therefore, is how we can interpret Scargill's attempt to frame Emery as being impolite by other means.

The first evidence of such an attempt occurs shortly after the beginning of the interview in example (11). The significant section of the sequence for our analysis is highlighted in grey:

(11)

[1]   E: peter taylor reporting\ well with me in the studio watching the film\ is mr arthur scargill\
president of the national union of mineworkers\ mr scargill\ (..) the issue causing (..) the
breakdown (.) was all last week/ the issue (..) at the front of the news\ and in everybody's
minds\ was the union's refusal to accept the closure of uneconomic pits\ are you now willing to
discuss uneconomic pits\

S:		(..) we're not prepared to go along to the national coal board\ and

2	E: you're not\ sorry if I interrupt you (.) there\ y/ I- I/ let me just remind you that—
	S: start— [er::] [er::] are you- are you going to let

3	E: you- you said you're not\ let's
	S: me answer the question\ you put a question\ for god's sake let me answer\

4	E: - let's have the (.) question again\ and see of we (..) get it right clear\ are you now willing to
	discuss uneconomic pits\ go ahead\
	S: (..) can I answer\

After introducing Scargill in stave 1, Emery goes on to contextualise the question he intends to put as being the issue "at the front of the news and in everybody's minds", thereby including the television audience through the pronoun *everybody*. The question concerns Scargill's and the NUM's willingness (or unwillingness) to discuss uneconomic pits. Scargill begins his answer in stave 1 but is stopped in his tracks by an intervention in stave 2, which Emery himself admits is an interruption. On being interrupted Scargill looks down and away from his interlocutor and compresses his lips with a down-turned corner of his mouth (Stillshot 1). The posture shows him as having leaned back slightly from the force of the interruption. In other words, Scargill's facial expression and posture at this point in the interaction reveal what could be interpreted as resigned exasperation.

Stillshot 1. Scargill's reaction to Emery's first interruption

Emery's "you're not" (stave 2) is a pre-empted answer to his question, even though it is as yet unclear how Scargill would have answered had he been allowed to continue. His way out of the face-threatening situation is to apologise for the interruption, but the brief bout of stammering following the apology is evidence of a certain amount of insecurity. Scargill realises this and immediately intervenes with two filled pauses "[er::]" at the same time as Emery is producing the somewhat highminded moralistic utterance "let me just remind you that–" (stave 2).

How does power play a role in the interpretation of this sequence? Emery has given the floor to Scargill but promptly restricts his freedom of action to answer in the way that he wants and not as Emery imagines he will. Restriction of Scargill's action-environment as the interviewee in a political interview is an exercise of power by Emery, and it is expressed through language. At the same time the restriction of an interviewee's action-environment is sanctioned to a certain extent in this interactional context.

In order to counter the exercise of power by Emery, it is essential that Scargill represents him as having acted rudely and aggressively without actually using either of these lexemes himself. His reassertion of the right to answer the question is accompanied by the emotional utterance "For God's sake let me answer!" indicating a negative evaluation of Emery's behaviour as violating the norms of appropriateness, as he frames them in this interaction, along the parameter of impoliteness. This is played upon in stave 4 when he mockingly asks for permission to answer the question when it is put the second time ("can I answer").

After example (11), Scargill is given the time to make a lengthy answer. Throughout, he avoids explicitly answering the question, although Emery (and presumably the television audience with him) infers that the preconditions that Scargill talks about at such great length are indeed preconditions placed on talks by the National Coal Board to the effect that uneconomic pits are indeed the issue. He changes tack in example (12), stave 2, by referring to BBC's Michael Eaton having "blown the gaff" the previous evening, only to be stopped once more by Emery:

(12)

1	E:
	S: those two points alone could resolve this dispute\ but you see\ michael eaton on bbc television

2	E: yes but bef- before we go on talking about what mr eaton said/ no\
	S: yesterday\ blew the gaff\ but you see/ listen\ no no\ no no\ no no\ you've stopped me

3	E: you can take it up with Mr Eaton\ I interrupted you because you said\ (.) you were not
	S: once\ he/ no\ you interrupted me once\ (...) well we can go on like this—

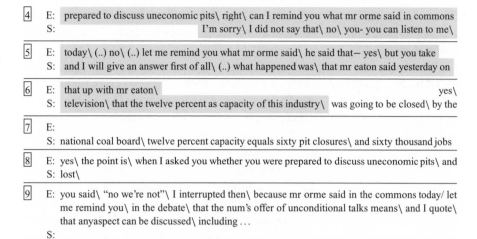

| 4 | E: | prepared to discuss uneconomic pits\ right\ can I remind you what mr orme said in commons |
| | S: | I'm sorry\ I did not say that\ no\ you- you can listen to me\ |

| 5 | E: | today\ (..) no\ (..) let me remind you what mr orme said\ he said that— yes\ but you take |
| | S: | and I will give an answer first of all\ (..) what happened was\ that mr eaton said yesterday on |

| 6 | E: | that up with mr eaton\ yes\ |
| | S: | television\ that the twelve percent as capacity of this industry\ was going to be closed\ by the |

| 7 | E: | |
| | S: | national coal board\ twelve percent capacity equals sixty pit closures\ and sixty thousand jobs |

| 8 | E: | yes\ the point is\ when I asked you whether you were prepared to discuss uneconomic pits\ and |
| | S: | lost\ |

| 9 | E: | you said\ "no we're not"\ I interrupted then\ because mr orme said in the commons today/ let me remind you\ in the debate\ that the num's offer of unconditional talks means\ and I quote\ that anyaspect can be discussed\ including ... |
| | S: | |

Emery's initial interruption just after the beginning of the interview has put Scargill on his guard and this results in a 20–second free-for-all in which each of the two participants tries to restrict the other's freedom of action to take or retain the floor. The consequence is incomprehensibility on the part of anybody listening to the programme. The discursive struggle for power here is again linked to the notion of the norms of appropriacy in relational work. It is also at this point in the programme that we get a diagonal camera sequence, which means that both participants are visible to the audience (Stillshot 2). Throughout this

Stillshot 2. The camera angle during the 20–seconds overlap

20–second sequence, Emery's manual gestures are evidence of an aggressive attempt to take over the floor, whereas Scargill uses his hands defensively to retain it.

We interpret the change of camera perspective as resulting from the necessity faced by the programme editor of deciding which of the two co-participants to focus on at that moment. The diagonal shot is evidence of his/her dilemma. One of the possible conclusions that members of the audience may have made at this point in the interview is that the two co-participants are not only inconsiderate to one another but also towards the wider audience.

The co-participants' utterances during this 20–second sequence may or may not have been understood by members of the wider audience, but when we look at the transcript, we realise after the event that both participants were closely monitoring what the other was saying. For example, Emery makes the following statement in stave 3: "I interrupted you because you said you were not prepared to discuss uneconomic pits". He then uses the discourse marker "right" to induce Scargill to corroborate this fact and is immediately countered by Scargill's "I'm sorry. I did not say that" (stave 4). Once again, Emery is trying to restrict Scargill's freedom of action by framing him as not being prepared to discuss this issue.

Now, the problem here is to decide whether the implicature Emery has inferred from Scargill's unwillingness to discuss preconditions set by the NCB is valid. Let us return to the socio-historical contextualisation of the interview itself. The audience and both Emery and Scargill are aware that by this time in the strike (after 11 months) the "preconditions" that Scargill mentions concern the need to discuss the issue of uneconomic pits. So when Scargill talks about those preconditions for negotiation with the NCB he can only mean the need to discuss those pits. We conclude from this that Emery's implicature is indeed valid. On the other hand, Scargill is still perfectly justified in claiming that he did not *say* anything about uneconomic pits. At all events, Emery's framing of Scargill appears to have been successful when he repeats his accusation once more without being contradicted this time by Scargill: "When I asked you whether you were prepared to discuss uneconomic pits, and you said, 'No, we're not' . . . " (staves 8–9, example (12)).

Three further sequences will now be looked at briefly in which Emery comes very close to insulting Scargill. The first of these concerns the list of promises which Scargill originally made to the miners, their failure to have taken effect and Emery's accusation that Scargill doesn't have "any clout" in example (13). Example (14) concerns the dispute over whether or not Scargill allowed the NUM to ballot the opinion of its members. Example (15) is the open accusation made by Emery but thinly disguised as being an opinion voiced by other trade union leaders and left wingers that Scargill is "a disaster" when it comes to negotiating:

(13)

1 E: but if- if- if that is a victory\ as you claim\
   S: as it does to keep him at work\ producing coal\ (..) it doesn't make sense\

2 E: (..) and you promised them\ let me remind you\ all last summer\ that coal stocks were running
      down\ that power cuts would soon come in august\ and by christmas\ and they wouldn't and so
      on\ the fact is\ (..) you've got no clout\ have you\ to deliver on those promises you made to
   S:

3 E: them\ how much longer are you going to ask your miners to suffer\
   S: let me make two points first

4 E:
   S: first of all\

(14)

1 E: look\ whatever the merits of your case\ let's look\ if we may\ at your tactics\ not having a
      ballot\ when many of your own people/ ronnie mott we heard there in that film\ believed that
      you might have won\ (..) had a ballot been held in favour of a strike\ not condemning picketing
      violence was another thing which he also mentioned\ which alienated a lot of opinion from
      your case\ making misleading promises\ as I mentioned\ having your funds sequestered\
   S:

2 E: haven't you in fact let your members down\
   S: (..) no\ I haven't\ I would let my members down if

3 E:
   S: I betrayed them\ and I'd never do that\ first of all\ (..) don't say that I didn't have a ballot\ (..) I

4 E: well you didn't\ did you\
   S: carried out the wishes on the instruction— if you're going to keep interrupting when you

5 E: no\ I/ you said\ "don't say that I didn't have a ballot"\ and you didn't\ (..) go ahead\ (..) you
   S: ask me a question\

6 E: didn't have a ballot\
   S: (...) I carried out the wishes and instructions of my members\

(15)

1 E: do you know what they say about you\ (..) other union leaders I've spoken to\ other left
      wingers\ they say that [er::] you make a marvellous advocate for your case\ but as a negotiator\
   S:

2 E: (..) you're a disaster\ (..) it's true\ isn't it\
   S: oh\ (..) well of course\ it means that you're [er::] talking as

3 E:
   S: silly as they [er::] are\

The major issue in each of these three sequences is whether or not Emery can be considered to have gone beyond the bounds of the redefined norms of appropriate behaviour for a political interview. If any of these three sequences contains a blatant face attack directed at Scargill with an attempt to malign Scargill's character, both Scargill and the television audience would be justified in evaluating his behaviour as at least *impolite*, if not *aggressive* or downright *insulting*.

To say that a co-participant does not have clout and cannot deliver on promises made in example (13) is, admittedly, a weak form of insult, but it is the kind of statement that one might expect in present-day political interviews. It is, in other words, sanctioned[10] behaviour, and it is highly likely to have been expectable in the early 1980s. Scargill's response does not display a show of indignation; he simply goes on with the utterance "Let me make two points first of all." We would therefore suggest that Scargill does in fact accept the redefined norms of appropriate behaviour for televised political interviews, which strengthens our interpretation that he has tried to frame Emery as being aggressive in example (11).

Accusing an interviewee of making misleading promises, implying that he has been undemocratic in not allowing the union to ballot the opinion of its members and is responsible for having the funds of his trade union sequestered in (14) are a little less severe, since, apart from Emery's personal evaluation of the promises having been misleading, it is true to say that the funds were sequestered and that the NUM did not have a ballot amongst its members. However, it is precisely these facts which are likely to damage Scargill's (and also the National Union of Mineworkers') public image if they are admitted. It is interesting to see that it is the accusation of not having held a ballot which causes the altercation which follows and not the accusation of being misleading or the sequestration of the union funds. Scargill chooses to challenge the one accusation which is a crystal-clear fact in the eyes of the general public (including Emery), and he resorts to the same strategy as at the beginning of the interview, viz. the framing of Emery as restricting his freedom of action to explain the matter by interrupting him.

By far the most damaging insult is the one put forward by Emery in (15), viz. that Scargill is a disaster when it comes to negotiating. The visual sequence of Scargill's reaction to this veiled insult shows an increased rate of blinking and a movement of the tongue across the lips possibly indicating a dry mouth at this point. This is the one point in the whole interaction, with the possible exception of Emery's initial interruptive sequence, at which Scargill might have been able to frame Emery as indulging in insulting behaviour. He is prevented from doing so by Emery's skilful embedding of the insult into alleged statements by third parties ("Do you know what they say about you, other union leaders I've spoken to, other left wingers? They say that . . ."; stave 1) and by inviting Scargill himself to comment on the truth of the proposition that he is a disaster ("It's true, isn't it?"; stave 2). Scargill's response is to frame both those who Emery claims have made this statement and Emery himself as "talking silly" (staves 2–3) and to launch into a self-righteous appraisal of his own past achievements as a negotiator in the Yorkshire coalfield.

In the absence of explicitly expressed evaluations of the co-participants' behaviour as going beyond the sanctioned norms of appropriate behaviour in a televised political interview, i.e. lexemes such as *impolite, rude, insulting, aggressive*, etc., we are forced to fall back on other utterances by the co-participant in the defensive position in a political interview, who is almost always the interviewee. What we have tried to do in this section is to demonstrate that we have to keep a close check on affective linguistic reactions such as "for God's sake let me answer" (example (11), stave 3), accusations of illicit behaviour such as "you interrupted me once" (example (12), stave 3), "don't say that I didn't have a ballot" (example (14), stave 3), "if you're going to keep interrupting when you ask me a question" (example (14), stave 4), or countering a perceived insult with another such as "it means that you're as silly as they are" (example (15), stave 2–3). We have suggested that a further rich source of evidence is to interpret the defensive co-participant's gestures, body posture and facial expressions as displaying frustration, indignation, shock, etc. Beyond that, one other method would be to record the reactions of the participants after the event, or in the case of the television audience to gather a set of verbalised reactions to what the viewers observed, which would be similar to collecting the various responses from an Internet discussion board such as the one looked at in Section 3. While there is a danger that there might be a discrepancy between the *in situ* reaction and reaction after the event, there must be some kind of overlap to give the researcher interpretative clues.

One point should have emerged from our analyses in Sections 3 and 4, and that concerns the desirability of working from genuine data collected in instances of social practice and working from first-order notions of what participants in social practice categorise as impolite behaviour rather than working from an idealised theory of what impoliteness is. We shall investigate the consequences of this approach to impoliteness in the final section.

5. Implications and conclusions

Relational work refers to all aspects of the work invested by individuals in the construction, maintenance, reproduction and transformation of interpersonal relationships among those engaged in social practice. In this sense it is equivalent to facework, but only if we accept that facework is always present in any form of socio-communicative verbal interaction. If facework is only taken to refer to rationally motivated means of mitigating face-threatening acts, which is implicit in the Brown and Levinson understanding of facework, then it cannot always be taken to be present in social practice.

Goffman (1955) conceptualises face as "a socially attributed aspect of self that is on loan for the duration of the interaction in accordance with the line or lines that the individual has adopted for the purposes of [the] interaction" (Watts 2003: 105). He tends to look at the social side of face, whereas Brown and Levinson focus on its cognitive nature. Relational work understands face as combining the two, in that what an individual develops as his/her continual construction of self depends on social interaction, and social interaction takes place between individuals.

Relational work is always inherent in all forms of social practice, and it involves every individual's conceptualisation of the behaviour appropriate to the forms of social practice in which s/he is engaged. At the same time different conceptualisations depend crucially on the conceptualisations made by others, i.e. the work invested in constructing, maintaining, reproducing and transforming ongoing interpersonal relationships is at one and the same time both social and individual. It is, in other words, intersubjective.

We cannot therefore expect that the relational work that we carry out in every instance of social interaction that involves us as participants is always at a level of personal consciousness, and where it is not (which we would take to be the default situation), we suggest that it is socially unmarked. It is simply social behaviour which goes unnoticed, a part of what Bourdieu (1990) calls our "feel for the game", or, to use the notion of frames of expectation once again, part of what we are used to and expect to occur.

At any point in ongoing social interaction, however, something might occur which lies outside this frame of normality and which demands our attention as a co-participant since it doesn't fit the frame, and at such junctures in the overall social practice it demands that we make some kind of moral judgement. Marked behaviour of this kind might elicit positive evaluations, one of which would be to judge the behaviour as *polite*. Negatively marked behaviour, on the other hand, will evoke judgements of impoliteness, but it is also likely to evoke a wide range of possible responses ranging from the relatively neutral *impolite*, through *rude* to *boorish, aggressive, insulting, inconsiderate*, as well as a host of other negative judgements.

Our understanding of relational work entails an understanding of these judgements, whether positive or negative, as being discursively constructed and as being individual evaluations of the social behaviour of others. In this sense, both "politeness" and "impoliteness" are what we call first-order constructs and are not second-order terms in a rational, universal theory of politeness.

In this chapter we have focused on the negatively marked side of relational work in an attempt to tease out how those involved in ongoing social interaction evaluate the verbal behaviour of their co-participants. We have noted that, while making judgements about the behaviour of others *after the event* could easily entail the metapragmatic use of lexemes such as those given above, they are far less likely to be used metapragmatically during the course of an interaction. This makes it much more difficult for a researcher (also after the event) to make interpretations of negatively marked behaviour. In the Emery–Scargill interview we thus needed to pay close attention to comments made by either of the two participants during the interview, to study closely the visual signals revealing negative evaluations, to consider the wider implications of what is involved in producing a television broadcast of this type (the significance of the documentary film shown immediately prior to the interview, the physical set-up in the television studio, the editing being carried out live with camera shots, etc.) and, above all, to contextualise the sequence of social practice within a wider socio-political, socio-historical context. If the researcher is prepared to do all this (and probably much more than we have indicated in this chapter), then it is indeed possible to tease out negative evaluations of co-participants' behaviour which would lie within the range of impoliteness in the relational work being carried out.

It is also possible to see how forms of impoliteness (just like forms of politeness), even though they may be discursively disputed terms, are intimately involved in the exercise of power. It would not be possible to attribute attempts to gain and exercise power if relational work were not seen as a continually flexible, continually changing attempt to negotiate meaning in social practice, and it is for that reason that impoliteness, like politeness, is only a human universal if we are prepared to see it as the product of individual instances of social interaction.

Appendix

Readers who are interested in seeing a full transcript of the interview should contact Richard J. Watts.

Comment on transcription conventions:

The transcript has been made with an adaptation of the Hiat transcription conventions (cf. Ehlich 1993) in which turns are represented horizontally in the form of musical staves rather than vertically as in a drama script. This takes up a little more space but is particularly useful to represent concurrent speech by two or more interactants.

Simplified transcription conventions:

\	end of a tone unit
/	"self-interruption" leading to a recycling of the turn
the- the	repetition
—	unfinished utterance
::	lengthened syllables (only apparent here in the filled pause [er::])
[er::]	material included within square brackets refers to non-lexical utterances
(.)	unfilled pause of under 0.5 seconds
(..)	unfilled pause of between 0.5 and 1 second in length
(...)	unfilled pause of more than 1 second

Notes

1. With many thanks to Derek Bousfield and Holger Limberg for valuable comments on this chapter.
2. At the same time, what some people consider to be marked socially appropriate behaviour might be interpreted by others as being inappropriate to a certain extent. This might lead to latently negative evaluative lexemes such as *standoffish, stuck-up, hoity-toity*, etc., thus indicating that an individual who expresses such an evaluation is aware that others would consider the behaviour as appropriate, but personally interprets it negatively. This is because individuals' mappings of how lexemes should be profiled against the wider concept of inappropriate behaviour are highly likely to differ (Watts 2006).
3. While Kienpointner (1997) uses the 'term' rudeness as an umbrella term, i.e. as a second order term, he still recognises that rudeness as well as politeness are not absolute terms.

4. There need be no one-to-one correspondence between what that person felt at the time of the interaction and what he/she reports at a later stage.
5. The poster equates *rude* with *impolite*. It is interesting to see that certain contributors to this volume make second order distinctions between these terms (Terkourafi, Culpeper, Bousfield).
6. Available at www.bbc.co.uk/guidelines/edguide/politics/politicalinterv.shtml [2006]. Although we don't have access to instructions given to editorial staff in the 1980s, we can assume that similar guidelines would have been issued at that time.
7. Scargill says "the fact is there was government intervention to stop it" and later "I condemn the f/ police brutality that I saw\ and massive state interference and intervention".
8. Our personal impression was that the physical set-up frames notions such as *distance* and *unreachability* and effectively turns the metaphor of the table as the locus of conciliation via negotiation into a metaphor of an unbridgeable gap between two irreconcilable points of view. In this way the sense of a gulf between interviewer and interviewee is heightened.
9. The term "frame" in this context should be understood slightly differently from the expectation frames posited earlier in this chapter, but nevertheless as being related to them. We use "frame" in the present analysis to refer to ways in which individuals engaged in social practice *represent* others (including co-participants) through the various semiotic codes at their disposal. The difference between the two uses of "frame" is this: whereas frames of expectation are formed through earlier experience of social practice, representational frames are constructed in ongoing instances of social practice to represent the character traits, ideas and opinions of and even statements made by others. They are used as a means of creating in third persons (here the television audience) expectations as to how the represented others are likely to behave. In the present sequence of social practice, the desired representation is one of inappropriate behaviour on the part of the other, i.e. Emery attempting to frame Scargill as behaving inappropriately, and vice versa.
10. Sanctioned behaviour does not automatically mean that it is normalised in its effect, i.e. that it does not hurt the recipient (cf. Culpeper 2005).

Chapter 5
Political campaign debates as zero-sum games: Impoliteness and power in candidates' exchanges

María Dolores García-Pastor

1. Introduction[1]

Although there has been a noticeable increase of research into different political genres adopting a politeness perspective in the last twenty years (e.g.
Agha 1997; Blas Arroyo 2001, 2002, 2003; Bolívar 2005; Chilton 1990; Christie
2002; Fernández García 2000; Galasinski 1998; García-Pastor 2002, 2006; Harris 2001; Harris, Grainger and Mullany 2006; Mullany 2002; Pérez de Ayala
2001; Rudanko 1995; Zupnik 1994), politeness studies of political discourse
in general, and electoral debates in particular, are still scarce. As for the latter, whilst some of these studies concentrate on politeness or face mitigation
(Galasinski 1998), and others centre on impoliteness or face aggravation (Agha
1997; Blas Arroyo 2001), common to all these debate investigations is that they
do not sufficiently consider other important aspects of candidates' discourses
intimately related to politeness phenomena in these events such as the issue of
power (cf. Locher 2004). This chapter aims to modestly attend to such weakness
by exploring the interface between impoliteness and power in the context of
political campaign debates of the 2000 U.S. elections. To this end, I focus hitherto on those interventions in which politicians principally address one another,
since they best exemplify the combative dimension of these encounters. It is in
and through these interchanges that debaters intend to damage and dominate
the opponent, thus showing the antagonism that underlies and shapes their relationship. Such antagonism is fundamentally prompted by the competition for a
determinate political office they experience in electoral campaigns. This is observed in debates in that a candidate's victory entails the defeat of the adversary
and vice versa, a debater's loss implies the rival's gain. Consequently, political campaign debates are zero-sum games, whose win-lose nature and hostile
character become salient in candidates' reciprocal exchanges.[2]

In this chapter, I employ a second order approach to impoliteness (Watts
2003), whereby this concept basically consists of a speaker's intended face aggravation or attack towards the hearer (i.e. the opponent in this article) (cf.

Culpeper 2005). Power, on the other hand, is viewed as "relational, dynamic and contestable" (Locher 2004: 37). In order to examine impoliteness and power in politicians' interchanges in debates, Lachenicht's (1980) aggravating language framework, and Culpeper's (1996, 2005), Culpeper, Bousfield and Wichmann's (2003) and Blas Arroyo's (2001) impoliteness models have been followed to analyse sixteen U.S. electoral debates. All these studies adopt a classical perspective on impoliteness, as they draw on the work of Brown and Levinson ([1978] 1987) to deal with aggravating language and impoliteness respectively in different contexts. Thus, the theoretical framework within which impoliteness is discussed here is closest to Brown and Levinson's theory. Taking these studies as a starting point, I suggest a data-driven framework of impoliteness strategies in the context of political campaign debates. This framework entails, among other things, that impoliteness in this chapter constitutes aggravation towards the hearer's positive face or his/her desire to be approved of, and his/her negative face or his/her desire to have freedom of action (cf. Brown and Levinson [1978] 1987). Moreover, positive and negative face aggravation are expected to take determinate shapes, and operate in specific ways, thereby illustrating a context-specific form and function of impoliteness in debates. Impoliteness strategies in this research were observed to comprise major discursive categories, viz, face aggravating moves. These moves appeared forming chains that yielded what I have labelled *negativity cycles* following Gottman's (1994) work on divorce talk. In these cycles debaters conveyed a high degree of hostility towards the counter candidate, and constantly attempted to exert power over him/her. This gave place to a discursive struggle, which, inter alia, clearly exemplified the zero-sum game essence of electoral debates.

2.   Politeness studies of electoral debates

As previously mentioned, politeness investigations of political discourse, and electoral debates as one of its manifestations, are relatively recent and fairly scant. These studies focus on political speeches in diplomatic encounters and other communicative situations (Bolívar 2005; Chilton 1990), public political statements on the whole (Bolívar 2005; Harris, Grainger and Mullany 2006), televised political panel discussions (Zupnik 1994), parliamentary debates (Christie 2002; Harris 2001; Pérez de Ayala 2001; Rudanko 1995), political broadcast interviews (Fernández García 2000; Mullany 2002), and electoral debates (Agha 1997; Blas Arroyo 2001, 2002, 2003; Fernández García 2000; Galasinski 1998). Among all these investigations, research on political campaign debates that partially or fully takes a politeness approach, centres on politeness or impoliteness without paying due attention to other facets of debaters' talk closely related to politeness matters like the issue of power. Jaworski and Galasinski (2000) already hint at a relation between power and impoliteness in debates by establishing that contestants normally bid for power through positive self-presentation and negative other-depiction. Locher's (2004) analysis of an excerpt from the second presidential debate between Al Gore and George W. Bush in the 2000 U.S. elections also points out the relationship between power and politeness phenomena in these encounters. Along these lines, Watts (2003: 201) affirms that relational work between interactants, i.e. the work they do in relating to others, of which (im)polite behaviour is part, always embodies "a latent struggle for power in which perceptions of politeness play a significant role". Thus, notions of power and politeness intertwine in social intercourse (Eelen 2001; Mills 2003), especially as regards impoliteness in communicative encounters where there is a conflict of interests between conversational participants (Blas Arroyo 2001; Culpeper 1996; Kienpointner 1997). It is precisely in these exchanges that a) the latent clash of interests that is subjacent to power is even more pronounced, and b) the restriction of an individual's freedom that power entails, also turns more visible. Evidence for this can be found in investigations within pragmatics that deal more implicitly or explicitly with power in contexts involving opposed interests among interlocutors, and face aggravation in relation to at least one of the conversational parties, whose freedom of action is curtailed as a result, e.g. police-suspect and inspector–constable interviews (see Harris 1995; Thomas 1985), magistrate–defendant interaction (cf. Harris 1995; Lakoff 1989; Levinson 1992; Penman 1990), etc.

As zero-sum games that entail confrontation between their principal participants, electoral debates are a paramount instance of contexts where the interrelation between power and impoliteness becomes evident. Nevertheless, researchers exploring (im)politeness in these events have not considered such interrelations seriously enough. Thus, in his study of the first 1996 Clinton–Dole presidential debate, Agha (1997) concentrates on combat and aggression showing how debaters commonly enact these by means of negative other-typifying utterances directed towards the opponent. Agha recognises the existence of a link between these utterances and power by indicating that power is at the core of aggression in debates. Yet he leaves such connection unexplored. In a similar vein, Blas Arroyo (2001) emphasises conflict and impoliteness in his research of two electoral debates of the 1993 Spanish elections offering a content-based classification of impoliteness strategies in these events. He acknowledges that power is prominent in debates due to politicians' conflicting goals, and that it is through impoliteness that candidates intend to exert power over the rival. I would argue that elaborating on these claims could shed more light on the issue of power and its interrelation with impoliteness. In his subsequent studies he concentrates on the form and role of mitigating devices in these Spanish debates (Blas Arroyo 2002, 2003).

Fernández García (2000) deals with (im)politeness in Spanish political campaign debates giving more weight to face aggravation in his analysis. Like the aforementioned scholars, Fernández García affirms that contenders' power is in play in debates, and indirectly associates this notion with the hostility they display when addressing one another. Further development of these statements on theoretical or analytical grounds could yield insight into the notion of power and its link to impoliteness in these events. Finally, in his piece on rule breaching behaviour in two 1995 Polish presidential debates, Galasinski (1998) focuses on face mitigation and proposes a series of mitigating strategies debaters utilise to license such behaviour. Notwithstanding the implicit connection he draws between a politician's attack against the adversary and power through the coercive action of the former over the latter, Galasinski does not make this connection explicit nor does he pursue its examination. It is my contention that by considering the interface between impoliteness and a key aspect of candidates' discourses in debates such as power, a more comprehensive picture of impoliteness in these encounters, i.e. its shape and functioning, and political interaction in general can be gained.

3.   Debates as zero-sum games: Impoliteness and power

This chapter focuses on impoliteness as a second order concept (Watts 2003), i.e., impoliteness as a theoretical concept which is established by the researcher. Therefore, in tune with Culpeper (2005), impoliteness is conceptualised here as a speaker's intentional communication of face aggravation or attack to the hearer, who perceives and/or constructs the speaker's behaviour as intentionally face aggravating or attacking. In a context like political campaign debates, where politicians compete for a determinate political office, and continuously attempt to damage and dominate the counter candidate as a result, it would be unimaginable to conceive of impoliteness towards the rival differently from intended impoliteness in terms of aggravation or attack against his/her persona. Additionally, some notion of face, regardless of the definition of this concept one entertains (e.g. Arundale 2006; Brown and Levinson [1978] 1987; Goffman 1967; Mao 1994; Spencer-Oatey 2000b, 2002), is particularly suitable in political communication, since a politician's image and/or its attribution by the public is crucial for him/her to achieve his/her political goals. It is Brown and Levinson's notion of face, namely, the self-image an individual wants for him/herself in a specific society, that has been adopted here. Notwithstanding all the criticism it has received, especially in the cross-cultural pragmatics literature (e.g. Ide 1989; Mao 1994; Matsumoto 1988), I believe Brown and Levinson's notion of face, appropriately contextualised, is still useful to explain politeness issues across communicative contexts (cf. Arundale 2006; Culpeper 2005). Thus, a speaker's intended impoliteness in debates has been viewed in this chapter as aggravation towards a) the hearer's positive face, i.e. "the desire to be ratified, understood, approved of, liked or admired" (Brown and Levinson [1978] 1987: 62), and b) the hearer's negative face, namely, "the want of every 'competent adult member' that his actions be unimpeded by others" (62). In light of all the above, impoliteness as defined in this chapter has been thought to come close to the reality of this phenomenon in electoral debates.

As for power, I follow Locher (2004) in that this concept is relational, dynamic and contestable. Therefore, 1) power cannot emerge but in social bonds; 2) it is always 'up for grabs' as opposed to static, and 3) it can be resisted, which I would argue is another way of exerting power too. Underlying Locher's claims is mainly the idea that power cannot be divorced from social practice; it entails a discursive struggle between interlocutors, who negotiate it in their exchanges with one another, and, most importantly, it comes into being through communication. In spite of the relational, fluid, contestable and interactional essence of power, I also believe that power has an abstract or metaphorical nature (Tannen 1987), which is based on those attributions of power individuals make without necessarily communicating these in discourse. Nevertheless, interlocutors need to constantly secure such self- or other-attributed power in interaction given the temporary and contestable condition of this concept (Locher 2004). As established elsewhere (García-Pastor 2002, 2006), power in electoral debates is interactional *persuasive power,* according to Lakoff's (1990) and van Dijk's (1997) depiction of power in political interaction on the whole. Such depiction primarily lies in the fact that politicians' ultimate goal in their interactions with the public is to attain its persuasion. Moreover, power related to politicians' political campaign debates is also *official power*, viz, power that is overt, and institutionally expected by all debate participants (cf. Lakoff 1989, 1990; Mills 2003; van Dijk 1997). Official power contrasts with the *unofficial power* associated with the audience in these events, which lacks institutional recognition and is power of a covert kind symbolically granted by candidates themselves in and through their persuasive attempts.

The interrelation between the persuasive and official power characterising candidates' discourses in debates and impoliteness as understood in this chapterer, i.e. intended face aggravation, is expected to become salient in contenders' reciprocal interchanges due to the zero-sum game nature of these events. In these exchanges politicians employ impoliteness to discredit the opponent, and implicitly score points for their own image. According to Jaworski and Galasinski (2000), this is the way contestants bid for power in electoral debates. However, I would add that this also creates a discursive situation in which a politician coerces the adversary into having to respond somehow to such discrediting action, and this results in the former exerting power over the latter too. The zero-sum game essence of these events explains that the opponent typically responds with an impolite counter-move, whereby s/he tips the power balance to his/her own side. Thus, debaters' distinct interactional moves clearly illustrate the attack–defence or defence–attack dynamics defining politicians' interventions in political campaign debates (Benoit and Wells 1996; Galasinski 1998). Attack comes down to any attempt by a candidate to damage his/her rival's image, whilst defence alludes to any intent to safeguard one's own image commonly before the adversary's attacks. This attack–defence or defence–attack dynamics brings about a tit-for-tat that evinces 1) the antagonism underlying debaters' social bond, and 2) a discursive struggle between them, all of which makes more patent the relational, dynamic and contestable quality of power. Consequently, impoliteness, power and their interrelation are prominent in candidates' reciprocal exchanges in electoral debates mainly because of the zero-sum game nature of these communicative encounters.

4.   Data and methods

Sixteen debates of the 2000 U.S. elections corresponding to a total of twenty hours of ongoing talk are the object of analysis in this chapter. Ten of these debates belong to the presidential race, and include six Democratic and Republican debates, three presidential debates, and one vice presidential debate. The remaining ones are three senatorial and three governor debates from the New York, Virginia and Minnesota senatorial races, and the New Hampshire, Missouri, and Indiana governor races. All these debates were transcribed according to Jefferson's (Atkinson and Heritage 1984) transcription notations, which underwent some modifications in light of the aims of this research (see Appendix). An analysis of micro strategies was first performed taking some impoliteness and aggravating language models as a starting point (e.g. Blas Arroyo 2001; Culpeper 1996, 2005; Culpeper, Bousfield and Wichmann 2003; Lachenicht 1980) to propose a data-driven framework of impoliteness strategies in these contexts.

Similar to these models and as previously mentioned, this framework is close to Brown and Levinson's ([1978] 1987) theory in that, among other things, it entails that these impoliteness strategies constitute intended aggravation towards the hearer's positive face and/or his/her negative face (see above). Furthermore, in this framework a) no hierarchy of impoliteness strategies from most to least aggravating is alleged, b) mutual exclusivity of strategies in the same stretch of talk is dismissed, c) the multifunctionality and multidirectionality of strategies is contemplated by accepting the possibility that a determinate strategy orients to both positive and negative faces and multiple addressees at the same time, and d) strategies are conceived of as discourse-spanning and context-sensitive. In this way, it is believed that this framework can somehow meet some of the expectations that a solid empirical framework of (im)politeness strategies needs to fulfil on the conceptual and analytical planes (cf. Craig, Tracy and Spisak 1986; Eelen 2001; Locher and Watts 2005; Penman 1990). Such a framework is outlined in the next section.

Impoliteness strategies were observed to give place to larger discursive categories, namely, face aggravating moves, with two major face orientations towards the hearer's positive and negative face respectively. Whilst micro strategies were seen to concurrently orient to both faces with regularity, impolite moves exhibited such dual face directionality only on occasion. Instead, one face orientation normally prevailed over the other. In spite of focusing on the figure of the hearer (the opponent here) in the examination of face aggravating strategies and moves in the debates, the speaker was not completely overlooked by taking into account the fact that candidates sometimes use self-face damage in debates for strategic purposes. Positive and negative face aggravating moves were found to spark highly aggressive interactional periods, i.e. negativity cycles (see Gottman 1994).[3]

5. Analysis and discussion

5.1. *Impoliteness strategies*

The analysis of face aggravating strategies in this study has centred solely on on-record attack with redressive action (cf. Brown and Levinson [1978] 1987). Consequently, the bald-on-record and off-record impolite categories entertained in some of the aforementioned models were not considered here. The resulting framework of impoliteness strategies in this research is summarised in Table 1.

Table 1.   Face Aggravating Stragegies

Positive face-oriented strategies	Negative face-oriented strategies
Convey dislike for, and disagreement with H* and close others (his/her/their things, actions, values and opinions).	State the communicative act(s) as common or shared knowledge.
Use aggressive punning.	Indebt H.
Be ironic/sarcastic.	Refer to rights, duties and rules not respected, fulfilled or complied with respectively.
Deny in-group status.	
Disassociate, distance from H.	Increase imposition weight.
Ignore H.	Refuse H and H's things, actions, values and opinions.
Belittle or diminish the importance of H and H's things, actions, values and opinions.	Challenge.
	Frighten.
	Dare.

*H refers to the 'hearer'

Some strategies, which either do not appear in other impoliteness models or, if appearing in these, do not have a strategy status, were established as impolite strategies in their own right here due to candidates' recurrent use of determinate linguistic devices, e.g. puns in the case of the strategy 'use aggressive punning', and performance of certain linguistic actions as distinctive tactics to hurt the adversary. Most of the strategies suggested, though, have been adapted from other models in view of what surfaced in the analysis. For instance, regarding positive face-oriented strategies, the strategy 'convey dislike for, and disagreement with H and close others (his/her/their things, actions, values and opinions)' stems from the unification of Lachenicht's (1980) positive face aggravating strategies 'express dislike for H and H's things', and 'disclaim common opinions'. The meaning of these two strategies has also been expanded to incorporate the things, actions, values and opinions of H's close or related others, because in attacking the rival a debater often included the family, friends, colleagues and political party of the former in the attack (see Gregori-Signes 2005). Bill Bradley's (BB) words against Al Gore in (1) illustrate this strategy:

(1) 1   BB: [...] ↑nineteen ninety six the welfare reform bill. (.)
     2   *and the ↑welfare refoorm biill that ↑Al ↑Gore urged*
     3   *↑president Clinton to siign in the middle of the*
     4   *cam↑paaign so as (.) to win the e↑lection (.) was*
     5   *truly a ↑GAAMBLE* [...]

The strategy 'deny in-group status' is analogous to Culpeper's (1996) and Culpeper, Bousfield and Wichmann's (2003) strategy 'disassociate from the other'. The only difference is that in political campaign debates this strategy involves the speaker's exclusion of the hearer from a group or collectivity that is commonly H's own political party to deny his/her political identity. Thus, this strategy ensued as a distinct one from the strategy 'disassociate, distance from the other', which in debates consists of politicians' deployment of formal and impersonal address terms to claim relational distance between themselves and the opponent. The following intervention by Al Gore (AG) exemplifies this strategy:

(2) 1   AG: [...] ↑for the ↑↑LAAST seven ↑years I've served as
     2   viice <u>president</u> (.) *and the ↑↑other ↑night in the*
     3   *debate uh senator Bradley criticized <u>mee</u> and other*
     4   *Democrats for being in what ↑↑he ↑caalled a*
     5   *'Wasshing<u>toon</u> <u>bunnker</u>'* [...]

As for negative face-oriented strategies, the strategy 'refer to rights, duties and rules not respected, fulfilled or complied with respectively' is a specific manifestation of Lachenicht's (1980) strategy 'refer to rights and obligations', and Culpeper's (1996, 2005) and Culpeper, Bousfield and Wichmann's (2003) broader strategy 'explicitly associate the other with a negative aspect' (see also Blas Arroyo's (2001) 'asocia directamente al interlocutor con intenciones, hechos, etc. negativos' (associate the interlocutor with negative intentions, facts, etc.)). The strategy 'increase imposition weight' is broader than Lachenicht's (1980), as it turned out to encompass many sorts of impositions ranging from inflicting a certain attitude or world view on H, to literal or metaphorical invasions of his/her space (cf. Culpeper 1996, 2005; Culpeper, Bousfield and Wichmann 2003). These two strategies combine in Steve Forbes' (SF) interchange directed at George W. Bush in (3):

(3) 1   SF: [...] *on education (.) you've dumped down the*
     2   *↑↑standards. to the point (.) where uh in ↑Texas (.)*
     3   *your S.A.↑Tt. ranking has gone from fortieth in the*
     4   *↑nation. to forty-sixth in the nation (.) what can you*

5	tell (.) the people of New Hampshire (.) and of
6	America (.) that you won't do in Washington what
7	you've done in Texas [...]

The strategy 'refuse H and H's things, actions, values and opinions' (cf. Blas Arroyo 2001; Culpeper 1996, 2005; Culpeper, Bousfield and Wichmann 2003; Lachenicht 1980) comes down to contenders' refusals of imaginary or real imposing offers from the adversary. The strategy 'challenge' covers impositions that materialised as demands from the speaker to the hearer that s/he proved his/her claims implying s/he could not do so, and conveying disagreement with him/her (see Muntigl and Turnbull 1998). In sum, the framework of face aggravating strategies put forward in this chapter provides further evidence to the idea that (im)politeness adopts specific shapes and operates in specific ways across communicative encounters as far as its aggravating side is concerned.

5.2. Negativity cycles

As already discussed, face aggravating strategies yielded positive and negative face aggravating moves, which formed chains constituting negativity cycles. Such moves did not necessarily correspond with a turn at talk. Rather, they consisted of a juxtaposition of impoliteness strategies constituting a coherent and identifiable chunk of speech by virtue of the overall aggravating function they performed as regards the opponent's positive and negative face. Negativity cycles sporadically contained direct and explicit face mitigation targeted at the moderator of the exchange, the audience or the rival, which was issued for strategic purposes linked to the speaker's (S) own image building in the case of the latter. These macro impolite units took place at any point in the unfolding event, frequently resulting in illicit talk that the moderator ended up stopping most of the time. An affiliative and/or disaffiliative response from the audience was also a typical end to these units. Impoliteness in these highly aggressive episodes was observed to be impoliteness of the *instrumental, strategic* or *systematic* sort as in debate interaction on the whole, viz, intended rule-governed aggravation utilised by individuals to attain certain goals in a given speech situation (Beebe 1995; Kasper 1990; Kienpointner 1997; Lakoff 1989).[4] Such impoliteness merged with *lack of affect restraint* impoliteness, which originates from the unrestrained expression of feelings or emotions (Kasper 1990; Kochman 1984). These episodes usually involved an emotion of anger, hence impoliteness of a *volcanic* kind (Beebe 1995).

Negativity cycles were almost equally composed of positive and negative face aggravation. The positive and negative face aggravating strategies 'convey dislike for, and disagreement with H and close others (his/her/their things, actions, values and opinions)', and 'increase imposition weight' respectively, surfaced as the most popular. Nevertheless, the negative face aggravating strategies 'challenge' and 'state the communicative act(s) as common or shared knowledge', and the positive face aggravating strategies 'be ironic/sarcastic' and 'belittle or diminish the importance of H and H's things, actions, values and opinions' were regular in these aggressive episodes too. The different extracts discussed below illustrate the presence of all these strategies in these cycles. Contrary to what was expected, face mitigation was seen to override impoliteness in one case. In this specific instance one of the two candidates involved in the exchange praises the opponent at some point, and partially agrees with the latter for strategic ends related to the presentation of a positive image of himself. Lastly, impoliteness in negativity cycles often escalated reaching its peak in a reaction of stonewalling from one of the interlocutors (cf. Vuchinich 1990). Stonewalling amounted to complete utterances a candidate repeated in an automatic non-interruptive manner to bespeak ignorance of the adversary, and block his/her speech: for example, utterances denying the truth of the rival's statements such as 'that's not true'. These findings back the argument in the politeness and conflict talk literature that impoliteness breeds impoliteness in social intercourse (Corsaro and Rizzo 1990; Culpeper 1996; Culpeper, Bousfield and Wichmann 2003; Lakoff 1989; Mills 2003; Vuchinich 1990).

Power in negativity cycles is interactional *persuasive power* as in political communication in general (Lakoff 1990; van Dijk, 1997). As already mentioned concerning power related to politicians in electoral debates, power in these cycles also appeared as power of an *official* sort (García-Pastor 2002, 2006), namely, power which is overt, and institutionally expected by all debate participants (cf. Lakoff 1989, 1990; Mills 2003; van Dijk 1997). Such power fundamentally surfaced as *expert* power or power based on individuals' knowledge or expertise of a determinate type (Spencer-Oatey 2000b; Tannen 1987; Thomas 1995). Its relational, dynamic and contestable nature became salient in candidates' instantiation of a tit-for-tat in these highly impolite interchanges, which illustrated a verbal duel or struggle between them. This struggle was found to consist of reciprocal positive and negative face aggravation at a content level, and a fight for conversational resources at a structural level, in particular, topic control and floor holding. Thus, contenders enacted power in negativity cycles by striving to 1) discredit the opponent and coerce him/her into a determinate course of action by means of positive and negative face impoliteness, and 2) control the topic of the interaction and hold the floor, which have normally been identified as the canonical ways of accruing power in discourse. This accounts for the outstanding presence of *overt disagreement*, that is, disagreement devoid of reluctance markers leading to unmodulated or unmitigated dissent (Gruber 1998; Kotthoff 1993; Locher 2004), and metacommunicative statements on structural properties of the talk, e.g. statements on who had the floor and for how long, claims about one's own rights in the interaction, etc. Politicians' discursive struggle in these antagonistic periods also explains the rapid tempo of the conversation and the abundance of interruptions and overlaps (cf. Fernández García 2000). All the above revealed the attack–defence or defence–attack system typical of electoral debates, where attack entails any intent to hurt the opponent's image, and defence implies any attempt to protect one's own (see extracts below for an illustration). As a result, the clash of interests and the restriction of freedom underlying power were prominent in these hostile macro sequences. In brief, negativity cycles are combative episodes, in which the interrelation between impoliteness and power in debates and the zero-sum game essence of these events becomes salient.

Excerpt (4) below is a negativity cycle that exemplifies the interface between impoliteness and power in a multiple candidates' debate held at the very beginning of Election 2000. This cycle is principally performed by the Republican contestants Gary Bauer (GB) and Steve Forbes (SF). Bauer starts an argument on most favoured-nation status for China, viz, the ascription of a normal trade relations status for this country, to implicitly suggest that Forbes and Bush have offered such status to the Chinese in return for financial contributions to their electoral campaigns. Karen Brown's (KB(M)) intervention allotting the next turn in the conversation to George W. Bush puts an end to the episode at the same time that it shows her institutional authority as one of the moderators (M) of the encounter:

(4) 1 GB: [...] ↑STEVE FORBES you <u>CAN'T</u> figure ↑out
     2   where you are on most favored-nation status for
     3   China
     4 SF: [oh come on Gary I've laid out a policy on China
     5   (.)
     6 GB: what we can say (.) one thing (.) what we can
     7   say (.) something else (.)]
     8 SF: [you should listen to it
     9 GB: governor Bush you agreee]
    10 SF: [Gary I'll give you a copy (.) I'll give you a copy
    11   of my book and you can find it

12	GB:	USE your own time USE your own time]
13		governor Bush you've got a policy on China that
14		looks just like Bill Clinton's when it comes to
15		most favored-↑nation <u>status</u> (.) so I think you
16		guuys (.) are <u>al</u>ready affected by some of these
17		big money contributions
18	JMC:	[could I mention some (.) I'm the
19	SF:	no one's ever bought me Gary and never will
20	JMC:	I'm the only guy that has [has a commercial]
21		running that
22	KB(M):	(unintelligible)]
23	JMC:	morphs Bill Clinton's face into mine
24		[(some of the candidates laugh)
25	KB(M):	governor Bush] you get to ask the next question
26		[…]

The discursive struggle Bauer and Forbes carry out in this negativity cycle illustrates how the two candidates 'do' power here, and how this is achieved through impoliteness in the form of positive and negative face aggravating moves constituted by some of the impoliteness strategies outlined in Table 1. From line 1 Gary Bauer, a former Reagan administration official, bids for expert power in asserting that Steve Forbes has not been coherent enough about his position on most favoured-nation status for China. Bauer thus claims expert power by means of a face aggravating move, in which, overall, he aims to damage Forbes' positive face using the impoliteness strategy 'belittle or diminish the importance of H and H's things, actions, values and opinions' (cf. Blas Arroyo 2001; Culpeper 1996, 2005; Culpeper, Bousfield and Wichmann 2003; Lachenicht 1980) combined with the strategy 'convey dislike for, and disagreement with H and close others (his/her/their things, actions, values and opinions)' (lines 1–3). Bauer's usage of the publisher's first name and surname alerts the audience about his attack (see Bou Franch 2006), and is evocative of the shape reprimands sometimes adopt in ordinary conversation. Accordingly, Bauer also seems to be admonishing Forbes for his lack of coherence in his position on China in this positive face aggravating sequence. This justifies the presence of the negative face aggravating strategies 'increase imposition weight', and very indirectly, 'refer to rights, duties and rules not respected, fulfilled or complied with respectively' in this move too.

Forbes reacts to Bauer's impolite sequence and his bid for expert power with a counter-move in which he defends himself from the latter's accusation, and attempts to invalidate his claim for expert power (lines 4–5). This counter-move consists of a positive face aggravating move constituted by the strategy 'convey dislike for, and disagreement with the hearer and close others (his/her/their things, actions, values and opinions)'. In this way, Forbes not only resists Bauer's power move, but simultaneously intends to exert power over the official. The publisher further attempts to exert power over Bauer via a negative face aggravating sequence in line 8, whereby he reprimands the latter, and another one in lines 10–11, where he stresses his imposition on the official. In so doing, Forbes persistently interrupts Bauer, who shows his anger at this interruptive conduct with a negative face aggravating move primarily compounded by the impoliteness strategy 'increase imposition weight' (line 12). This sequence is based on two imperatives, which amount to metacommunicative statements that depict Forbes' behaviour as illegitimate, hence a breach of the interactional rules of the debate. Bauer's loud voice signals his anger, hence the presence of volcanic impoliteness, and reinforces his impinging action upon the publisher's negative face here (cf. Culpeper, Bousfield and Wichmann 2003).

By means of this impolite move Bauer aims to exert power over Forbes again. The fact that the official regains the floor and once more controls the topic of the interaction facilitates this. Bauer bids for expert power at this point in the conversation by means of a positive face aggravating move against Bush consisting mainly of the impoliteness strategy 'deny in-group status' (lines 13–15), and a negative face aggravating move against both Bush and Forbes principally based on the strategies 'increase imposition weight', and 'refer to rights, duties and rules not respected, fulfilled or complied with respectively' (lines 15–17). Therefore, in these sequences Bauer counter-attacks and intends to exert power over Forbes and Bush by way of impoliteness. Forbes takes offence at Bauer's charge, and reciprocates with impoliteness to defend himself in line 19. Face mitigation in this extract is instantiated by John McCain through a permission request from the moderators (line 18), and an ironic/sarcastic joke about Clinton and the Democrats (lines 18, 20–21, and 23). In short, Bauer and Forbes 'do' power in this episode by means of positive and negative face aggravating sequences, which show a discursive struggle between them that evinces how power and impoliteness intertwine in negativity cycles in electoral debates, and underscores the relational, dynamic and contestable character of this concept. The attack-defence or defence-attack dynamics that characterises politicians' talk in these events is also patent in this example.

Similarly, the negativity cycle enacted by Al Gore (AG) and Bill Bradley (BB) in (5) comprises a verbal duel between both politicians that shows how impoliteness and power intertwine in debates. This cycle belongs to a debate held in February 2000, and moderated by Bernard Shaw (BS(M)). As in (4), this antagonistic episode finishes with the moderator' calling time on the candidates.

The audience also intervenes here as a collective entity (A) and individually in the form of an anonymous audience member (AAM19):

(5)	1	AG:	[. . .] senator Bradley ↑you must be the ↑only
	2		Democrat in America who misses ↑Ken <u>Starr</u>.
	3	BB:	[yeah. (.) yeah
	4	A:	(16. collectively laughs, applauds and screams)
	5	BS(M):	senator ↑Bradley
	6	BB:	UUh (.) ↑Iii did <u>NOt</u> propooose] (.) aa (.)
	7		especial ↑prosecutor (.) I <u>saaid</u> (.) thaaat (.) the
	8		↑DEmocratic party will <u>looo</u>se its <u>MAN</u>tle as a
	9		re<u>form</u> party (.) if we don't come to ↑terms (.)
	10		with what happened in nineteen ninety <u>six</u> (.)
	11		and I think the ↑<u>BEST</u> way to come to terms
	12		with what happened in nineteen ninety six (.) is
	13		for ↑you to tell people exactly what happened
	14		(.) in your own woords (.) so that (.) let me tell
	15		you (.) if ↑YOU AARE=
	16	BS(M):	=time=
	17	AG:	=WELL (.) LET ME JUST uh (0.5) (taking a
	18		piece of paper from the lectern) read you the
	19		front (.) th 'The New York Tiimes' to↑daay (.)
	20		recall'n uh (.) reporting on your statement
	21		[yesterday
	22	BB:	incorrect
	23	AG:	(reading from paper) 'for]mer senator Bill
	24		Bradley (.) publicly endorsed today the
	25		appointment of a especial ↑PROsecutor=
	26	BB:	=it's incorrect=
	27	AG:	=[for the Clinton-Gore
	28	AAM19:	BOOOOO
	29	AG:	<u>CAM</u>paign] in ninety six'=
	30	BB	=in[correct
	31	AG:	well take it] up with 'The New York Times'=
	32	BB:	=[yeah
	33	AG:	you're] the one that (.)
	34	A:	[(collectively applauds and boos)
	35	AG:	that is reported as having SAID <u>THAT</u>.
	36	BB:	NO
	37	AG	in the transcript

38	BB:	it's incorrect
39	A:	(6.5 collectively applauds)
40	AG:	THE TRANSCRIPT (1.) ↑I READ the
41		transcript f of <u>what</u> you saaid.] (.) now (.) th the
42		<u>point</u> is (.) the point is <u>this</u> (.) ↑we haave a=
43	BS(M):	=time= […]

In this cycle both Gore and Bradley 'do' power through reciprocal face aggravation bringing about a discursive struggle, in which Gore first attempts to exert power over Bradley with an ironic/sarcastic remark that is intended to attack the senator's positive face (lines 1–2). In this remark Gore uses the impoliteness strategies 'be ironic/sarcastic' and 'deny in-group status', thereby exhibiting the 'go-for-the-jugular' style distinctive of him (Connolly 2000). The vice president denies the senator's in-group status as a Democrat in establishing that he 'misses Ken Star', the Republican lawyer responsible for the attempted impeachment of Bill Clinton in 1999. Gore's remark produces the collective laughter of the audience (line 4), which participates actively in the encounter to the extent that some anonymous audience members individually join in the interaction (line 28).[5] Bradley defends himself against Gore's charges, and attacks the latter through a positive face aggravating move (lines 6–15), which consists of the impoliteness strategy 'convey dislike for, and disagreement with H and close others (his/her/their things, actions, values and opinions)', and the negative face aggravating strategies 'increase imposition weight', and 'challenge' (lines 11–15). In this way, he counteracts Gore's power move by concurrently exerting power in the interaction. The senator's defence–attack hitherto resembles interlocutors' offensive-defensive or defensive–offensive moves in other communicative situations (cf. Culpeper, Bousfield and Wichmann 2003; Kienpointner 1997).

Nonetheless, this dynamic progressively turns into an attack–attack or attack–counter attack one as the aggressive exchange unfolds. This underlines the discursive struggle between Gore and Bradley in the episode. Gore's immediate negative face aggravating sequence (lines 17–21, 23–25, 27 and 29), in which he deploys *material evidence* (Martel 1983), namely, an article from *The New York Times*, constitutes the turning point for this change in the discourse. The vice president bids for expert power here mainly by way of the impoliteness strategy 'increase imposition weight'. The senator reciprocates straight away with a positive face aggravating move where he bluntly denies the truth of Gore's statements and tries to invalidate his bid for power simultaneously exerting power in the interaction (line 22). Bradley reproduces this impolite move, which is constituted by overt disagreement (Gruber 1998; Kotthoff 1993; Locher 2004), in lines 26, 30 and 38. It is in this fashion that the senator instantiates his stonewalling reaction in the exchange. The pace of the conversation increases, as revealed in the debaters' incessant interruptions and overlaps, which accentuate the discursive struggle between them. This struggle reaches its summit in the vice president's loud affirmations in lines 40–41. These underscore the volcanic impoliteness ubiquitous to the episode, and show Gore's aim to strategically score a point for himself in the contest in which both contestants are involved. This makes more apparent the zero-sum game condition of the debate in question. This negativity cycle illustrates how Gore and Bradley negotiate power by means of impoliteness bringing about a discursive struggle especially prominent in this excerpt.

From the third debate between Al Gore (AG) and George W. Bush (GWB) in their quest for the presidency of the U.S., example (6) further substantiates the idea that negativity cycles epitomise the interrelation between impoliteness and power in political campaign debates. Like (4) and (5) above, the moderator, Jim Lehrer (JL(M)), ends the cycle by announcing a new stage in the conversation. The audience (A) participates in the interaction at some point too. This extract also illustrates Gore's continuous breach of the interactional rules established for this event, whereby candidates are not allowed to address one another directly or ask each other questions:

(6)	1	AG:	[...] he said if affirmative aaction means quotas
	2		he's a↑gainst it. (.) affirmative aaction (.) doesn't
	3		mean=
	4	GWB:	=[↑good
	5	AG:	quotas] (.) are you ↑for it with<u>out</u> quotas
	6	GWB:	I may not be for ↑your version Mr. vice president
	7		but I'm for what I just des↑criibed to the lady (.)
	8		[she <u>heard</u> my answer
	9	AG:	=are you for what the Su]↑<u>preme</u> Court saays is
	10		(.) a a <u>constitutional</u> way of having affirmative
	11		aaction
	12	GWB:	Jim is ↑this
	13	JL(M):	let's go on to another (.) anotheeer [uuuh
	14	A:	(collectively laughs)
	15	JL(M):	and it's a it's a question
	16	AG:	I think that speaks for itself
	17	GWB:	no (.) [it doesn't ↑speak
	18	JL(M):	and it's a question

19	GWB:	for itself Mr. vice president it speaks for the <u>faact</u> that
20		there are certain ruules in this that we all
21		a↑gree to. but evidently rules don't ↑<u>mean</u>
22		anything (laughs)=
23	JL(M):	=the question is for yooou vice president Gore
24		[. . .]

This negativity cycle is actually encouraged by Jim Lehrer, who, in his role of provoker (Blas Arroyo 1998), asks the vice president a question in which he implicitly questions the clarity of Bush's previous answer. Gore and Bush 'do' power here through positive and negative face aggravation producing a discursive struggle in the exchange that culminates in Bush's angry reaction at its end. Such struggle begins with a negative face aggravating move from Gore mainly constituted by the impoliteness strategies 'increase imposition weight' (lines 1–2), and 'state the communicative act(s) as common or shared knowledge' (lines 2–3). In this way, Gore produces a metacommunicative statement that summarises Bush's words and position, and lectures the governor, thus bidding for expert power. The vice president continues exerting power over his adversary through a negative face aggravating move based on the impoliteness strategy 'challenge' (line 5). By directly positing a challenging question to Bush, Gore attacks him and transgresses the rules set up for the debate. Bush defends himself and resists the vice president's power move with a counter-move consisting of a positive face aggravating sequence, in which he disagrees with the latter (lines 6–8). Besides exemplifying a discursive struggle, through which power is negotiated by means of reciprocal impoliteness, Gore's and Bush's negative and positive face aggravating move respectively show the attack–defence or defence–attack dynamics characterising politicians' talk in debates.

The vice president responds to Bush's positive face aggravation with a negative face aggravating sequence, through which he increases his imposition on the governor, and challenges him implying that he cannot adequately answer (lines 9–11). Gore persists in trying to exert power over Bush here, and breaks the interactional rules of the debate to this end again. This brings about Bush's indirect request to Jim Lehrer, the moderator, that he intervene and somehow stop Gore's illicit behaviour (line 12) coupled with the audience's laughter at the vice president's conduct (line 14). By shifting addressee from Gore to Lehrer and using face mitigation, Bush intends to invalidate the vice president's power move and exert power in the exchange altogether. However, Gore's negative face aggravating move in his unequivocal statement (line 16) counteracts Bush's bid for power, and implicitly summarises what he has been attempting to prove in this negativity cycle: that Bush does not have sufficient knowledge about the

issue under discussion, hence does not know where he stands on it. Gore therefore coerces Bush and implicitly presents a negative image of the governor and
a positive image of himself to attain power in the interaction (cf. Jaworski and
Galasinski 2000). Bush's instant *opposition format* (Kotthoff 1993), i.e. disagreement in which S uses H's words to make the opposite point, aims to bid
for power and offer a negative image of the vice president. All the above shows
how power and impoliteness intertwine to yield the discursive struggle between
Gore and Bush defining this negativity cycle.

Extract (7) exemplifies a negativity cycle performed by Charles Robb (CR)
and his Republican opponent George Allen (GA) in a senatorial debate from the
2000 Virginia race. By contrast with the above, the discursive struggle between
both debaters hitherto clearly tips the power balance on Allen's side. The audience as a collective entity (A) and an anonymous audience member (AAM4)
also takes part in the exchange, which is finished by Douglas Wilder (DW(M)),
the moderator:

(7)	1	CR:	it it ↑wasn't for my benefit] incidentally
	2		George=
	3	GA:	well. but you were there. (.) [you
	4	CR:	ooh.]
	5	GA:	were there. (.) and introducing and so forth=
	6	CR:	=yeeah.=
	7	GA:	so I'm sure you've got none of those funds that
	8		were raised there for your <u>campaign</u> and all
	9		those good negative ↑ADS we've [seen (.) in
	10		Virginia for the last several months
	11	CR:	(bursts into laughter)
	12	AAM4:	(bursts into laughter)]
	13	GA:	here you want you wanted to (.) ↑build the
	14		particulars on where I disagree with <u>your</u> votes
	15		and those of of of (.) of <u>president</u> Clinton (.) and
	16		↑whyy I think he really (.) he's the one you
	17		agree with the most. (.) here you are (.) you
	18		vote with him eighty-seven per cent of the time
	19		(.) more than <u>any</u> other <u>member</u> of our
	20		delegation (.) Republican <u>D</u>emocrat or
	21		Indep<u>end</u>ent (.) in Virginia (.) ↑<u>heck</u> I don't
	22		think that ↑<u>Hillary</u> (.) agrees with Bill [eighty-
	23		seven per cent of the <u>time</u>
	24	A:	(immediate collective applause)

25	GA:	but Virginia's junior senator ↑does] (.) you vote
26		↑with him you ↑talk about school ↑safety (.)
27		the ↑Clinton administration did <u>not</u> (.) all↑ow
28		was to ex<u>pel</u> students who brought [↑<u>guns</u>
29	CR:	mhm.]
30	GA:	to schools you voted ↑wroong. time after time
31		(.) and senator Warner <u>stood</u> with us (.) where I
32		disagree with you a↑gain. is on the (.) and and
33		president Clinton is on the marriage ↑penalty
34		<u>tax</u> (.) a↑<u>gain</u> there were Democrat Cong (.)
35		members of <u>Congress</u> (.) who voted for that
36		marriage penalty tax relief that <u>you</u> and
37		president Clinton (.) have prevented uuh (.)
38		from being eliminated this <u>year</u> (.) you had
39		voted five ↑tiimes. (.) a<u>gainst</u> (.) requiring able-
40		bodied people on (.) <u>food</u> stamps no welfare to
41		↑work (.) [and you stood
42	DW(M):	time (.) time [has gone by [...]

In this extract, Charles Robb and George Allen jointly enact power in the interaction by way of impoliteness. This generates a discursive struggle that begins
with Robb's positive face aggravating move (lines 1–2). In this move, Robb
disagrees with Allen defending himself before the latter's accusation that he
had attended a gathering with president Clinton to raise funds for his campaign.
Robb thus resists Allen's power move here bidding for power himself at the
same time. Allen's accusation is part of a global strategy of casting Robb as a
Washington politician, who merely acts as if he were Clinton's puppet. In this
way, Allen intends to take advantage of the unpopularity of the president, and the
fact that most Virginians reject Washington politics for their state. The Republican politician reacts to Robb's power move with a counter-move, in which he
impinges upon the latter's negative face based on the impoliteness strategy 'increase imposition weight' (line 3). This produces Robb's reaction of 'insincere
agreement' (Culpeper, Bousfield and Wichmann 2003) (lines 4 and 6), whereby
he tries to invalidate Allen's bid for power, whilst exerting power too. Allen
keeps on claiming power by aggravating the Democrat's positive face with a
series of ironic/sarcastic remarks (lines 7–10) that cause Robb's laughter, and
that of an anonymous audience member (lines 11 and 12). Contrary to the affiliative meaning of the audience member's laughter, the Democratic debater's
stresses disagreement, as it seems to indicate that he views his opponent's turn
as non-serious dismissing it in consequence.

At this point, Allen starts to monopolise the floor and the topic under discussion attacking Robb and intending to exert power over him up to the end of the cycle. Allen instantiates a negative face aggravating sequence for this purpose, which contains, on the one hand, the positive face aggravating strategies 'convey dislike for, and disagreement with H and close others (his/her/their things, actions, values and opinions)' (lines 13–17 and 30–34) and 'be ironic/sarcastic' (lines 21–23). On the other hand, it includes the negative face aggravating strategies 'increase imposition weight', 'indebt H', and 'refer to rights, duties and rules not respected, fulfilled or complied with respectively' (lines 18–21, 25–28, 30 and 34–41). By means of all these strategies Allen builds his argument that Robb's voting record and president Clinton's are basically identical. He further reinforces this argument in his ironic/sarcastic remark in lines 21–23, which stresses the idea that Robb is Clinton's marionette. The audience's positive collective reply (line 24) signals the Republican politician's success in 1) indirectly constructing an alliance with audience members here (see Hutchby 1997), and 2) damaging his rival's image, and exerting power over him. Allen strategically exploits pitch contour in this final part of the episode to intensify his disapproval, thus showing his anger and the volcanic impoliteness underlying this negativity cycle. In sum, Robb's and Allen's exchange of positive and negative face aggravation illustrates their enactment of power evincing a discursive struggle between the two in the interaction.

6. Conclusions

In this chapter I have intended to explore the interface between impoliteness and power in electoral debates of the 2000 U.S. elections. I would argue that politeness investigations of debates have not contemplated the issue of power seriously enough notwithstanding the close relationship between this concept and politeness phenomena. Power in debates becomes salient and its link to impoliteness is evident due to the zero-sum game essence of these events. Politicians discredit the opponent, and coerce him/her into a specific course of action in their interchanges. This gives place to a discursive struggle which 1) evinces the interrelation between impoliteness and power in debates, and 2) underscores the relational, dynamic and contestable features of these concepts. Such struggle illustrates the attack–defence or defence–attack dynamics characteristic of these contexts too. I have labelled these exchanges negativity cycles, and I have described them as chains of positive and negative face aggravating moves compounded by a series of impoliteness strategies that, inter alia, reflect how impoliteness adopts a determinate shape and operates in a particular way in electoral debates. Whether the same, similar or different strategies of face aggravation emerge in other political genres is an area that could benefit from future investigation to help elucidate the form and function of impoliteness in political communication. Impoliteness in negativity cycles was found to be strategic and volcanic, and had a tendency to escalate. Therefore, negativity cycles epitomise the interrelation between impoliteness and power in political campaign debates, and make more salient the inherent characteristics of this concept.

Appendix

(1.5)	Pause in tenths of seconds.
(.)	Pause shorter than a tenth of second.
[ ]	Overlap.
=	Latching.
ooo	Sound stretch.
↑Oh	Rise in pitch.
.	Fall in pitch
YES	Louder volume.
yes	Stress.
(nods)	Actions, gestures and noises.
y'cd	Contraction.
'Times'	Latin or foreign words, direct quoting, and proper nouns.

Notes

1. My thanks go to Miriam A. Locher, Derek Bousfield and Stephanie Schnurr for their valuable comments on this chapter.
2. Even though electoral debates are first and foremost persuasive events where politicians ultimately aim to persuade the audience (García-Pastor 2002, 2006), in this chapter I will be focusing on their antagonistic aspect.
3. The presence of these impolite episodes in electoral debates and their cyclical condition have already been recognised by debate researchers like Blas Arroyo (2001) and Fernández García (2000). García-Pastor and Sanjosé (in preparation) are currently investigating their semantic representation and their cyclical character in statistical terms.
4. Although one may think that all impoliteness is, on some level, instrumental, I would argue that this is contingent upon the definition of impoliteness one adopts in a second order approach to this notion. Thus, the instrumental character that may be attributed to impoliteness vanishes if one considers, for instance, unintended impoliteness as

part of the definition of this phenomenon (cf., e.g. Bou Franch and Garcés Conejos 1994).
5. The active involvement of the audience in this negativity cycle makes this hostile episode resemble confrontational sequences in tabloid talkshows (see Gregori-Signes 1998, 2000a/b).

Part 3. Interaction with legally constituted authorities

Chapter 6
Impoliteness in the struggle for power

Derek Bousfield

1. Introduction: Impoliteness, abuse and violence[1]

Locher and Bousfield (this volume) note the disproportionate number of studies dealing with politeness when compared to impoliteness. Even if we are not going to accept at face value such academic (Lakoff 2006) and lay (Truss 2005) insistences that the paradigms of polite interaction (in western societies) are undergoing a negative change, it is still of paramount importance that we study impoliteness. After all, 1999–2000 saw medical and other employees working within the British National Health Service (NHS) suffer 65,000 reported 'violent and/or abusive incidents', primarily at the hands of members of the public. The following year, 2000–2001, saw this rise to 84,273 reported incidents (UK Dept of Health 2002).[2] These figures, indicating that abusive/violent attacks are far from isolated incidents, prompted the publication of a comprehensive position statement entitled *Withholding treatment from violent and abusive patients in NHS trusts*. This text defines 'abusive behaviour' as including (but by no means limited to), "Threatening or abusive language involving excessive swearing or offensive remarks"; "Derogatory racial or sexual remarks"; "Malicious allegations relating to members of staff, other patients or visitors"; "Threats or threatening behaviour"; "Name calling, including personal comments about physical looks" and "Language that belittles a person's abilities". Furthermore, this publication outlines the NHS's definition of *violence* against staff as being:

> ... any incident where staff are abused, threatened or assaulted in circumstances relating to their work, involving an explicit or implicit challenge to their safety, well-being or health ... [furthermore, the definition of violence] can incorporate some of the behaviours identified in harassment and bullying, for example, verbal violence. *Verbal aggression is frequently used by patients, relatives and carers to intimidate healthcare professionals, to alter priorities or to vent anger and frustration.*

(UK Dept of Health 2002, my emphasis)

There are three main points to be made here. First, whilst the actual term 'impoliteness' is not used here, we can, nevertheless, compare the above definitions of what the NHS considers to be 'abusive' and '(verbally) violent behaviour' with the linguistic output strategies which Culpeper (1996) suggests can be deployed for impolite purposes. Second, when we consider the final, italicised sentence in the quotation above, it seems clear that for the NHS at least lay-users', or members' own interest in the phenomenon (of what I here consider to be impoliteness) appears to be concerned with the role that power seems to have in such antagonistic situations. Third, the example above is from but one institution within one western society – the NHS cannot be alone in terms of its members being the targets of verbally violent/abusive exchanges by members of the public.

Given that Eelen (2001), Watts (2003), Locher and Watts (2005) amongst others advocate the need for theoretical conceptualisations of im/politeness (impoliteness$_2$) to follow, and be informed by 'lay' understandings of the phenomenon (impoliteness$_1$), and given what has been mentioned above it follows that researchers should look at the interplay of im/politeness with power. This is especially important given that impoliteness would appear to be ubiquitous not only in many different types of discourse (see Culpeper, Bousfield and Wichmann 2003: 1545–1546; Locher and Bousfield, this volume), but also on different societal levels (see Lakoff 2006). For example, just prior to the 2003 war against Iraq, in the face of France's refusal to support military action in the Gulf region, supporters of the Bush Administration in the U.S. reportedly called the French 'Cheese-Eating Surrender Monkeys'[3] (Critchmar 2005), which is clearly an impolite, racist epithet. When we consider the wide range of discourse types in which impoliteness has been found to play a significant role against the dearth of published research on the phenomenon, then it appears that considering the exercise of power through the communication of impoliteness within multiple, different discourses, across all levels of a society, is a crucial and critically pressing area of research. Indeed, it is crucial not only for academic understandings of the dynamics of interpersonal communication but also for such fields as institutional-discourses, behaviour in organisations, cross-cultural relations and studies relating to conflict resolution.

Given such an obvious and pressing need for models concerned with all forms of dynamics of communication to account for aggressive/abusive linguistic communication, it is a surprise that research into power and impoliteness has not been expanded upon before now – hence this very collection. As a contributory step towards redressing the balance, I will discuss the following in the rest of this chapter: In section 2 the data sets utilised in this study. In section 3 I will define my own understanding of impoliteness and propose a model following a critique of existing work. Whilst I present a data driven definition and model I should note here that I am taking a broadly theoretical, or 'impoliteness$_2$' approach to the phenomena under scrutiny. This said, and as I hope I show here, this impoliteness$_2$ approach both considers and describes phenomena observed as impoliteness$_1$ (see Eelen 2001: 44).

In section 4 I will explicate my understanding of the concept of power and its interrelationship with the phenomena of politeness and impoliteness. In section 5 I will apply the outlined approach to power and the model of impoliteness adopted here to a range of extracts from the data sets studied. Finally, in section 6 I will summarise my argument and draw some conclusions, including making explicit links between this chapter and those in the present collection and also outlining areas for future research into power and impoliteness.

Before we continue ...

Imagine, for a moment, that we are both at a large Linguistics Conference. I am presenting, and you are listening attentively to what you think might be an interesting paper. Imagine, further, that after introducing myself, I make it clear that I want you to stand up. Consider, then, the following utterances that might be deployed for this purpose:[4]

1. Sorry to ask, but could I ask you to stand up for a minute? I'll explain why in full later but it would really help me out if you could stand now.
2. Could I ask you all to stand up?
3. Stand up.
4. Stand up, *now*!
5. You either get off your backside or I come over and break your legs! Which is it to be, Monkeyboy/girl?

With which utterance(s) are you more likely to remove yourself from your seat and actually stand up? Why? How do you feel about it? I refer back to this exercise further in section 4 of this chapter. Until then, I will simply point out that it is my belief that the exercise of power is both ubiquitous and inescapable when dealing with any aspect of politeness and impoliteness. Indeed, there is and can be no interaction – linguistic or otherwise – without power being an issue (see Locher 2004).

2. The data sets

The data utilised were all selected because they appeared to contain some form of impolite, linguistically aggressive behaviour which appeared to be damaging the face of interactants for the purposes of power expression and manipulation.

The data have all been taken from a number of television 'docusoaps', or 'fly-on-the-wall' documentary serials. The examples for this chapter are drawn from two data sets taken from *Soldiers To Be* and *Raw Blues.*

Soldiers To Be is a BBC serial television documentary programme dealing with the military training of recruits to the British Army. It would appear to be a common factor of many military organisations that confrontational and impolite linguistic behaviour is produced during the training process. This appears to be for two main reasons: (1) the extreme inequality of power obtaining between recruits and those who train them; (2) the particular training philosophy which, Culpeper (1996) theorises, aims to depersonalise recruits in order to break them down physically and psychologically. This would appear to be done in order that they may be remoulded as model soldiers. Given the aggressive language use, this BBC programme series has been chosen.

Raw Blues is a BBC serial television documentary programme which concerns the training and everyday policing activities of newly trained police officers in London's Metropolitan Police Force. Again, as one might imagine from the range of activities and events which pervade police officers' work, there is a potential for conflictive, impolite discourse to occur. These make police–public discourses typified by *Raw Blues* rich sources of data for study (see also Limberg, this volume, who draws on televised data from German Police–Public exchanges).

Following Culpeper, Bousfield and Wichmann (2003) there are two caveats worth noting here. The first is that the observer's paradox is clearly a potential issue. A camera crew following the trainees in either data set could cause those filmed to alter their 'natural' behaviour in such situations. Additionally, we should be extremely careful about generalising norms of behaviour on the basis of the limited data set deployed here. It would be folly to suggest that the communication of impoliteness within these examples is *the norm* for these types of discourse just because it seems that way from the limited number of examples available for analysis and discussion (see Culpeper 2005; Bousfield 2007b, section 2.1 for an elaboration and discussion of this latter point). Thus noted, we can explore definitions and understandings of impoliteness, below.

3.   Definition/understanding of *impoliteness*

Definitions of impoliteness vary amongst researchers working on the phenomenon. They vary even amongst those who have worked together in the past. Culpeper, Bousfield and Wichmann (2003: 1545), building on the definition in Culpeper (1996), defined impoliteness as "the use of strategies designed to attack face, and thereby cause social conflict and disharmony". Culpeper (2005) refined this definition into the following:

> Impoliteness comes about when: (1) the speaker communicates face-attack intentionally, or (2) the hearer perceives and/or constructs behavior as intentionally face-attacking, or a combination of (1) and (2).
>
> (Culpeper 2005: 38)

There are a number of issues here which have caused later researchers to disagree as to whether to adopt this re-definition or not (compare the discussions in Cashman [2006] and Rudanko [2006], for example). The main issue with Culpeper's (2005) conceptualisation lies in the fact that, under one reading, there appears to be a contradiction in the understanding of what constitutes impoliteness. In preparing to give the definition above of what impoliteness is, Culpeper (2005) first describes what impoliteness *is not*. For Culpeper (2005: 37) "... [i]mpoliteness is not unintentional".[5] Whilst I wholeheartedly agree, this definition could be construed as contradicting what Culpeper says when he defines what impoliteness *is*. After all, if, given the definition under (2) (in the quotation above) the hearer can construct a speaker's behaviour as constituting impoliteness even where that speaker's intention to attack face *does not exist* (see Culpeper 2005: 39), then this could be construed as contradicting Culpeper's (2005: 37) own earlier remark that "... [i]mpoliteness is not unintentional".

However, I think it fair to say that the construction of a contradictory definition is, clearly, not Culpeper's intention. What is perhaps required here is a clarification and elaboration, both of what was meant and of the issues surrounding speaker intention and hearer interpretation. A fairer reading would suggest that Culpeper (2005) is suggesting that a hearer can *construct* what that hearer *believes* to be the speaker's intention. However, followed to its logical conclusion, despite the obvious competence that most interlocutors have regarding communication, the correct assignation of intention is by no means guaranteed as the speaker *may not have actually intended* what the hearer believes they have accurately perceived. In short, Culpeper is suggesting that impoliteness can exist where the hearer could *construct* a face-damaging intention on the part of the speaker where one does not exist. That is, the hearer believes the speaker to have been impolite but the speaker her/himself may not have had that intention.

While it is laudable that Culpeper is attempting to incorporate the role of the hearer in the construction and communication of impoliteness – something that has been somewhat lacking in approaches previous to that study – ironically he risks doing so at the expense of the role of the speaker and the speaker's intent.

Because of this, Culpeper's (2005) definition of impoliteness is, in my view, not one which could be considered to be always *co*-constructed by participants in interaction (though see Cashman, this volume, for a different view). Given that researchers such as Arundale (2006), Locher and Watts (2005), Mills (2003, 2005), amongst others argue for the necessity of a model of im/politeness which considers and accounts for the constructed nature of the phenomenon, this appears to be something of an issue for Culpeper's otherwise attractive but still developing approach.

Given the necessity of describing a model which accounts for both speaker and hearer (or, more accurately, one which accounts for those in a producer role and those in a receiver role) I take impoliteness as constituting the issuing of intentionally gratuitous and conflictive face-threatening acts (FTAs) that are purposefully performed:

1) Unmitigated, in contexts where mitigation (where mitigation equates with politeness) is required and/or,
2) With deliberate aggression, that is, with the face threat exacerbated, 'boosted', or maximised in some way to heighten the face damage inflicted. (adapted from Bousfield 2007b)

Furthermore, for impoliteness to be considered successful impoliteness, the intention of the speaker (or 'author') to 'offend' (threaten/damage face) must be understood by those in a receiver role. (Bousfield 2007b)

With this definition, quite obviously, impoliteness does not exist where one but not both of the participants (in two party interaction) intends/perceives face-threat. Whilst this might appear to be problematic, it is explained thus:

i) If the Speaker (or someone in a producer role) *intends* face-damage and the Hearer (or someone in a receiver role) *perceives* the Speaker's (Producer's) intention to damage face (cf. Goffman 1967: 14), then *impoliteness is successfully conveyed*. We should note that such impoliteness may later be defended against by the hearer or a third party using a counter-strategy (see Culpeper, Bousfield and Wichmann 2003; Bousfield 2007b).
ii) If the Speaker/Producer *intends* face-damage but the Hearer/Receiver *fails to perceive* the speaker's intent/any face-damage, then *the attempt at impoliteness fails*.[6]
iii) If the Speaker/Producer does *not intend* face-damage but the Hearer/Receiver *constructs* the Speaker's/Producer's utterance as being *intentionally* face-damaging then this could be one of the following: *accidental face-damage* (as opposed to *incidental* or *intentional face-damage*; see Goffman 1967: 14), which could be caused by one or more of: *rudeness* (e.g. inadequate levels of politeness); *insensitivity* (on the part of the

Speaker/Producer); *hypersensitivity* (on the part of the Hearer/Receiver); *a clash of expectations*; *a cultural misunderstanding*; *misidentification* (by the speaker or the hearer*) of the community of practice or activity type in which they are engaged*; some combination of these, or some other hitherto unidentified means of inadvertently causing offence or of perceiving offence when none was intended.

iv) If the Speaker/Producer does *not intend* face-damage but the Hearer/Receiver *constructs* the Speaker's/Producer's utterance as being *unintentionally* face-damaging, then this could be one, or more, of the following: *incidental* or *accidental face-damage* (as opposed to *intentional face-damage*; see Goffman 1967: 14), which could be caused by one or more of: *rudeness* (e.g. inadequate levels of politeness); *insensitivity* (on the part of the Speaker/Producer); *hypersensitivity* (on the part of the Hearer/Receiver); *a clash of expectations*; *a cultural misunderstanding*; *misidentification (by the speaker) of the community of practice or activity type in which they are engaged*; some combination of these, or some other hitherto unidentified means of inadvertently causing offence or of perceiving offence when none was intended.

Within this chapter I am interested in the phenomena under (i) above – where impoliteness is successfully conveyed. I will not, here, tease out the nuances of meaning and behaviour of giving and taking of offence that are inherent in (ii), (iii) and (iv) above. Exploration of these categories remains an area for future research.

The model of analysis I will deploy here for the purposes of exploring the notion of impoliteness and its relationship with power is, broadly, an adapted version of the one developed by Culpeper (1996, 2005) and his co-authors (Culpeper, Bousfield and Wichmann 2003). At this point it needs to be noted that Culpeper and his co-authors have constructed a model of impoliteness that was initially based on the classic Brown and Levinson model of politeness ([1978] 1987). However, the Brown and Levinson model is flawed in a number of ways. Many of these flaws have been extensively discussed (most notably in Werkhofer 1992) and, indeed, it is not my intention to uncover old arguments or re-invent existing solutions here. Rather, I am going to concentrate on those apparent deficiencies which remain in the model of politeness and which mean that, despite the corrective strides already taken, the Culpeper (1996, 2005) and Culpeper, Bousfield and Wichmann (2003) conceptualisations still require some amendment and modification to more accurately account for the phenomenon of power through the communication of impoliteness in interaction.

A model of impoliteness

In its 2005 incarnation, the model proposed and developed by Culpeper suggests a shift in the focus of intentional, impolite face-attack away from a Brown and Levinson style 5–point model of offensive superstrategies (Bald, on Record; Positive Impoliteness; Negative Impoliteness; Sarcasm; Withhold Politeness). This 5–point type of model had been propounded by Lachenicht (1980) and Culpeper (1996) and followed by others since. However, Culpeper (2005: 40) wisely begins to argue for the adoption of a more contextually and culturally sensitive model of face. The one he suggests should be adopted is Spencer-Oatey's (2002) approach.[7] However, as Cashman (2006) has argued, despite his promising move here, Culpeper (2005: 41–42) still refers to the original 5–point model and does not fully integrate Spencer-Oatey's approach into his own. However, with Culpeper *relating* Spencer-Oatey's approach to the existing, classic model this allows Culpeper to produce an evolutionary development of this approach to impoliteness. In doing so his approach remains sympathetic and complementary to the work done previously on this model. However, I would suggest that the evolutionary steps that Culpeper (2005: 41–42) makes have not yet gone far enough to solve the issues facing the model.[8]

The 5-point model identifies a number of separate ways ('superstrategies') in which impoliteness can be generated and conveyed. I should stress here that what follows is a paraphrased explanation of the model in its most recent (2005) incarnation.

(1) <u>Bald on record impoliteness</u>
According to the developments of the model (Culpeper 1996, 2005), *bald, on record impoliteness* is seen as typically being deployed where there *is* much face at stake, and where there *is* an intention on the part of the speaker to attack the face of the hearer and/or where the speaker does not have the power to (safely) utter an impolite utterance. That is, the utterance is deployed in a direct, clear and unambiguous manner (fully in accordance with Grice's ([1975] 1989a) maxims), "... where face is not irrelevant, or minimized" (Culpeper 2005: 41).

(2) <u>Positive impoliteness</u>
(Attacking your want to be approved of, which Culpeper (2005: 40) explicitly links with Spencer-Oatey's (2002) *quality face* and elements of *sociality face).*
Positive Impoliteness, according to the latest instantiation of the model (Culpeper 2005: 41) involves "the use of strategies deployed to damage the recipient's positive face wants". Examples of such strategies from Cul-

peper (1996) include 'ignore, snub the other', 'exclude the other from the activity', 'disassociate from the other', 'be disinterested, unconcerned, unsympathetic', 'use inappropriate identity markers', 'use obscure or secretive language', 'seek disagreement', 'make the other feel uncomfortable (e.g. do not avoid silence, joke, or use small talk)', 'use taboo words', 'call the other names', etc.

(3) Negative impoliteness (Attacking your freedom of action, which Culpeper (2005: 40) explicitly links with Spencer-Oatey's (2002) *equity rights*. Further, he (2005: 41) suggests that this negative face also overlaps with *association rights*, to some extent.)
Negative Impoliteness, according to the latest instantiation of the model (Culpeper 2005: 41) involves "the use of strategies deployed to damage the recipient's negative face wants". Examples of such strategies from Culpeper (1996) include 'frighten', 'condescend, scorn, or ridicule', 'invade the other's space', 'explicitly associate the other with a negative aspect', 'put the other's indebtedness on record', etc.

(4) Off-record impoliteness.
This superstrategy was introduced by Culpeper (2005: 43–44) as a replacement to the 'meta-strategic' nature of sarcasm (which had previously been considered on the same level as the other superstrategies; cf. Culpeper 1996). 'Off-record impoliteness' is one where the offence is conveyed indirectly by way of an implicature and could be cancelled (e.g. denied, or an account, post-modification or other type of elaboration offered, etc.) but where, according to Culpeper (2005: 44), "... one attributable intention clearly outweighs any others".

(5) Withhold politeness (Keep silent or fail to act where politeness work is expected)
Culpeper (1996: 357) notes that impoliteness may be realised through, "... the absence of politeness work where it would be expected." Culpeper (2005: 42) gives the example that "failing to thank someone for a present may be taken as deliberate impoliteness". Culpeper further notes that Brown and Levinson would appear to agree with the face-threatening aspects and implications surrounding the withholding of politeness when they claim:

... politeness has to be communicated, and the absence of communicated politeness may, *ceteris paribus*, be taken as the absence of a polite attitude.
(Brown and Levinson [1978] 1987: 5, as cited in Culpeper 1996: 357)

Now that the model has been re-stated here, it must be noted that there are a number of issues with it that need to be considered. First, *bald, on record impoliteness* cannot and does not exist outside of the theorist's vacuum. The problem here stems from the fact that the model that Culpeper and his co-authors Bousfield and Wichmann have adopted is inherited from Brown and Levinson ([1978] 1987). There is, essentially, a 'form-function' mismatch here. Brown and Levinson's ([1978] 1987) model of politeness, despite their own protests, would appear to be predicated on the belief that certain linguistic structures, defined lexically and grammatically, are inherently polite (or rather inherently 'face-threat mitigating'). However, as many researchers have noted since, politeness (and, indeed, impoliteness) does not exist in any lexically and grammatically defined structure when such structures are taken out of context.[9] By way of elaboration around the point being made here I wish to revisit the example of *bald, on record impoliteness* which was offered by Culpeper, Bousfield and Wichmann (2003):

> The following interaction, which we cite to illustrate 'bald on record impolite-ness', involves S1, a clamper who is preparing to ticket a car in a road next to a primary school, and parents of children who often park in order to drop their children unto the school. Prior to this interaction, a number of parents have been ticketed and one has had her vehicle removed. The conversation between S1, and S2, S3 (both are parents) and S4 (the school's headmistress) has been confrontational up to this point.

> S1: we'll start with you madam <to S4> I work for TFM parking okay
> S2: has made no attempt to respond
> S3:   excuse me excuse me you are a parking
> S4:

> S1: I did the first time I met you   okay where's you car?
> S2:
> S3: attendant alright act like one okay *shut up and act like a parking attendant*
> S4:

> Bald on record impoliteness occurs when S3 says *shut up and act like a parking attendant*. Here we see two imperative commands that are deployed baldly with the purpose of aggravating the face of the parking attendant. It might also be noted that S3 is in a position of relative powerlessness, and so this does not match one of the contexts in which Brown and Levinson (1987:69) attribute to bald on record *politeness.*
>
>   (Culpeper, Bousfield and Wichmann 2003: 1556, original emphasis)

What is of most interest here is that Culpeper, Bousfield and Wichmann (2003), when discussing *negative impoliteness*, refer back to the above example and say:

> Note also that *shut up*, which we commented on under the heading bald on record impoliteness, *is also an aggressive means of impeding speech.*
> (Culpeper, Bousfield and Wichmann 2003: 1559, my emphasis)

We must accept that, if we are 'impeding speech', then that is, in Brown and Levinson's ([1978] 1987) terms, *a negative face threat* as we are imposing on the target's freedom of action. We must therefore understand that *every single bald, on record* utterance attacks or threatens some (or both, if we retain the Brown and Levinson distinction) aspect(s) of face in *functional* terms.[10] As such, even if we were to retain the positive/negative face distinction from Brown and Levinson ([1978] 1987), then *bald, on record im/politeness* does not and cannot exist when we take into account (a) context, and, more importantly here, (b) the fact that there is no communication without face (see Locher 2004; Scollon and Scollon 2001; Terkourafi, this volume, for an elaboration of this point). After all, even in the example above, Culpeper, Bousfield and Wichmann (2003: 1556) note, "[h]ere we see two imperative commands that are deployed baldly *with the purpose of aggravating the face of the parking attendant*" (emphasis in original). As Brown and Levinson ([1978] 1987) insist on two and only two aspects of face, we must accept that (at least) one of them is aggravated/damaged here. Therefore, *bald, on record impoliteness* or *politeness* cannot and does not exist outside of the theorist's vacuum – it is superfluous as it simply describes formal aspects of utterances and does not adequately account for the functional aspects of those utterances. As such, it has no place in a model of impoliteness that attempts to capture real-world interactions.

Given the earlier discussion regarding the fusion of Brown and Levinson's concept of face with Spencer-Oatey's notion of rapport-management, I think it might be safe to say that a pure and unadulterated version of the negative/positive face dichotomy has almost run its course in contemporary academic work. Even the enhanced version suggested by Culpeper (2005) does not fully address the many issues that the positive/negative distinction to face suffers from. Given that (a) face is always an issue in interaction, and (b) the systematic way in which 'positive' and 'negative' face strategies have been found to regularly *combine* in interaction (see Culpeper, Bousfield and Wichmann 2003: 1560–1562; Harris 2001) then it would appear that the positive/negative face distinction is simply superfluous. Indeed, even elaborated models of face, such as that developed by Spencer-Oatey (2002, 2005) and adopted by Culpeper (2005) merely operate to *assist* our current understanding of im/politeness in interaction. They are far from being integral to it. As such, the model of superstrategies that Culpeper

(1996, 2005) and Culpeper, Bousfield and Wichmann (2003) have proposed and modified could be restructured along simpler lines with two overarching 'tactics',[11] thus:

(1) <u>On-record impoliteness</u>
The use of strategies designed to *explicitly* (a) attack the face of an interactant, (b) construct the face of an interactant in a non-harmonious or outright conflictive way, (c) deny the expected face wants, needs, or rights of the interactant, or some combination thereof. The attack is made in an unambiguous way given the context in which it occurs.

(2) <u>Off-record impoliteness</u>
The use of strategies where the threat or damage to an interactant's face is conveyed indirectly by way of an implicature (cf. Grice [1975] 1989a) and can be cancelled (e.g. denied, or an account/post-modification/elaboration offered, etc.) but where "... one attributable intention clearly outweighs any others" (Culpeper 2005: 44), given the context in which it occurs.

Sarcasm, and the *Withholding of Politeness where it is expected* would also come under the heading of off-record impoliteness, as follows:

(a) <u>Sarcasm</u>
Sarcasm constitutes the use of individual or combined strategies which, on the surface, appear to be appropriate but which are meant to be taken as meaning the opposite in terms of face-management. The utterance that appears, on the surface, to positively constitute, maintain, or enhance the face of the intended recipient(s) actually threatens, attacks and/or damages the face of the recipient(s) (see Culpeper 2005) given the context in which it occurs.[12]

(b) <u>Withhold politeness</u>
More specifically, withhold politeness where politeness would appear to be expected or mandatory. Withholding politeness is within the Off-Record category as "... politeness has to be communicated ... the absence of communicated politeness may, *ceteris paribus,* be taken as the absence of a polite attitude" (Brown and Levinson [1978] 1987: 5).

We should note that the individual strategies postulated by Culpeper (1996), Culpeper, Bousfield and Wichmann (2003), Cashman (2006) (amongst others), which can combine in multitudinous ways for the purposes of enhancing or boosting the face damage inflicted, are all deployable with(in) any of the above tactics chosen. Furthermore this model is, I believe, robust, in that it is deployable alongside traditional (e.g. Goffman 1967), culture-specific (e.g. Brown and Levinson [1978] 1987), or more contextually and culturally sensitive (e.g. Spencer-Oatey 2002, 2005) models of face. The point is that this modified model of impoliteness is an adaptable adjunct to existing models of face. It is on the basis of this simplified model that I analyse and comment on the examples in section 5, below. Before this, though, I explore the relationship between power and im/politeness.

4. Power and im/politeness

What I would like to make explicit here is the relationship between the concepts of impoliteness, on the one hand, and power, on the other.[13] Instrumental impoliteness – that is, impoliteness with the primary goal of affecting the target(s) of the impoliteness so that she/he acts in certain setting-specific, (extra)linguistic ways – is *necessarily* concerned with the concept of power. I follow Watts' two-part definition of power being (a) *power to*, and (b) *power over*. Watts (1991) defines having *power to* as follows:

> An individual *A* possesses power if s/he has the freedom of action to achieve the goals s/he has set her/himself, regardless of whether or not this involves the potential to impose *A*'s will on others to carry out actions that are in *A*'s interests. (Watts 1991: 60)

Additionally, Watts defines having *power over* thus:

> *A* exercises power over *B* when *A* affects *B* in a manner contrary to *B*'s perceived interests, regardless of whether [or not] *B* later comes to accept the desirability of *A*'s actions. (Watts 1991: 61)

In addition to Watts' conceptualisation of power, I also follow Limberg in taking Wartenberg's (1990) three-fold distinction of power: (i) force, (ii) coercion and (iii) influence. As Limberg (this volume) explains:

> Whereas 'force' presupposes a physical action to restrict the addressee's action-environment, 'coercive' power requires both the force to affect the addressee as well as a threat with which the speaker's intentions are revealed. If neither verbal threat nor physical force is applied, the exercise of power in a more fine-grained way is considered by Wartenberg as 'influence' (1990: 105). Wartenberg conceives of 'manipulation' as a specific form of influence upon others that involves, on the one hand, a particular manner in which the dominant agent exercises power, and, on the other hand, is achieved by "morally questionable means" (1990: 111; cf. van Dijk 2006). (Limberg, this volume: 161–162)

I suggest that Wartenberg's three-fold view of power, being 'force', 'coercion' and 'influence' can be linked to instrumental impoliteness as follows:

When instrumental impoliteness is successfully conveyed, it is:

(a) in every case, *on some level*, an impingement of what Brown and Levinson ([1978] 1987) would call 'negative face', in so far as an inter-actant's freedom of action is restricted (see also the discussion regarding the restriction of an interlocutor's 'action environment' in Locher 2004);

(b) intended to harm. Often the reasons for that are made clear in cases of instrumental impoliteness within the data sets studied; and,

(c) socially proscribed[14] in broad terms[15] and can thus, in Wartenberg's terms (1990), be considered 'morally questionable' (see quotation above).

However, as Culpeper (2005) has argued, just because impoliteness is *sanc-tioned* in certain discourses does not necessarily mean that such impoliteness is *neutralised* (see also Culpeper, this volume). The reason for this is that the dis-courses in which instrumental impoliteness more regularly occurs still have links to, and draw from the widely-held belief that the use of impoliteness is socially proscribed. It is because of this link that discourses which more regularly deploy impoliteness get their instrumental power. For without the proscribed nature of impoliteness (in terms of face-attack or negative relational work, depending upon the approach taken) impoliteness would not actually *be* impoliteness or, more importantly for the army training data set, instrumental. For further fuller discussions around this issue see Bousfield (2007a/b), Culpeper (2005) and Mills (2003, 2005).

All this relates to Watts' (1991) view of having, or gaining, *power over* and having, or creating through im/politeness usage, *power to*. Taking the latter of these first, we can see that having or creating the *power to* act as one wishes through the use of successful impoliteness, one has or creates the *power to* force, coerce or influence their interactant(s) into acting as the powerful agent wishes. In having this *power to,* one must necessarily have, or through im/politeness gain *power over* one's interactant(s) (note, the reverse is not necessarily true). Essentially, if accepted, the above argument makes Wartenberg's (1990) three fold view of power (force, coercion and [manipulative] influence) into sub-varieties of Watts' (1991) *power to* which is in turn a sub-variety of Watts' (1991) *power over*, at least in contexts where instrumental im/politeness is concerned.

Indeed, the exercise or contestation of power can be enacted through polite-ness as much as it can through impoliteness. Think back, now, to the exercise I asked you to do in section 1 above. What would you have done? When the above test was conducted during a panel paper on politeness and impoliteness most people in the auditorium happily got to their feet (some with a smile) when I asked them to stand up using (1) *Sorry to ask, but could I ask you all to stand up for a minute? I'll explain why in full later but it would really help me out if you could stand now.* When asked, none (at least admitted to having) felt they had just had their faces threatened or damaged by the request, or of feeling that negative relational work had taken place, despite the fact I had restricted their action environment which can be explained by the request's impingement upon their individual notions of negative face (Brown and Levinson [1978] 1987) or upon their equity rights (see Spencer-Oatey 2002, as cited in Culpeper 2005: 40). With this utterance I had *influenced* (and, with those I knew reasonably well, I had arguably *coerced*) action through politeness. However, when asked, most interactants admitted that the final option (5), being, *You either get off your backside or I come over and break your legs! Which is it to be, Monkeyboy/girl?* would, if used and meant sincerely, almost certainly have offended those in the auditorium, primarily because there would have been no attempt to mitigate the face threat or to positivise the essentially negative relational aspects of asking one to stand up in the middle of an academic paper presentation. Indeed, rather the opposite is the case as the face-damaging/negatively-oriented relational aspects of the 'request' have been *boosted* precisely for the purposes of offending the addressees – this would have been an attempt to *force* or otherwise *coerce* (precisely which would be dependent upon the particular individuals concerned) action through impoliteness. Indeed, had (5) been said in an army training setting, I contest it would still have been face-damaging and hurtful to the addressees (if they were recruits, and if the utterer was a training sergeant or corporal) despite the interactants' increased level of expectation regarding such linguistic behaviour (when compared to a lecture hall during a conference presentation). This is because face-damage and hurt is *precisely* what such linguistic behaviour is designed to do in such settings. Indeed, I will even go so far as to suggest that such instrumentally impolite comments are more successful (in terms of the perlocutionary effects matching the utterer's interactional goals) in army training settings than in academic paper presentation settings *because* they are more expected in army training.

Essentially then, linguistic politeness (of the type shown in (1)) is (an attempt) to exercise power over one's interlocutors whilst simultaneously ensuring that one's interlocutors *are not* (overly) offended in the process. Conversely, linguistic *im*politeness is (an attempt) to exercise power over one's interlocutors whilst simultaneously ensuring that one's interlocutors *are* (overly) offended in the process. Indeed as I have been arguing, and as I now hope to show in the analysis section immediately following, the 'causing of offence' (to paraphrase Culpeper 2005) through impoliteness is crucial to the actioning of one's power in these cases. That is, the communication of offence through one's impolite utterance(s) (if successful and left uncountered (see Culpeper, Bousfield and

Wichmann 2003; Bousfield 2007b)) is, context permitting, a device *par excellence* for the (re-)activation of one's power over one's interlocutors within an interactional exchange.

5.   Analysis: Impoliteness and power

5.1.   *Impoliteness and the re-assertion of power*

The following extract, taken from *Soldiers To Be*, is one in which we can clearly see the deployment of *on-record impoliteness* for the purposes of re-asserting the power hierarchy in the British Army setting. In this example, Platoon Sergeant 'Tich' Lovall (S1) is about to send the recruits, who have finished the first three weeks of their training, on to C.M.S.R.[16] – the final eleven, and much more difficult weeks of their basic training. The recruits are late for parade. Furthermore, Sgt. Lovall (S1) feels the need to give recruit Downes (S2) a word of advice before sending him on. S3 here represents an unidentified member of the recruits. The time is a little after 7 a.m. I am particularly interested, here, in the interaction between the platoon sergeant S1 and recruit S2 beginning at the end of stave 4 and continuing until the end of the extract:[17]

[1] *Soldiers To Be*

1. S1: what time were you told to be outside on parade in the drill shed . who can
   S2:
   S3:

2. S1: remember what time you were told   you were told
   S2:
   S3:   seven o'clock sergeant

3. S1: to be outside here at seven o'clock you are now late.. you are already late for
   S2:

4. S1: day one C M S R .. DO YOU UNDERSTAND   Downes
   S2:
   ALL: YES SERGEANT

5. S1: ... come here .... stand there . look at me . listen . top tip of the day
   S2:

6. S1: when you get down to C M S R shut your fucking mouth   do you
   S2:   <indistinct>

7. S1: understand . it's simple . you carry on the way you are going down there and
   S2:

8. S1: you will be broken   is that clear   you take a fucking step
   S2:   <sergeant>   sergeant

9. S1: back and you shut your grid . because not only will you come unstuck you
   S2:   sergeant

10. S1: will be a disruptive influence on the remainder of the platoon because you
    S2:

11. S1: cannot keep it shut stop telling other recruits what to do and concentrate on
    S2:

12. S1: getting it right yourself which is something you have a problem with do I
    S2:

13. S1: make myself perfectly clear   shut your fucking mouth do as
    S2:   yes sergeant

14. S1: you're told and worry about yourself for the first two weeks if not ..
    S2:

15. S1: your life will become extremely uncomfortable is that clear
    S2:   yes sergeant

What is interesting here in terms of impoliteness is *not* the first four staves. As Mills (2005: 270) argues the type of shouting in staves 1–4 is hardly likely to be considered impoliteness by either the issuer (the sergeant) or the recipients (recruits). The impoliteness comes after the recruits, as a collective (identified as ALL in the extract above), have answered the platoon sergeant.

It is at this point (stave 4) that S1 now singles out recruit Downes (S2) in order to give him some advice before Downes moves on to the next stage of his training. This advice is given impolitely but this impoliteness is primarily instrumental. After all, the sergeants and corporals who train the recruits have the overall goal that they need to be effective in their training. The British Army philosophy (like the philosophies of many military forces the world over) is predicated on the belief that the hierarchy of power is necessarily rigid, concrete and inflexible – for the good of all within the service and for its effectiveness as an organisation. As such, the recruits' understanding of who is on top of the power structure, and who on the bottom, needs to be very clear and totally unambiguous. From what we can see of the impolite utterances S1 directs at S2 in the above extract, it is apparent that S2 (in S1's eyes) has not learnt this simple fact of British Army life to S1's satisfaction. Hence, S1 uses instrumental impoliteness as a way of outlining S2's apparent failings and re-emphasising S1's relative power. Note the following in Staves 5–6: *Top tip of the day. When you get down to C M S R shut your fucking mouth.* Here we can see the deployment of two on-record strategies designed to limit his future action environment. The first is the rendition of a direct command: *shut your mouth,* the illocutionary force of which is boosted (cf. Holmes 1984) through combination with the second on-record strategy. This second strategy is the use of taboo language (cf. Culpeper 1996): *fucking.* Consider, also, the context in which this impolite directive takes place. It occurs after the *not* impolite directives to Downes to leave the squad and walk to a point of relative secrecy (away from earshot of the other squad members but still within sight of them all) and being told to *stand there* (with gestural deixis of a pointed finger), and to *look at me.* Note also the facetious utterance *Top tip of the day.* Where 'tip' has a positive semantic prosody: it is understood as something akin to 'friendly, light-hearted, and helpful advice'. 'Top tip', therefore is apparently out of place in a somewhat serious situation where the unambiguous (and repeated) threat exists of extremely negative sanctions on Downes should he fail to keep quiet and do as he is told by the superior-in-power NCO trainers.

The overall threat is *repeated* through the use of elegant variation with different lexico-syntactic structures. This can be seen in Staves 7–8 (*It's simple. You carry on the way you are going and you will be broken*), and in Staves 13–15 (*Shut your fucking mouth, do as you're told and worry about yourself for the first two weeks. If not, your life will become extremely uncomfortable. Is that clear?*).[18] Staves 13–15 also act as a summary to the overall Activity Type (cf. Levinson 1992) of a 'verbal warning' following instances of clear criticism (based on S1's evaluation of S2's past actions and (in)abilities). Note the use of questions such as *Is that clear?* (stave 8), which is *repeated* in stave 15. Note also the propositional repetition of this aggressive question in staves 12–13, with *Do I make myself perfectly clear?* As I have argued elsewhere (see Bousfield 2007a), such questions (and repetition of questions), in an appropriate context, aid in the success of impoliteness as they *force a response* from the target of the question. Such forced responses are primarily limited to answers which self-damage – or confirm other's damage to – the face of the responder. Indeed, such face-aggressive questions doubly restrict the target's action environment here. This is because (i) the target here, S2, has to respond (given the overall Community of Practice and the specific Type of Activity within which he is involved) and cannot safely 'opt out' without the risk of greater face damage for doing so, and (ii) because of the power relations (which have been somewhat bluntly reinforced) obtaining between sergeants in general (and S1 in particular) and recruits in general (and S2 in particular). To clarify, S2's 'allowable' type of response option (see Bousfield 2007b) is limited to verbally agreeing with the propositional content of S1's turns – however face damaging or limiting to S2's present or future action environments that such agreement may be. So, as we can see, impoliteness in such settings can not only be used to re-emphasise the relative power of the utterer (when it is the powerful uttering impoliteness) over the recipient, but also to limit the available responses (and thus limit the freedom) of the recipient. Such is the role of impoliteness in concrete power hierarchies with limited occupational restraints on language usage.[19]

5.2.   Impoliteness and the challenge to power

Example [2] is one where combined On-Record and Off-Record Impoliteness is used to challenge and limit the power of an institutionally more powerful addressee. Taken from the Police Training data set in *Raw Blues* the context is one in which newly qualified Police Constable Mike Walsh (S1) has arrested a member of the public (S2) on suspicion of causing criminal damage. Mike Walsh and a fellow officer (S3) are leading a handcuffed S2 down the steps and out of the residential block of flats where they made the arrest. As they descend, S2 begins to complain to S1 about the tightness of the restraining handcuffs:

[2] *Raw Blues*

1. S1:
   S2: do you understand do you understand I know I'm black and you're white

2. S1:   allright   allright
   S2: yeah but can you let that hur these are hurting me yeah <indistinct> fucking

3. S1: I'm going to put you in the back of the van alright [puts S2 in the police van]
   S2: hurting . these are fucking hurting me   no hold on hold on hold

4. S1:   we're not going to beat you up just sit just
   S2: on <you're going to beat me up>

5. S1: sit down there and calm down alright mate
   S2:   I'm calm [doors are closed: S2

6. S1:
   S2: kicks the door and sides of the van: muffled shouting] YOU DON'T GIVE

7. S1:
   S2: A FUCK DO YOU I KNOW I'M A BLACK PERSON YEAH . I KNOW

8. S1:
   S2: I'M A FUCKING NIGGER..YOU'RE FUCKING. FUCKING. I KNOW

9. S1:

S2: I'M TREATED LIKE FUCKING BAGGAGE YEAH .. I KNOW I'M A

10. S1:

S2: FUCKING NIGGER [Scene fades]

Here the overall (or 'global') tactic of S2 is to use a combination of both *on-record* and *off-record impoliteness* as an aggressive power renegotiation device. He goes off-record by implicitly accusing S1 in particular (and, by association, The Metropolitan Police in general) of racism. This is coupled with accusations of a lack of consideration (on the part of S1) for S2's well-being.

Implicit (off-record) accusations of racism are evidenced through his repeated references to race which become more stark and offensive through the use of boosting devices (see Holmes 1984) these being shouting (Culpeper 1996) and taboo language use (Culpeper 1996) beginning from staves 1 to 2 (*I know I'm black and you're white yeah but …*), continuing through to stave 7 (*I know I'm a black person*), and coming to full fruition in staves 7–8 ((shouted) *I know I'm a fucking nigger,* which is *repeated* in staves 9–10 for effect). The impoliteness discussed here concerning racism, whilst powerful and shocking, is nevertheless off-record as it seems apparent (to this researcher at least) that the impolite attitude/beliefs (Leech 1983) being expressed are not obviously the ones that S2 actually holds about himself and those who share his racial identity. In fact, the implicature generated is one in which S2 appears to be claiming that S1 (as a Caucasian police officer) holds about S2 (as a person of Afro-Caribbean origin). The implicature is achieved by flouting the Gricean ([1975] 1989a) maxims of *manner* (the way in which he expresses himself through the use of shouting and extreme taboo language (Culpeper 1996) within a conflictive exchange), *relation* (his racial/cultural heritage and the way in which police officers deal with him appear to have nothing in common), *quality* (he is not, as he implies in staves 1–2, deserving of rough treatment) and *quantity* (in terms of the volume (through shouting) and repetition of his impolite beliefs).

Further impoliteness is evident through the use of the direct (on-record) repeated accusations of a lack of consideration in staves 6–7 (*You don't give a fuck, do you?*) and in staves 8–9, combined with taboo language usage (Culpeper 1996) (*I know I'm treated like fucking baggage, yeah*) and in the off-record hostility enacted by the on-record expression of fear in stave 4 (*You're going to beat me up*). These all express the impolitely communicated belief (Leech 1983) that the police officer is going to unlawfully harm S2. We should, perhaps, further note that the comment in staves 8–9, being, *I know I'm treated like fucking baggage, yeah*, takes on greater face-damaging weight given the linguistic juxta-positioning within the off-record (implied) accusations of racism.

Overall, it appears that S2 is indirectly constructing a *hypothetical* ideological point of view of S1 which is extremely negative. S2, in short, is *apparently* 'self-damaging' his own face, through the use of some rather extreme on- and off-record impoliteness, as means of attacking S1. In doing so S2 is, therefore, limiting some of the powers of S1 to such an extent that S1 may feel forced to treat S2 differently when compared to how he treats other suspected criminals. Indeed, PC Mike Walsh (S1) admitted to camera, as the scene faded, that he was scared that a 'racially aggravated complaint' would be made against him by S2. Thus, the *fear* of a total curtailment of S1's future action-environment (in that, if found guilty of racism by a police enquiry, PC Walsh could be dismissed from the Police service) has been generated by S2's off-record impoliteness.

5.3. Sarcasm and power

In extract [3], taken from *Soldiers To Be*, Sergeant 'Tich' Lovall (S1) has all the recruits within his charge lined up along the corridor wall outside of their barrack rooms. They are expecting the Company Sergeant Major to arrive shortly for barrack room inspection. S1 has had all the recruits under his charge practicing shouting out both their names and the unit to which they hope to become full members (as these will be the answers to a stock question asked of each of them by the Company Sergeant Major). They have just finished doing this as S1 addresses them as a group. S1 further addresses S2, recruit Downes, individually:

[3] *Soldiers To Be*

1. S1: you've now all had one good shout at it so you should be confident when the
   S2:

2. S1: sar'nt major comes to you we have absolute confidence in all of you . Downes
   S2:

3. S1:   I have confidence in you Downes   thanks for
   S2: sergeant   excellent sergeant .

4. S1: agreeing with me anytime you want to be platoon sergeant you give me a
   S2:

5. S1: shout
   S2:

What is interesting here is the sarcasm of S1 in staves 3–5 which appears to be used for power re-activation purposes. This serves to remind not only S2 as the ostensible addressee (Thomas 1986) but all those in the squad (as sanctioned overhearers (Thomas 1986)) of the relative power of the sergeant over the recruits. The sarcasm is two-fold. First, note S1's utterance in staves 3–4, *thanks for agreeing with me*. This is insincere politeness and is, therefore, off-record impoliteness. It is identified, here, as insincere politeness for two reasons.

First, such politeness is totally unexpected and unnecessary (and is hence, foregrounded and, thus, highly interpretable) in this setting. As such it can only be interpreted as operating sarcastically, that is, as its apparent opposite. This is because such types of politeness, expressed from sergeants to recruits in instructional activity types, is a break from the expected norms in that setting.

Second, the utterance *thanks for agreeing with me* (staves 3–4) is identified as insincere politeness given the immediately following (juxta-positioning of) the facetious and sarcastic *anytime you want to be a platoon sergeant you give me a shout* (staves 4–5). We can see that this utterance appears to be an off-record (sarcastic) impolite criticism (cf. Culpeper, Bousfield and Wichmann 2003) of the apparent assumption of power and status by S2 when S2 said *excellent sergeant* in stave 3. The *excellent sergeant* utterance was in response to S1's apparently 'banter-like' (cf. Leech 1983) singling out of Downes with *I have confidence in you Downes* earlier in stave 3 after S1 had already said he had confidence in all of the recruits (which would presumably include Downes as a recruit).

Overall, it appears that S2 might have misinterpreted the type of activity he was in given S1's apparent 'banter-like' behaviour. Thus, S2 might have thought his *excellent sergeant* utterance was appropriate within that Activity Type. The sergeant S1, quite obviously from his response to the *excellent sergeant* utterance, did not share S2's understanding of the Activity Type they were in, and used sarcastic impoliteness as a power-reactivating device to reprimand S2's assumptive behaviour and to clarify just precisely what was what.[20]

6.   Summary and conclusion

In this chapter I have added my voice to the call for models of impoliteness to be developed further (see Locher and Bousfield and many others in this volume). I have shown how institutional organisations are beginning to realise the significance that aggressive linguistic behaviour can have on the ability of individuals to work and provide essential services. The NHS cannot be alone in this. Indeed, Culpeper, Bousfield and Wichmann (2003: 1545–1546) list a number of diverse discourses in which impoliteness, in their words, plays a central role. Also, chapters in this very collection either corroborate the range of discourses in which impoliteness is to be found, or further identify discourses in which it plays a part. This collection shows that linguistically aggressive phenomena such as impoliteness are to be found in historical courtroom discourse (Archer), in code-switching discourses (Cashman), in online, computer mediated interaction (Graham), in political discourses (García-Pastor; Locher and Watts), police–public interactions (Limberg) and in the workplace (Mullany; Schnurr, Marra and Holmes). Despite the concerns of researchers such as Lakoff (2006) or Truss (2005) we must accept that impoliteness is genuinely ubiquitous in that it is likely to exist across all discourses within human interaction as suggested by the wide – and widening – range of discourses (both synchronic and diachronic) in which it is to be found. Impoliteness must have been with us (almost) as long as humans have been communicating. It is also here to stay. To that end, it behoves us to have models of interaction which can capture and account for such behaviour. Here, I have suggested one such model. This is a re-structured version of the one that was proposed by Culpeper (1996) and developed in other works (Culpeper, Bousfield and Wichmann 2003; Culpeper 2005; Cashman 2006; Bousfield 2007b). The model was problematic in some crucial ways, most notably in its previous dependence on Brown and Levinson's ([1978] 1987) notion of face, and its retention of the idea of *bald, on record impoliteness*. Here, I have offered a much simplified approach to the Culpeper-led framework by conflating the original five superstrategies (and the "meta-strategy" of *sarcasm* [Culpeper 2005: 42]) for performing impoliteness into two 'tactics' with which the existing linguistic strategies for performing impoliteness (e.g. 'Use taboo language'; 'Condescend, scorn, ridicule') can be deployed. These two tactics are, quite simply, *on-record impoliteness* and *off-record impoliteness*. It is important to point out here that I make no claim that *off-record impoliteness* is always somehow less damaging than the more direct, *on-record impoliteness*. As argued in Culpeper, Bousfield and Wichmann (2003; see also Culpeper 2005: 44) who refer to Leech (1983: 171), there is reason to believe that the more indirect (i.e. off-record) forms of impoliteness can be more offensive than the direct (on-record). Offensive weightings of *on-* or *off-record* varieties of impoliteness are entirely dependent upon the context in which they occur. Further benefits for a model such as the one proposed here is that it presupposes no dependence on one model of face. Indeed the proposed model should work with all the main, existing approaches to human linguistic interaction concerned with im/politeness which consider the centrality of face (Brown and Levinson [1978] 1987; Goffman 1967; Locher 2004; Locher and Watts 2005; Spencer-Oatey 2000b, 2002, 2005; Watts 2003). In this way, should any given model of face be systematically critiqued, falsified and subsequently revised or replaced, the model of impoliteness suggested here should be able to adapt to accommodate.

Further, I have linked the concept of (instrumental) impoliteness with the exercise of or challenge to power. It should be noted at this point that when we wield power we are not necessarily being impolite. However, as would appear to be apparent from the discussion and analysis of the examples above, when we are (sincerely) impolite, we are either (a) creating/activating/re-activating some aspect of our own *relative power,* or (b) we are *challenging someone over their (assumption of) power* (or [c] a combination of both). Furthermore, whilst I have identified the use and abuse of impoliteness for expressing or challenging power in settings with rather strict and concrete hierarchies, what this chapter has left undiscussed are such settings as those which do not have such strict power hierarchies. Impoliteness can and does occur in negotiably hierachical settings as well as strictly hierarchical ones. Therefore, this is also an area for future research to consider in some considerable depth. Indeed, once explored, a comparison can be made across both strict and negotiable power hierarchies.

Given the very obvious relationship between power and impoliteness more research into this area, as well as into those areas identified and outlined by the other contributors to this volume, would seem to be both vital and pressing.

Notes

1. Thanks to Miriam Locher, Holly Cashman, Dawn Archer, Lesley Jeffries and Dan McIntyre for their patience and invaluable comments on earlier ideas and draft sections of this chapter. Any errors or weaknesses which remain are, of course, entirely my own.
2. These figures can be interpreted in one of two ways. (1) Attacks on NHS employees did, indeed, rise from 1999–2000 to 2000–2001. (2) Attacks have not appreciably risen; rather more incidents of verbal or physical abuse have been officially reported during this period than the previous year. In either case, research into the phenomenon of impoliteness is clearly needed.
3. This phrase is originally attributed to *The Simpsons'* character Groundskeeper Willy during the 'Round Springfield' episode (first aired, April 30th 1995) who, when substituting for a French class following budget cuts, greets the students with 'Bonjour ya cheese-eating surrender monkeys!'. This phrase was made, according to Younge and Henley (2003), 'acceptable' (sic!) in official diplomatic channels around the globe by Jonah Goldberg's (National Review) description of French nationals as being, "Primates capitulards et toujours en quête de fromages" – a slur based on cultural stereotype and historical accident.
4. I uttered this as part of a paper presentation on 'The Power of Impoliteness' at Sociolinguistics Symposium 16 at Limerick in Ireland. July 6–8th 2006.

5. Culpeper (2005: 37) casts "failed politeness" – being the misjudging of required politeness work – as an unwitting, unintended (i.e. accidental [cf. Goffman 1967: 14]) threat to face. This, in my view is not "impoliteness". This is, in fact, a type of "rudeness" (see also Culpeper, this volume; however, see Terkourafi, this volume, for an alternative view).

6. Though it should be noted that two of the possible defensive counter strategies identified by Culpeper, Bousfield and Wichmann (2003: 1566–1567) and discussed by Bousfield (2007b), of 'dismiss, make light of face damage, joke' and 'ignore the face attack' mean that it is virtually impossible for the analyst to identify whether (i) the impoliteness was successfully conveyed, but defended against; or (ii) the attempt at impoliteness failed. Such is the nature of impoliteness in interaction. Further, within this category is the possibility of the speaker intending face-damage, the hearer understanding that face-damage was intended but the face-damaging effects on the hearer are negligible. For example, my nephew calling me a 'pooh-pooh head!' or daughter saying 'naughty daddy!' when, in the name of safety, I stop them from engaging in life-and-limb risking acts of fun and horseplay that they really want to try. I am not at all offended by such comments in these situations but I understand they are intended to (a) harm and, (b) exert power over me. These thankfully rare occurrences in my family discourse are instances of what I would term "failed impoliteness". Quite obviously this is where researchers working with an impoliteness₁ approach would differ from those who, like me, are working with an impoliteness₂ approach. I see a theoretical distinction based on intent and successful perception of that intent.

7. Spencer-Oatey's approach (2002: 540–542) identifies two distinct but associated phenomena: *face* and *sociality rights*. *Face*, she considers as being made up of *quality face* – the desire to be viewed positively, and *social identity face* – the desire to be respected and accepted in our social roles. *Sociality rights* she considers as being made up of *equity rights* – the desire to be treated fairly and not unduly imposed upon by others, and *association* rights – a belief that we are entitled to associate with and have positive relationships with others.

8. As indeed, I am sure Culpeper would agree.

9. Though as Culpeper (2005: 41) argues, quite rightly in my view, many phrases such as "Hello, how are you?" and "You fucking cunt!" are conventionally considered, across many different discourses, as being polite and impolite respectively. We should also note that Terkourafi (this volume) points out that some linguistic expressions – conventionalised ones for example – do 'facework' more frequently (and therefore, more economically) than others. It therefore stands to reason that whilst no utterance is inherently polite or impolite, some, if not all utterances, are not value-neutral with regard to face-orientation either.

10. This is not to say that Brown and Levinson [1978] 1987) would consider the *Bald, on record* strategy to be devoid of face issues. Rather, the point I am making here is that *Bald, on record* is a *form* based superstrategy, whereas 'Positive Im/Politeness' and 'Negative Im/Politeness', being oriented towards Positive and Negative face respectively, are essentially *function* based superstrategies. When we also consider that the

Off-Record superstrategy can include off-record utterances which are orientated to positive and/or negative face, then we can see that Brown and Levinson have inter-mixed and linked *form* and *function* in their 5–point model. Indeed, this is perhaps unsurprising when we consider that *Bald, on record-in-form* utterances also have a *function* (as do, arguably, all communicative utterances). Indeed, because *Bald, on record-in-form* utterances have in Brown and Levinson's terms a positive/negative face-oriented *function,* it seems odd that such utterances would not be captured under the positive or negative im/politeness superstrategies. It therefore makes sense to simply do away with the *Bald, on record* superstrategy, as part of wider reforms to the model, as it does not operate in the same way or on the same level as the positive, negative and off-record superstrategies do when we separate *form* from *function.*

11. I choose the term 'tactic' to clearly differentiate what I propose here from the concept of '(super)strategy'. However, I do recognise that both are unhappy terms. In military discourse, 'strategies' are grand plans which, necessarily, require the successful completion of 'tactics' within them to succeed. In short, the terms 'strategy' as adopted by Brown and Levinson are misnamed – they should have been 'tactics' and the 'tactics' I name here, should be identified as 'strategies' – but historical nomenclatures have a way of sticking.

12. Note: I take Sarcasm (cf. Culpeper 1996, 2005) to be the opposite in *functional* terms to Banter (cf. Leech 1983) despite the apparently identical nature of the forms that each 'tactic' takes. Therefore, Banter, being the functional opposite to Sarcasm, is Sarcasm's polite 'mirror-tactic' (for want of a better phrase). As ever, every tactic and strategy in interaction is context-dependent for its effectiveness and understandability.

13. Note here that there is no claim being made that where someone is exercising power, one is necessarily being impolite. Rather where one is using or defending against instrumental impoliteness, one is projecting/contesting power.

14. Socially proscribed impoliteness refers to both impoliteness which is primarily instrumental and impoliteness which is primarily a vent to anger and frustration.

15. Though, of course, there are discourses in which impoliteness is *sanctioned* (though not necessarily *neutralised*), for example Army Training discourses. Being *sanctioned impoliteness* would mean that its use is not socially proscribed. See Culpeper (2005) and Mills (2005) for interesting discussions on this score.

16. C.M.S.R. training means 'Common Military Syllabus Recruit training' – Part of 'Phase 1' or 'Basic' military training which includes training in the basic military skills required of all soldiers and incorporates weapon handling and shooting, drill, physical fitness, field tactics, map reading, survival in nuclear, chemical and biological warfare and general military knowledge. It is an intensive course and requires the recruit to show considerable determination and courage to succeed.

17. Throughout the study I have used the stave transcription method for representing interaction. Within this approach (S1), (S2), for example, represent particular speakers; a full stop (.) represents an audible pause of more than one second; CAPITALS signal

increased volume, e.g. SHOUTING; non-verbal actions, contextual information and transcription difficulties are placed in brackets <thus>.

18. We should perhaps note here that the impoliteness is deemed to be instrumental as S1 is clearly trying to help S2 by forcing S2 to address 'failings' in his behaviour which could, ultimately, result in his ejection from the army. It is a way of 'being cruel to be kind'.

19. What I mean by this is that some British Universities purport to have a rigid hierarchical system in terms of staff and their structural-administrative roles. However, impoliteness from a head of subject to a more junior member of staff could be met with an official complaint and even legal proceedings against the head of subject (given the broadly, societal-wide belief that impoliteness is 'morally questionable' (see Limberg, this volume, on Wartenberg 1990) under present UK and EU laws. This may well be less likely to happen in a British Army setting where such language use appears to be tolerated. This is an area for future research.

20. 'What was what' here relates to the activity type that both speakers were in, and, therefore, the relative power relations obtaining between them both, given their rigid, hierarchical roles within the British Army Training setting.

Chapter 7
Threats in conflict talk: Impoliteness and manipulation

Holger Limberg

1. Introduction

In social interaction interlocutors can become involved in conflicts in which they exploit their linguistic repertoire in order to intentionally cause offence to others. This chapter addresses one specific type of offensive behaviour in conflict sequences between the police and citizens. It focuses particularly on the use of *verbal threats*, which are used to manipulate the target's conduct. In this context I wish to discuss: i) whether or not a particular threat utterance can be labelled as impolite; and ii) providing that it can, how perceptions of *impoliteness* are interactively created over a series of turns.

Research into linguistic politeness phenomena has been extensive compared to its impolite, conflictual, offensive counterpart. Under the influence of the most seminal theory on politeness, proposed by Brown and Levinson ([1978] 1987), impoliteness has traditionally been passed over as a secondary product of social interaction, often pictured as a simple deviation from certain politeness principles (cf. 'traditional' views in Lakoff 1973; Leech 1983; Brown and Levinson [1978] 1987, versus 'post-modern' views in Mills 2003; Watts 2003). In the wake of criticism launched against Brown and Levinson's theory, some researchers have started to shift the focus towards the disruptive side of social interaction, and explore impoliteness from a new perspective. Culpeper (2005: 38), for example, proposes that "[i]mpoliteness comes about when: (1) the speaker communicates face-attack intentionally, or (2) the hearer perceives and/or constructs behavior as intentionally face-attacking, or a combination of (1) and (2)". Although there is much work still to be done in this area of sociolinguistic research, the apparent 'dark' side of social interaction (Austin 1990) has become increasingly accepted as a common part of human linguistic behaviour.

Instances of intentional face attacks in verbal interaction are often transparent for the interlocutor as well as the analyst (Kasper 1990; Watts 2003). However, these instances of impolite behaviour tend to be used infrequently in informal social interaction and therefore remain unpredictable. For this reason, several researchers have turned to language use in institutional or 'quasi-institutional' settings (Heritage and Greatbach 1991) in search of impoliteness. In particular, settings such as army training, political discussions, or courtroom trials have served as sites for overt examples of impoliteness (cf. Culpeper 1996; Harris 2001; Lakoff 1989). This is, inter alia, understandable, considering the (high) frequency of occurrence of impolite linguistic behaviour in these contexts, but also because of the degree of deviation from 'normally' expected behaviour. In institutional contexts the power distribution between speakers is often disproportionate, which can encourage displays of inappropriate, salient behaviour. It may also be the case that interactants perceive an utterance as impolite in institutional settings simply because they are relying on the norms of other communities of practice.

My research is situated in line with previous approaches which analyse impoliteness in language use in a specific context that is both power-laden as well as conflict-sensitive. Documentaries of police work serve as interactional scenarios which exhibit incidents with high conflict potential. At the same time, police interactions also present a context in which an institutional framework authorises as well as constrains certain actions (cf. Thornborrow 2002). The police may insist on their right to exercise institutionalized power to make the offending party comply with their demands in situations where an offence has been perpetrated (cf. example 3a in section 5.3). Conversely, the offender can resist police control and try to use strategies in order to reverse the existing power imbalance. The combination of offensive communication and institutional framework leads to an interesting question: How do participants in these encounters bend the interactionally-negotiated and institutionally-purported norms when pursuing a particular goal (e.g. when taking offenders[1] into custody)? I wish to show this by investigating the use of verbal threats in three instances of confrontational clashes between citizens and the police. This strategy is often exploited by the more powerful interactant in a specific situation to manipulate the addressee's behaviour. Even though manipulation can also be achieved by other (often less face-threatening) means, police scenarios frequently indicate that only specific forceful (linguistic) strategies are successful when dealing with persistent resistance (cf. Hunter and Boster 1987; Kellermann and Shea 1996).

In Section 2 a sketch of my research design is presented, highlighting the advantages and weaknesses of using documentary data as empirical material to study impoliteness. Section 3 reflects on the co-occurrence of institutional authority, interactional asymmetry, and power in police work. In doing so, I discuss the concept of power as it relates to the emergence, progression and termination of a conflict in police officers' encounters with (alleged) offenders. Following this, I outline my conception of verbal threats, with particular reference to the conditional form of threats. I relate the notion of impoliteness to the use of threats in police work and discuss the problems involved in applying this concept in the present context. Finally, three exemplary scenarios from my data are presented to exhibit the use of threats in police–citizen interaction. Here I outline their manipulative potentials and reveal the dynamic interplay of several factors that can contribute towards perceptions of impoliteness in the course of these interactions.

2. Research design

The data used in this study originate from a German documentary series broadcast on private television in 2005. The show is called *Ärger im Revier* ('Trouble in the Precinct'), and it is a documentary series about the work of police officers on patrol. In several small and large-scale German cities, the custodians of the law are accompanied by a camera crew, who capture the police's response to emergency calls. The scenes are thus composed of a variety of incidents that police officers encounter when carrying out their daily business on the streets. Prototypical examples contain cases of disturbances of the peace, traffic violations, dealing with drunkards, conflicts among citizens, or occasionally a fight. On the whole, the cases tend to be restricted to minor delinquencies and infractions of the law. Compared with other crimes such as aggravated assault, murder and other capital offences, the series only covers unlawful acts which are suitable for a public audience, and for which official authorisation for television broadcasting has been given.

Despite the diversity of cases portrayed in this programme, the majority of the scenarios show a conflict or confrontation either between the police officers and citizens, or among citizens themselves. In the latter case, officers intervene in order to sustain or re-establish a social equilibrium. The use of verbal threats is not necessarily a part of the confrontation in these scenes; in fact, threat utterances in police work (at least according to my data) do not seem to occur as systematically as in other institutional contexts (cf. Harris 1984a). As far as the distribution of threats is concerned, they are predominantly issued by the police against the offender, but occasionally the tables are turned, and the offender issues a threat against the officer in a heated argument.

Any form of documentary is the result of an editing process which makes the recordings appealing for the audience. The police cases in my data are never exhibited in their entirety because the confrontations between the disputants are cut into several scenes. This is certainly a major drawback of these television formats from the point of view of linguistic analysis because we can never know which details might have been edited out. However, the tapes do not conceal direct confrontation or the use of verbal offences, which makes it a useful pool for studies into impoliteness phenomena.

Documentary data and the study of impoliteness

Examining this type of data requires a certain awareness of what it is about these shows that make them so appealing to a television audience. The format of these shows is designed to entertain the public, thereby assuring that the audience will continue watching. Conflict situations are particularly gripping for an audience because people become emotionally involved in the scene while watching it from a safe distance (Culpeper 2005). Furthermore, 'abnormal' social behaviour is more likely to arouse attention or is generally more salient and considered worthy of commentary (particularly from the audience's perspective) than 'normal' unobtrusive behaviour (cf. Watts 2003). Culpeper (2005) successfully illustrates how certain television shows blend verbal creativity and impoliteness to create an entertaining performance. Private television, in particular, depends heavily on advertising revenue; therefore, its primary marketing strategy is to attract a wide range of viewers. These television programmes are produced to appeal to a mass audience.

As far as data authenticity is concerned, a word of caution needs to be added about the recording process of this data material. Since a camera crew follows every step the officers take and records, though not necessarily broadcasts, every instance of their (non)verbal contributions, a certain effect on the officers' as well as on the citizens' (verbal) conduct has to be expected. These documentary formats put the public face and reputation of the police on display.

In spite of this shortcoming, I still consider these documentaries as authentic representations of the work police officers perform during daily patrols. The value of documentary data and their authenticity are important in studying language in conflict situations (cf. Bousfield 2007a). Instances of explicit face-attack are not always predictable in everyday life, and it is not a simple matter to record them empirically. Moreover, interactions in documentaries are not based on scripts, so participants' contributions are neither pre-established nor artificial. This assumption is supported by Shon, who compares naturally-occurring police data with documentary recordings of the same type and concludes that "they are essentially the same in their structural and social organization" (2003: 153). Another advantage of using video material is that it allows researchers to investigate non-verbal elements, which along with prosodic aspects play a decisive role in the interpretation of impolite strategies (see Beebe 1995; Culpeper, Bousfield, and Wichmann 2003; Locher and Watts, this volume).

3. Institutional framework, interactional asymmetry, and power in police work

There are certain discourse contexts in which individual contributions are considered to be unevenly distributed among the interactants. Prototypical examples of interactional asymmetry are found in institutional settings, in which speakers of different affiliations (i.e. typically an institutional representative and a 'client') actively engage in talk (Drew and Heritage 1992). In encounters between the police and citizens, prevailing asymmetries are marked in several dimensions, which encompass both the participants' extra-discursive identities as well as the corresponding linguistic and non-linguistic output (cf. Drew and Heritage 1992; Shon 1998).

Interactional asymmetry results, among other things, from the distribution of power between the interactants. Power is one important factor that influences the course as well as the outcome of these interactions. It has frequently been argued that power is an ingredient of any type of interaction between human beings, and that it is not restricted to those settings that are institutionally anchored (Drew and Heritage 1992: 48; Watts 1991: 2; Watts 2003: 201; Locher 2004: 9). Yet institutional settings (and talks) are often, at least in comparison to most informal interactions, distinctive sites for power negotiation, which is why power has been a subject for linguistic study in specific institutionalised settings (e.g. O'Barr 1982; Ainsworth-Vaughn 1998; Locher 2004; and Watts 1991, for a study on power in family discourse). In police work, several dimensions of power play a decisive role in negotiations between officers and offenders, particularly when some form of resistance occurs (see section 3.1).

In this study I will treat power as well as interactional asymmetry on the whole as dynamic, discursive concepts that are subject to change throughout the ongoing interaction (cf. Drew and Heritage 1992; Diamond 1996; Thornborrow 2002). Similarly, we must accept that the identity of the police as well as the institutional status they assume (as a law-enforcement agency) are to some degree established (or known) prior to the start of the interaction (Thornborrow 2002). This view does not necessarily contradict the discursive construction of identity because we must consider that the background of the interlocutors and especially the societal role that the police play are important variables in these interactions. In police interactions this view assumes that the relative status of the police does not automatically invest them with the power to control the interaction in all respects (although this may be the case). Similarly, the designated 'less powerful' interactant (i.e. the offender) can still attempt to assert discourse control by employing certain strategies or showing resistance against influencing strategies employed by the police (see example 3b in section 5.3). Thornborrow (2002), for instance, reveals how an apparent victim in a police interview manages to challenge the controlling discourse practices of the police and block the allegation (of false testimony) against her by reversing the interactional order of questioning. Yet how successful these attempts are at resisting the discourse control exerted by the dominant interactant depends, inter alia, on the type of strategy used, its placement in the situated discourse, and on the professionalism of the institutional party.

Police interactions as a type of institutional discourse are not restricted to an institutional setting such as the police station, in which cross examinations or victim interviews are conducted. The crux of police work, both in quantitative and qualitative terms, is performed in public (Whitaker 1982). It is, to a large extent, on the street that patrolling officers implement their law-enforcement duties. Thus, the institutional framework in the focus of this paper is the public work of police officers who deal with minor offences perpetrated by citizens in several German cities.

3.1.   *Power and manipulation in police interaction*

In studying the interrelationship between power and language, several researchers argue for a processual and dynamic notion of power in a three-fold manner: power is open to negotiation, it involves an 'action-restriction' of (at least) one interlocutor, and it presumes a conflict of interest (Wartenberg 1990; Watts 1991; Locher 2004, inter alia). The term 'negotiation' implies that a power relationship exists between at least two interactants (e.g. police and offender), and it refers to something that is vied for (Diamond 1996). A distinction has been proposed between the notions of 'power-to' which refers to a person's ability to act out power, and 'power-over', which emphasises the relational aspect of power (Wartenberg 1990).[2] Along this line, Watts defines the exercise of power as

> A exercises power over B when A affects B in a manner contrary to B's initially perceived interests, regardless of whether B later comes to accept the desirability of A's actions. (Watts 1991: 62)

In the case of police interaction, the offender's freedom of action is restricted by the intervention of the police, irrespective of the offender's acceptance of this intervention. From the police (viz. legal) perspective, the intrusion into citizens' lives is a form of police action that is institutionally authorised. Shon (2005) emphasises that the police are invested with the bureaucratic power to take certain measures, such as stopping drivers in traffic. From a legal point of view (viz. the institution), an authorised (and justified) intervention by the police as well as the linguistic strategies used in this intervention would be in accordance with the hypothesised norms of appropriacy of this 'Community of Practice' (see Mills 2003; and section 4).

The judgement about 'appropriacy' is a controversial matter in police work because it is strongly tied to the narrow space between certain allegations and factual evidence. One has to assume that the police only intervene on the basis of justified suspicion. If we follow this view, then the verbal behaviour that constitutes the police intervention does not transgress the norms in this context, assuming the action is institutionally sanctioned. This, however, does not imply that police action automatically comes with a set of linguistic strategies that are appropriate in any context, but instead that the police must choose strategies that are appropriate to the local circumstances. From the offender's point of view, police actions are not always justified. In fact, as my data show, offenders frequently display opposition to police intervention.

Power over others is not always wielded responsibly; in fact, at times it leads to abuse. In the heat of a conflict, there is always the risk that the interactional moves of both interlocutors might transgress the operative norms for the ongoing interaction. This can be seen especially when a conflict is about to escalate into physical violence. The threat of physical force can constitute an abuse of power by the police if the threat is not justified (cf. example 1). Conversely, if offenders reverse the power imbalance and threaten the police physically, such a move can also be construed (by the officer) as transgressing acceptable and appropriate behaviour (cf. example 3).

In any case, police measures against the offender constitute a form of 'action-restriction' that can be exercised in various ways, depending on the source of restriction, the intensity of the impact and the effectiveness in making the other person comply (Wartenberg 1990). Along this line, Wartenberg (1990) proposes a three-fold distinction of power, consisting of 'force', 'coercion', and 'influence'. Whereas 'force' presupposes a physical action to restrict the addressee's action-environment, 'coercive' power requires both the force to affect the addressee and a threat with which the speaker's intentions are revealed. If neither verbal threat nor physical force is applied, the exercise of power in a more fine-grained way is considered by Wartenberg as 'influence'[3] (1990: 105). Wartenberg conceives of 'manipulation' as a specific form of influence upon others that involves, on the one hand, a particular manner in which the dominant agent exercises power, and, on the other hand, is achieved by "morally questionable means" (1990: 111; cf. van Dijk 2006). I do not consider it morally questionable for the police to use such threats as long as they are not precursors to brute force. In reality, this practice generally operates justifiably and expediently. Verbally manipulating the offender into performing an undesirable action conforms to the *institutionally-sanctioned* practices in taking assertive action against resistant offenders. Moreover, in contrast to forceful imprisonment, the use of verbal strategies to make an offender comply with one's demands is, by all means, somewhat less 'menacing' and 'aggressive' (it can, however, still be perceived as face-threatening). Although the possibility of 'force' and the coercive aspect inherent in Wartenberg's sub-division of power should not be neglected in analysing threats, conditional threats allow the target some space to reconsider his/her conduct and possibly circumvent more forceful actions (see section 4).

It is often difficult to conceptually detach 'manipulation' from the other two forms of power exercise proposed by Wartenberg. This is because manipulation is present in all dimensions of power, and is, therefore, an inherent element of any power-exercise and power negotiation. Thus, the three elements, 'exercise of power', 'action restriction' and some form of 'influence' upon the other party (viz. manipulation) are dynamically tied to each other (cf. Wartenberg 1990). In addition, the police's own action-environment is restricted by the offender's conduct as well as the institutional alignments and regulations they have to observe.

3.2.   *Conflict and resistance in police – citizen encounters*

Police intervention is implemented to halt social disruption and re-establish a lawful equilibrium. What makes some of these encounters discursively interesting from the perspective of impoliteness research is citizens' resistance towards the accusations. This resistance forms the basis of the conflict between the police and offenders, which the former are called upon to resolve verbally, and, if necessary, physically.

From a discourse perspective, the participants are overtly at cross-purposes. The offending party has either committed, or is about to commit an offence against a third party, thereby violating the law or an existing social norm. The police, on the other hand, have the responsibility to prevent citizens from committing offences, and to penalise offenders if they violate established rules and regulations. It is not uncommon for the offender to deny having committed the act, or to resist the imposed penalty, even if it is only a verbal warning. This situation constitutes a delicate matter for the police officers. Not only do they have to distinguish between 'alleged' and 'established' facts, but they also have to be explicit in communicating to the offender the breaches s/he has committed. If any further course of action is to proceed smoothly, the offender has to accept the reprimand as well as admit (at least implicitly) to his/her misconduct. Following this, relevant measures have to be taken by the police to pursue the breach.

According to my data, two general patterns of offenders' resistance emerge during the negotiation process (i.e. while the offence is communicated to the alleged offender). Both patterns aim at circumventing (or at least reducing) the imminent penalisation. Some offenders try to ignore the accusations, perhaps because they do not want to further incriminate themselves. This type of resistance can be described as implicit or 'tacit' (see example 1 in section 5). On the other hand, in a more direct, 'on-record' manner, the offender may become rebellious and directly challenge the accusations. Such oppositional moves can go so far as to severely threaten the police officers' face, and are thus subject to being assessed as impolite by the targets (cf. section 5, example 2 and 3). With this in view, the police have to resort to verbal (and in some cases also physical) means to reprimand the offender and to re-establish social equilibrium.

In the course of this endeavour, officers have to utilise expedient strategies to achieve their ends without themselves violating social and legal norms. In Germany, a police officer who immediately draws a gun on a person who has committed a minor offence would violate the professional and legal code of conduct. Thus, *situationally-appropriate* means have to be utilised in exercising the police officers' duty. Several examples of the recordings reveal an increase in force and intensity on the (non)linguistic level depending on the course of the interaction; i.e. the more resistance is exhibited by the offender (overtly or covertly), the more face-threatening and unmitigated the response of the police will be. This does not imply a direct link between the directness of a strategy and its face-threatening or impolite value, but the police seem to adapt their strategies to the reaction(s) of the offender. Whereas initially the officers may draw on other forms of directives (e.g. requests) to influence the offender's conduct, in the course of the exchange the face-threatening potential of those strategies sometimes increases. Accordingly, in heated interactions certain linguistic strategies are deliberately employed which can exhibit strong (illocutionary) forces depending on their situated usage and the effect they have on the target.

4.   Threats as a powerful and manipulating linguistic device

Police work almost naturally involves different confrontational situations between the police and alleged offenders, during which the conflict can shift into
a disruptive and 'unmitigated' sequence, resulting in perceptions of inappropriate behaviour. It is particularly when the offending party attempts to avoid
penalisation that abusive and face-threatening language is utilised; this can then
cause the police to resort to more drastic measures in order to resolve the conflict.

A linguistic device that participants may employ in conflict situations is the
verbal threat. I regard verbal threats as a speech activity, or, according to Searle's
terminology (1969), a 'speech act' that coerces and manipulates target B into
(not) doing something which B considers to have an unfavourable outcome,
and which may cause the threatener (directly or indirectly) to initiate negative
consequences upon B's non-compliance (cf. similar definitions of threats in
Fraser 1975; Nicoloff 1989; Storey 1995; Shon 2005). Despite the significance
of other semiotic factors that contribute towards threatening perceptions in these
scenarios, e.g. a police uniform, the police car with ringing sirens, or the pistol
officers carry, my focus is restricted to the verbal implementation of (conditional)
threats without 'life-threatening' implications (cf. Shon 2003).

Power in this speech activity is produced by the co-occurrence of the three
elements: force, coercion, and influence (i.e. manipulation). A conditional threat
can coerce the target into compliance on grounds of the entailed proposition.
Coercion is achieved by making explicit the anticipated consequence, which is
communicated in the threat utterance. This often involves B's potential physical removal by the officers, who theoretically possess the *force* to take an offender into custody. The manipulative dimension is closely related to the former
two aspects. *Manipulation* can occur on five interrelated levels: cognitively,
emotionally, linguistically, behaviourally, and socially.[4] In practice, a threat can
change the way the offender views his/her misconduct as well as alter his/her
emotional sensitivity towards the act or towards the police intervention. Linguistic manipulation is made transparent, for instance, by an expression of acceptance of the anticipated action (e.g., 'okay' or 'yes', as in example 1b),
which should be followed by obeying the police order (i.e., non-verbal compliance). Social manipulation may occur when offenders act in accordance with
what is regarded as socially and legally established conduct beyond the scope
of this encounter. Even though this explanation is far from being exhaustive,
successful manipulation may *eventually* and *ideally* lead to compliance with
the threat token. This is an important step towards the termination of the conflict.

In a similar power-laden as well as highly asymmetrical context, Harris (1984a) investigates the form and function of threats in courts. She concludes that

> [a] threat becomes in this context just such a 'pragmatic and symbolic act'; pragmatic in attempting to bring about a particular act or series of acts and symbolic of the power and control of the court system and ultimately the social structure. (Harris 1984a: 268)

The two-fold distinction of threats proposed by Harris reveals both their controlling function ('pragmatic power' or 'power to') as well as the possibility of exercising 'power-over' somebody ('symbolic power'). When a threat is issued by a judge or a police officer, the symbolic power inherent in the institutional position and professional rights (i.e. their 'power to') turns into strong pragmatic power (i.e. their 'power over' the target), resulting in manipulation of the target and his/her social conduct. Hence, the use of threats is one particular linguistic strategy which is extremely sensitive in terms of the power relationship between the interactants and the institutional network in which it operates.

Thus far, the conception of verbal threats proposed in this chapter delineates a linguistic device which can exercise strong 'power over' the addressee; usually for the benefit of the threatener and to the disadvantage of the threatened person. In Goffmanian terms, this speech activity manipulates the addressee's face; i.e. "the positive social value a person effectively claims for himself [*sic*] by the line others assume he [*sic*] has taken during a particular contact" (Goffman 1967: 5). In addition, it has consequences for the threatener's face because his/her self-image is constructed and constantly altered by the social attributes assumed by the opponent in an ongoing conflict. According to Brown and Levinson's conceptualisation of face ([1978] 1987), one could attribute this face-threatening strategy towards the positive as well as the negative aspect of face.[5]

However, two controversial questions remain unanswered thus far. Are threats considered to be *impolite*, particularly in this context? And secondly, due to their 'powerful' nature, can this speech activity only be successfully exercised by the more powerful interactant?

Threats and impoliteness: Sanctioned or neutralised?

Mills (2005: 265) suggests that certain acts are conventionally associated with impoliteness. Using the example of the speech act 'threat', she emphasises that "hypothesizing of intention is essential to assessing an act as impolite" (Mills 2005: 266). The cognitive concept of intentionality is an important aspect in the exercise of power, and therefore also for the use of threats in this context (see

Wartenberg 1990; Culpeper, Bousfield, and Wichmann 2003; Locher 2004).[6] Despite the illusive character of this term, one has to assume some form of intention behind the exercise of power, and consequently in the use of verbal threats, since the threatener is trying to manipulate another person into doing something against his/her will.

Impoliteness in threat utterances is highly context-dependent and, to some extent, institutionally-bound. In one sense, the institutionalised nature of police talk sanctions the use of threats by officers because it allows them to state the expected penalty to the offender. On the other hand, despite official authorisation of this strategy one would expect that the target of a threat would be likely to assess the exploitation of institutional power through the use of verbal threats as face-threatening (i.e. impolite or rude) because his/her action-environment is severely restricted. This would imply that the manipulative use of language can be sanctioned by virtue of the institutional and professional rights of one of the interactants, but it simultaneously creates an impolite linguistic tactic under certain circumstances (cf. Bousfield 2007a).

One way to explain the use of face-threatening strategies in institutional contexts is to make a distinction between *sanctioned* behaviour (i.e. that which is permissible given the roles and power relations between the interactants) and *neutralised* behaviour (i.e. FTAs that are neutralised lose their face-damaging character; see Culpeper 2005). We can assume that the use of a threat by an officer is an institutionally sanctioned strategy. However, not every form of a threat in police interactions can be regarded as sanctioned. Neither can we assume that a threat is always neutralised in this context just because the target does not explicitly comment on it. According to Harris (2001) there are institutional contexts which not only sanction, but also reward systematic impoliteness. In political discourse, for example, impoliteness becomes part of the institutional 'game' without leading to the breakdown of interpersonal relationships (Harris 2001: 469). Police interactions, on the other hand, occur in an institutional context with a high asymmetrical relationship between the interlocutors. The offender may not realise that threats are regarded as an accepted practice in police encounters. Instead, s/he perceives the interfering move by the officers as personally restrictive and face-threatening. Police norms sanction the use of threats against offenders, providing they are not overused or abused. On the other hand, the target of a threat can perceive this strategy as inappropriate or 'impolite', depending on the salience of the strategy and its appropriateness from the target's point of view.

The question arises as to whether the lexeme 'impolite' can be used to describe such behaviour in this context, particularly if brute force and abuse of power are involved (cf. section 5.1). By the same token, it is problematic to call somebody 'impolite' who has harmed a person physically. Even if threats are 'only' used to manipulate the target *verbally*, they can nevertheless be considered as going beyond the sanctioned norms of appropriate behaviour in certain circumstances. Regardless of whether or not the target evaluates this behaviour explicitly, other interactional moves as well as information about the context might support such an assessment. Threats are not impolite *per se*; it is the institutional application (viz. as a sanctioned matter) on the one hand and the target's perception on the other hand that help us to identify this behaviour. For want of a better term I use the lexeme 'impoliteness' in this study to describe certain moves by either of the participants, who, in uttering a threat in a confrontation, go beyond appropriate conduct and deliberately attack the other person's face.

Finally, it is the *cumulative* view of impoliteness that plays a significant role in this context (cf. Mills 2005). It is not merely the threat utterance itself that stipulates perceptions of impoliteness. Instead, the dynamic unfolding of the conflict scenario with several face-threatening turns, which may eventually lead to the triggering of a threat, contributes significantly towards this assessment. In particular, strong perceptions of impoliteness are created when the offender 'turns the tables' and directs a threat against the police (see example 3b).

5. Threats in police work

In the following sections, three exemplary types of threat utterances in police work are presented which draw attention to their manipulative as well as their impolite dimensions. The instances are taken from three different police interactions, and they show how face-threatening, and to some extent highly conflictive, police interactions can proceed. As I have argued above, perceptions of impoliteness are not exclusively influenced by a single verbal threat, but by a number of turn sequences which exert strong influence upon these assessments.

5.1. Issuing a police threat

The first scenario presented in this section deals with a homeless person (H), who is loitering in the men's section of a department store. The manager has called the police to have the homeless man removed from this location because his presence apparently disturbs the customers. In spite of the manager's complaints and the arrival of the police, H prefers to read the newspaper on a couch while drinking from a can of beer.[7] P1 (male officer) and P2 (female officer) repeatedly ask H to leave the store and to continue reading his paper in a public place. After H refuses to comply with the police officer's demand to leave the locale, P1 resorts to harsher means:

Example (1a):[8]
083 P1: *auf geht's*
         'let's go'
084   *sonst trag ich Sie hier raus*
         'or I'll carry you out'
085   *dann gibt's Pfefferspray in die Augen*
         'then you'll have pepper spray in your eyes'
((*TV commentator briefly describes the scene*))
086   *ja auf geht's*
         'ok let's go'
((*Commentator continues describing the scene*))
087   *(x) wir wollen los*
         '(x) we're going'

H's refusal to leave the store triggers a verbal threat by P1 (lines 83–85). The actual wording of the threat is put in a conditional form (*'Let's go, or I'll carry you out'* - *'then you'll have pepper spray in your eyes'*). Harris (1984a: 248–249) notes that, despite slightly divergent forms of threat utterances (i.e., for example, 'If you do X, (then) I will do Y'; 'Do X or I will do Y'; 'Do X and I will do Y') and the options they realise in a particular semantic network, these threats appear to have the same meaning. The threat token is made transparent by the 'X or Y' structure in this scenario. If the homeless person does not leave the store of his own accord, the officers will remove him forcefully. The face-threat in this scene results to a large extent from the type of punishment that H can expect. The forceful 'booting out' is emphasised by a threat of physical punishment (viz. by means of pepper spray), and is subsequently repeated to boost the face-threat and increase the manipulative forces that is meant to coerce H into compliance. Because H is drowsy, which is probably the result of his alcohol consumption, he does not respond directly to the threat. Therefore, the face-threatening implications of this move are not readily observable, but can only be inferred from the interaction that precedes the first threat utterance by P1. Here, H responds to the police orders (to leave) with self-defensive moves and accounts for his behaviour such as "*I haven't harmed anybody here*" and "*I was only reading my newspaper*" (due to lack of space, this excerpt is not part of the transcript). This shows that H feels his action-environment to be severely restricted, and that he defends his presence in the department store.

In example (1b) the scene continues after a scene cut:

Example (1b):
088   (pause) ((*scene cut before*))
089 P1: *ich sach das jetzt kein zweites Mal*
        'I won't repeat myself'
090   *ich trach Sie hier raus*
        'I'll carry you out'
091   *an allen Vieren*
        'on all fours'
092   (2.5)
093   *und Sie landen in der Gewahrsamszelle*
        'and you're going into the holding cell'
094   *und Sie haben hinterher wahrscheinlich eine blutende Nase*
        'and you will probably have a bloody nose afterwards'
095   (2.0) ((*voice from walkie-talkie*))
096 H: *ja: (x) muss ich mir langsam mal überlegen*
        'ye:s (x) I'll have to think about that'

In line 96, a weak form of (verbal) compliance is reached when the homeless person verbalises second thoughts regarding his behaviour. This signals that, as a result of several threat tokens, manipulation has been, at least partially and tentatively, successful. P1 repeats the original threat (as seen in lines 83–85) because H shows no form of compliance in the first instance. What is interesting in this respect is that the officer introduces the second threat by an utterance (*'I won't repeat myself'*, line 89) which is in contrast to what he does in the subsequent turn. P1 reiterates the threat, but this time more elaborately and with a higher threat potential. He specifies the physical pain H may be about to endure if he does not make a move. At this point the threat is only verbal, and there is no physical contact between P1 and H.[9] H is prompted to reconsider the officer's demands in order to avoid being hurt and forcibly removed (*"Yes. I'll have to think about that"*, line 96).

The repetition of the threat is realised by rephrasing the threat token (*'You're going into the holding cell'*, line 93) and combining it with the threat of physical violence (*'bloody nose'*, line 94). Both turns serve to intimidate H and bring about successful compliance (cf. Fraser 1975, 1998, who puts forward 'intimidation' as one condition for verbal threats). Since H shows no signs of compliance after the first threat, the use of a second threat can certainly be considered appropriate at this point. However, as far as the offensive content is concerned, the blatant threat of physical violence overstates police power and may thus constitute an abuse of their power, even though they are implementing their authority

against a resistant offender. The data do not give explicit evidence of H's evaluation of the officer's second threat. What we do find is a tentative compliance
response and several explanations about his presence in the store. H's responses
could be interpreted as an indication that he considers the violence expressed
in the threat as inappropriate (or impolite). This would be understandable since
his well-being is at stake, and he feels forced to defend himself.

5.2. Verbal duelling

In the following situation, the conflict exhibits a kind of verbal duel between
offender and officer. The offender openly protests against the police orders,
whereas the police officer opposes the verbal protest by resolute behaviour, and,
finally, by uttering a threat. The context is as follows: the police are chasing a
suspicious motor cyclist (F) who is trying to escape from a routine traffic control.
The officers follow him into the countryside, and finally manage to stop him.
The facts of the case become immediately clear to the police. The motorcyclist
seems to have committed several offences, including resisting arrest, driving
without a licence and driving whilst under the influence of alcohol. As a matter
of routine, the police (two male officers, P1 and P2) demand that F takes a
breathalyser test to determine the level of alcohol in his blood. The offender is
cooperative in taking the test, but then shows resistance when it comes down to
following the police to the station (in the police car) and leaving his motorcycle
unattended in the meadow. The conflict is exacerbated when the offender tries
to move his vehicle off the meadow to a nearby hedge:

Example (2a):
049 P1: *ne*
         'nope'
050   *das Ding bleibt jetzt hier stehen=*
         'the thing stays here now'=
051 F: *=ne ich schieb ihn bloß [zur Hecke]*
         '=no I'm just going to move it [to the hedge]'
052 P1: *[ne das Ding] bleibt hier*
         '[nope the thing] stays here'
053   *ne:=*
         'no:pe='
054 F: *=wo die Hecke ist=*
         '=where the hedge is='
055 P1: *=ne::*
         '=no::pe'

056   *das Ding bleibt [jetzt hier stehen]*
       'the thing stays [here now]'
057 F: *[ich kann ihn doch*
       nicht so] im Gelände stehen lassen=
       '[I can't leave him
       (it) out in the open like that='
058 P1: *=das steht das bleibt jetzt [so stehn]*
       '=it remains it's not [going anywhere]'

The conflict (of interest) is verbalised by two types of resistance that co-occur in this scenario. The offender (F) opposes the police order to follow immediately, and the police officer (P1) forbids the offender to move his vehicle. This pattern portrays the verbal duel between P1 and F that propels the conflict along. Noticeably in this scenario, the police make use of orders repeatedly, almost all of them in the same wording, preceded by a dispreferred marker combined with an account: *'No. The thing stays here'*. By repeating this directive towards F, the officer not only resists giving in to the offender's request, but also emphasises his authority (viz. exercise of power) over the offender. Additionally, the sequence indicates signs of annoyance on P1's part about the resistance he is confronted with. Repeating the same order seems to be an attempt to achieve cooperation from the target without overstepping the boundaries of what is institutionally-sanctioned as well as legally acceptable in these circumstances. Hence, the police's conduct cannot be regarded as impolite despite its directness and the face-threatening implications resulting from a demonstration of their power. Further signs that may allow for an interpretation of annoyance and conflict intensification can be seen in the elongation of the non-compliance marker *'nope'* (lines 53, 55) and the use of the derogatory term *'thing'* by P1 to refer to F's motorcycle (line 56). By contrast, F uses the male pronoun *ihn* ('him') in line 57 to refer to his vehicle as a personified object which must be treated with respect and care.

So far, impolite behaviour is not present in this interaction, but a conflict is clearly emerging in the struggle between F's desire to remove his vehicle and P1's refusals to allow him to do so. A few turns later, F is still trying to move his vehicle to a safer place; the police then resort to a more face-threatening and power-exerting strategy than the directive uttered in the previous excerpt:

Example (2b):
070 F: *=ne lassen Se ma*
        '=nope leave it'

071 P1: *[((inaudible))]*
072 F: *[ich schiebs] doch bloß bis zur*
          [Hecke]
          '[I'll just move] it to the
          [hedge]'
073 P1: *[Sie] schieben das nirgendswohin=*
          '[you're] not moving it anywhere='
074   *=Sie bocken das jetzt hier öf*
          '=you put that here on its stand
          now'
075 F: *und da [ist doch (xxx)]*
          'and there [is (xxx)']
076 P1: *[SIE BOCKEN DAS JETZT HIER]*
          SOFORT HIER ÖF,
          '[YOU PUT THAT HERE] ON ITS
          STAND NOW,'
077   *ODER ICH WERD RICHTIG UNGEMÜTLICH*
          'OR I'LL GET REALLY UNPLEASANT'

In lines 76/77, P1 emphatically utters a verbal threat – *"YOU PUT THAT HERE ON ITS STAND NOW, OR I'LL GET REALLY UNPLEASANT"*. The threat amounts to direct coercion and manipulation of F's behaviour. Moreover, the negative consequences that F can expect should he continue to resist can be directly derived from the use of the conditional. The very fact that P1 remains vague about the precise action he will take, apart from saying it will soon become unpleasant, intensifies the conflictual atmosphere and the severity of the threat. F does not know what it means if P1 is unpleasant. In this respect, the target cannot directly respond to a specific proposition, nor react towards the anticipated consequences entailed therein. The actual consequence of the threat is not tangible for F. It seems as if the vagueness of the action that the threat communicates creates a strong uncertainty in F and thus encourages him to comply. Since the police have already communicated the charges against F, it should be clear to him that his situation is not open to negotiation and that any further attempts to move his vehicle will be countered more forcefully by the officers. As this scenario exhibits, the threat utterance itself is within the bounds of acceptable behaviour in this context. It is in accordance with the professional rights of police officers, and only implemented after other, less threatening strategies have failed.

F does not respond towards the threat. Instead, he focuses on gaining power over the police to get permission for his request. Contrary to the police conduct, it is F's fruitless attempt to gain temporary power over the police (against their will) and to be given permission for moving his vehicle that could be considered as 'impolite' by P1. Clearly, F is not in the position to be giving orders or making demands on the police (e.g. as in line 70). The officer seems to be annoyed about F's behaviour and his persistent attempts to move his motorcycle, as exhibited, for example, in this ironic remark *"What are you saying? You aren't sneaking off – Yeah, we saw that"* (uttered by P1 in the excerpt between examples 2a and b; not included in the transcript).

The 'impoliteness' on the part of the offender in this respect results not only from the presence of severe resistance towards police orders, but, more importantly, from the types of resistance and how they are communicated. Over the course of several turns he employs rather 'bald-on-record' and face-threatening strategies in objecting to the orders and rebelling against official conduct (cf. Culpeper 1996). Particularly in line 70, F reverses the use of directives to address an implicit order to the officer not to touch his vehicle. Since the police are acting within their rights to confiscate the vehicle and take the offender to the police station for further questioning, F should not be responding in the way he does. In this respect, the dynamic and face-threatening unfolding of the scenario, as exhibited by the offender's resistant behaviour through several turns, can be interpreted as inappropriate (or impolite) by the officers.

5.3. Turning the tables: A threat–counterthreat sequence

As a final example in this chapter I would like to present a case in which the offender issues a counterthreat against an officer. Such a scenario is theoretically possible in police–citizen encounters due to the emotional involvement of the conflicting parties. Although its occurrence is very rare (especially if the police are targeted), the example demonstrates the face-attacking consequences officers may face in these conflict situations. Two police officers (P1 & P2, both male) from Stendal, a city in Eastern Germany, are called to a block of flats in which one tenant (A) has called the police because tenant B, who lives one floor above him, is disturbing his sleep. The incident is broadcast in two parts. In the first part, the officers check the tenant's personal details and remind him to keep the noise down. During this short exchange, P1 and P2 notice a certain degree of indifference on the part of B towards them, which, from visual scrutiny of the episode in question, may be drug-induced. This becomes transparent to some degree in B's unconcerned responses, such as *'whatever you say'* (line 76) or *'that, too'* (line 78).

In this scene, P2 delivers the warning about being too loud more directly by way of a threat token. In doing so, he establishes the facts of the case and explicates potential consequences for B if the disturbance continues. Example (3a) is taken from the first encounter in which the threat is uttered in order to prompt B to keep the volume down:

Example (3a):

073 P2: *und sollten Sie dat nich lassen mit der Musik,*
          'and if you don't keep the music down'
074   *kommen wa hier noch einmal*
          'we'll be back'
075   (1.6)
076 B: *wie Sie meinen*
          'whatever you say'
077 P2:   *dann nehmen wa Ihre Anlage mit*
          'then we'll take your stereo'
078 B: *hohoho ha (.) auch das noch*
          'hohoho ha (.) that, too'
079 P2:   *ja?*
          'yes?'
080   *dazu ham wa dat Recht*
          'we have the right to do that'

P2's utterance in lines 73/74 constitutes the threat in this scene, which makes the proposition clear to B ('*If you don't keep the music down, we will come back again*'). If B does not keep the noise down, the police will come back and confiscate his stereo. The threat is uttered in a normal and straightforward way without any voice-raising or threatening gestures. In doing so, the officer acts in accordance with police norms and his profeesional right to reprimand this behaviour. He makes this explicit by saying "*We have the right to do that*" (line 80) to emphasise his legal position with respect to B.

The second part begins back in tenant A's flat, when P1 and P2 try to find out more about the troublesome neighbour. Shortly into this scene, the officers hear more noise coming from the flat above, which immediately triggers their next move. As a result, tenant B is forced to spend the night at the police station. Even though B hardly resists this intervention due to the physical predominance of the officers, he addresses a question at P2 which has considerable consequences for the officer's face (lines 161–164):

Example (3b):

158 P2: *ist der Spass vorbei*
'the fun is over'

159 (2.0)

160 *werden wa wohl noch ne*
Hausdurchsuchung machen müssen hier
wa?
'we'll have to search this house too
right?'

161 B: *kommen Sie aus Stendal?*
'are you from Stendal?'

162 P2: *ik komm aus Stendal=*
'I am from Stendal=

163 *=kene sorge*
=don't worry'

164 B: *na ja denn viel Spass noch*
'well then have fun'

165 P2: *wollen Sie mir jetzt noch drohen oder wie*
'are you threatening me or what'

As an act of resistance and reluctance towards the police intervention, B tries to make a last move against his 'opponent' (P2) by giving vent to a verbal threat against the officer (*'Are you from Stendal – well then have fun'*, lines 161/164). The threat implies that B might seek revenge against the officer in the near future for having treated B 'unfairly'. It is introduced by B asking P2 whether he lives in the same town (viz. Stendal), and is then followed by B stating *"Well then have fun"*. Despite the intransparent consequences in B's threat, P2 directly orients towards the tenant's utterance in lines 161/164, recognizing it as a threat (*"Are you threatening me or what"*, line 165). What is interesting in this respect is that the counterthreat by B is not directed against P2 as an officer or against the police as an institution, but it targets P2 as a *private person*. It appears as if the force of this utterance can only be sustained by targeting the officer as an individual (cf. Culpeper, Bousfield and Wichmann 2003: 1565). Clearly, B's move transgresses the norms of what is admissible and appropriate to say to an officer. Therefore, B's turn in lines 161/164 exhibits a transparent case of 'impoliteness' as well as a face attack that is directed against the officer and his ('personal') face.

Although the officer does not evaluate this utterance explicitly in terms of 'impoliteness', we must assume that this counterthreat crosses the line of what is acceptable in such conflicts. Apart from recognising B's utterance as a threat, P2's comments express annoyance and reprimand B's behaviour after this incident (literally: *"You're going to the end of the line – I'll tell you that"*; figuratively: *"You're in no position to talk"*), implying that B has no right to speak to the officer in this manner (examples not included). The officer's response can be interpreted as an attempt to ward off B's threat to his face as well as to reassert the police's institutional authority. The officer's ability to remain calm during this altercation is undoubtedly a reflection of his experience in dealing with offenders in a professional manner.

6. Conclusion

Police threats are an institutionally-sanctioned device which is often strategically employed in conflict exchanges in which the offender displays strong resistance towards the legal authority. Its primary function is to make the target comply with the threat token, thereby advancing the conflict resolution. This chapter has tried to explore the role of such threats in conflict talk with reference to cases of police–citizen (viz. offender) interaction. By focusing on a particular institutional context, the *pragmatic* as well as the *symbolic* power that is created and exercised by verbal threats was investigated. It has become clear that verbal (conditional) threats function as a powerful linguistic device that coerces and manipulates the target into doing something which is against his/her will.

The institutional role invests police officers with the authority to employ these means for their professional tasks as long as they do not deviate from the institutional code of conduct. Verbal threats are not inherently impolite in this context; rather, they can be appropriate to the prevailing circumstances from a police perspective. However, threats can also constitute a face-threatening act that exercises an influence on the target's social identity and the freedom of action s/he enjoys. Threats restrict the offender's action-environment, and coerce him/her into compliance with police orders. Assessments about impoliteness and the use of threats can only be made on the basis of the situational usage of this strategy and whether it has been implemented appropriately.

We have seen that the data do not yield evidence for explicit assessments of interactants' behaviour in terms of these lexemes ('impolite', 'rude'). This calls for a close contextualisation of tokens that are subject to interpretation as inappropriate (cf. Watts 2003; Locher and Watts, this volume). If we accept that a verbal threat is: i) an extreme form of face-attack, uttered intentionally to manipulate the target's behaviour (beyond the institutional norms); and ii) perceived by the target as restricting (or manipulating) one's action-environment, then it is suitable to use the lexeme 'impoliteness' (or a similar term) in this context. However, we can only judge the appropriacy of this strategy by analyzing each scenario individually and working out clues for such assessments. This is sometimes difficult, as we have seen from my data, when participants do not explicitly refer to such behaviour as 'impolite' or 'rude'. Moreover, bearing in mind that certain rights and constraints encompass this institutional framework, the police are expected to resort to 'less direct' means at first to encourage the offender to co-operate. If these attempts fail, more severe and face-threatening devices can be used to achieve the desired ends. The police work discussed in this chapter displays such a procedure.

The three exemplary cases of threat utterances in conflict scenarios of daily police work have revealed the following: it is not the institutional status of the speaker alone that equips an individual with the privilege to utter a threat. Threats may also be performed by the offender against the police. Particularly in heated arguments between the two parties, in which resistance and objection is conveyed by the offender's conduct and the participants therefore become involved in a verbal duel, the offending party may resort to a (counter)threat strategy as an ultimate resource to avoid being taken into custody. Even though the effect of this threat will most likely be unsuccessful and will likely be responded to with professional detachment and authority, counterthreats transgress the norms of what is considered appropriate in these encounters.

Ideally, a successful conditional threat will manipulate the target's conduct because it makes the anticipated consequences transparent, which are not in the target's interest. It is thus a powerful linguistic device that can manipulate the target both on a linguistic and non-linguistic level. In conflicts, alleged offenders frequently assume an oppositional stance against police intervention in order to refute the accusations. Verbal threats can, in this respect, serve as a vehicle to terminate the conflict and to re-establish (at least temporarily) social equilibrium. While the police prefer a signal of compliance with the threat token, offenders initially do the opposite in pursuit of their own interests. However, if they fail to show compliance, more forceful modes are exercised (i.e. even physical action), including taking the offender into temporary custody.

Threats in police work show that the symbolic and the pragmatic sides of power are inextricably connected as well as important for the success of a threat utterance. Persons endowed with strong symbolic power due to their institutional rank or position (e.g. police officers, judges, or army trainers) are most likely to gain compliance from the target when they turn their symbolic power into pragmatic power, e.g. the power to prevent an offender from behaving in an unac- ceptable manner. The pragmatic power is then made transparent either through the use of certain linguistic strategies (e.g. a threat) or by exploiting general conversational mechanisms (cf. Bousfield 2007a). Hence, the symbolic power of the institution is transformed into a very pragmatic power, communicating one person's 'power over' another.

As far as the use of threats in this institutional context and the subject of impoliteness are concerned, it is clear that we must extend (im)politeness theory to include institutional forms of discourse (cf. Harris 2001; Culpeper 2005). We must also re-evaluate the assessments of impoliteness made by participants in these contexts. In particular, the issue of sanctioned versus neutralised behaviour can reveal whether impoliteness actually occurs or is, in fact, equilibrated on the account of the relevant framework. This leaves us with a more 'context-dependent' analysis of instances of impoliteness.

Notes

1. The term 'offender' is used generally throughout this work as referring to a person in my data who has allegedly or actually committed an offence against a third party or an established legal (or social) norm.
2. It is the latter concept ('power over') that is of primary interest in this study. This distinction is closely tied to Fairclough's (1989) distinction between 'power behind discourse' and 'power in discourse' (cf. Watts's [1991] distinction of 'power over' and 'power to'). In the police scenarios, the former includes "the physical sanctions underpinning an order . . . given by a policeman", and the latter might be, for example, "instantiated in the use of an agent-less passive" (Chilton 2002: 6).
3. The loose character of this notion is noted by Wartenberg (1990: 104) himself, who points to the wide range of phenomena that this concept entails.
4. It is beyond the scope of this chapter to explain these dimensions in great detail. Therefore, I have only given a short description of how this manipulative device can influence our linguistic and non-linguistic behaviour. For a more detailed discussion see van Dijk (2006), Chilton (2002) and Wartenberg (1990: 110–112).
5. It must be mentioned that Brown and Levinson ([1978] 1987: 66) list 'threats' as one of those acts that threaten only the addressee's negative face. The face-threatening implications of this act make it necessary to extend the area of influence of threats to include both positive and negative aspects of face. In addition, it is important to investigate the effects of the threat on the speaker as well as on the addressee.
6. The concept of intention in uttering a threat is intuitively understood from two perspectives: the speaker has the intention to threaten the addressee, and, in case of non-compliance, bring about the predicted consequences. The addressee, on the other hand, also hypothesises this intention in the speaker based on several linguistic and non-linguistic cues.
7. It should be noted here that drinking alcohol in public places does not constitute an offence in Germany.
8. The examples cited in this work are transcribed according to well-known transcription notations; CAPITALS, for example, signal increased volume (cf. Atkinson and

Heritage 1984). For reasons of readability, the transcription has been kept to a minimum. Individuals' names have been left out to conceal their identity. The first line of each transcript presents the original language (i.e. German; transcribed, to some degree, in non-standard forms), and the second line gives an idiomatic translation of the turn.

9. According to German police practices, physical force can only be applied as a last resort. Since this point has not yet been reached in the conflict, physically removing H at this point could be considered inappropriate.

Chapter 8
Verbal aggression and impoliteness:
Related or synonymous?

Dawn Elizabeth Archer

1. Introduction

Culpeper (1998: 86) has suggested that "impoliteness is a type of aggression",
and the courtroom is a "legitimate form of [that] verbal aggression" in that
"prosecutors are licensed to aggravate a witness's face". He further suggests
that this "legitimate" aggravation of face may well explain why the "courtroom
has provided the basis of ... many plays, films, and television dramas". Culpeper's interest in impoliteness is well known, of course. Indeed, he has devised
an impoliteness model (Culpeper 1996), which he, Bousfield and Wichmann revised in 2003, Culpeper again revised in 2005 and which Bousfield critiques and
further revises in this edited collection. Although the original or revised models
were not designed with the courtroom in mind, Culpeper and his co-authors
have explored activity types (Levinson 1992) that, like the courtroom, involve
a high level of "conflictive talk" (i.e. US army training data [Culpeper 1996],
the television quiz show *The Weakest Link* [Culpeper 2005] and the docu-soap
The Clampers [Culpeper, Bousfield, and Wichmann 2003; Bousfield 2004]).

In the first of these studies, Culpeper (1996: 359) made the point that impoliteness is not always "a haphazard product of say a heated argument" in some
activity types, but can be deployed by the participants "in a systematic way as
part of what they perceive to be their job". Some researchers find the idea of
systematic impoliteness problematic, however. Indeed, they argue that impoliteness that is systematic should be regarded as a *norm* for a given community of
practice and, as such, as politic as opposed to salient behaviour (Watts 1992,
2003; Locher and Watts, this volume; see also Mills 2003, 2005). They also
query whether the participants involved in activity types where conflictive talk
plays an important role (i.e. is the norm) would consider impoliteness to have
taken place (Mills 2005: 270).[1] The main aim of this chapter is to investigate
the usefulness of Culpeper's impoliteness model and its revisions in a historical
courtroom context, in light of this "systematic" debate: more specifically, I am
interested in determining whether we should be talking about *impoliteness* in

a context in which some courtroom participants are legally *licensed* to aggravate the face of other participants because of their role, and in which there is likely to be a high expectation of conflictive talk amongst participants. This will necessitate establishing whether verbal aggression and impoliteness are actually/always synonymous in a historical courtroom context. To help in this regard, I will be seeking to determine whether there is something unique about the courtroom that distinguishes it from other activity types involving conflictive talk. I particularly want to discover if/the extent to which:

(i) the legal (and therefore institutional) sanctioning of the use of verbal aggression by certain participant groups (i.e. lawyers and judges) within the historical courtroom serves to over-ride the receiver(s)'s assessment of face-damage having taken place (especially when the role of the receiver serves to restrict his/her action-environment: Wartenberg 1990)

(ii) impoliteness is deemed to have taken place when verbal aggression techniques are utilised by members of those participant groups whose *right* to aggravate face is not legally sanctioned by their role in the historical courtroom.

I should make it clear from the outset that I am not suggesting that *sanctioning* guarantees *neutralisation* of the face attack in this activity type or any other (cf. Culpeper 2005). Rather, I am trying to tease out the relationship between the *rights* of the various participant groups and the *acceptability of face attack* in a historical courtroom context, so that I can better assess which strategies are likely to be perceived as verbally aggressive and which are likely to be perceived as impolite. As such, I will be paying close attention to the strategies utilised by the different participant groups (i.e. lawyers, judges, witnesses and defendants), whilst exploring a central theme of this edited collection: the relationship between power and impoliteness.

Why focus on the historical as opposed to the modern courtroom? Researchers who study impoliteness in a modern courtroom context tend to concentrate on the interaction between lawyers and witnesses during cross-examinations, i.e. the "talk" that is more likely to be characterised by conflicting goals. Not surprisingly, they are able to produce evidence of participants engaging in face-attacking strategies whilst simultaneously seeking to enhance/protect their own face (and/or the face of their client). Yet if we are to tease out the differences between "impoliteness" and "verbal aggression" in the courtroom (modern and historical), we need to investigate examinations-in-chief as well as cross-examinations – i.e. those interactions when examiners are more likely to use supportive rather than aggressive questioning strategies, because it is in their interest to have the cooperation of the witnesses (1) when seeking to confirm/clarify information that had been given previously, and/or (2) when establishing their version of events through questions and answers. The English historical courtroom (1649–1722) is particularly interesting in this regard, as there was not the strict division between examination-in-chief and cross-examination that there is today. Consequently, small stretches of interaction can involve both activities.[2] Another important difference which may influence our "impolite" versus "verbally aggressive" distinction relates to the questioner role: rather than being a "non-transferable marker of power" as it is today (Walker 1987: 62), it was a role largely undertaken by defendants (when able) and judges (more typically) at the beginning of our period (lawyers did not begin to adopt the questioner role we associate with them today until the eighteenth century).

I will be drawing from the transcripts of four treason trials as a means of teasing out the differences between "impoliteness" and "verbal aggression" in a historical courtroom context: Charles I (1649), Coleman (1678), Francia (1716) and Layer (1722). These trials represent the period in which defence lawyers were introduced to the courtroom, and the courtroom began a slow process of change towards an adversarial procedure (Langbein 2003). The transcripts were originally taken down by professional scribes during the speech event, and later published as verbatim accounts. Claims of complete accuracy/fullness are technically untrue, of course, but the reliability of trial reporting has been shown to have improved markedly towards the end of the seventeenth century (Langbein 1978: 265). The compilers of the *Corpus of English Dialogues*[3] (from which these texts are taken) have also checked the transcripts against related data (i.e. manuscripts and alternative contemporary accounts) to ensure they represent the best available record.[4]

In Section 2, I introduce the impoliteness model proposed by Culpeper (1996) and revised in Culpeper, Bousfield and Wichmann (2003), Culpeper (2005), Kryk-Kastovsky (2006) and Bousfield (this volume), and use this opportunity to discuss the difficulties associated with defining – and categorising – impoliteness. In Section 3, I summarise my findings in relation to the English historical courtroom, evaluating them in respect to the debate surrounding the systematic use of impoliteness. In particular, I suggest that, although the courtroom is associated by many researchers with impoliteness, (prototypical) impoliteness is relatively uncommon in the historical courtroom. I further suggest that we should therefore consider distinguishing between impoliteness and verbal aggression, and propose a way of doing so using Goffman's (1967) three distinctions relating to face damage (i.e. *intentional, incidental* and *unintended*: cf. Culpeper, Bousfield and Wichmann 2003). In Section 4, I summarise my opinion as to the usefulness of applying impoliteness models to an activity type for which some verbal aggression techniques are legally sanctioned, and reiterate a view argued throughout this chapter, namely, if we are explicit about the fact that the Culpeper-inspired models actually deal with *face-threat* (Locher and Watts 2005), we can use them to explore "verbal aggression" (as well as "impoliteness") strategies.

2. Categorising impoliteness

Until relatively recently, the courtroom was perceived by many politeness researchers as an arena in which a kind of "formal protocol . . . regulate[s] potential conflicts"; that is to say, aggression is proactively disarmed/eradicated (if possible, before it surfaces) so that "communication between potentially aggressive parties" becomes possible (Brown and Levinson [1978] 1987: 1, 51: note 2; see also Lakoff 1989). But Penman (1990: 18) is amongst a number of researchers to argue (convincingly) that facework in courtroom interaction can be directed towards face *aggravation* as well as face *enhancement*. Culpeper (1998) adheres to Penman's (1990) view, of course, and proposes a number of impoliteness super-strategies to help us capture the different means by which we might attack the face of our interlocutor in his 1996 article. I outline these *aggravating* strategies below.

2.1. Culpeper's (1996) impoliteness super-strategies

Culpeper (1996) identifies five super-strategies to explain impoliteness phenomena, the first four of which *mirror* the "politeness" strategies developed by Brown and Levinson ([1978] 1987):

1) Bald on record impoliteness = strategies that attack the addressee's face directly, clearly and unambiguously even though face is deemed to be relevant in the given circumstances.[5] Culpeper, Bousfield and Wichmann (2003) provide the example of a disgruntled driver who told a parking attendant to *Shut up and act like a parking attendant!* (but see Bousfield, this volume).

2) Positive impoliteness = strategies designed to damage the addressee's positive face wants (i.e. the desire to be appreciated/approved of). Examples include "ignoring the other" and/or "excluding [him/her] from an activity", "being disinterested . . . unsympathetic", "using inappropriate identity markers", "obscure or secretive language" and/or "taboo words", "seeking disagreement" and "calling the other names".

3) Negative impoliteness = strategies designed to damage the addressee's negative face wants (i.e. the desire for freedom of action/to be unimpeded). Examples include "frighten[ing]" the other, being "condescending, scorn[ing] or ridicul[ing]" and "invad[ing] the other's face".

4) Sarcasm or mock politeness = politeness strategies that are obviously insincere, and thus remain surface realisations.[6] Culpeper, Bousfield and Wichmann (2003) pro-

vide the example of a driver who, on receiving a ticket from a parking attendant, sarcastically told the latter to *Have a good day!*

Culpeper's (1996: 357) fifth strategy is equivalent to "withholding politeness" where politeness would normally be expected. Examples of withheld impoliteness are hard to identify with any degree of certainty, as instances can only be clearly identified when an interactant goes on record to withhold politeness that may be expected at a particular juncture (Bousfield 2004: 156–157). This raises the issue of context – something that Culpeper, Bousfield and Wichmann (2003) discuss in detail. They point out, for example, that:

> ... if it were not part of someone's role (as a tutor, say) to make a criticism, and if it were known that the addressee was particularly sensitive to criticism, then *It was bad*, as a description of the addressee's work, would seem to be impolite. It should be noted [then] that a key difference between politeness and impoliteness is *intention*: whether it is the speaker's intention to support face (politeness) or to attack it (impoliteness). (Culpeper, Bousfield and Wichmann 2003: 1549–1550)

The above quote captures two of the revisions to Culpeper (1996) which Culpeper, Bousfield and Wichmann (2003) propose – that is:

1. the need to better account for context, which includes looking for an explanation for impoliteness that moves beyond the level of the single utterance, and
2. the need to consider speaker intention.

Culpeper, Bousfield and Wichmann also highlight a third revision: the need to take account of prosodic clues when determining whether impoliteness has, in fact, taken place.[7] Historical data does not provide us with prosodic information, of course. Consequently, I will only discuss the need to (1) better account for context and (2) consider speaker intention in more detail in Section 2.1.1. This section will also pick up on Culpeper's (2005) own further revisions to his original definition of impoliteness, including his addition of an "off-record" impoliteness strategy. In addition, I will discuss Bousfield's (this volume) critique of Culpeper's (2005) revisions and his simplification of the six impoliteness super-strategies to two only: "on record impoliteness" and "off record impoliteness".

2.1.1. The difficulties of (de-)coding impoliteness: A closer look at the super-strategies

A number of researchers have criticised some of the individual super-strategies that are meant to capture im/politeness. Mills (2003: 14), for example, argues that one of the super-strategies for promoting social harmony – that of banter (or mock impoliteness) – can be manipulated in context so that, although superficially non-serious, it is actually "closer to [the speaker's] true feelings" than perceived to be by the hearer and, in consequence, is surreptitiously face damaging. Conversely, acts that seem to be overt *attacks* on face may not be taken to be such in context (Mills 2003: 136). Mills goes on to state that impoliteness should therefore be seen for what it is – "a very complex assessment of intentions and not a simple either-or category, as some theorists seem to suggest" (2003: 14). She also emphasises that, given the tendency of impoliteness to "escalate" (Culpeper 1996: 355), we should view it in a cumulative way (rather than at the level of the single utterance). Mills' (2003) criticisms raise a number of important issues in my view, but I want to focus here (and in subsequent sections) on three in particular. They are:

1. whether we should automatically equate the occurrence of certain super-strategies in a given context with the occurrence of impoliteness,
2. whether the super-strategies (highlighted by Culpeper and others) can be in operation simultaneously, and
3. whether identifying the cumulative effect of impolite acts might help us to better identify what constitutes a threat to face in a given community of practice.

In respect to the first issue, it is worth noting that Culpeper, Bousfield and Wichmann's (2003) own revisions to Culpeper (1996) make much of speaker intent: they define impoliteness as "communicative strategies *designed* to attack face, and thereby cause social conflict and disharmony" (2003: 1546, my italics). As if to emphasise the point even further, they also spell out the overlap between their definition and the first of Goffman's (1967: 14) "three types of actions which constitute a threat to face", i.e. "the offending person may appear to have acted maliciously and spitefully, with the *intention* of causing open insult" (my emphasis). However, it's also worth noting that Culpeper (2005) has since identified a number of weaknesses in the 2003 definition, which he suggests are occasioned by an assumption that face-attack will (automatically) "cause social conflict and disharmony" and a failure to adequately account for what the hearer is doing. Following Tracy and Tracy (1998), Culpeper (2005) thus offers a revised definition:

> Impoliteness comes about when: (1) the speaker communicates face-attack intentionally, or (2) the hearer perceives and/or constructs behaviour as intentionally face-attacking, or a combination of (1) and (2). (Culpeper 2005: 38)

According to Culpeper (2005), the key aspect of this revised definition is that it makes clear that impoliteness is constructed in the interaction between *speaker* and *hearer* (i.e. the dynamics of interaction in context become crucial). He then goes on to suggest that the prototypical instance of impoliteness probably involves both (1) and (2); the speaker communicating face-attack intentionally and the hearer perceiving/constructing it as such. That said, other permutations of (1) and (2) are possible:

> Face-attack may be intentionally communicated but fail to find its mark in any way, or, conversely, the hearer may perceive or construct intentional face-attack on the part of the speaker, when none was intended. (Culpeper 2005: 39)

Some researchers are not completely satisfied with Culpeper's (2005) revisions. For example, Bousfield (this volume) fears that Culpeper's idea that "[im]politeness is not unintentional" could be construed as contradicting the idea that a hearer can "construct intentional face-attack on the part of the speaker, when none was intended" (Culpeper 2005: 37, 39). Bousfield is also suspicious of Mills' (2003) assertion that utterances can be surreptitiously face-damaging. Indeed, he contends that we should only speak about "impoliteness" in relation to "intentionally gratuitous and conflictive face-threatening acts (FTAs) that are purposefully performed" (this volume: 132). This includes acts that:

1) [are] unmitigated in contexts where such mitigation is expected/required and/or,
2) [utilise] deliberate aggression, that is, … the face threat [is] intentionally exacerbated, "boosted", or maximised in some way to heighten the face damage inflicted (Bousfield 2007a: 7).

In essence, then, Bousfield is arguing that real (or "successful") impoliteness is marked not just by intention on the part of the speaker, but, rather, the intention of the speaker must also be understood by those in a receiver role (Bousfield 2007b, this volume). Put simply, there cannot be a mismatch between the perspectives of the speaker and hearer(s) (cf. Culpeper 2005). If we explore the above characteristics in detail, we find that (2) captures the *markedness* characteristic of impoliteness highlighted by relational theorists such as Locher (2004) and Watts (2003), and (1) shares similarities with Culpeper's (1996) "withholding politeness" strategy.

Bousfield (this volume: 138) goes on to reduce Culpeper's (1996, 2005) super-strategies to two only – i.e. "on record impoliteness" and "off record impoliteness". Bousfield defines the former as involving an interactant *explicitly* and unambiguously attacking the face of another, in a Goffman (1955, 1967) sense. As such, it appears to share some similarities with Culpeper's (1996) bald-on-record impoliteness strategy, even though Bousfield is critical of the latter's viability. That said, it is also meant to subsume the positive and negative super-strategies (Bousfield, personal correspondence). Bousfield's "off record impoliteness" also shares similarities with Culpeper's (2005) off-record super-strategy. Indeed, he quotes from Culpeper's (2005) definition to explain the latter:

... the threat or damage to an interactant's face is conveyed indirectly by way of an implicature ... and can be cancelled (e.g. denied, or an account/postmodification/ elaboration offered, etc.) but ... "one attributable intention clearly outweighs any others" (Culpeper 2005: 44) given the context in which it occurs. (Bousfield, this volume: 138)

However, Bousfield's understanding of off record impoliteness now subsumes Culpeper's "sarcasm" meta-strategy, even though the latter is a second-order (rather than a first-order) principle, according to Culpeper.

2.1.2.   "Impoliteness" as a sub-category of "verbal aggression"

Bousfield's insistence that "successful" impoliteness *has to be co-constructed* (i.e. intended and also perceived as "impoliteness") is markedly different from that proposed in Culpeper, Bousfield and Wichmann (2003). For Bousfield and his co-writers go as far as suggesting that a particular impoliteness strategy might occur "frequently" in the 2003 paper and still not be perceived as being impolite in some contexts (Culpeper, Bousfield and Wichmann 2003: 1576).

In my view, Bousfield's new stance allows him to side-step an accusation that has been levelled at the other Culpeper-inspired models, namely, that the impoliteness strategies they outline are, in fact, strategies for the *aggravation* of (or *non-attendance* to) face, which can (but may not necessarily) lead to "impoliteness" in the lay sense of the term (Locher and Watts 2005). This is important, as there has been a concern over labelling within im/politeness research for some time. Indeed, problems relating to terminology led Watts (2003) to propose that we distinguish between existing theories of im/politeness – which he describes as (im)politeness₂ – and 'folk' interpretations of im/politeness – which he describes as (im)politeness₁ – so that we do not fall into the trap of using im/politeness terms in a way that bear little resemblance to lay interpretations of what is (and is not) deemed to be im/polite in a given context. Yet, for me, the answer is not to abandon the Culpeper-inspired models completely but, rather, to *extend* their applicability so that they explicitly capture verbal aggression at a broader level. Let me elucidate: Culpeper, Bousfield and Wichmann (2003) draw from Goffman's (1967) three-way distinction between face threat that is *intentional*, face threat that is *incidental* and face threat that is *unintended*. They then maintain that their "impoliteness" super-strategies *only* relate to impoliteness that falls *within the intentional category* – i.e. where the intention is to cause face damage (Goffman 1967: 14; Culpeper, Bousfield and Wichmann 2003: 1550). I would contend that a better approach is to understand "impoliteness" as a sub-category of "verbal aggression", so that we can begin to use the Culpeper (1996, 2005) and Culpeper, Bousfield and Wichmann (2003) strategies to investigate *all* of

Goffman's (1967) distinctions – that is, face threat that is *intentional*, face threat that is *incidental* and face threat that is *unintended*. We would then distinguish "impoliteness" from "verbal aggression" by determining whether the linguistic behaviour in question was motivated by some *personal sense of spite*, following Culpeper, Bousfield and Wichmann (2003).

My approach – seeing impoliteness as a sub-category of verbal aggression – is conceptually similar to the approach to workplace incivility adopted by Pearson, Andersson and Wegner (2001). That is to say, both approaches are attempting to capture the point at which behaviour transgresses the norms of acceptability (as dictated by the activity type) to become *marked*[8] by "incivility" or "impoliteness".[9] That said, there are some serious terminological differences, the most obvious being our differing understanding of "aggression". Indeed, for Pearson, Andersson and Wegner (2001), "aggression" cannot be part of a workplace *norm*. Instead, it must be viewed as a type of antisocial behaviour that violates workplace norms *intentionally*, unlike "incivility" (which is ambiguous as to intent):

> ... like aggression, incivility is a deviant behaviour. In contrast to aggression [where there is "intent to harm"], incivility is less intense and ... is ambiguous as to intent to harm. (Pearson, Andersson and Wegner 2001: 1403; see also Andersson and Pearson 1999)

Using the historical courtroom context as my example, I will show that verbal aggression is not necessarily *deviant* in some professional settings and, in fact, only becomes so when the *primary* goal is to harm (i.e. cause intentional or deliberate face threat, in a Goffman 1967 sense). I will also marry the idea of courtroom participants having multiple goals (see Penman 1990) with Pearson, Andersson and Wegner's (2001) insightful comments in respect to the potential ambiguity of intent (to harm), as a means of suggesting that one may be able to deliberately manipulate the ambiguity generated by multiple goals to one's advantage when constructing (counter) crime-narratives (see, in particular, Section 3.1).

2.1.3. Re-labelling the super-strategies

As part of my approach I am advocating that we take on board the criticisms of the relational theorists such as Locher (2004) and Watts (2003) and re-label the Culpeper-inspired strategies *face-aggravating* strategies (rather than impoliteness strategies). I recognise that this re-labelling would probably be insufficient for Mills (2003) given her call for im/politeness researchers to move away from the notion of fixed categories completely and move towards the adoption of an im/politeness continuum (following Kienpointner 1997). In my defence I should acknowledge that I am attracted to the idea of an impoliteness continuum in principle. However, as far as I am aware, there is (as yet) no real agreement as to what the various points on the continuum might be, and how they, in turn, may inter-relate with other variables – such as "the degree to which institutions have routinised the use of certain types of language" (Mills 2003: 125), and the degree to which "discursive resources and identities available to participants to accomplish specific actions are [therefore] weakened or strengthened in relation to their current institutional identities" (Thornborrow 2002: 4). It is also worth remembering that, whilst a continuum would allow for a fuzziness in categorisation that Culpeper's (1996) original model does not, the latter was designed so as to allow for the addition of new strategies and the revision of existing strategies as and when necessary.

I have already discussed one example of such revision – that of Bousfield (this volume) – in some detail (but see also Section 4). Another revision that is similar to Bousfield's is that of Kryk-Kastovsky (2006: 216), who calls for a semantic/pragmatic category that can distinguish between utterances which are *overtly* impolite "by virtue of [their] literal meaning" and utterances which are *covertly* impolite, i.e. rendered impolite by the speaker and/or interpreted as such by the hearer. Kryk-Kastovsky advocates that we also adopt a "structural (syntactic)" impoliteness category (I find the terminology of this category problematic, however, as it may give one the false impression that impoliteness exists at the word or grammatical level *out of context*). Finally, as she explores two trials dating from 1685 (Oates and Lisle), she argues (rightly) that we need to be sensitive to the socio-historical context. As Kryk-Kastovsky and I both study "impoliteness" in the historical English courtroom, I will be evaluating some of her findings in relation to my own in Section 3 whilst also suggesting some further revisions to the Culpeper-inspired super-strategies.

Revisions offer one means of coping with fuzziness. In addition, we might also consider capturing potential fuzziness by allowing for the concurrent operation of the various super-strategies, as Culpeper, Bousfield and Wichmann (2003) and Bousfield (2004) do when studying impoliteness in extended, real-life interactions. Bousfield's (2004) work, in particular, suggests that the identification of the cumulative effect of impolite acts can help us to better identify what constitutes a threat to face in a given activity type as well as the extent to which threats to face differ from one activity type to the other. Of course, as soon as we begin to study how impoliteness is enacted in particular activity types, we must take heed of other "important aspect[s] of the evaluation of utterances as polite or impolite" (Mills 2003: 125) – such as the extent to which the perceived (institutional) norms of interaction within a given activity type allow for verbal aggression and, by so doing, effectively constrain the impoliteness potential of such behaviour. When exploring historical data, we also need to be sensitive to possible diachronic differences in (institutional) norms of interaction and/or evolutionary changes to those norms (see Section 1 and also Archer 2005).[10] The most important aspect to consider, then, is probably whether the participants within a particular activity type deem that impoliteness has taken place (given the context and, more specifically, the legal sanctioning of conflictive talk) – which means that we need to ascertain how the participants themselves assess the interaction(s) of which they are a part (Locher and Watts 2005).

2.2. Measuring participant perception

Culpeper, Bousfield and Wichmann (2003: 52) point out (rightly) that most "interlocutors do not wear their intentions on their sleeves". However, they also highlight an argument put forward by Grimshaw (1990) with respect to conflictive talk, which suggests that one *can* reconstruct the "plausible" intentions of speakers, given adequate evidence:

> [Whilst, most] researchers ... [would accept] that what is in people's heads is accessible neither to analysts nor to interlocutors (nor even, ultimately, fully accessible to those whose behaviour is under investigation) ... most of them ... argue ... that the availability of ethnographic context *and* of an optimally complete behaviour record permits analysts to make such inferences and attributions which are 'for-the-most-practical-purposes' ... no less plausible than those of actual participants. ... [That is to say] the disambiguation process is [purported to be roughly the same as] that which we ourselves employ in interaction. (Grimshaw 1990: 281)

At the risk of further pointing out the obvious, it is worth remembering that participants within a particular activity type may differ in respect to their perceptions as to whether impoliteness has taken place. Such a *mismatch* between speaker intent and receiver understanding would probably lead Bousfield (this volume) to argue that we are dealing with "rudeness", conflicting world views and/or different schematic expectations rather than impoliteness in such instances. In contrast, Culpeper's (2005: 36–40) revised definition allows for the possibility that "the hearer may perceive or construct intentional face-attack on the part of the speaker, when none was intended". I would argue, then, that Culpeper's (2005) approach is likely to prove more useful in a courtroom context – if we allow for the fact that the Culpeper-inspired models can capture "verbal aggression" at a broader level (i.e. linguistic behaviour that, although not motivated by some personal sense of *spite*, can result in offence being taken) as well as "impoliteness" (i.e. linguistic behaviour motivated by some personal sense of *spite*) (see Section 2.1.2). Indeed, the courtroom is an especially interesting activity type in respect to differing perceptions of verbal aggression as research suggests that defendants, in particular, come to court expecting to have their behaviour questioned and, as such, frequently anticipate accusations before they are made and, interestingly, offer defences to apparently neutral questions (Atkinson and Drew 1979). Likewise, witnesses are said to assume their questioners really want them to confirm the *version* of the truth they are constructing for the jury, which may help to explain why (like defendants) their answers can be defensive, evasive and ambiguous, even when their questioners are not intending to be overtly confrontational (Danet et al. 1980).

2.3. The barristers' use of questions as a means of "controlling" the evidence

I do not mean to suggest that barristers do not use "conducive" questions, however, for there is plentiful evidence to suggest that they are very aware of the importance of designing their question(s) in such a way as to restrict what respondents do in an answer (cf. Wartenberg 1990) – not least because of the need to communicate their view of what happened indirectly, through testimony they elicit; officially, they may not assert, claim, or attempt to persuade during questioning in the modern English courtroom – they may only ask (Atkinson and Drew 1979: 66; Danet et al. 1980: 223).

Interestingly, a number of linguistics researchers have been able to identify patterns of use from their studies of the modern courtroom, which suggest a "continuum of control" (where open-ended *wh*-questions represent the least amount of control and tag questions represent the most amount of control: see Woodbury 1984: 212; Luchjenbroers 1997: 482). As I have shown in Archer (2005), this "continuum of control" is also relevant to the historical courtroom (but see Section 3.1). More recently, Kryk-Kastovsky (2006) has suggested that the powerful participants within historical trials also utilised the more "controlling" question-types (i.e. *yes/no*, declaratives and tag questions) to attack the positive and/or negative face of their interlocutors by confusing or intimidating them and/or by casting doubt on their testimony. In Section 3, I undertake my own analysis of historical English courtroom data, and use this opportunity to argue that, whilst Kryk-Kastovsky (2006: 223) is right to signal that the questioning strategies of the judges and the lawyers "constitute[d] an instrument of power", she is wrong to assume that these potentially face-aggravating strategies were "covertly impolite", in the main. Indeed, I will suggest that perceptions of impoliteness having taken place were dependent, to some extent, on the institutionally-sanctioned roles of the "interrogator" and the "interrogated" (to use Kryk-Kastovsky's terms) and the type of examination sequence(s) in which they were engaged. As such, I will be attending to the two central aims of this chapter: 1. the relationship between individual assessments of face-damage and the legal "sanctioning" of the use of verbal aggression by certain participant groups, and 2. the relationship between power and impoliteness in this particular setting.

3. Questioning strategies in the historical English courtroom: "Verbally aggressive" and/or "impolite"?

As previously established, Kryk-Kastovsky (2006: 223, 227) believes that questions not only provided a means of controlling witnesses in the historical courtroom (cf. Section 2.3) but also a means of threatening their face and, by so doing, engage in impoliteness. By way of example, she provides the following adjacency pair between a witness, Mrs Ireland, and the Lord Chief Justice (LCJ) from the Trial of Titus Oates (1685):

(1)
L.C.J.   And you are sure he went out of Town the Saturday after?
Mrs. *A. Ireland.* Yes, I am sure he went out of Town then; for I asked him, why he would go on a Saturday? And he told me, he would go but to Standen that Night.

In respect to the above, Kryk-Kastovsky claims that:

> It is obvious how by virtue of its form the judge's question forces Mrs. Ireland to provide an answer where the choice is restricted to two options only. Additionally, its form starting with the *you are sure* clause casts doubt on the truth of the whole proposition, i.e., it constitutes a face threatening act directed at Mrs. Ireland's negative face (an instance of covert impoliteness). However, this did not confuse Mrs. Ireland, who was in control of her emotions and, despite the judge's impoliteness ... spoke exactly to the point. (Kryk-Kastovsky 2006: 226)

Whilst I accept there are face issues at work here (i.e. that Mrs Ireland's *linguistic* freedom is restricted), it does not follow that the Lord Chief Justice was *automatically* being impolite. Indeed, we could merely see this as an example of a judge exercising his *right* to seek clarification as to the correctness of the information the witness had given. As such, any perceived face damage would be *incidental* as opposed to *intentional*; that is to say, an unplanned "by-product" of the interaction as opposed to a malicious and spiteful act (Goffman 1967: 14). I would also contend that Kryk-Kastovsky's (2006: 226) comment respecting Mrs Ireland is a little premature, given that it seems to be based on one adjacency pair. Indeed, it is equally possible that Mrs Ireland's response was not occasioned by a desire to confirm apparently dubious testimony (and, by so doing, protect her positive face) but, rather, was prompted by a belief that the judge might find such information useful. I highlight the above so that I can emphasise the importance of having sufficient evidence to interpret face attack as intentional (and thus impolite as opposed to verbally aggressive: see Section 2.1.2). I would also add that, prior to investigating impoliteness in a (historical) courtroom, we should determine whether we believe every question in the courtroom serves a coercive function and, by so doing, effectively forces respondents to adopt a defensive counter-position.

3.1.   Do courtroom questions always serve a coercive function?

In Archer (2005: 154), I take the view that questions can be used *coercively*, i.e. they can be used to demand specific information (cf. Walker 1987: 59–60) in a way that restricts the participants' action-environment (Wartenberg 1990) and, by so doing, take on additional "controlling" and, on occasion, "accusing" functions (see Harris 1984b: 6, 22). However, I argue against our assuming that questions are always used *coercively* – even when their form suggests that a high level of *conducivity* is likely (cf. (negative) *yes/no*, declaratives and tag questions). For example, in the following extract taken from the Trial of Francis Francia (1716), the defence lawyer (Hungerford) asked a witness for the defence (Mary Meggison) a couple of *yes/no* questions before being "interrupted" by the Attorney General (i.e. one of the main prosecution lawyers):

(2)

Mr. *Hungerford.*	Do you know of any Offers that were made to the Prisoner, and by whom?
Meggison.	Upon the Twenty Eighth of *September* last I was in Mr. *Francia's* Room, and Mr. *Buckley* came in and told him he should be tried suddenly, and there were a great many Witnesses against him; and he would swear against him, because, says he, you have cheated my Master of Five Guineas, and won't swear against Mr. *Harvey.*
Mr. *Hungerford.*	Was you in the Room then?
Meggison.	I sat upon a little Box at the Bed's Feet, and it was so dark he could not see me.
Mr. *Att. General.*	How came you to Newgate.
Meggison.	I have been a great many times in *Newgate.*
Mr. *Att. General.*	You dwell there sometimes, don't you?
Meggison.	No, I never did.
Mr. *Att. General.*	Are you a married Woman?

As well as demonstrating the blurring of examination-in-chief and cross-examination sequences I highlighted earlier (Section 1), this particular extract provides a useful example of the different ways in which questions were interpreted by the same witness, depending on whether she viewed her questioner as *friendly* or not (Section 2.2). Indeed, as a witness for the defence, Meggison was happy to provide the information requested by the defence lawyer (Hungerford), even though the interrogatives addressed to her requested quite specific information and, by so doing, restricted her *linguistic* action-environment (Wartenberg 1990). Moreover, she supplied information in her initial response that appeared to confirm previous testimony given by the defendant (i.e. that Townshend had not given the defendant money out of generosity: see Section 3.2 for a discussion of this interaction).

Meggison was then questioned by the Attorney General, who initially asked a seemingly innocuous question: "How came you to Newgate?". Although an information-seeking question, Meggison appeared to infer an incriminatory element, and thereby provided a rather evasive answer, "I have been a great Many times in Newgate". The Attorney General immediately picked up on Meggison's "evasiveness" in his second question to her, as a means of implying that she had been an inmate at (rather than a visitor to) Newgate: "You dwell there sometimes, don't you?". When Meggison refuted the Attorney General's insinuation, he asked another seemingly innocuous question. However, because of the questions that had preceded it, its function was clear – to once again call into question Meggison's reputation, by suggesting that she associated with men who were not her husband.

As previously highlighted (Section 2.1.1), Culpeper, Bousfield and Wichmann's (2003) definition of impoliteness draws upon Goffman's (1967) intentional category to argue that impoliteness must involve some personal sense of spite. Such a definition is problematic in this particular context, however, as we could easily argue that the Attorney General was acting *within his sanctioned role* rather than out of some *personal* sense of spite (such as an intensely *personal* dislike of Meggison and/or her behaviour). As such, we should probably see any face damage that arose as *incidental* (Goffman 1967). Yet there is a sense in which the Attorney General, in having multiple goals, was strategically manipulating the ambiguity inherent within *intent to harm* as identified by Pearson, Andersson and Wegner (2001) (see Section 2.1.2). Indeed, whilst the Attorney General's *primary* goal may not have been to "insult" Meggison, he was nevertheless attacking her "image of self delineated in terms of approved social attributes" (Goffman 1967: 5) in an attempt to characterise her as a loose woman and, by so doing, damage her effectiveness as a witness. Not surprisingly, Meggison appeared to be offended. Although there are some problems with therefore seeing this as an *incidental* offence (in Goffman's 1967 sense of the term), the resulting face threat has more in common with this category than with "insults" which, by their very nature, are "malicious" and "spiteful" (Goffman 1967: 14).

Given this type of linguistic behaviour typifies cross-examination sequences (in both modern and historical courtroom contexts), I am advocating that we can make better use of the Culpeper-inspired super-strategies by seeking to identify "verbal aggression" rather than "impoliteness" – which, in this instance, was achieved by an "off record" strategy, that is to say, the threat or damage to Meggison's face was conveyed indirectly by way of several implicatures that, if necessary, could be cancelled (via a denial) and/or modified via an account, postmodification and/or elaboration (Culpeper 2005; Bousfield, this volume; see also Section 3.2). However, our identification of "verbal aggression" in this way would need to take account of the fuzziness/overlap between Goffman's (1967) intentional and incidental categories, occasioned by the difficulty in identifying any *personal* sense of spite (see Section 4).

3.2.   Face-damaging activities between defendants and witnesses: Did it equate to "impoliteness"?

As the previous section has revealed, the context of the historical courtroom could affect the conducivity of questions to the extent that even apparently non-conducive questions took on additional "accusing" and "controlling" functions (cf. Harris 1984b: 6, 22). This does not mean that all question-types automatically became conducive, of course. Indeed, example (2) above suggests that the controlling capacity of questions (in the historical courtroom) had more to do with the *institutionally/legally inscribed roles* of the participants and the *type* of examination sequence in which they (believed they) were engaged than any inherent characteristic of the question-types themselves (see also Archer 2005).

As extracts like example (2) are plentiful in my historical trial data, it is nevertheless tempting to conclude that questions were a marker of power in the historical courtroom, as they are in the modern courtroom (Walker 1987). But we must remember that defendants were allowed to ask questions of witnesses during the period under investigation. That said, defendants were not always able to question witnesses directly; rather, as demonstrated by the following extract taken from the Trial of Edward Coleman (1678), they sometimes had to ask their questions *indirectly* through the judge. As example (3) also highlights, their role was such that they often struggled to procure "answers" that would help them prove their version of events and, by so doing, their innocence:

(3) [Context: The prisoner, Edward Coleman, had been asked whether he had any questions to ask the witness, Oates, by the judge]

Prisoner. Pray ask Mr. Oates, whether he was not as near to me as this Gentleman is, because he speaks of his eyes being bad?

Mr. Oats. I had the disadvantage of a Candle upon my eyes; Mr. Coleman stood more in the dark.

Prisoner. He names several times that he met with me in this place and that place, a third and fourth place about business.

Mr. Oats. He was altered much by his Perriwig in several Meetings, and had several Perriwiggs, and a Perriwigg doth disguise a man very much; but when I heard him speak, then I knew him to be Mr. Coleman.

I have included this particular extract as a further demonstration of how a Culpeper-inspired approach may be used to identify verbal aggression more generally, and not just impoliteness (see Section 2.1.2). Notice, for example, that Coleman's first "question" to Oates appeared to have a "confirmation-seeking" function (i.e. that Oates was physically close to Coleman at the particular time in question). However, it was worded in a way that suggests Oates had not been honest in his previous testimony respecting his ability to clearly identify Coleman. Put simply, Coleman was indirectly accusing Oates of lying (and, given Oates's indictment for perjury in 1685, Coleman was probably right).[11] Given the multiple functions in evidence, we can only really highlight the *possibility that one of Coleman's subsidiary goals was to attack Oates's positive face, albeit indirectly*. I would therefore advocate that we understand this particular utterance as an example of an *indirect face attack that was incidental in nature*; that is to say, its *primary goal* was not to wilfully cause face damage (i.e. undertaken "out of [some personal sense of] spite") but face damage nevertheless arose as an "anticipated by-product" of an action that was performed (i.e. "*in spite* of its [potentially] offensive consequences" (Goffman 1967: 14, my emphasis; see also Section 3.1.

In my view, the indirectness/subsidiary nature of the goals in examples (2) and (3) were far from accidental; rather, they were occasioned by a perceived need to be able to deny any implicature that was deemed to be potentially damaging to one's own (counter) crime-narrative and/or self-incriminatory in some way. The need for deniability is even greater in other conflictive activity types, of course (e.g. police interrogations). Consequently, we may want to revise present "off record" strategy definitions when seeking to capture verbal aggression (as opposed to *intentional* impoliteness), so that "one attributable intention" does *not* have to "*clearly* outweigh any others" (Culpeper 2005: 44, my emphasis).[12]

If we analysed the first adjacency pair in example (3) using a relational approach (i.e. from the perspective of the hearer), I would contend that the result would be the same (i.e. that impoliteness had *not* taken place). By way of illustration, although Oates immediately attended to Coleman's face-damaging accusation by providing an account for his not seeing clearly, it is noticeable that he did not engage in any metatalk and/or behaviour that signalled he found Coleman's questions to be *impolite* (compare Meggison's responses in example (2) and, in particular, her strong denial of "No, I never did", which suggests that offence was taken). I would also contend that our conclusion that this is not impoliteness holds when we consider how this particular interaction *panned out* over the rest of the exchange (Culpeper, Bousfield and Wichmann 2003). Notice, for example, that Coleman's next utterance, "He names several times that he met with me in this place and that place, a third and fourth place about business", intimated that, if Oates had seen him as many times as he claimed, he should have had no problem recognising him and, at the same time, affirmed Coleman's earlier point that Oates was lying. Interestingly, Oates' response to this second (albeit indirect) "accusation" appears to have had both primary and secondary goals (suggesting that lawyers were not the only participants to utilise multiple goals in the historical courtroom). The primary goal was one of *explaining* and was non-face-threatening: Oates explained how Coleman's appearance was altered through his wearing of periwigs to the extent that it was only when Oates heard Coleman speak, that he was certain of his identity. In contrast, the subsidiary goals were inter-related and face-threatening in nature (but was not equivalent to impoliteness): Oates wanted the judge (and jury) to see Coleman's changing of wigs as a deliberate attempt to disguise himself and, in turn, that it was Coleman rather than himself who was being dishonest.

3.3.   *Identifying the power variables in operation in the historical courtroom*

The last utterance in example (3), "He was altered much by his Perriwig [. . .]", ably demonstrates that a (defendant's) legally-sanctioned right to ask questions was not the same as having the power to "compel responsive answers" from respondents in the historical courtroom (cf. Walker 1987: 58). I would argue, therefore, that questions could only be used to exercise control in the historical courtroom when asked by participants who not only had *a legally-sanctioned right to ask them,* but also a *recognised position of authority within the courtroom* itself. In other words, when three of French and Raven's (1959) five classifications of power – "expert power", "legitimate power" and "coercive power" – were in operation; that is to say, the questioners had specialist knowledge/expertise, their authority allowed them to prescribe or request certain things from others, and they could control negative outcomes by virtue of their role (see also Fairclough 1989; Wartenberg 1990: 85).[13]

The following example, taken from Francia (1716), is one of several examples of defendants addressing "conducive" interrogative-types (i.e. declarative questions and negative polars) to witnesses, yet struggling to *control* their responses (i.e. securing the information they wanted):

(4) [Context: Lord Townshend was initially questioned by the prosecution counsel and stated how, having been informed that the prisoner, Francia, was involved in – and the "Channel" for – "a Treasonable Correspondence", he had seized his letters, and examined him on two occasions regarding their contents. The defence counsel, including Mr Ward, then took over the questioning.]

Mr. *Ward.*	I desire to ask your Lordship whether you heard that Declaration read over to him?
Ld. *Townshend.*	I dare say I did.
Mr. *Ward.*	Did he not endeavour to excuse himself from signing it, till he had read it himself?
Ld. *Townshend.*	I don't remember that, I don't know that he made any Difficulty of signing it; but I am sure it could not be because he was refus'd to read it.
Prisoner.	Was not there any Reluctancy in me to sign it?
Ld. *Townshend.*	What do you mean? Have not I answer'd that already?
Prisoner.	Did not you offer me some Money to sign it?
Ld. *Townshend.*	I hope you can't say a thing of so much Infamy [.]

We cannot really make sense of Francia's conducive questions unless we first attend to Ward's negative polar to Townshend, "Did he not endeavour to excuse himself from signing it [...]?", which assumed – and asked Townshend to confirm – that Francia did not want to sign the written account of his examinations until he had read them. Significantly, Townshend's response to Ward referred back to an accusation that Francia's defence counsel had made to another witness: that Francia had not been permitted to read the account (see Archer 2005: 254–256 for a discussion of this interaction). Presumably, Townshend reintroduced this evidence to emphasise his belief that Francia was neither "refus'd to read" nor reluctant to sign the account. I would argue, then, that the witness felt that it was important to protect his own face at this point in the cross-examination.[14] Notice that the defendant's first negative polar to Townshend, "Was not there any Reluctancy in me [..]?", picked up on Townshend's response to Ward to intimate there was indeed "Reluctancy" on his part that he believed Townshend could confirm. Effectively, Francia was signalling to the court – and, in particular, to the jury (as they would ultimately decide upon his guilt or innocence) – that Townshend was not telling the truth. Townshend's response to Francia, "What do you mean? Have I not answered that already?", suggests some annoyance on his part at being asked such a question by the defendant. In addition, I would argue that Townshend interpreted Francia's implicature (that he was in some way withholding information) to be a deliberate (i.e., intentional) attack on his character (see Goffman's 1967: 5 notion of self-image, i.e. "an image of self delineated in terms of approved social attributes"). But Francia ignored the witness's rhetorical question and, instead, asked a second negative polar, "Did not you offer me some Money to sign it", which contained another face-damaging accusation: that Townshend had attempted to bribe Francia into signing his examination/confession.

The use of damaging presuppositions is well-documented in the courtroom. As evidenced in the above extract, they also play an important face-aggravating purpose. Indeed, this becomes especially acute when one participant, as in this case, refuses to accept the denials (or alternate view) of the other and/or there is a clash of goals (in respect to expected outcomes). Townshend's response, at this point, was not to enter into a verbal duel with Francia, however, but to intimate that the accusation was too scandalous to be taken seriously: "I hope you can't say such a thing of so much Infamy", and then address a 177–word utterance to the whole court:

(5)

Ld. Townshend.   After he had been examin'd, he complain'd to me of the Misery he was reduc'd to, that his Wife and Family must starve, and represented himself as if he were at loss for a Supper: I told him he had nothing to hope for, or any room to expect any Favour, but by making a clear Confession. He went on begging, and said that his Wife was starving; I do not certainly know whether it was the very Night that he sign'd his Confession or not; but I am sure it was not for that, but in pure Alms, and because he begg'd so hard, I put my Hand in my Pocket, and gave him three, four, or five Guineas, I know not which, in Charity; and it was what I never could refuse any Man that apply'd to me in that manner, and begg'd so hard. He said his Brother would not look upon him, because he was taken up for High Treason, and he desir'd me to give him something in Charity, which I did.

As highlighted previously, the relational approach to impoliteness makes much of the interactant's *perception(s) of the communicator's intentions*. Indeed, Locher and Watts (this volume: 80) maintain that "the uptake of a message is as important if not more important than the utterer's original intention". I would contend, therefore, that Townshend's "Infamy" outburst provides us with a clear example of impoliteness from a relational perspective.

Locher and Watts (this volume: 88) also draw upon the notion of "framing" to show how interactants will often construct each other in a deliberately conflictive light. I believe this notion provides a particularly useful means of understanding Townshend's long address to the jury for, although the primary goal of the address was an "informing" one (i.e. informing the Court why he had given Francia some money), Townshend was ultimately signalling that Francia was the sort who "begg'd so hard" that *good people* like Townshend felt compelled to give him "Charity". In response, Francia chose to *frame* Townshend as someone who was not generous, but, rather, had ulterior motives for giving Francia the money:

(6)

Prisoner.   I desire to ask you whether you ever bestow'd on any body else the like Charity? Pray my Lord, name the Man under your Examination, you ever gave five Guineas to before?

As before, I am happy to classify example (6) as an "off record" strategy signalling verbal aggression, if we first amend the need to see "... one attributable intention" as "clearly outweigh[ing] any others" (Culpeper 2005: 44). That said, the fact that the Lord Ch. Baron answered on behalf of Townshend may signal that Francia's linguistic strategy was deemed to be marked in some way by the judge (Watts 2003). Indeed, Francia was instructed to "Propose [his] Question to the Court" and, when he did so, the judge made it clear to him that (as far as he was concerned) Townshend had "acted out of Charity".

The Trial of Charles I (1649) provides us with another interesting example of framing as a face-aggravation strategy (Locher and Watts, this volume). It occurred at the point that Charles was being critical of the Court he faced: he had stated that he "value[d] it not a Rush", and could not "acknowledge a new *Court* that [he had] never heard of before". Significantly, when he sought to be "give[n] time", so that he could explain why he could not answer his charge, he was interrupted. The king appeared to take offence at this, for he told the Lord President that he "ought not to interrupt" him. The Lord President's response, however, was to *frame* Charles as a "Delinquent":

(7)

Lord President.   [...] you may not be permitted to fall into those discourses; you appear as a Delinquent, you have not acknowledged the authority of the Court, the Court craves it not of you, but once more they command you to give your positive Answer

Notice that the Lord President made explicit reference to the intended pragmatic force of his "command" in addition to *calling* the king a *name* (see Culpeper's 1996 positive impoliteness strategy). When used by dominant speakers, such "metapragmatic acts" are thought to "effectively remove any possibility of 'negotiating communicative intent'" (Thomas 1986: 194). Indeed, the power relationship is such that the interlocutor is meant to back down (or at best remain silent). But Charles opted to "risk aggravating the confrontation" (Thomas 1986: 195) by requesting that he be excused from having to answer, because to do so would "alter the fundamental Laws of the Kingdom". As a direct result, the Lord President restricted the king's freedom of action (Wartenberg 1990) both *verbally and physically*, by informing him that he would not be allowed to speak until he pleaded, and forcibly removing him from the courtroom.

It is worth noting that participants who enjoyed "expert power" and "legitimate" power (French and Raven 1959) were also occasionally censured for *inappropriate* behaviour (Watts 2003). By way of illustration, in the Trial of Christopher Layer (1722), one of the defence lawyers, Mr. Hungerford, tried to insist that his opposite number should "not go into Overt-Acts committed in any other County" as a means of preventing the prosecution lawyer from admitting evidence that was detrimental to his client's case.[15] Although the use of "objection tactics" (to give them their legal label) is thought to have been on the increase during the eighteenth century (Landsman 1990: 543–547), the judge's response here would seem to suggest that he was either not used to – or did not appreciate – such adversarial innovation. Indeed, he appeared to think that Hungerford was impinging on his role as judge:

(8)

Ld. Ch. Jus.   Sure never any Thing was like this! It is our Province to give Directions, and we think it not proper to interrupt the King's Counsel, but that they should proceed in their own Method: You shall be heard as long as you please, when you come to make your Observations.

Interestingly, the prosecution counsel cleverly used the judge's unease to their advantage by immediately complaining about the prisoner's behaviour in respect to "talk[ing] privately with the Jury" or "to his Counsel so loud, that the Jury may easily hear every Word". The insinuation was clear: the defendant was trying to influence the jury. As such behaviour was "inappropriate", the judge immediately addressed a further instruction to Hungerford – "He must not speak so loud" – which appeared to contain an implicit criticism (that Hungerford was not sufficiently controlling his defendant), and, as such, was damaging to Hungerford's positive face (Culpeper, Bousfield and Wichmann 2003). Like most of the lawyers in the trial data under discussion, Hungerford appeared to appreciate the importance of "maintaining" – and where necessary, "repairing" any perceived damage to – the face of the judges, even if that meant backgrounding his own (and/or his client's) face wants. Consequently, he was very quick to apologise to the judge. That said, he immediately sought to protect his own face wants from further damage after making the apology (in a way that served to damage his client's face still further): he assured the judge that Francia had received "no Encouragement ... for any such Conduct" from the defence team and would not do so.

I would argue, based on examples (7) and (8), that the most powerful professionals in the historical courtroom – the judges – were the final arbiters on whether impoliteness had taken place. And it would seem that they were happy to allow other "professional" participant groups to engage in verbal aggression techniques – as long as they (and/or their clients) stayed within institutional parameters. Yet they would often censure the defendants for employing similar verbal strategies to the lawyers (for example, providing a counter crime-narrative in a way that intimated that previous witnesses had been less-than-truthful). This is not meant to imply that some individual defendants and, indeed, witnesses did not experience personal face damage, because they obviously did (see, for example, my earlier discussions of examples [2] and [4]). Rather, I am suggesting, firstly, that their own personal assessment was usually superseded by the judges' assessment and, by implication, the institutional assessment and, secondly, that their lack of power (and, in most cases, lack of expertise) was such that they could not easily complain and/or achieve some sort of face repair (French and Raven 1959).

One exception to this was Townshend, of course. It's worth noting that Townshend was able to successfully utilise his dual strategy of appealing to the judges/jury and challenging/opposing the evidence given by the defence. It is difficult to know for certain why Townshend was as successful as he was, but he was undoubtedly aided by his occupation as the Secretary of State, which (as well as affording him status in the eyes of the judges) would have meant that he had a familiarity with courtroom procedure that many other witnesses and defendants did not. I would suggest, then, that the issue of "verbal aggression" versus "impoliteness" is also important when one considers the apparent differences in attitudes both within and between the participant groups, as occasioned by their (non-)familiarity with courtroom practices. Indeed, evidence from my trial data suggests that the judges and the lawyers had very different expectations as to what was normal (verbal) behaviour than the majority of the defendants and witnesses who were unfamiliar with courtroom procedure.

4.   Reassessing "impoliteness" in a historical courtroom context

Historical courtroom interaction typifies institutional talk in that the linguistic contributions of the various participants were determined (to a greater or lesser degree) by the roles assigned to them (Levinson 1992). Put simply, there was evidence of asymmetry – and where we find asymmetry, we will also find power.[16] This book has set itself the task of exploring the relationship between power and impoliteness in a number of settings. However, I have sought to show that, in the context of the historical courtroom, we should consider power to be an issue for verbal aggression generally, and not just one of its subcategories. Indeed, my data suggests that, in this particular context, power tended to be exerted/challenged through verbal aggression rather than impoliteness, in the main.

1To fully appreciate the difference between the two, I have advocated that we make use of *all* of Goffman's (1967) face-damaging categories, that is, face threat that is *intentional*, face threat that is *incidental* and face threat that is *unintended* (cf. Culpeper, Bousfield and Wichmann 2003). I have also suggested that we distinguish primary goals and subsidiary goals (Penman 1990), and would advocate, in addition, that we develop an *"intentionality* scale". Let me elucidate: based on the data I have analysed in this chapter, I would contend that judges from the eighteenth-century onwards "perfom[ed] actions consistent with the duties and constraints [their role] impose[d]" in a way that was similar to the adjudicator in Culpeper, Bousfield and Wichmann (2003: 1551). That is, the judge's role was increasingly becoming that of an arbiter seeking some sort of verbal and legal resolution, based on the evidence. As such, any FTAs they committed were most likely to be *incidental* in nature.[17] Although the lawyers also sought resolution, their growing involvement in constructing (counter) crime-narratives (that best fitted the evidence as they wished the jury to perceive it) meant that, whilst their primary goal may not have been to "insult", they managed to offend some of their interactants, nevertheless. In addition, some of the lawyers (and, for that matter, witnesses and defendants) appeared to utilise multiple goals in a way that deliberately problematised any perceived intent to harm (see Section 3). Consequently, whilst Goffman's (1967) *incidental* categorisation does not provide a completely adequate account for the offence caused during such interactions, I have suggested that the resulting face threat has more in common with this category than with "insults" that, by their very nature, are "malicious" and "spiteful" (Goffman 1967: 14). I believe, however, that an *intentionality scale* (which can differentiate between a strong and weak *intent to harm* in a way that takes account of the presence of multiple goals) might prove a useful means of further enhancing our understanding of the relationship between verbal aggression, its sub-category of impoliteness, and the fuzzy area that seems to exist between them (Pearson, Andersson and Wegner 2001).

One consequence of this *"misfit"* or fuzziness between the categories is that we cannot utilise Culpeper, Bousfield and Wichmann (2003) in a courtroom context, unless we first accept that "impoliteness" is actually a sub-category (albeit with fuzzy edges) of "verbal – or, in the case of written texts, linguistic – aggression" and are then explicit about the fact that the Culpeper-inspired super-strategies really capture *the aggravation of face which can (but may not necessarily) lead to impoliteness* (Locher and Watts 2005). Of course, once we do so, we can begin to distinguish "impoliteness" from "verbal aggression" by determining whether, in the first instance, the user's primary goal was to "insult", following Culpeper, Bousfield and Wichmann (2003). As much of the face damage exhibited in my trial data seems to have been achieved via presuppositions, Kryk-Kastovsky's (2006) distinction between "overt" and "covert" face-aggravating strategies also appears to be of some use in a courtroom context. Unfortunately, Bousfield's (this volume) distinction between "on record" and "off record" impoliteness is not as useful, in spite of their similarity. The reason? Bousfield's super-strategies seek to capture face damage that was intended by the speaker *and* understood as such by the receiver (see Section 2.1.2). In consequence, they can only really account for prototypical impoliteness and, as I demonstrate throughout Section 3, prototypical impoliteness was *extremely uncommon* in the (1649–1722) courtroom.

Notes

1. In response to the second point, Culpeper (2005) and Bousfield (this volume) contend that, even in cases where there is an increased level of expectation of conflictive talk, we should not assume that addressees will not experience face-damage.
2. One of the main reasons for this "blurring of the sequences" (Archer 2005: 161) was that cross-examination was still a developing discourse practice at this time.
3. The Corpus of English Dialogues was constructed by Merja Kytö, Uppsala University (with the help of Terry Walker), and Jonathan Culpeper, Lancaster University (with the help of Dawn Archer).
4. By way of illustration, Kytö and Walker (2003) compared three imprints of the trial of Charles I: A Perfect Narrative and the first and second editions of King Charls His Tryal (see pp. 231–235 for a detailed description of the process adopted).
5. The assumption that face can be "irrelevant" (see Culpeper 1996: 356) is problematic today, given the claim by some that face issues always play a role in interaction (Locher, personal correspondence).

6. Sarcasm (or mock politeness) is the opposite of banter (or mock impoliteness); that is, the desired effect is social disharmony (as opposed to social harmony).

7. Culpeper, Bousfield and Wichmann (2003: 1576) particularly focus on the attitudinal aspect (although they also explore loudness and speed of delivery), and conclude that "it is sometimes the prosody that makes an utterance impolite – giving truth to the common view that the offence lay in how something was said rather than what was said" (cf. Grice's 1975 Maxim of Manner).

8. Pearson, Andersson and Wegner (2001) prefer to use the term "deviant".

9. Notice, also, the obvious similarity with relational approaches that argue for the need to identify norms when investigating im/politeness.

10. Archer (2005) provides a detailed account of the differences between the discursive norms of the historical courtroom (1640–1760) and the discursive norms of the modern courtroom, whilst also signalling the impact that the advent of defence lawyers had upon the former.

11. Coleman was brought to trial because Oates had named him in a fictitious 'popish plot', the essence of which was that English Catholics were about to assassinate King Charles II, subvert Protestantism in England, and reconvert the Country to Romanism "by fire and sword". Although Oates was later found guilty of perjury and imprisoned, the charges were widely believed at the time and caused a great panic. Indeed, Coleman was one of 35 persons executed on the testimony of Oates.

12. See my gloss of Culpeper (2005) and Bousfield (this volume) in Section 3.1.

13. French and Raven (1959) also identify "reward" and "referent" categories, which relate to A's ability to control positive outcomes (by providing, or helping to "provide, things that B desires, and to remove or decrease things that B dislikes" (quoted in Spencer-Oatey 1992: 108)), and B's identification with and desire to become more like A, respectively.

14. Townshend's re-introduction of this evidence also serves as a useful reminder that, if we are to fully appreciate verbal aggression strategies (as utilised in a historical courtroom context), we may need to attend to interaction that did not directly involve the participant(s) we are studying. Indeed, as the English trial became more adversarial in nature, defence and prosecution lawyers began to construct their crime-narratives over a series of questioning sequences (as they do in a modern courtroom context). Like their modern counterparts, they were also beginning to ask different witnesses about the same evidence, but from a perspective which supported their own crime-narrative (see Section 3.1 and also Archer [2005: 213]).

15. In criminal law, an "overt act" is an action which might be innocent of itself. However, if it is deemed to be part of the preparation and active furtherance of a crime, it can be introduced as evidence of the defendant's participation in that crime.

16. As Foucault (1980: 142) points out, whilst "there are no relations of power without resistances", institutional power is such that it affords some more power than others.

17. The term "arbiter" implies a sense of neutrality. However, in practice, judges would sometimes assume guilt (rather than innocence) at this time. I have already found evidence for a guilty but unwilling to confess paradigm when studying the magis-

trates involved in the infamous Salem Witchcraft Trials of 1692 (see Archer 2002). Moreover, I found that this paradigm not only affected the function of the magistrates' questions – transforming many into accusations (cf. Harris 1984b) – but also impeded the magistrates' inferencing processes to the extent that they did not infer or chose to ignore evidence from the defendants that contradicted their *guilty* perspective.

Part 4. Workplace interaction

Chapter 9
Impoliteness as a means of contesting power relations in the workplace

Stephanie Schnurr, Meredith Marra and Janet Holmes

1. Introduction[1]

Politeness norms are particularly important in the workplace because so much depends on good collegial relationships and conflict avoidance. An investigation of the ways in which norms of appropriate and accepted behaviour are negotiated and instantiated in a workplace setting thus seems a very worthwhile enterprise. The importance of politeness norms is especially salient in workplace teams. In our extensive analyses of a number of teams across very different workplaces, we have identified considerable differences with regards to what counts as appropriate and unmarked verbal behaviour in interactions between team members (see Schnurr, Marra and Holmes 2007; and also Holmes and Marra 2002a, 2004; Holmes and Stubbe 2003a; Daly et al. 2004). Moreover, previous research has illustrated that there is a close connection between politeness and power (e.g. Holmes and Stubbe 2003b; Watts 2003), so that while adhering to politeness norms people may at the same time reinforce existing power relations. Challenges to the norms of accepted and appropriate behaviour, on the other hand, often constitute attempts to contest and subvert existing power relations.

In this chapter, we focus on the issue of what constitutes impolite discursive behaviour in the workplace. We aim to identify and illustrate some of the ways in which people in New Zealand workplaces use impoliteness in order to challenge their superiors and to subvert existing power relations. Using a range of examples of negatively marked and inappropriate behaviours in different working teams, we illustrate that the intersection between what counts as appropriate and inappropriate is often far from clear, and requires a great deal of local contextual knowledge in its interpretation.

Despite a large amount of research on politeness (much of it with a cross-cultural focus), until recently the area of impoliteness has received relatively little attention (e.g. Culpeper 1996, 2005; Culpeper, Bousfield and Wichmann 2003; Kienpointner 1997). Since Brown and Levinson's seminal work on politeness theory, research on politeness has moved on to view linguistic politeness as a means for expressing consideration for others (e.g. Holmes 1995: 4), and to highlight the importance of the listeners' interpretation, and hence the speaker's *perceived* intention (e.g. Mills 2003; Watts 2003). Recent models regard politeness as a matter of subjective judgements about social appropriateness.

Impoliteness, by contrast has received relatively little attention from researchers, and has only recently been identified as an area of interest. Previous studies on impoliteness have identified a number of subcategories, such as motivated and unmotivated impoliteness (Kienpointner 1997; see also Mills 2003). Following Watts (2003), Culpeper (1996, 2005) mentions another category of impoliteness, 'mock impoliteness', or 'sanctioned aggressive facework' (Watts 2003: 260). This refers to impolite behaviours that are not truly impolite but reflect the shared knowledge and values of a group, and which have the effect and intention of reinforcing solidarity among group members (see also Mills 2003; Daly et al. 2004). In what follows, we will illustrate some of these concepts from our workplace data.

Linguistic politeness can be defined as discursively strategic interaction: i.e. linguistic devices (perceived as having been) used in order to maintain harmonious relations and avoid conflict with others (Kasper 1990), while impoliteness is generally understood as the use of strategies and behaviour oriented to face-attack, and likely to cause social disruption (Beebe 1995; Culpeper, Bousfield and Wichmann 2003; Tracy and Tracy 1998). However, despite these differences in meaning, politeness and impoliteness do not constitute polar opposites but should rather be viewed as points along a continuum (Mills 2003; Watts 2003). This idea has been developed in some detail by Watts (2003) and Locher (2004; see also Locher and Watts 2005) in their comprehensive framework of relational work. They describe a continuum ranging from over-polite to polite and non-polite to impolite behaviour. While most behaviours are actually unmarked (and hence constitute politic behaviour which goes unnoticed), both extremes of behaviour, overly polite as well as impolite, are marked.

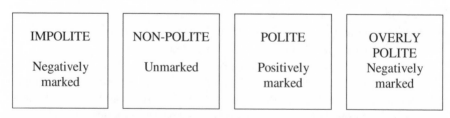

IMPOLITE	NON-POLITE	POLITE	OVERLY POLITE
Negatively marked	Unmarked	Positively marked	Negatively marked

Figure 1.   An integrated model of (im)politeness and markedness (adapted from Locher and Watts 2005: 12)

In this chapter we focus on the categories located at the ends of this continuum: impolite and overly polite behaviour (cf. Culpeper's 1996 "insincere politeness"). Both types of behaviours are described as marked and non-politic/ inappropriate. We use this continuum as a starting point and argue that not only does over-polite behaviour constitute non-politic behaviour, but in some contexts such behaviour may be perceived and conventionally thought of as impolite, whereas behaviours typically perceived as impolite (such as swearing) may actually be considered perfectly appropriate, and thus politic, in certain contexts. We focus particularly on the intersection between the categories of negatively marked, non-politic versus unmarked or positively marked politic/appropriate behaviours.

As with the notion of politeness, behaviours that are considered as inappropriate, marked and impolite vary depending on the context in which they appear. Locher (2004: 90) notes, for example, that "[p]oliteness cannot be investigated without looking in detail at the context, the speakers, the situation and the evoked norms." In other words, notions of what counts as polite and impolite are always contingent on the situational and discourse context in which the utterance occurs (Eelen 2001; Mills 2003; Watts 2003). This is as true of workplace interactions as it is of interactions in other social contexts.

Workplaces typically develop their own distinctive and preferred ways of expressing (im)politeness, and members of different workplaces tend to differ substantially in the ways in which they "do politeness", as well as the extent to which, and the ways in which, they are deliberately impolite or socially disruptive. Norms concerning what counts as unmarked and appropriate behaviour are negotiated among the members of workplaces or working groups who form distinct communities of practice (we have explored this point in great detail elsewhere; see Schnurr, Marra and Holmes 2007).

The notion of a community of practice (henceforth CofP) evolved from a social constructionist theoretical framework, i.e. a CofP approach focuses on the ways in which people construct their membership of certain groups through their language use. Eckert and McConnell-Ginet (1992) define a community of practice as:

> An aggregate of people who come together around mutual engagement in an endeavor. Ways of doing things, ways of talking, beliefs, values, power relations
> – in short, practices – emerge in the course of this mutual endeavor. (Eckert and McConnell-Ginet 1992: 464)

Wenger (1998) identifies three crucial criteria for distinguishing different CofPs, namely, mutual engagement (including regular interaction), a joint, negotiated enterprise (e.g., the shared organisational objectives of the team or group), and a shared repertoire developed over a period of time (which may include specialised jargon, routines, running jokes, etc). Using this framework highlights the importance of membership of a particular CofP in relation to distinct ways of behaving appropriately in the workplace, and in particular of adhering to and perhaps challenging prevailing norms of politeness and impoliteness.

Ways of doing politeness and impoliteness are influenced by the community within which organisational members are communicating; and conversely their ways of doing (im)politeness actively contribute to the construction of different kinds of CofP. By adhering to the norms of acceptable and appropriate behaviours negotiated among members of a CofP, interlocutors not only reinforce those norms but at the same time accept existing power relations. Conversely, by challenging these norms and by doing impoliteness, they question and attempt to subvert existing power relations. Hence, there appears to be a close relationship between doing (im)politeness and power.

Beebe (1995) comments that one of the main functions of impoliteness is to abrogate power. She notes a number of ways in which rudeness may serve to "get power" for the speaker: to appear superior, to get power over actions (which includes getting someone else to do something, and avoiding doing something yourself), and to get power in an interaction (which includes making the interlocutor talk, making the interlocutor stop talking, getting the floor, and shaping what the interlocutor tells you [or how they communicate this to you]) (Beebe 1995: 159–160). Beebe further outlines some discursive strategies which interlocutors may draw on in order to achieve these functions, such as sarcasm, turn-taking, interruptions, overlaps, and floor-management.

Of course, any struggle for power by the interlocutors needs to be understood against the background of the CofP's negotiated norms, and in particular the routinised language patterns which form "part of the politic behaviour of the social interaction reciprocally shared by participants" (Watts 2003: 156; see also Mills 2003). A failure to abide by these norms of politic behaviour (whether intended or unintentional) may lead to "the attribution of impoliteness" (Watts 2003: 201; see also Mills 2003: 135). Hence, context, and in particular the linguistic repertoire negotiated among members of CofP, is crucial in understanding the occurrence of impoliteness.

As noted earlier, we focus in this chapter on an investigation of the two ends of the continuum of relational work outlined above. By discussing a range of examples of negatively marked behaviours, we aim to illustrate that the intersection between politic and inappropriate/unpolitic behaviour is often imprecise and unclear. Some behaviours which may superficially appear to be impolite may more accurately be interpreted as unmarked, and hence politic behaviour in the context in which they appear. Other apparently polite discourse moves may in fact be perceived by participants as inappropriate or rude, and hence unpolitic and marked.

2.   Data and methodology

In order to illustrate our claims, we draw on naturalistic data collected by the Wellington Language in the Workplace (LWP) Project located at Victoria University. Over the past decade, the LWP Project has been collecting and analysing authentic workplace interactions from a range of New Zealand workplaces. With a focus on effective communicators, the research team typically identifies suitable contributors and asks them to record a range of their everyday work interactions. This data is augmented by video recordings of larger meetings in which they participate. Currently the growing corpus comprises more than 1500 (mainly spoken) interactions from over 20 organisations. The recordings cover a wide range of interaction types: short telephone calls, one-to-one informal interactions and also formal weekly meetings as well as one-off day-long meetings. The organisations who have agreed to contribute recordings include government departments, corporate organisations, small businesses, factories and a hospital ward (see Holmes and Stubbe 2003b for a fuller description of the data collection methodology and the demographic make-up of the participants and the workplaces).

The data that we explore in this chapter has been selected from three workplaces with distinctive communities of practice. These communities are: a highly profitable and productive team of workers in a Wellington factory; the IT section of a large institution; and a project team from the New Zealand headquarters of a multinational corporation. Because understanding the community's customs is crucial in the process of identifying and interpreting politic behaviour, a description of the relevant norms is provided alongside the examples in the analysis below.

In addition to the data gathered in each workplace, we collect background information on the organisations, teams and participants. This information supports our analyses by providing details about organisational hierarchies and group responsibilities. Knowledge of the respective hierarchies has been important to our discussion; because our focus is the ways in which impoliteness may be used as a means to challenge and subvert existing power relations, we focus on the use of impoliteness by subordinates which is directed upwards at their superiors.

3.   Doing impoliteness in the workplace

Perhaps unsurprisingly, we found relatively few instances of on-record explicit impoliteness in our large workplace data set. Most of the behaviour displayed by organisational members can be described as politic: it constitutes appropriate behaviour which is in accordance with the discursive and behavioural norms established among members of the various working groups (which form CofPs) where we recorded data (cf. Mills 2003).

Moreover, the majority of impolite discourse moves in our data set were produced by superiors towards their subordinates. All the same, on many occasions we classified challenging and potentially impolite behaviour displayed by superiors towards their subordinates as politic and unmarked rather than as negatively marked and impolitic, because subordinates' reactions did not provide any indication that they perceived their bosses' behaviour as marked in any way. These observations clearly illustrate the signficance of power and status in this context: it is clearly acceptable for higher-status interlocutors to employ discourse moves which are potentially more threatening and challenging, while the same behaviour is often perceived as negatively marked and inappropriate if displayed by subordinates. For the purpose of our analysis, then, we understand impoliteness as infringing the norms of appropriate behaviour that prevail in particular contexts and among particular interlocutors (cf. Mills 2005: 269–270).

The various working groups we recorded differ significantly in the ways in which members interact with each other, not only with regard to what counts as appropriate and politic behaviour, but in particular in respect to what is considered as impolite and rude behaviour. Thus, in order to account for these differences, we decided to concentrate on just two categories of impoliteness encountered in our data:

Category 1: discourse moves which appear superficially POLITE or POLITIC but which convey a very impolite, contestive or subversive message. Instances of category 1 impoliteness are utterances which seem to be polite in their form, but which clearly express impolite or rude content.

Category 2: discourse moves, which appear inherently IMPOLITE but which on closer examination, taking account of the norms negotiated among members of the work groups or communities of practice (CofPs), can be characterised as politic behaviour. Instances of category 2 impoliteness are typically restricted to the CofP in which they occur: if such utterances appeared in a different social context, they could be perceived as inappropriate and rude.

In the next section we provide examples of each of these categories and illustrate ways in which members of the various CofPs employ these two categories of impoliteness to challenge the existing power relations. In particular, we focus on the ways in which subordinates make use of a range of different strategies to realise impoliteness, thereby challenging their superiors and subverting existing power relations.

3.1.   Polite utterances with an impolite message

In this section we provide examples of discourse moves which appear superficially polite but which convey an impolite message. Our first example nicely illustrates the importance of considering the norms that prevail in a particular context in assessing appropriately politic versus inappropriately impolite behaviour. It demonstrates how even superficially very polite behaviour may sometimes constitute an instance of impoliteness in context. The example is taken from data collected in a factory involving interaction between blue-collar workers. Ginette, the team-coordinator and most senior person in the team, is speaking to her team member, Peter, over the factory's intercom system:

Example (1)[2]
Context: Wellington factory packing floor. Ginette, the team co-ordinator, radios Peter (in the control room) to update the team on the packing line situation
1. Gin.:   copy control copy control +
2. Pet.:   oh + good afternoon where have you been +
3. Gin.:   who wants to know
4. Pet.:   well we do + + +
5. Gin.:   um we're just gonna- run our fifth [product name]
6.   and see how this packaging holds if it's okay
7.   i- and then wait and we'll get back to you
8. Pet.:   **( ) thank you very much for your information**

Ginette opens an interaction with Peter with her routine formula for contacting the control room, *copy control copy control*. On the basis of his response *oh + good afternoon where have you been* (line 2), we can infer that Peter has been expecting her call. Hence, it appears that Peter's *oh + good afternoon* is not intended as a criticism, but, in the context of the following rather contestive query *where have you been,* rather expresses genuine surprise that she has not contacted him earlier. Ginette's response is equally challenging (*who wants to know,* line 3), and it nicely illustrates the typical style of interaction between members of this team. This direct and challenging interchange is perfectly normal and representative, and appropriate in tone for members of this workplace team who constitute a well-integrated CofP (see also examples [4] and [5] and Daly et al. 2004). In most white-collar workplaces in which we have recorded our data, such an exchange would almost certainly be perceived as inappropriately direct, and interpreted as highly impolite or rude. However, in the context of this factory CofP, it constitutes politic behaviour (see also Daly et al. 2004 and Newton 2004).

Interestingly, Peter's question about Ginette's whereabouts never gets answered by her. This refusal to respond to his challenge and to share information about her activities could be seen as a way of doing power. Moreover, the considerable pause after his reply to her question *well we do* (line 4) could also be interpreted as an indication of Ginette's disapproval of his questioning and a means of asserting her control. Her reply *wait and we'll get back to you* (line 7) represents a further challenge of Peter's entitlement to know where she has been. Ginette thus reinstates and asserts her power quite clearly in response to his challenge.

In this chapter, however, we draw attention to another aspect of this interaction, namely Peter's comment at the end of this interaction. In the context of normal interaction between team members in the CofP within this particular workplace, Peter's superficially polite utterance *thank you very much for your information* (line 8) can be interpreted as an instance of inappropriate and impolitic behaviour. The fact that it can be interpreted in context as almost certainly intended sarcastically (cf. Culpeper 1996) does not detract from the fact that its superficial form is hyper-polite. Sarcasm and irony are often not linguistically marked and always require attention to context and background knowledge (Barbe 1995; Seckman and Couch 1989). To any naïve listener from outside this CofP Peter appears to be expressing himself with appropriate respect to his superior. He is in fact conveying his annoyance at Ginette's failure to inform him of her activities.

As described elsewhere in more detail (Holmes and Marra 2002a; Daly et al. 2004; Holmes and Stubbe 2003b), interactions in this workplace are characterised by a generally rough and tough tone, frequent challenging humour and banter, and a large amount of swearing. On the basis of extensive contextual information, then, we can confidently classify Peter's comment as inappropriate in this context: the form of his utterance is excessively polite, i.e. overly exaggerated, so that it can only realistically be interpreted as an instance of inappropriate or impolite behaviour. Although this behaviour would certainly go unremarked in a white-collar workplace, it is decidedly marked in this blue-collar context, and in particular in the CofP of Ginette's team. So while appearing superficially polite, the content of Peter's comment can be confidently interpreted as impolite in intent: the message that Peter is in fact conveying with this remark is that Ginette should have contacted him earlier. But instead of expressing his annoyance with her behaviour overtly, he packages his critical and clearly impolite comment in a form that appears to be polite, but which in fact constitutes inappropriate, and clearly marked behaviour in this context.

This example is thus a prime example of what Watts (2003) and Locher and Watts (2005) consider negatively marked, overly-polite behaviour in their continuum of relational work: this kind of overly polite behaviour is inappropriate, exaggerated and thus negatively marked and non-politic behaviour in the factory workplace. Thus, Peter's behaviour is another example of the notion that polite and impolite behaviour are highly context dependent: not only is the intended message of his utterance impolite and challenging, but despite the fact that his remark looks politic at first glance, once one takes account of the norms of the context, and in particular the discursive norms negotiated among members of this particular CofP, it becomes clear that it constitutes marked and inappropriate behaviour.

Our second example occurred at the opening stages of a regular management meeting in the IT section of a large white collar organisation. Some participants would habitually arrive late at these meetings, and those present would wait for them before opening the meeting. In the interviews which were conducted with individuals after collecting the recorded data, some participants reported that they found this regular late arrival behaviour rather annoying, but due to the strong client focus of the work which some managers were engaged in, their lateness (e.g. when a client had an urgent problem) appeared justifiable or excusable. Nevertheless, the regular late arrival of some managers generated frustration and irritation among some of their colleagues. This background information is necessary in order to fully understand what is actually going on in example (2):

Example (2)

Context: Fortnightly managers' meeting of the IT department in a larger organisation chaired by Tricia, the department director. The meeting involves six managers, an external HR consultant, as well as Tricia and Evelyn, her personal assistant. Participants are waiting to begin the meeting. Serena, a manager, arrives late for the meeting.

1. Tri.: good afternoon
2. Ser.: [in a light hearted tone of voice]: sorry I'm late:
3. Eve.: **it's been noted**
4.   **chocolates expected next meeting**
5.   [laughter]
6. Ser: **(that's right) cos I was considering whether you'd**

7.   **notice if I didn't turn up**
8.   [laughter] [. . .]
9. Tri.:   [in a friendly tone of voice]: we noticed:

The meeting participants have already been waiting for some time when Serena finally arrives. Indeed, Tricia, the director of the department and chair of the meeting, has instructed someone to give missing participants a call and check whether they intend to attend the meeting. When the last missing participant Serena finally arrives, Tricia greets her with the ironic remark *good afternoon*. Since the meeting was supposed to start at 10 a.m., this comment clearly indicates her disapproval. However, rather than criticising Serena explicitly, Tricia uses ironic humour to hedge her critical comment and save Serena's face. Serena responds with an apology *sorry I'm late* (line 2), but her tone indicates that she is not treating her breach very seriously.

Interestingly, it is Evelyn, Tricia's PA, and the least senior person in the meeting, who then responds by overtly criticising Serena for her lateness *it's been noted* (line 3). Evelyn here humorously takes on the role of a more senior person. She then continues to rebuke Serena in a friendly tone with her comment *chocolates expected next meeting* (line 4), a comment which refers back to a long instance of conjoint humour that participants had developed previously, when they discussed various ways of making latecomers pay for their lateness (e.g. chocolates, wine and beer). Evelyn's humorous comment evokes laughter from all participants. Evelyn's behaviour can be interpreted as a way of doing power without threatening anyone's face.

However, instead of apologising again, or playing along with the humour by adopting the role of being guilty of lateness, Serena does not accept the criticism, but rather challenges Tricia quite directly by saying *cos I was considering whether you'd notice if I didn't turn up* (lines 6 and 7). Serena thus skilfully transfers the responsibility to Tricia by implying that her attendance is not really necessary, and perhaps implicitly even raising questions about the usefulness of the meeting (cf. Grice 1975). From interviews we have conducted in this workplace, we know that some managers feel concerned about the usefulness and need for so many meetings. In this context Serena's comment, albeit humorous, can be understood as containing a challenging and impolite message. Her remark again evokes a gale of laughter, and Tricia responds with *we noticed* (line 9) in a friendly voice, thus bringing this episode to an end.

While there are a number of very interesting observations that could be made with respect to "doing power" in this example, we here concentrate on the comment by Serena which challenges Tricia. Serena's remark *cos I was considering whether you'd notice if I didn't turn up* is a very good example of category 1 impoliteness: with regard to its form, her utterance appears to be politic, but the context makes it very clear that its content is basically impolite. Not only does Serena turn her initial apology (*sorry I'm late*) into a challenge to her director, but she also attacks Tricia by implying that she fails to see the usefulness of her presence at these meetings in general. Her impolite behaviour thus challenges the existing power relations by indirectly questioning Tricia's authority. However, the context in which the impoliteness occurs, in particular because it is embedded in some humorous comments and lots of laughter, considerably mitigates its potentially face-threatening impact. (This mitigating role of humour and laughter in the context of impoliteness is further illustrated in some of the examples of category 2 impoliteness discussed below.) However, Tricia's final remark skilfully counters Serena's attack and her attempt at reverting the power relations: Tricia is the one who has the last word on this topic, and with the friendly voice that characterises most of her interactions, she effectively puts Serena in her place and restores the balance of power. After this short episode Tricia opens the meeting and begins the discussion of the first item on the agenda without being challenged or questioned further.

Example (3) is taken from another interaction between Tricia and two of her managers, Isabelle and Noel. At this point in the meeting Isabelle has just brought up a sensitive topic on which Noel has a completely different opinion to his director, Tricia. Noel thus feels bound to express his disagreement with Tricia's point of view, but he does so in a way that indicates he is trying hard to make his disagreement sound polite.

Although the impoliteness in this example is not as obvious as in the previous example, it nicely illustrates some of the points that we wish to make. In order to understand what is going on in this interaction, and in particular why we have classified Noel's behaviour as impolite in content, some background knowledge is necessary: this interaction takes place shortly before an important meeting in which Tricia and Noel are supposed to present a particular issue to a larger section of the organisation. Although Noel and Tricia have discussed this issue at length in previous interactions, he is still not convinced by her opinion and does not seem to be prepared to support her point of view at the upcoming meeting. His disagreement in lines 1 and 2 thus poses a potential threat to Tricia's face.

Example (3)
Context: Interaction between Noel and Isabelle (managers) and their boss Tricia (director), all members of IT department in a larger organisation.
1. Noe.:   **so Tricia and I might have a different story about that**
2.   **of course you realise that +**
3.   //slightly different I mean we might\
4. Tri: /[in a contestive tone of voice]: why would\\

5.	we have a different story:
6. Noe.:	well because I think the reason I think that we might
7.	//just\ slightly (veer) different
8. Tri.:	/mm\\
9. Noe.:	I mean I'm not saying totally different
10.	is because one is such a big issue for the support //teams\
11. Isa.:	/mm\\
12. Noe.:	is that we haven't really kind of sorted out
13.	the centralisation that happened last year [. . .]

Noel's initial comment *so Tricia and I might have a different story about that of course you realise that* (lines 1 and 2) appears to be directed at Isabelle rather than Tricia. This is a rather skilful strategy for indirectly conveying to Tricia the unwelcome information that he holds an opposing opinion to hers. Nevertheless, this utterance clearly comprises a challenge to Tricia's power and authority with regard to the particular issue on which they disagree. However, it seems that when he realises the potential face-threat of his comment, he begins to relativise his initial utterance, utilising a variety of mitigating strategies, including hedges and modals: *slightly different I mean we might* (line 3). And when Tricia simultaneously directly asks him to clarify his accusations in a rather contestive tone of voice, *why would we have a different story* (lines 4 and 5), he retreats to a statement which considerably hedges his initial remark, using numerous pragmatic *particles (well, I think, just, I mean, really, kind of)* and a modal (*might*) in addition to various restarts and even a pause (lines 6, 7, 9, 10, 12). He is obviously trying very hard to retrieve, obscure, or at least relativise the threat of his inappropriate comment. We have classified Noel's utterance as impolite because his expression of disagreement could not have come at a worse moment in time considering the upcoming meeting.

According to our distinction, then, Noel's remark can be classified as another instance of category 1 impoliteness since his comment obviously has an impolite and potentially face challenging content (i.e. a very inconvenient disagreement with his boss), although its form appears to be politic at first glance. However, Noel's subsequent discourse, in particular his extensive justification and explanation, as well as his high use of mitigating devices, suggests that he realises that he has overstepped the boundaries of politic behaviour with his challenging remark. His intensive attempt to mitigate and qualify the impact of his disagreement further suggests that the form of his comment was not politic (i.e. probably too direct).[3] At this point in the interaction Noel seems to be walking a fine line between communicating his (opposing) opinion to his boss while at the same time sticking to the politic formalities of communicating such a potentially face-threatening message.

This example thus illustrates the fine line between politic and impolite behaviour, whilst also raising the question of whether these two are always strictly distinguishable from each other, or whether perhaps there is a grey area of overlap. The content of Noel's disagreement and criticism is impolite because it challenges Tricia's authority; however, the form in which he delivers it and particularly his subsequent attempts at minimising its negative impact could be considered both politic as well as inappropriate. It is politic because the numerous hedging devices seem to be aimed at mitigating the negative impact of Noel's initial utterance, as well as providing redress for the fact that he seems to have overstepped an unspoken boundary of respect for a superior's opinion. At the same time, however, these discourse markers appear to be inappropriate in their sheer quantity which seems excessive and over-the-top. But the contestive tone of voice in which Tricia responded to Noel's disagreement may have motivated Noel to employ such elaborate hedging strategies in response.

In the next section we analyse utterances which at first glance appear inherently impolite in form and content, but which on closer examination constitute examples of politic behaviour – behaviour which conforms to the norms developed between members of a particular CofP.

3.2. *Superficial impoliteness but politic behaviour*

In our review of the literature on impoliteness, we noted the category labelled 'mock impoliteness' by Culpeper (1996), i.e. utterances which appear superficially impolite but which constitute politic behaviour in context. Below we provide two examples of such a category.

Example (4) is another example that was recorded in the Wellington factory. It occurred in an interaction between Ginette and her two subordinates Russell and Ivan. The three team members are discussing the progress they are making on the packing line:

Example (4)
Context: Wellington factory. Ginette, the team co-ordinator for the packing line with two team members Ivan and Russell.

1. Rus.:   how was the meeting gee [Samoan]: ua uma:
                                    is it finished
2. Gin.:   [Samoan]: te lei alu: [voc]
                   I didn't go
3.   trying to get the lines going brother
4. Rus.:   oh were you down there all the time ( )
5. Iv.:   **(that) you left the fucking packing lines going like hell**
6. Rus.:   //[laughs]\

7. Gin.:   /I'm there all the time bro\\
8. Rus.:   [laughing]: yeah but I think you're the problem: [laughs]
9. Gin.:   [in mock anger]: you just keep an eye on your screen:
10. Rus.:   //**[chortles]: oo hoo hoo:**\
11. Iv.:   /[chortles]: oo hoo hoo:\\
12. Gin.:   if I get any shit powder from you
13.   I'm coming up here to box your ears

This extract clearly illustrates category 2 impoliteness: it contains a number of discourse moves which appear inherently impolite, but which on closer examination and in the light of contextual information, are, we argue, more accurately interpreted as instances of politic behaviour. The first such utterance is Ivan's comment *you left the fucking packing lines going like hell* (line 5). Here Ivan accuses Ginette, his boss, of being partly responsible for some problems they are experiencing on the packing lines. This message is picked up by his colleague Russell a few utterances later when he directly, albeit humorously, accuses Ginette of having caused the problem. His comment *yeah but + I think you're the problem* (line 8) is more direct and thus potentially more face-threatening and impolite than Ivan's critical remark. Not only the content of Russell's utterance, but also its directness and teasing element make it appear inherently impolite and potentially face-threatening. Although Russell laughs during and after uttering this remark, which may mitigate its negative impact, it can nevertheless be regarded as very direct and potentially face-threatening. It is very unlikely that such direct and confrontational behaviour would occur in most of the white-collar workplaces in which we recorded data. However, as we have argued above (see example [1]), this kind of superficially impolite and challenging behaviour, and in particular aggressive and sometimes even abusive banter (cf. Leech 1983) and teasing is typical of interactions between members of Ginette's team. Thus Russell's teasing can be regarded not as impolite behaviour, but rather as politic behaviour in the context of the norms negotiated among members of this CofP.

This interpretation is supported by Ginette's reaction to Russell's superficially rude remark: she plays along by pretending to be angry and humorously rebuking him, *you just keep an eye on your screen* (line 9). But, instead of leaving it at this, Russell challenges his boss again by chortling at her attempt to display her power and authority (line 10). This behaviour could be regarded as even more face-threatening than Russell's initial teasing, since it could be interpreted as signalling his unwillingness to comply with her, as questioning her authority and subverting existing power relations. However, based on the large amount of data that we have recorded in this workplace, we would argue that Russell's more challenging and face-threatening behaviour is still within the boundaries of acceptable behaviour for this CofP (see also Daly et al. 2004). This is further supported by the subsequent development of the interaction: rather than getting upset or angry, Ginette continues her teasing exchange with Russell, and even humorously threatens to box his ears should he not comply with her (lines 12 and 13). On this basis we feel confident in characterising Russell's behaviour as having been co-constructed within the context as politic rather than impolite.

It is also worth noting that this example is particularly interesting with regard to the enactment of power: Russell's initial challenging teasing of his boss could be interpreted as an attempt to subvert existing power relations and to challenge Ginette's authority and status. The disrespectful laughter with which he responds to her mock display of authority and power (i.e. her humorous threat *you just keep an eye on your screen*) could be interpreted as a further attempt at challenging Ginette. But her final reply in lines 12 and 13, in which she humorously threatens her subordinate, firmly reinstates her power and leaves no doubt that she is the one in charge.

A similar point is illustrated in example (5), which occurred in an interaction between Ginette and Dirk (an Engineering Officer):

Example (5)
Context: Wellington factory packing line. Ginette, the team co-ordinator, is talking to Dirk about assigning tasks to people.

1. Gin.: it's be better to use when (don't know) and
2.   [in a funny voice]: I mean this in the most nicest possible
3.   way: + to do some work when we've either got Jake or
4.   Charles rather than Doug ++
5. Dir.: I know exactly what you're saying +
6.   **I hear what you're saying woman**
7. Gin.: [laughs] but it'd be good to um
8. Dir.: (yep)
9. Gin.: I (don't know) just check the belts (in feed)
10.   belts fans shit like that +

Dirk's comment *I hear what you're saying woman* (line 6) could be interpreted as impolite behaviour towards his superior, Ginette. Not only his tone and the content of his utterance (i.e. impertinently suggesting she is stating the obvious) but also his use of the address term *woman* towards his superior could well be interpreted as derogatory and rude if this utterance had occurred in a different context. In particular, in a white-collar workplace in New Zealand this kind of challenging response would almost certainly be perceived as unacceptable and impolite as a sexist and degrading term.[4] However, as described above, the working climate (including the ways in which employees communicate with each other) in the factory differs significantly from that of a typical white-collar workplace with respect to levels of directness, frequency of potential face-attacks, challenging humour and verbal abuse. Hence, Dirk's behaviour in this example can be classified as politic behaviour which draws on the norms of appropriate behaviour in this CofP. Referring to Ginette as *woman* conveys a cheeky, disrespectful attitude, and the use of this term could be interpreted as subtly subverting Ginette's supervisory status within the organisation. However, as noted by Dickey (1997: 255) "terms which have derogatory literal meanings [can] function as forms of address with positive social meanings", and, on the basis of our ethnographic observations, this is clearly a case in point. There are numerous examples in the data where Ginette is referred to as *woman* by her subordinates. The interpretation of this otherwise belittling and challenging term as a solidarity marker is further supported by Ginette's reaction to Dirk (she gives no indication that she finds the term objectionable, but simply laughs at him and continues to spell out her request).

It is also worth noting the contrast between examples (4) and (5). In example (4) the content is superficially impolite but the face attack is clearly interpreted as politic, while in example (5) the offensive term is interpreted as a term of familiarity. In example (6) below, we see another utterance which could appear impolite to outsiders, but is in fact in keeping with the interactional patterns of the group, thus constituting politic behaviour.

Elsewhere we have described this third CofP (a project team at the Wellington office of a large multinational) as a highly competitive but entertaining and good-humoured group (see Holmes and Marra 2002a). Their weekly meeting is peppered with humour and with examples of one-upmanship. The aim for the group is not to put colleagues down, but instead to come up with the best humorous quips. The project manager, Smithy, does nothing to discourage this behaviour and is, in fact, one of the leading contenders in the ongoing battle of wits:

Example (6)[5]
Context: Jock "Smithy" Smitherson, the manager of a corporate project team, is chairing the team's reporting meeting. Each Tuesday morning, the various subprojects report on their weekly progress. Following the end of Vita's report, he nominates Matt as the next speaker

1. Vit.:   Friday would be perfect
2. Smi.:   hey Matt did you get all of your things completed
3.   by Friday
4. Matt: **I was just about to say if Mr Smitherson wasn't so**
5.   **rude as to interrupt um**
6.   [general laughter]
7. Matt: ditto for me all the contents are there (with me)

| 8. | this week is fine |
| 9. | tweak things with with Tessa um |

In this example, the apparent impoliteness arises from an accusation by a subordinate that his superior is being impolite. Smithy, as the meeting chair, is acting well within the perimeters of his role when he hands the floor to Matt with his question in lines 2 and 3; he names Matt as the next speaker and asks about his progress over the previous week. Matt's response, which evokes general hilarity from the group, suggests that this nomination by Smithy is an unnecessary and unwanted interruption to the flow of the meeting.

Although Matt is being impolite at the surface level, he is going on-record as being impolite through the humorous tone with which he makes his accusation. His overtly scathing tone (a tone which would not be acceptable for this easy-going and tight-knit group if it were meant to be taken at face value) is a signal to the group that the utterance is not intended to be a serious reaction to Smithy's attempt at facilitation, i.e. it flouts the maxims of quantity and manner to create a humorous effect. The use of the respectful form *Mr Smitherson* rather than the normal brief nickname *Smithy* could be interpreted as inappropriately overpolite for this group as in the examples discussed in category 1. Instead we have included this example in the second category because of what we regard as the more relevant mock impoliteness. When Matt accuses his superior of interrupting, he is also accusing the meeting chair, who is responsible for the smooth running of the meeting, of poor meeting etiquette. In this team Smithy frequently signals the end of a report by nominating the team member who should take the next turn, regardless of whether or not this is obvious to the group (for example where the group is taking turns in order around the table). That he has behaved within the norms for meeting behaviour for this group is without question. Matt is also operating within the norms, but is orienting to the importance of quick wittedness and humour for this group. For Smithy's team, displaying a good sense of humour is politic behaviour.

Interestingly, like many of the examples in both categories, the response to the impoliteness (whether mock or perceived) is laughter. This could well suggest that in all three communities, laughter is an acceptable audience reaction to impoliteness, possibly signalling discomfort at the upward challenge (see Marra 2007).

4. Conclusion

The examples discussed have illustrated different ways in which the analysis of impoliteness is relevant in interpreting what is going on in workplace interaction, and especially in the analysis of challenges to superiors and to subverting existing power relations. We have identified two categories of impolite behaviour in our data: i) discourse moves which appear superficially polite or politic but which convey a very impolite, contestive or subversive message, and ii) discourse moves, which appear inherently impolite but which on closer examination, taking account of the norms negotiated among members of the working groups or CofPs, turn out to be politic utterances. Focusing on power relations, however, utterances in both categories, may effectively contribute to subverting the status quo.

The analysis further suggested that the boundaries between politic and impolite behaviours are far from clear cut, and that context (and the uptake) is crucial in analysing and classifying these discourse moves. In particular, the challenging and abusive behaviour regularly displayed by the factory workers towards their team leader Ginette would be completely inappropriate and certainly perceived as impolite in both working teams in the white-collar organisations. The same is true for behaviour, which clearly constitutes the norm in most white-collar workplaces, but which would most certainly be perceived as overly polite, and hence inappropriate, and in some cases even offensive in the factory context.

Moreover, most of the instances of impoliteness that we found in our data were directed downwards, i.e. from superiors to their subordinates, which clearly indicates the significance of power relations in this context. Interestingly, when such behaviour was displayed by superiors it was rarely perceived as impolite, but rather as simply direct. When adopted by subordinates, on the other hand, impolite behaviour was generally regarded as an attempt at subverting existing power relations. This interpretation is supported by the observation that most instances of impoliteness upwards in our data were followed by a range of different hedging strategies aimed at mitigating the negative impact and potential face-threat of the impoliteness act.

These findings suggest that the relationship between the various points on the continuum of relational work are far from straightforward and that there seems to be a connection between the overly polite and the impoliteness end (see also Watts 2005). Moreover, the analysis has clearly illustrated that both form and content of discourse moves need to be considered in deciding whether an utterance constitutes an instance of impolite or politic behaviour in the context in which it appears.

Appendix

Transcription conventions

[laughs]: :	Paralinguistic features and additional information in square brackets; colons indicate start and end
+	Pause up to one second
-	Incomplete or cut-off utterance
... // ..... \ ... ... / ..... \\ ...	Simultaneous speech
(hello)	Transcriber's best guess at an unclear utterance
[...]	Section of transcript omitted
[voc]	Untranscribable noise
translation	Translated section in italics below original

All names are pseudonyms.

Notes

1. The authors would like to express appreciation to the participants who allowed us to record their interactions. We also thank other members of the Language in the Workplace team, especially Dr Bernadette Vine (Corpus Manager) along with the research assistants who helped to collect and transcribe the data. The research described here was made possible by grants from Victoria University of Wellington's Research Fund.
2. The utterances highlighted in bold mark the impolite discourse move that the analysis focuses on.
3. Similar behaviour by Noel in the same interaction is discussed in Schnurr, Marra and Holmes (2007).
4. In preparing this chapter we struggled to find an equivalent male form of address which we felt would elicit a similar negative reaction in a typical white collar workplace. After extended discussions, the term we suggest is 'boy' although this is far from ideal, given the recognised negative ethnic connotations of the term. Nevertheless the derogatory sense is clear.
5. This example has been previously analysed as an example of subversive quip in Holmes and Marra (2002b).

Chapter 10
"Stop hassling me!" Impoliteness, power and gender identity in the professional workplace

Louise Mullany

1. Introduction[1]

It has now been well-established by a number of researchers that theories of politeness must include conceptualisations of impoliteness in order to be deemed comprehensive (see Lakoff 1989; Culpeper 1996, 2005; Eelen 2001; Culpeper, Bousfield and Wichmann 2003; Mills 2003; Watts 2003; Locher 2004; Spencer-Oatey 2005). A growing number of empirical analyses of impoliteness in the fields of pragmatics, discourse analysis and sociolinguistics have started to be produced in a range of contexts, helping to emphasise the fruitfulness and overall importance of producing research which addresses impoliteness. This chapter adds to this expanding field by focusing on the interplay between impoliteness, power and gender identity in the interactions of business managers within corporate organisations.

The notion of power is deemed to be of key importance to studies of (im)politeness (as well as to gender), though as Harris (2007) points out, there have been difficulties in fusing politeness and power together (Harris uses "politeness" in an all-encompassing manner here to also include impoliteness). She argues that these difficulties are due to the "huge theoretical baggage" that surrounds both terms (2007: 123). Despite such "baggage", Harris (2007) points to the recent work of Eelen (2001), Holmes and Stubbe (2003a), Watts (2003), Mills (2003) and Locher (2004) as providing very useful insights into politeness and power. She sees such work as representing a clear departure from the view of power applied within Brown and Levinson's ([1978] 1987) model. Brown and Levinson place power as one of the key components within their formula used to assess the *weightiness* of a face-threatening act. Power is therefore perceived to be static and easily calculable. As Harris (2001) rightly points out, such a conceptualisation of power is too rigid, resulting in the power dynamic between interactants being seen as pre-existing discourse, as well as being taken for granted. Harris (2003) easily disproves Brown and Levinson's formula by demonstrating that those in positions of power within institutions make widespread use of politeness strategies, which is not predicted or accounted for by the rigidity of their model.

Drawing on the work of Lakoff (1989), Harris (2001, 2007) advocates that, in order for the relationship between (im)politeness and power to be properly explored, investigations need to take place in institutional and professional contexts. As asymmetrical power relationships and differing levels of status already formally exist in such contexts, Lakoff's view is that conducting analyses within such spheres will enable researchers to see (im)politeness from a very different perspective than studies simply examining language in informal contexts. I firmly agree with this position, and in this chapter I intend to demonstrate how the institutional interaction of managerial professionals can inform us a good deal about the complex interplay between impoliteness and power. Indeed, it is no coincidence that there is a key focus on language within institutional contexts in a range of chapters that appear in this volume, including other "workplaces" (Bousfield; Limberg; Schnurr, Marra and Holmes), the courtroom (Archer) and political spheres (García-Pastor; Locher and Watts).

In addition to being part of a recommended area of study for (im)politeness and power research, the professional workplace in particular has also recently become a growing area of research within the discipline of language and gender studies. This is inextricably interlinked with the political importance of investigating language and gender in the workplace on a global scale, where women are continuing to enter previously male-dominated professions in greater numbers than ever before. As Thimm, Koch and Schey (2003: 531) observe, "talk at work has received attention from feminists worldwide, reflecting the growing importance of professional communication for women in different countries". This study thus contributes to this expanding arena of investigation.

In order to examine how impoliteness and power interact with gender, this chapter focuses on the interactions of men and women business managers in a UK manufacturing company. There has been a plethora of research conducted on politeness within language and gender studies, perhaps the most oft-cited and seminal contributions being the works of Lakoff (1975), Brown (1980) and Holmes (1995). Recent research has also explored politeness and gender in the workplace (see Holmes and Schnurr 2005; Mullany 2006). However, with the exception of a handful of recent publications (see Mills 2002, 2003, 2005; Mullany 2002), very little work has considered gender and impoliteness. There is thus a real need for more empirical research to be carried out in order to enhance understandings of impoliteness and gender identity. As Mills (2005) highlights, a focus on gender and impoliteness can reveal a range of crucial information about identity construction and gender stereotyping.

In the next two sections of the chapter, I will outline the theoretical approaches that I am taking to conceptualising impoliteness, power and gender identity, including a consideration of the complex interplay between them. I will then move on to introduce the data, followed by the analysis and a discussion of the results. Conclusions will then be drawn as to the implications this study has for the field of gender and (im)politeness research in particular relation to power.

2. Theorising impoliteness, theorising power

The influence of Brown and Levinson ([1978] 1987) is still clearly visible in some more recent theorisations of impoliteness, albeit in significantly revised and more sophisticated forms (Culpeper, Bousfield and Wichmann 2003; Culpeper 2005, this volume; García-Pastor, this volume). However, other researchers have significantly distanced themselves from the Brown and Levinson model, rethinking the manner in which impoliteness and politeness are conceived. Harris (2007) observes a difference between what she terms the "normative" model (i.e. Brown and Levinson-influenced models) versus a newer approach which she terms "contestable", associated with the theories of Eelen (2001), Watts (2003), Mills (2003) and Locher (2004). Like Harris, Terkourafi (2005a) has also observed two differing camps in politeness research, which she classifies as "traditional" approaches (Brown and Levinson [1978] 1987; Leech 1983) and "post-modern" approaches (Eelen 2001; Watts 2003; Mills 2003). However, as Terkourafi (2005a) points out, it is important to bear in mind that the two approaches are not mutually exclusive. Indeed, in this chapter, whilst my theoretical positioning is closest to the "post-modern" approach to conceptualising impoliteness and power (as well as gender, see Section 3), most heavily influenced by Mills' (2003) work, there is also an observable influence of Culpeper (2005) when defining and analysing impoliteness (see below and Section 5). Also, whilst Harris' (2007) and Terkourafi's (2005a) grouping of theories into two different camps provides a useful overall distinction which aids in clarifying the finite details of theoretical developments in conceptualising (im)politeness, it is also important to acknowledge that there are differences and divisions between researchers *within* the "postmodern" camp as well as *within* the "traditional", "normative" camp.

These differences should not be glossed over. Indeed, classifying all studies which draw upon Brown and Levinson/Leech under the "traditional" approach obscures the advancements that have been made. I therefore suggest reserving the category of "traditional" for those studies which still closely adhere to the original principles of Brown and Levinson and Leech, and contrast this with the more advanced "normative" models that have been developed by researchers including Culpeper, Bousfield and Wichmann (2003), Culpeper (2005, this volume) and Bousfield (this volume).

Within the more recent, "post-modern" approach, Eelen (2001), Watts (2003), Mills (2003), Locher (2004) and Locher and Watts (2005) all argue that impoliteness and politeness should be seen as forms of social practice. They are strongly influenced by Bourdieu's (1990, 1991) theory of practice and, within this, his notion of *habitus*: the "set of dispositions which incline agents to act and react in certain ways" (Thompson 1991: 12). According to Harris' (2007) classification, (im)politeness within the social practice perspective is not constituted as a set of normative structures, but is deemed to be *contested*, with participants within interactions making assessments themselves as to what is impolite or polite. These assessments will vary depending upon context and the habitus of differing individuals. From this perspective, (im)politeness should not be perceived as being contained within language (associated with Brown and Levinson-influenced views), but instead as something fluid which is enacted within interaction. Furthermore, as participants' assessments of impoliteness are made over stretches of discourse, there is a need to abandon analyses that just focus on (im)politeness being enacted within a single utterance, associated with a traditional Brown and Levinson approach. Culpeper, Bousfield and Wichmann (2003) and Culpeper (2005) also reject this perspective in favour of the view of impoliteness being constructed within interaction.

Indeed, both the "postmodern" and the more advanced Brown and Levinson-influenced approaches distance themselves from the traditional perspective that a politeness model revolves around speaker intention only, often assessed solely by examining a single utterance. By conceptualising (im)politeness as something that emerges within discourse, as opposed to being contained within a decontextualised utterance, the focus of the analysis is broadened out to include the crucial role of the hearer, and the hearer's perceptions of intentionality. Culpeper (2005) provides a useful distinction of the role of intentionality as part of his revised definition of impoliteness:

> Impoliteness comes about when: (1) the speaker communicates face-attack intentionally, or (2) the hearer perceives and/or constructs behaviour as intentionally face-attacking, or a combination of (1) and (2). (Culpeper 2005: 38)

From my perspective, whilst I do not deny the overall importance of speaker intention, as this intention *on its own* is so difficult to interpret, I instead place key emphasis on the second part of Culpeper's definition, the importance of combining the reactions of the hearer in response to the speaker, to assess if the hearer perceives the behaviour of the speaker to have been intentionally face-attacking. This perspective neatly emphasises how impoliteness is constructed *within* interaction, across stretches of discourse, enabling a combined focus on speaker and hearer, in order for the analyst to use all available cues to interpret whether impoliteness has taken place within a particular community of practice (see below). In this way, the analyst is not relying solely on an attempt to ascertain speaker intention her/himself, but is utilising the hearer's reactions as evidence of whether the hearer perceived the speaker to have been intentionally impolite.

Coming back to the social practice approach to politeness and impoliteness, Mills (2002, 2003, 2005) utilises the communities of practice (CofP) model, which has been highly influential in language and gender studies through the work of Eckert and McConnell-Ginet (1992, 1995, 1999, 2003). In previous work (Mullany 2004, 2006), I have developed a modified form of Mills' CofP approach when examining politeness in professional workplace data, and a similar framework will be followed in this chapter in order to assess impoliteness, power and gender identity.

Mills (2002: 82) argues that "the notion of a CofP can provide a framework for analysing the complexity of judging an utterance as polite or impolite". She elaborates on this, arguing that impoliteness (and politeness) should be characterised by an assessment or a judgement about someone's behaviour within a specific *community of practice*, as opposed to being perceived as "a quality intrinsic to an utterance" (2005: 265), as would be the case with a traditional Brown and Levinson approach (though not the more advanced Brown and Levinson-influenced models). Within the CofP perspective, Mills (2002: 79) argues that impoliteness exists "when it is classified as such by certain, usually dominant community members and/or when it leads to a breakdown in relations". Within CofPs there is a set of norms and conventions which dictate what is perceived as "appropriate" behaviour within that particular context. It is against such norms that assessments of impoliteness will be made.

Mills (2003, 2005) argues against dividing impoliteness and politeness into two polarised categories to avoid oversimplifying what is instead a far more complex picture. This viewpoint is also shared by Locher (2004). Locher (2004) devises a detailed system of classification, advocating that politeness phenomena should be subsumed under the category of "relational work". This includes a whole range of behaviour from impolite, non-polite and over-polite, and integrates Watts' (1992) definition of "politic" behaviour within this model. Whilst Locher's framework is useful for clarifying the importance of inappropriateness as a feature of impolite behaviour, like Mills (2003) and Harris (2005), I have reservations about the distinctions between "politic" and "polite" behaviour.[2] Therefore, as an alternative, I instead favour Mills' perspective that simply the two categories of impoliteness and politeness should be viewed at either end of a continuum, albeit on "a continuum of assessment" (Mills 2005: 266). The continuum approach accounts for the fact that often it can be very difficult to assess if someone has been impolite or polite.

In particular regards to defining impoliteness, Mills makes the following observation which will be applied to the data analysed in this study:

> Impoliteness can be considered as any type of linguistic behaviour which is assessed as intending to threaten the hearer's face or social identity, or as transgressing the hypothesized Community of Practice's norms of appropriacy. (Mills 2005: 268)

As with Culpeper (2005), Mills (2002, 2003, 2005) also demonstrates the crucial importance of analysing hearer's responses and reactions in order to assess if impoliteness has intentionally taken place. Of particular relevance to this study, she also points out that, when an interlocutor has made an accusation of impoliteness, such accusations are often concerned with problems of agreement in relation to perceptions of power and social status:

> Accusations of impoliteness generally signal to participants that there has been a mismatch in the judgement of status, role or familiarity and thus perhaps also a mismatch in their assessment of their position in the particular Community of Practice. (Mills 2005: 268)

This observation will be tested when analysing my data.

A further point worth emphasising, interrelated with the polarised view of impoliteness and politeness, is my agreement with Mills' perspective that impoliteness should not be seen as either rare or irrational. Such accusations are a consequence of traditional Brown and Levinson-influenced models of conflict-avoidance, due to their reliance on Grice's (1975) co-operative principle. Engaging in impolite behaviour is perfectly rational, and is far more 'normal' than is predicted by Gricean-based theories of human communication (Kienpointner 1997; Culpeper, Bousfield and Wichmann 2003).

The real point of departure between Mills' theory and my own perspective is concerned with who is able to comment on the judgements and assessments of impoliteness. I disagree with Mills' argument that it is only those members who belong to the specific CofPs that are being investigated who are able to judge whether particular acts are impolite or polite. If this perspective is followed, researchers who *do not* belong to the CofPs they are studying are unable to make judgements, and are thus restricted to interviewing members after interactions have taken place in order to attempt to gain their assessments and judgements of impoliteness and politeness. Alternatively, researchers could limit themselves to analysing CofPs where *they* are members, as Mills does successfully in her

2002 and 2005 publications. However, as I have argued elsewhere (Mullany 2006), judgements and assessments of (im)politeness can and should be made by linguistics researchers through examining the interactions of speakers and hearers across stretches of discourse. As Holmes and Schnurr (2005: 122) point out, arguing against doing this "seems to us like shooting oneself in the foot".

Provided that analysts are careful about the claims they make, using all verbal, non-verbal material and observations that are open to them to come up with what they consider to be the most justifiable reading of what has taken place within an interaction, then it is perfectly acceptable for analysts to play a role in judging whether or not (im)politeness has taken place. Interviewing after discourse has taken place can perhaps be useful in some circumstances, but in itself it produces yet another text which has its own range of problems, and it should never be taken at face value as being a definitive account of "what really went on" in an interaction (Silverman 2000). Mills herself openly acknowledges such problems. A further argument against such an approach made by Holmes and Schnurr (2005) is that participants do not have enough metalanguage to be able to articulate their intentions anyway (see also Terkourafi 2005a for a critique of this methodological approach). Furthermore, limiting oneself to requiring interview data to assess perceived intentions of previously recorded interactional data could result in a whole host of different contexts no longer being open to you as a researcher, particularly institutional settings. In my experience of recording interactional business communication within professional workplaces, convincing busy managers to sit down and tell an interviewer about what they thought their intentions were in previous interactions would be extremely difficult to achieve (see Mullany 2007).

The "post-modern" principles which we have seen behind newer conceptualisations of (im)politeness also figure heavily in definitions of power that are adopted in this chapter (as well as gender, see Section 3). As an alternative to the rigid and fixed view of power from within Brown and Levinson's perspective, power, like (im)politeness, is also conceptualised from a social practice perspective. Foucault's (1972) work on power has also been influential to these "postmodern" approaches. Power is defined as active and fluid, which accords with Foucault's (1972) idea of power as a web or net, a view that has proved to be very useful within language and gender studies (Baxter 2003; Mills 2003).

Whilst participants within workplaces are still allocated positions of power based upon the formal position that they occupy on the institutional hierarchy, from this perspective power "is no longer an objective external force but becomes relative to how it is used by those occupants" (Eelen 2001: 114). Mills (2002: 74) makes a very similar observation, arguing that from a Foucauldian perspective "language can be seen as an arena where power may be appropriated, rather than power roles being seen as frozen societal roles that are clearly mapped out for participants before an interaction takes place". In their analysis of politeness and power in the workplace, Holmes and Stubbe (2003a: 3) ascribe to the view that power is fluid and enacted *within* discourse. They make the useful observation that every interaction consists of "people enacting, reproducing and sometimes resisting institutional power relationships in their use of discourse". They also utilise, from Critical Discourse Analysis, the concepts of repressive and oppressive discourse, whereby power can be expressed either covertly (repressively) or overtly (oppressively) by individuals, and this enactment of power can depend upon dominant ideologies that influence the interaction.

As one of the only volumes on (im)politeness which thoroughly discusses power from this "post-modern" perspective, Locher (2004) produces an excellent summary which is worth quoting here:

> [P]ower is regarded as relational, dynamic and contestable. Thus, power cannot be possessed like a commodity: it is constantly negotiated in and around relationships. More powerful interactants who have more freedom to act will have to secure their position. By comparison, less powerful interactants may resist, align themselves with other members of a group or attempt to exercise their own power. Negotiating power in interaction is thus part of how interactants shape and present their identity. (Locher 2004: 37, emphasis removed)

Just like (im)politeness, power should not be seen as being contained within language; instead it is enacted through discourse when interactants engage in identity performance. Those who occupy formal positions of power on institutional hierarchies constantly have to re-enact their power through discourse, whilst those in relatively more powerless positions can both resist power as well as attempt to gain it for themselves. (See Mills 1997, for a discussion on how secretaries within university departments accrue power for themselves over their superiors.) As Harris (2007) points out, both her own examination of politeness in the interactions of individuals in positions of power, including magistrates, police officers and doctors, as well as Locher's (2004) analysis of a media interview with the then US president Bill Clinton, demonstrates how there can be a surprisingly large amount of negotiation of both identity and power, regardless of the positions on the institutional hierarchies that interlocutors may occupy prior to interaction taking place.

3.   Gender identity, impoliteness and power

In this chapter, gender identity is conceptualised as a performative social construct following Butler (1990). Like power, from this social constructionist perspective gender is seen as fluid and dynamic, something that speakers "do" within discourse as opposed to being something that they already are. The combination of the performativity approach and the CofP framework has proved to be a very useful analytical model in language and gender research (Mills 2003; Holmes and Stubbe 2003b; Holmes and Marra 2004; Holmes 2006; Mullany 2004, 2006), and it is also the approach taken here.

It is now well-established that the differences which were found between female and male speech in earlier language and gender studies should be perceived as stereotypical expectations of gender-appropriate behaviour, against which women and men are evaluated and judged (Freed 1996; Holmes 2000; Mills 2003; Holmes and Stubbe 2003b). Recent gender and language studies which have utilised the performativity and CofP model in workplace investigations have found evidence of women performing stereotypically masculine speech styles and vice versa, depending upon the particular CofP norms and conventions within which the interaction is taking place (Holmes and Stubbe 2003b). However, it is important to remember that, in using the stereotypical norms associated with the other gender, women may be subject to negative evaluation and thus experience a double bind (Lakoff 1990, 2003).

Mills (2003) views politeness as a gendered concept, with impolite behaviour being stereotypically associated with masculinity, whilst politeness is stereotypically associated with femininity.[3] Successfully performed impoliteness is a good example of a pragmatic strategy which accrues power for the speaker (Beebe 1995). Therefore, when members of CofPs enact impoliteness, they can thus be seen as performing stereotypically masculine interactional styles. Based on Mills' view of gender identity and politeness, there is a stereotypical, societal expectation that white middle-class women will avoid impolite behaviour and are instead expected to be more polite than men. It is through such stereotypical expectations, kept in place by gender ideologies, that gender roles are reaffirmed. As a consequence, "women may feel that they have to temper their use of these powerful and masculine speech forms in order that their speech is not judged by others to be aberrant" (Mills 2005: 272).

In this study I present evidence of men and women managers enacting impoliteness in mixed-sex business meetings. The examples of women managers being impolite demonstrate them breaking stereotypically gendered speech norms by enacting impoliteness, illustrating how they do not appear to have tempered their use of impoliteness strategies on these particular occasions. By presenting examples of women being impolite, the aim is to go some way towards fulfilling Mills' (2005) view, following Bucholtz (1999a), that as researchers we should be highlighting exceptions to stereotypically gendered interactional styles. Particularly with regard to impoliteness, Mills argues that it is important for the view of women being "nicer" than men to be challenged by producing analyses which show exceptions to this. Additionally, the analysis also focuses on impoliteness being enacted from men to women managers. Further information on how these CofP members evaluate and judge one another according to the performance of their gender and professional identities will also be carefully examined in conjunction with the interactional analysis.

4.   Data

The data that are analysed in this chapter are taken from an ethnographic case study of a manufacturing company based in the UK. Business meetings provide very fruitful speech events through which the performance of gender, professional identity and power can be gained. As Mumby (1988: 68) points out, meetings are "the most important and visible sites of organisational power". The analysis focuses on interaction that takes place within the business meeting discourse of two different CofPs within the manufacturing company. In the managerial meeting interactions that took place in this workplace, impoliteness occurred infrequently, which accords with Holmes and Stubbe's (2003b: 5) view that politeness, not impoliteness, is expected in workplace interaction: "most workplace interactions provide evidence of mutual respect and concern for the feelings or face needs of others, that is, politeness" (though see Schnurr, Marra and Holmes, this volume). However, within the data, there are a handful of examples of impolite interactions which warrant further investigation.

As well as audio-recording business meetings, where I was also present as an observer, the ethnographic approach I undertook additionally included shadowing, conducting interviews and analysing written company documents. This multi-method approach was adopted in order to attempt to gain a detailed picture of the organisation to enhance my linguistic analysis of business interactions. It has already been pointed out above that the interviews did not aim to get participants to talk about their intentions behind particular stretches of interaction. Instead, my interview data attempted to gain participants' attitudes and evaluations on the topic of gender and language and gender more generally in relation to the enactment of professional identities. These data provide crucial background information regarding the relationships between CofP members, as well as revealing the manner in which managers perceive the enactment of each others' professional identities through gendered lenses (Bem 1993).

The manufacturing company is made up of a range of different teams and departments which warrant classification as CofPs in their own right (see Mullany 2007). Data are taken from two different CofPs, the *Product Review Team* and the *Business Control Team*. The Product Review Team consists of 6 male and 4 female members, who are engaging in their monthly business meeting. The Business Control Team consists of 6 female and 4 male members, though one male, the direct superior of all participants, is absent. They are engaging in their weekly business meeting.

There is some cross-over in CofP membership. Female manager Sharon and male manager David, speakers who provide a key focus within the first part of the analysis, are members of both CofPs, thus providing the opportunity to assess their relationship in two different CofP contexts.

5. Analysis

The first interaction to be analysed is taken from a stretch of discourse that took place between Sharon and David in the Product Review Team meeting. Sharon and David are status equals who occupy exactly the same middle-managerial position on the broader institutional hierarchy of the manufacturing company. They have very similar levels of experience, although David has been in post with this particular company for three years longer. Sharon and David have a very tense working relationship, confirmed in separate dyadic interviews which I conducted. Shortly after this meeting was recorded, Sharon left the manufacturing company, and my interview with David took place after she had gone. In this encounter, David informs me of his view that Sharon was appointed to do exactly the same job that he was already doing. According to him, Sharon only managed to get transferred from another company because of her "relationship" with one of the company's male directors who had also previously worked at this other organisation.

David explicitly sexualises Sharon's managerial identity (see below). He goes on to express his view that having Sharon in the business held him back in terms of career progression. He had to perform his role in conjunction with her, whereas before he was able to perform his professional role by himself, and gain kudos for his achievements. Whilst I was interviewing Sharon, before she left the company, she makes disparaging comments about David's ability to fulfil his role, which she attributes to his personality. When this example of impoliteness takes place, Sharon and David have been jointly allocated the floor by their superior/meeting Chair Rob to report back on a task they had been allocated to fulfil together (transcription conventions are presented in the Appendix):

Extract (1)
Sharon and David are jointly reporting on yearly sales figures

1. David: So that's gone up from three something up
2.   on the autumn side it
3. David: [(.) side side   ]
4.   [((Sharon repeatedly whistles))] ((She waves
5.   a piece of paper at David and then throws this
6.   across the room at him))
7. David: I'm SOOO sorry (.) ((picks up a different sheet
8.   but not the one Sharon has thrown))
9. David: on page five of the autumn winter one

Instead of attracting David's attention through speech, the conventional way of gaining one another's attention in this CofP, Sharon instead chooses to whistle repeatedly at David to attract his attention, as well as simultaneously drawing attention to herself as the one with the correct information. In conjunction with whistling, Sharon waves a sheet of paper at him to convey the message that the figures he is reading out are incorrect. She then throws this paper rather aggressively across the meeting table in David's general direction. Whilst it is perhaps possible to argue that Sharon's actions could be identified as "incidental face-threat" (Culpeper 2005: 36), the ethnographic information gained regarding the relationship between these participants, the fact that Sharon breaks the norms and conventions of attracting her colleague's attention in this CofP, and most importantly, the manner in which David reacts as hearer firmly indicate that Sharon can be interpreted as intentionally choosing to attack David's face, drawing attention to the fact that he is inefficiently presenting the wrong information to the rest of the team.

At line 7 David strongly indicates that he has interpreted Sharon's behaviour to be intentionally impolite, responding with impoliteness himself using sarcasm. David's interactional strategy fulfils Culpeper's (2005: 42) sarcasm criteria: He performs what can be classified as an "obviously insincere" apology, with the sarcasm further signalled by the verbose use of "SOOO" as an excessive intensifier (see Holmes 1984), emphasising his insincerity. It is also notable that he does not use the sheet that Sharon has thrown at him, but instead finds the correct sheet in his own bundle of papers. This extract therefore presents evidence of both a male and female manager enacting a stereotypically masculine interactional style, with both of them being impolite and attacking each other's face needs. The struggle for power and status between status equals Sharon and David can thus be seen through their use of linguistic impoliteness towards one another.

The next instance of impoliteness is taken from the Business Control Team CofP. It too is directed at David and involves Sharon, but it also includes a number of other female CofP members. In this meeting, Simon, the overall superior of this CofP and regular Chair, pulled out at the last minute and appointed David as his stand-in. Therefore, whilst David occupies the same middle-management status level as all other participants outside of the meeting (with the exception of Julie, who is subordinate to other managers) in this specific, localised context of discourse management, David occupies a superior position of power, having been allocated the role of Chair.

Extract (2) takes place ten minutes after Sharon had already criticised David for his time-keeping skills using indirectness, and shortly after the absent Chair Simon had briefly entered the room to suggest David should bring the meeting to a close, using an indirect directive (see Mullany 2007):

Extract (2)
David is detailing how certain product codes are calculated

```
 1. David:    There are you know thirty forty different {xxx}
 2.           codes depending whether it's colour {red} non-colour
 3.           {red}{charcoal} erm you know whatever it might
 4.           be [er  ]
 5. Carol:       [mm]
 6.           [((laughter from all women managers))
 7. David:    [I realise [I'm  ]
 8. Becky:             [sorry] David we'll all stop [laughing]
 9. David:                                          [I realise ]
10. Becky:    ((laughs))
11. David:    I'm boring you but the scary
12.           [there is an important point to all this]
13. Carol:    [((laughs)) yes yes come on then       ]
14. David:    [there's a scary] scary footnote to all of this erm
15. Kate:     [((laughs))     ]
16. David:    having looked at the
17.           [export side of things                ]
18. Becky:    [((bangs cup on the table repeatedly))]
19. David:    Stop hassling me
20. Becky:    I wasn't I was giving you a drum roll
21.           ((laughter from all women managers))
22. David:    Oh right
23. Julie:    Important excit[ing bit  ]
24. Becky:                   [important]
25.           ((Becky and Sharon bang cups again in the
26.           sound of a drum roll))
```

Carol signals her frustration and impatience with David here with her minimal response "mm" (line 5). The intonation with which she issues this firmly signals that she is disinterested in what David is saying, resulting in amusement from all women managers, signalled through their collective laughter. Instead of bringing the meeting to a close, David has opened up another topic and goes into great detail to illustrate his point. Becky then interrupts David and enacts impoliteness, using the strategy of mock politeness (Culpeper 2005: 42), attacking David's face by insincerely apologising and continuing to laugh at his expense (lines 8 and 10). David indicates that he has assessed Becky's comment and the laughter of the women managers to be intentionally impolite by explicitly stating that he knows that he is 'boring' them, but nonetheless he has an important point to make. David is then interrupted by Carol, who extends the humour by engaging in banter, laughing and issuing a direct, unmitigated directive. Becky then enacts impoliteness again by the paralinguistic action of banging her cup repeatedly on the table (line 18). At this point David signals that he has perceived Becky's behaviour to be intentionally impolite again, responding on this occasion with a direct, aggravated directive, explicitly commanding her to "stop hassling" him. This clearly indicates that David perceives Becky's actions to be inappropriate for this CofP context, and thus impolite and challenging.

In response, Becky continues with this episode of impoliteness, under the guise of humour, by directly denying that she was "hassling" him, alternatively claiming that she was giving him a "drum roll", paralinguistically mocking David's evaluation of the seriousness of the point he is trying to make. The humorous justification for Becky's response makes it difficult for David to challenge her, and he simply acknowledges her explanation with "oh right". Becky has thus managed to maintain her challenge through impoliteness, and Julie then joins in, enacting power for herself by sarcastically mocking David's view that his information is both "exciting" and "important", despite being the CofP member with the least power and status on the institutional hierarchy. Becky engages in supportive simultaneous talk with Julie here (lines 23–24), repeating part of her turn. Sharon then joins Becky in banging their cups, under the guise that they are now both providing David with a drum roll.

The female members of this CofP thus collectively enact power together, jointly engaging with each other in this episode of impoliteness towards David to encourage him, in the interests of time and efficiency, to bring the meeting to a close. Interestingly, they draw upon stereotypically feminine speech strategies, using supportive simultaneous talk and collaboratively engaging with one another, but they do this in order to enact banter and impoliteness, challenging one of their male colleagues, who, in this particular context, is their superior at a local level of discourse management. It is important not to under-estimate the role of humour here, though, as it provides these women managers with a guise they can use, as Becky does, to deny that they are being serious. Humour is a very powerful and ambiguous linguistic device, and the humorous strategies that women managers adopt make it very difficult for David to challenge their impolite actions (see Mullany 2007).

In the interview conducted with Sharon she directly comments on David's chairing style and his talking time more generally in meetings, negatively evaluating his behaviour in stating that "he'd go on all day if we'd let him". Her comment strongly implies that she views it as the responsibility of her and others in the group to ensure that David does not "go on all day". Similarly, Becky states that "David will go on all day" in her interview. However, both Sharon and Becky explicitly attribute this to David's personality as opposed to gender. In David's interview, whilst he does not make any direct comment regarding Sharon's behaviour towards him in meetings, he does negatively evaluate her on gender grounds, as mentioned briefly above. He makes the following comment:

Extract (3)
> I have no (.) doubt in my mind that she has used her
> sexual (-) erm wiles if that's the right word ((laughs))
> er you know (-) to get what she wanted in the business
> and that probably to some degree (.) er has had a negative
> effect on me (.) so I've found myself (.) less able to exert
> (.) my influence based on skill (.) er in the light of others'
> er ability to (.) apply their sexual influences.

David's sexist comments reduce Sharon's success in the business to her ability to sexually manipulate, which has hampered his ability to use his managerial "skill". I will come back to assessing the consequences of David's attitudes and evaluations in a moment.

The final example of interactional meeting data is also taken from the Business Control Meeting, and involves Becky in interaction with another of this CofP's male managers, her status equal Martin:

Extract (4)
Becky is feeding back on a problem with one of her customers
1. Becky: I'll do it as a call off [account] [er   ]
2. Sharon: [yeah] [yeah]
3. Martin: Well the other thing is get estimates from them and
4.   [then we could have that as well   ]
5. Becky: [well that's what I mean that's what I'm working on] (.)
6.   honestly believe me I'm trying to sort it ((smile voice))
7.   I keep getting picked on [and I am trying
8. Martin: [((laughs))

9.	Sharon:	[((laughs))
10.	Becky:	[to sort it out]
11.	Martin:	[((smile voice)) we're] not picking on you
12.		((laughter from all))
13.	Becky:	the {xxx} can summary come on (xxx)
14.	Martin:	you'll know when we're picking on you
15.	Sharon:	((laughs))
16.	Becky:	It was actually the uk sales director [who offered
17.	Martin:	[mhm
18.	Becky:	it to them ((laughs))
19.	Martin:	yeah ((laughs))

Becky has come up with a solution to a problem that she has been having with one of her customers, and Sharon supportively agrees with this (lines 1–2). However, Martin then issues a direct, unmitigated directive, commanding Becky to "get estimates from them". Becky disruptively interrupts Martin, and her competitive, defensive response, where she rebuffs his command and informs him that she has already done this, indicates that she has perceived Martin to have attacked her face needs, being impolite by undermining her authority/being condescending. Whilst his directive may appear at a surface level to be helpful, as Becky's status equal, Martin does not have the institutional power, authority or expertise to tell her what to do about this particular issue. He issues his directive without mitigation, whereas the established norm for issuing directives in this CofP is to use a range of mitigation strategies. Mills' (2005: 268) view of a "mismatch in the judgement of status" resulting in impoliteness can thus be seen here. Whilst Martin appears to think that it is appropriate for him to issue Becky with a directive, it is clear from her response that she does not think that he has the status or power to do so. She has already come up with and reported her solution to the CofP, a problem which has been solely her role responsibility to sort out.

Becky performs stereotypically masculine strategies by interrupting Martin, assertively declaring that she has already done what he commanded (line 5). She then explicitly commands him to believe that she is being 'honest' when she states she is trying to sort out the problem. Becky then draws on humour to continue her response, using a smile voice and inappropriate register to accuse Martin of 'picking' on her. Becky's register, most commonly associated with the performance of a child's identity in interaction (line 7), mitigates the overall force of her challenge to Martin, and the inappropriacy of her utterance is the source of laughter for both him and Sharon. Martin then adds to Becky's humour, denying that she is being "picked on", a source of amusement for all. He then uses stereotypically masculine banter (line 14) to function as a denial that he was criticising her, and expands out responsibility from himself to the collective "we". Becky then deflects responsibility for this problem away from herself, using humour to criticise the company director who is ultimately responsible for creating this problem. Martin then agrees with her, thus signalling an end to this period of conflict.

Whilst there is no apparent overt tension between Martin and Becky in the company, in David's interview, he makes the following comment, which he later reveals to be in reference to Becky, Kate, and Martin as one of the "other males":

Extract (5)
> Two female account managers here are not slow to
> use the combination of will and gender to good effect
> when they can see an opportunity to do so and that's
> usually in the direction of a male person get what they
> want I've no doubt about it . . . that's causing erm
> resentment from other males you know there are other
> account managers who were who were certainly were
> at the same level as them who feel they're dropping
> behind because of the ability of the two females to
> exert their will gender mix to good effect.

David's reporting of Martin's perspective (and indeed, the view shared by "other males") that Becky and Kate use their sexuality to "get what they want" portrays women as cunning and devious sexual manipulators who use their sexuality instead of skill (the male norm) to enact their professional roles. In Martin's own interview, he backs up David's view of women managers in the company being sexually manipulative in the following observation:

Extract (6)
> Some women can play (.) the fact that they are a
> woman (.) and other women erm just tend to be
> more emotional I've found th-than men which isn't
> someone I particularly want to wor- I I don't
> particularly want to be working for a person who's
> (.) got emotional highs and lows you know I want
> to be working for someone that I know where I am
> (.) when I'm with them.

Martin thus presents two categories that women managers fall into: the sexual manipulator, or the emotional, irrational woman who is not competent to fulfil her role due to her biological predisposition. Martin further expands upon his perspective:

Extract (7)

> I just find men in general I mean in the workplace
> and in general I just find them to be more stable and
> straight really than women ... If you look at sort of even
> just on the biological clock you know you've got one
> week a month when women are you know not as they
> are the other three weeks of the month you know and
> and that is bound to have an effect.

Martin thus argues that women are more unsuitable for management due to their biological make-up, a prime example of this essentialist position being used to justify his perception that women are less suited to working in the professional sphere. These interview extracts are particularly revealing if viewed from the perspective of gendered discourses (Sunderland 2004; Mullany 2007). 'Discourse' in this sense is conceptualised from a Foucauldian perspective as "practices that systematically form the objects of which they speak" (Foucault 1972: 49). These gendered discourses carry gender ideologies, and are maintained by dominant gendered stereotypes which dictate norms of gender appropriate behaviour (Talbot 2003). One of the most enduring, overarching examples of a gendered discourse that operates within society is the "discourse of gender difference" (Sunderland 2004: 52), which, as its name suggests, works to emphasise distinct differences between women and men, often drawing on biological essentialism as a justification. Within the interview extracts from David and Martin, the discourse of women as emotional/irrational and the discourse of female sexualisation can be identified. These discourses over-emphasise distinct differences between women and men and account for these differences as a consequence of biology, and can thus be perceived within the overarching gender differences discourse. The consequences of the persistence of these dominant gendered discourses will be fully considered in the next section, along with a discussion of the key points of this chapter.

6.   Discussion

The interactional meeting analysis has demonstrated how interlocutors assess and judge whether impoliteness has taken place within discourse in particular CofPs. As analyst of these data, I have assessed how impoliteness emerges within interaction by examining stretches of discourse between speakers and hearers as opposed to just analysing a speaker's single, decontextualised utterance. A key part of this analysis has focused on how hearers signal their judgement of speaker intentionality by analysing hearer's responses as well as the speaker's discourse within particular CofPs. It is hoped that the analysis has emphasised the fruitful nature of integrating the CofP model of conceptualising impoliteness with certain aspects of Culpeper's (2005) impoliteness definition, particularly his second point (see Section 2 above), where he emphasises the importance of the role of the hearer.

The analysis of the impolite stretches of meeting discourse which took place between participants in two different CofPs demonstrates how women managers use impoliteness strategically to enact power over their male colleague David, even when he occupies a more senior position of power as meeting Chair. Whilst older language and gender studies in public spheres have shown how men dominate talking time (Eakins and Eakins 1979; Edelsky 1981), used as evidence of men exerting interactional power over women, there is evidence of resistance to this by the women managers in this CofP. They accrue power for themselves by negatively evaluating David's abilities to fulfil his professional role responsibility as an effective meeting Chair. It is not the intention to assess the rights and wrongs of this type of behaviour, but instead to present evidence that questions the stereotypical view of women as "nicer" interactants.

There is clear evidence of Sharon and Becky, along with other women managers in Extract (2) breaking the stereotypical norms of "appropriate" middle-class feminine behaviour, enacting power for themselves by engaging in stereotypically masculine, impolite behaviour when enacting their managerial identities. Furthermore, in Extract (4), Becky's response in retaliation to her perception of Martin's impoliteness demonstrates her performance of a wide range of stereotypically masculine, assertive styles. She then combines these with more mitigated, stereotypically feminine styles. Performing both stereotypically masculine and feminine strategies can be interpreted as indicating evidence of a wide-verbal-repertoire (Marra, Schnurr and Holmes 2006).

However, the analysis of meeting interaction only presents part of the picture. Examination of these CofP members' attitudes and evaluations of one another clearly demonstrates negative evaluation of women managers based on their perceived biological shortcomings. These dominant gendered discourses clearly highlight how women are negatively evaluated in the workplace, being seen as less suitable for the public sphere by their male peers. Therefore, whilst the linguistic analysis illustrates women performing assertive speech strategies and gaining power for themselves through impoliteness or in response to impoliteness directed at them, by going beyond a linguistic analysis and looking at broader gendered discourses, these successful, assertive women are subject to negative evaluation on gender grounds. The examination of gendered discourses presents potential explanations for the range of social and political problems that women still face in the professional sphere, including the persistence of the glass ceiling, unequal pay and sexual harassment. This moves the focus away from more localised issues of power, to global, overarching issues of gender and power within social institutions (see McElhinny 2003; Mullany 2007).

There is a plethora of data from other studies which supports this evidence of gendered discourses, firmly demonstrating that these problems exist in a wide range of professions, not just in this particular company. Sexualising women to reduce their achievement has been found by several other researchers (see Halford and Leonard 2001; Appelbaum, Audet and Miller 2002; Lakoff 2003; Olsson and Walker 2003). Furthermore, negatively evaluating women as being too "emotional and irrational" to fulfil managerial roles effectively, unlike the unemotional, rational male norm, has also been found in a range of work including Wajcman (1998), Olsson (2000), Brewis (2001) and Vinnicombe and Singh (2003).

Interview data, collected as part of an overall ethnographic approach, has been drawn upon in this chapter both to enhance the linguistic analysis, providing background information on participants' relationships to suggest reasons why impoliteness may be taking place, as well as providing a broader layer of analysis to assess gendered discourses. This goes some way towards accounting for how gender is deeply embedded within institutional structures (McElhinny 2003). Overall this method illustrates an alternative use for interviews, instead of using them to try and decipher participants' intentions behind their speech.

7.   Conclusion

In this chapter, the empirical analysis of meeting interaction has highlighted how impoliteness, power and gender identity are all enacted within discourse, as well as demonstrating how impoliteness can be identified by analysing the judgements interactants make across stretches of discourse. The fluid and dynamic nature of power and gender has been emphasised, along with the value of using the CofP model, integrated with certain aspects of Culpeper's (2005) model, to produce analyses of (im)politeness and gender. It is my intention that combining aspects of the "postmodern" approach with the newer conceptualisations of (im)politeness based on significant re-writings of Brown and Levinson demonstrates how the two broad approaches to impoliteness should not be seen in direct opposition – they can inform and enhance one another.

It is also the intention that the fruitfulness of analysing interaction within the institutional setting of the workplace has been emphasised. The data analysis has presented clear evidence of women acting assertively, using impoliteness or responding assertively towards impoliteness deemed to have been intentionally directed at them. However, the dominant gendered discourses demonstrate that negative evaluation and sexist comments towards women in the public sphere are not far away, regardless of how much evidence there is of women managers enacting power through discourse.

Appendix

Transcription conventions

(.)	indicates a pause of two seconds or less
(-)	indicates a pause of over two seconds
(xxx)	indicates material that was impossible to make out
{xxx}	indicates material that has been edited out for the purposes of confidentiality
[ ] [ ]	closed brackets indicate simultaneous speech
% %	percentage signs indicate material was uttered quietly
RIDICULOUS	capital letters indicate material was uttered loudly
((laughs))	material in double brackets indicates additional information
=	equals signs indicate no discernible gap between speakers' utterances

Notes

1. I am indebted to Derek Bousfield, Miriam Locher and María Dolores García-Pastor for providing me with a range of insightful and meticulous comments on an earlier draft of this chapter. I also wish to express thanks to my workplace participants for helping to make this research possible.
2. Whilst I believe that the distinction between "politic" behaviour and "politeness" can be a useful one in some circumstances in order to clarify the distinction between socio-culturally determined behaviour ("politic"), and behaviour which aims to make someone feel better about themselves ("polite"), I agree with Mills (2003: 68) that often this is a "counter-intuitive" distinction, as in some studies "politic" behaviour is taken to stand for politeness, particularly if interactants' perceptions of politeness are assessed. As Harris (2005) points out, the distinction often creates more problems than it solves, and also it can be difficult to see when one definition ends and the other begins.
3. Mills (2003) also draws a distinction between social class here, with politeness being associated with middle-class femininity and impoliteness being associated with working-class masculinity. It is thus particularly notable that the data analysis in this chapter highlights white middle-class females breaking stereotypical expectations by performing impoliteness to white middle-class males.

Part 5. Further empirical studies

Chapter 11
"You're screwed either way": An exploration of code-switching, impoliteness and power

Holly R. Cashman

1. Introduction: Code-switching, (im)politeness and power[1]

Code-switching is a topic that has received a great deal of attention from linguists with a wide range of interests and diverse theoretical approaches in the past half century. Similarly research on politeness, and more recently impoliteness, has grown exponentially in the last quarter century. Traditionally, politeness research has tended to focus on the monolingual. Although a great deal of research examines politeness in second language acquisition contexts (e.g., Barron 2003; Achiba 2003; Kasper and Rose 2002, just to name a few recent book-length works), comparatively little research has focused on politeness or impoliteness in other, natural bilingual contexts (cf. Cashman 2006, 2008). Several studies of conversational interaction in bilingual communities, which will be summarized very briefly below, indicate that speakers may exploit code-switching and language choice in the construction of politeness and impoliteness in interaction, although the question of (im)politeness is not central to these studies and with few exceptions no explicit use of (im)politeness models or theories is made. Valdés (1981) argued early on that, far from being random or meaningless, code-switching could be a functional strategy adopted by speakers in interaction. She concluded that code-switching was used strategically to both aggravate and mitigate requests (Valdés 1981: 106). Li Wei (1995) notes that speakers' choice of a language variety and code-switching in interaction occurs within the context of a language community, which implies certain code-switching norms and speakers' language preferences. He finds that in intergenerational, bilingual interactions, non-compliant language choices may serve to maximize the face threat of a request, while compliant choices may do the opposite (2005: 208–210). Cromdal (2004) observes that bilingual children use code-switching strategically in disputes to highlight opposition and constrain interactants' opportunities to engage in talk. In this way, he indicates, code-switching works in concert with other devices. Valdés, Li Wei and Cromdal all emphasize that in many cases the direction of the switch is not important; rather, it is the contrast created by the juxtaposition of the two language varieties that is used as an interactional resource (Valdés 1981: 105; Li Wei 1995: 212; Cromdal 2004: 53). In some cases, however, the direction of the switch may be important, as bilingual speakers' may exploit the association of the language varieties in their repertoire with different levels of status or power in the wider social context of the interaction. Jørgensen (1998: 343), for example, describes code-switching as a 'power wielding tool' in interaction among young bilinguals who were developing an awareness of the relative status of their mother tongue vis-à-vis the country's national language in the school environment. Similarly, in a recent study Garder-Chloros and Finnis (2003: 526) demonstrate that in addition to other uses, code-switching in the London Greek-Cypriot community they study could be used to mitigate directness, particularly in instances of women addressing men.

It should be pointed out at the outset that there is no attempt in this chapter to describe code-switching as inherently impolitic or impolite. The reason for this is two-fold. First, as has been argued convincingly elsewhere (cf. Watts 2003: 168 and Culpeper 2005: 41), specific words, expressions or speech acts (or, it seems reasonable to add, linguistic resources such as code-switching) cannot accurately be described as inherently polite or impolite. Second, the small, eclectic sample from one very specific community and the qualitative analysis of same would, of course, not provide a sufficient basis from which to generalize about a practice that is found in nearly every bi- and multilingual community around the world. What this chapter will do, it is hoped, is tease out the complexity of the intersection of code-switching, impoliteness and power, discuss in detail several examples of code-switching and impoliteness, and, based on that discussion, make several preliminary observations about code-switching and (im)politeness in bilingual communities.

2. Theoretical approach

The theoretical approach that is taken in this chapter is informed by several recent research threads. First, the taxonomy of *impoliteness* strategies outlined in Culpeper (1996, 2005) and Culpeper, Bousfield, and Wichmann (2003) not only elucidates the variety and heterogeneity of ways of being impolite, but the most recent article provides a useful working definition of impoliteness that guides the approach taken in this chapter. Culpeper explains that

> [i]mpoliteness comes about when: (1) the speaker communicates face-attack intentionally, or (2) the hearer perceives and/or constructs behavior as intentionally face-attacking, or a combination of (1) and (2). (Culpeper 2005: 38)

This definition importantly takes into account the role of the hearer as well as that of the speaker in constructing impoliteness, although Bousfield (2007b, this volume) signals this as a problem. Culpeper (2005: 37), as Bousfield points out, asserts that impoliteness is not unintentional, but in the above definition an unintentional face attack could be construed as intentional by the hearer and, therefore, by Culpeper's definition, be impolite. While Bousfield's (2007b) definition of impoliteness attempts to remedy the contradiction in Culpeper's definition, it in effect eliminates from consideration within impoliteness the case of a hearer, or person in a receiver role, who intentionally constructs an utterance (intentional or not) as impolite. I would argue that this specific type of situation belongs in an examination of impoliteness, and that the Culpeper definition, despite Bousfield's reservations, gives enough but not too much importance to the role of the hearer.

While the distinction between super strategies (e.g., positive and negative impoliteness) in many ways ties Culpeper (1996) to Brown and Levinson's ([1978] 1987) politeness theory, subsequent modifications in Culpeper, Bousfield, and Wichmann (2003) and Culpeper (2005) seem to indicate that the approach might be more flexible and able to be integrated into other frameworks. For example, Culpeper (2005) tentatively aligns his impoliteness strategies with Spencer-Oatey's (2002, 2005) rapport management framework, which develops the notion of face by recognizing within it two components (called quality face and social identity face) and complements the notion of face with the concept of sociality rights, which is also comprised of two components (equity rights and association rights). Cashman (2006) attempts to flesh out this alignment, which can be summarized briefly as seen in Table 1.

2.1. Relational work and the discursive struggle over impoliteness

Relational work (Locher 2004; Locher and Watts 2005) is a second key concept that contributes to the theoretical approach taken in this chapter. According to Locher, relational work is basically the "process of defining relationships in interaction" (2004: 51). A departure from Brown and Levinson's ([1978] 1987) politeness theory, relational work comprises a much broader spectrum of language behaviour, from the negatively marked, impolite behaviour to the negatively marked, over-polite behaviour, with unmarked politic behaviour and marked polite and politic behaviour in between (Locher 2004: 90). The concept of relational work is key to the approach taken here in part because of its capacity for dealing with issues of identity and power in interaction. Summarizing the interrelatedness of power and identity within the relational work framework, Locher (2004) explains that

Table 1. A summary of the provisional alignment of impoliteness strategies with Spencer-Oatey's (2002) concept of rapport-management, adapted from Cashman (2006: 241)

Attacks on face	Definition of desire/belief	Impoliteness strategies
Quality face	desire to be evaluated positively in terms of personal qualities	attack the other's appearance; attack the other's ability/work
Social identity face	desire for acknowledgement of our social identities or roles	condescend, scorn or ridicule
Attacks on sociality rights		
Equity rights	belief that we are entitled to be treated fairly by others	frighten/threaten; hinder or block the other – physically or linguistically; challenge the other; impose on the other
Association rights	belief that we are entitled to associate with others in accordance with the type of relationship	ignore or snub the other; disassociate from the other

> ... power is regarded as relational, dynamic and contestable. Thus, power cannot be possessed like a commodity: it is constantly negotiated in and around relationships. More powerful interactants who have more freedom to act will have to secure their position. By comparison, less powerful interactants may resist, align themselves with other members of a group or attempt to exercise their own power. Negotiating power in interaction is thus part of how interactants shape their identity. (Locher 2004: 37)

The gist of Culpeper's (2005) above definition of impoliteness fits within the concept of relational work as long as it is seen not as the opposite of politeness alone, but as one, negatively marked, non-politic, inappropriate part of a spectrum of language behaviours that comprise relational work.

Additionally, Watts' (2003) notion of the *discursive struggle* over (im)politeness is key to the approach to code-switching and impoliteness in this chapter. Watts distinguishes between folk interpretations of *(im)politeness* (first order) and sociolinguistic interpretations of *(im)politeness* (second order), and he emphasizes that the definition of first order (im)politeness is "an ongoing struggle over the differential values of appropriate social behaviour" (2003: 25). While

Culpeper's (2005) distinctly second order definition of impoliteness is used as the jumping off point in this chapter, the focus will be on how participants themselves define impoliteness and how they construct and negotiate it in interaction, or first order interpretations of impoliteness. Therefore, this notion of appropriateness and the context of social norms is key for the present analysis, even if relatively absent from Culpeper's definition.[2] Also, it is important to note that a duality similar to the first and second order distinction in (im)politeness exists with the definition of code-switching. What analysts consider the juxtaposition of material from two distinct language varieties in a single turn at talk or within a single interaction may not be considered code-switching by participants. In other words, the folk interpretation of code-switching may not always align with the analyst's interpretation.

Integrating Culpeper's (2005) definition of impoliteness, Locher's (2004) concept of relational work and Watts' (2003) notion of discursive struggle, this present chapter will attempt to treat impoliteness in a contextualized way that focuses on how speakers themselves construct, evaluate and negotiate impoliteness in interaction. Despite the use of Culpeper's second order definition of impoliteness, this chapter focuses primarily on first order notions of politeness and attempts, while recognizing the dangers inherent in the enterprise, to use these two notions complementarily.

2.2. Language choice and code-switching

The study of bilingual talk is an area in which terminology is often confusing and contradictory. In this chapter, language choice and code-switching describe two related, but distinct phenomena. Language choice is understood as the selection of one language variety over another (or others) to address an interlocutor. Code-switching is seen as the juxtaposition of more than one language variety in a single utterance or interaction. In discussing language choice, the language variety chosen is of primary importance, but in the analysis of code-switching, the direction of the switch (i.e., from Spanish to English or from English to Spanish) may or may not be relevant. Where it is considered relevant in this chapter, this is discussed. Where it is not, the switch itself as a contextualization cue is the focus.

2.3. Research questions

In this chapter, the use of code-switching as a resource in the construction, interpretation and negotiation of conflict in a Spanish/English bilingual community in the U.S. is examined. The following research questions are addressed: First, do bilingual speakers see code-switching as a resource for constructing and evaluating impoliteness? Second, do the bilingual participants in a small set of role-play and spontaneous interaction data use code-switching as a resource for constructing/interpreting impoliteness in interaction? Third, (how) are code-switching and impoliteness involved in the emergence and alteration of power relationships and participants' identities in interaction?

3.   Methods and data

While much research on linguistic (im)politeness relies solely on the analysis of spoken interaction (either spontaneous and naturally-occurring or deriving from experimental, role-play situations) or questionnaire data (including discourse completion tasks), Mills (2003: 12) advocates the analysis of a more eclectic set of data, including anecdotes and interviews in addition to recorded spontaneous conversation and questionnaires. Traditionally, research on linguistic politeness has favoured the questionnaire and the role-play as data collection instruments, while research on linguistic impoliteness has employed a variety of sources of data from recalled spontaneous interactions (Beebe 1995), to recordings of spontaneous conversations (Cashman 2006), to literary texts (Culpeper 1996) and media data (Culpeper, Bousfield and Wichmann 2003; Culpeper 2005). While it is not within the scope of this chapter to weigh the advantages and disadvantages of these diverse data collection instruments and sources, as others have already done in detail (e.g., Kasper and Dahl 1991), it is necessary to briefly discuss, if not justify, the use of the interview, which is less common and may be misunderstood. The discourse completion task-style questionnaire and the role-play attempt to elicit participants' authentic responses to prompts or situations. In contrast, the interview seeks to elicit participants' evaluations of interactions, either retrospectively through the playback of recordings or, as in the present case, simply through more or less direct questioning about the concepts of politeness and impoliteness and the elicitation of relevant anecdotes. Given the growing interest in first order notions of politeness and impoliteness, accessing participants' evaluations would, it would seem, be a priority, leading researchers to want to "take native speaker assessments of politeness seriously and to make them the basis of a discursive, data-driven, bottom-up approach" (Locher and Watts 2005: 16).

Although there may be agreement on the importance of non-specialist beliefs about language in general and first order notions about language in particular, how to access that information is the difficult question, as the interview has been seen as a problematic and unreliable source of data in linguistics for a variety of reasons. For example, the use of the sociolinguistic interview (cf. Labov 1984) as a means of accessing a variety of styles has been criticized on the basis that the interview is not a natural speech event and the elicited data does not approximate spontaneous conversation (cf. Wolfson 1976; Briggs 1986). Furthermore, participants' evaluations of their use of linguistic variables have been found to be unreliable (cf. Labov 1966: 470–472), which calls into question the reliability of metalinguistic tasks in interview data. In recent research on politeness, rapport management and relational work, these same reservations about interview data have also been expressed. Mills (2003: 44), for example, points out that politeness is an area in which a gap exists between what participants do and what they think (or report) they do. Spencer-Oatey (2000b) notes that in research on intercultural rapport management, there was a danger that participants might act as cultural representatives rather than individuals and provide stereotypical notions rather than their own individual evaluations. Locher and Watts add that they do not "ask the participants themselves how they felt about what they were doing" (2005: 17) because the retrospective-style interview, in which speakers reflect on the interaction (such as a conversation or a role-play) that they have participated in, imposes a polite–impolite parameter on the participants.

Milroy and Gordon (2003), however, argue that

> ... we should not assume that all self-reported data are less accurate than those collected through observation of actual usage ... Direct questioning may, in fact, provide a more accurate usage picture for some variables than would less metalinguistic approaches. Included here would be items that appear infrequently in free conversation and are difficult to elicit through indirect questioning. (Milroy and Gordon 2003: 54–55)

Although their discussion relates specifically to the use of metalinguistic approaches such as surveys and interviews to access use of phonological and morpho-syntactic variables, their point is, I would argue, equally valid for the elicitation of first order notions of politeness and impoliteness. While it is certainly possible to use analysis of spontaneous conversation, as Watts (2003) and Locher and Watts (2005) advocate, to uncover participants' in-situ evaluation of politeness and impoliteness, it is not unreasonable to suspect that in the open-ended interview that is used here, in which ideas about what participants consider polite and impolite are explored through the elicitation and evaluation of anecdotes and other recalled events, speakers' first order notions of politeness and impoliteness can be accessed. It is believed that in this interview style, inspired by the cognitive anthropological approach described by Quinn (2005), the participants themselves determine the relevance of that parameter for their experiences and interactions, making it possible to recover their first order notions of impoliteness through their analyses of their experiences. It is, of course, recognized that, as Mills (2003: 45) explains, interview data is a necessarily partial and interested type of data. She also notes, however, that other types of data often seen as impartial and unbiased are actually not, including recordings of spontaneous conversation. Analysts' transcripts of conversations, Mills (2003: 45) points out, though often quite detailed, are nevertheless incomplete renderings of the complex layers of linguistic and non-linguistic elements of conversational interactions.

Due to the aforementioned, widespread reservations about the use of interview data, it is important to point out here that this data is used in the analysis below to complement other types of data, namely role-play and spontaneous interaction, just as those other types of data are used to complement the interview data. It is also necessary to point out that the interviews analyzed here were exploratory in nature; that is, a good deal more, and more in-depth, interviews would need to be carried out in order to approximate the technique described by Quinn (2005).

The data analyzed in this chapter are the following: (1) a set of three exploratory interviews conducted with students at Arizona State University between the ages of 21 and 37. Of the three participants, one is an undergraduate, two are graduate students; two are female, one is male. All three were born in Mexico and later immigrated to the U.S. as children. They consider themselves bilingual, with Spanish as their native language and English as their second language. One still considers Spanish her dominant language, while the other two now consider English their dominant language; (2) a set of audio-recorded role-plays. The entire set includes nine different situations organized around three areas (requests, apologies and invitation refusals) and thirty speakers (15 male, 15 female). These data were collected by a bilingual, Mexican-American, male graduate student. The example examined from this data set in this chapter is from a request role-play between peers; (3) a corpus of 25 hours of audio-taped, spontaneous interaction in a second grade classroom in a central Phoenix, Arizona, dual language immersion elementary school with a student population of roughly 850 students, that is predominantly Mexican and Mexican-American: 90% of the students identify as Hispanic. These data were collected by the author while working as a participant observer in a second grade classroom at the school from January through June 2003. Spontaneous student–student and student–teacher interactions among the 22 students, two teachers (one for English, one for Spanish), and one student teacher in the classroom, on the playground and in the cafeteria were recorded. While it is hoped that these three sources of data provide a more complete and complementary picture of code-switching and impoliteness, it is not claimed that this is an exhaustive investigation nor that the claims are generalizable to any other bilingual community (or even this specific one for that matter).

4.   Analysis: Power, code-switching and being impolite

4.1.   Evaluating impoliteness

The three bilingual Mexican-American participants interviewed seemed to agree on several key areas related to code-switching, impoliteness and power. First, when asked about the topic of impoliteness, none of the three interviewees initially raised the issue of code-switching, or even language choice. Rather, the first topic related to linguistic interaction that arose in the interviews was children's participation in adult conversation. Two participants, both female, commented that children were not allowed to participate in adult conversation. One participant, for example, said:

(1)   it was always kind of an unspoken rule that I do not interject myself into an adult's conversation um very little you know I remember my parents would visit friends of the family or whatever and they would have their conversation and me being young you do not you know speak up you do not interrupt the conversation because it's an adult conversation you're a child (Alicia,[4] 21)

Another participant summed this up more succinctly:

(2)   I was always told not to speak 'now don't do that don't speak you don't know how to speak' you know (Noemi, 37)

The male participant commented more generally that:

(3)   I always look at the Spanish or Mexican culture you know so I would consider polite speaking with respect to your elders (Carlos, 27)

These evaluations, of course, do not imply that no child ever interrupts an adult conversation in Mexican-American communities of practice.[5] Instead, it would seem that the participants are describing here what Watts might call the latent network, or the "objectified social structures produced by 'historical practice'" (2003: 153). To choose appropriate, politic behaviour would be to re-enact or reproduce these structures, while to choose inappropriate, non-politic behaviour (either impolite or over-polite) would be to attempt to reconstruct or re-negotiate those latent networks through the creation of emergent networks. Of course, with the adult–child relationship the element of power is relatively obvious. The adults, as more powerful interactants, will often be able to maintain their position as legitimate participants in a conversation, while children, as less powerful interactants, may attempt to renegotiate their less powerful position by inserting themselves into adult conversation. To bring in the second order notion of rapport management, I would suggest that this insertion could be considered an attack on the adults' association rights: the children impose on the adults the requirement to associate with them, even though, according to the norms of the community, the adults are not required to interact with the children. Age or generation in the participants' description of politeness in the latent network has interesting implications for the evaluation of language choice and code-switching, as will be explored below.

Also related to the topic of code-switching and impoliteness, the topic of language choice and (im)politeness was something that resonated with all three participants. In their responses, all three participants deemed the language proficiency of the interlocutor the most important aspect of the context for evaluating the (im)politeness of language choice. For example, one interviewee summed up his ideas about language choice succinctly:

(4)   if I know that somebody doesn't speak English I really- or Spanish I won't speak Spanish in front of them just because I- I think it's kind of rude ((laughs)) you know to because my parents were always you know 'don't speak a language around people that- that don't speak it because it's kind of rude' so ((laughs)) (Carlos, 27)

The same interviewee described how he would choose which language to use with someone he did not know:

(5)   I guess um in- there's an unspoken kind of rule that if it's an elderly person that's of Hispanic descent like I'll probably talk to them in Spanish um just because that's- that- I would be like accommodating myself to them because they're like you know kind of higher than me ((laughs)) and uh- and with I guess with English I would just use it with normal- just my normal activities with most people (Carlos, 27)

In his description of his approach to language choice, Carlos points out two key aspects of the issue: first, that it is, to use Locher's framework of relational work (2004: 90), inappropriate and negatively marked to speak a language in front of someone that he or she does not understand, and second, that it is appropriate and either unmarked or positively marked to speak to an older adult in their preferred language. Furthermore, it is implied that, in Carlos' latent network, Spanish is the preferred language of older Hispanic adults and English is the preferred language of everyone else.

A second interviewee commented on language choice in the family context, which was relevant to her since she has several family members who are Spanish monolingual (including parents and a sister) as well as children who are English-dominant bilinguals who prefer to speak English. She explains:

(6)   I have family um who speak English most of the time like ((laughs)) my daughter (1.0) she speaks Spanish very well but she speak it never never and she knows my family is there and they don't- like my mom my dad or my older sister they don't speak English my other- other siblings do um and they speak English and they know they don't supposed to be speaking English I say 'mija [my daughter] you're not speaking Spanish your tía [aunt] doesn't understand what you're saying' (Noemi, 37)

Like Carlos in example (5), Noemi hinges her assessment of the appropriateness of language choice on the language proficiency of the hearer as well as the relationship between interlocutors. In a way, her statement echoes in the present what Carlos reports his parents telling him as a child, that the appropriate language choice is the preferred language of your interlocutor, especially if that person is older, as in the case of Noemi's daughter's Spanish monolingual aunt and grandparents. In addition, Noemi implies by mentioning that her daughter speaks Spanish very well that the language proficiency of the speaker is also an important factor in assessing the appropriateness of language choice. Because her daughter speaks Spanish very well, her choosing to speak English to or even in front of elder, Spanish monolingual family members can be evaluated as inappropriate and negatively marked.

A third participant described the appropriateness of language choice more specifically in the context of a work setting, which was relevant to her at the time, as she had just started a new job where many staff members were bilingual:

(7)   I think if you have the ability to use both of them especially if you're in a work setting where you're supposed to be conducting specific chores if it's something as simple as 'can you please pass me the pencil' and you feel the need to say it in Spanish knowing that it makes other people uncomfortable that kind of goes into like the impolite ((laughter)) so it's just a matter of making you feel comfortable I can understand it if you don't know how to say a certain word but (1.0) just out of- I don't want to say respect because I think (1.0) we're all entitled to speak in whichever language we choose to but you're working (1.0) so (1.0) it's- it really depends on who you're interacting with and whether they can understand you in either one (Alicia, 21)

Like Carlos in example (5) and Noemi in example (6), in example (7) Alicia couches her evaluation of the appropriateness of language choice in the language proficiency of the hearer(s), and like Noemi in example (6) she recognizes also the proficiency of the speaker as a factor in language choice. It seems that a speaker's lack of proficiency in the hearer's preferred language might, in the dynamic nature of the emergent network, result in what might ordinarily be considered a non-polite language choice, if not appropriate, at least not inappropriate. The additional aspect of the work setting introduced by Alicia brings with it a conflict, in her evaluation, between language rights and what she reluctantly calls respect. Although Alicia recognizes that bilingual speakers have the right to speak either language, this power to choose either language is in her estimation checked by the institutional context in which demonstrating mutual respect with one's co-workers is appropriate and by the aforementioned aspect of the latent network in which speaking a language a hearer does not understand in front of him or her is inappropriate and negatively evaluated.

To sum up the discussion of examples (4) to (7), language choice is a central issue for bilingual speakers, and these choices are an important aspect of relational work for bilingual speakers. The politics of language choice seem to accord a fair amount of power to monolingual members of the communities over bilingual members, as their language proficiency often determines what is considered appropriate in a given interaction. Within the family and in the workplace, bilingual speakers' language choice is policed, and monolingual speakers may secure their power over bilingual speakers by evaluating as impolite the use of a language they do not understand in their presence. By choosing a language not preferred or understood by one's interactants or even overhearers of one's interaction, bilingual speakers may use impoliteness to resist this policing and/or to align oneself with other bilingual speakers in order to assert one's own power. The use of a language not understood by others in a given context could be evaluated as an attack on the association rights of the monolinguals, or those who do not understand the interaction, as they are, in effect, excluded from the interaction.

When asked if they could think of a time when they were impolite to someone or when someone was impolite to them, each of the three participants told at least one anecdote that involved language choice or code-switching and impoliteness. One interviewee, interestingly, told two very similar anecdotes in which language choice was interpreted as impolite. In example (8), the interviewee is the 'hearer/recipient' of the impolite language choice:

(8)   my family and I went to- it was kind of like a festival um here in one of the parks
       in the area and it was mainly catering to the Hispanic community because it had

artists you know who- from Mexico or whatever and it really irritated me and I couldn't tell you why but it really irritated me that the person who was collecting the tickets asked to see my purse- to open up my purse but in Spanish I was like I speak English too because he had been speaking English to somebody else and the moment he saw me he was like 'open- abre su su bolsa por favor [open your your purse please]' and I was like 'dude I don't know what you're saying' so I don't know I think people have different ideas as to what it means to be addressed in one of the languages or the other (Alicia, 21)

In her contextualization of the security guard's utterance in example (8), Alicia provides information about two factors affecting her evaluation of her inter- locutor's language choice, the ethnicity of participants and the language of the preceding talk. Although Alicia claims not to be able to identify why she as- sessed the language choice to be inappropriate and non-politic, she does hint at what the reason might be. By asserting her proficiency in English, claiming a lack of proficiency in Spanish, and referring to being addressed in one language or another as having meaning, Alicia indicates that for her in this situation to be addressed in Spanish meant that the security guard had determined that she did not speak English; this assessment and the language choice that resulted from it, it seems, were seen as impolite by Alicia. While we do not know why this is the case, we can guess that several factors may play a role in what being addressed in Spanish meant to Alicia in that situation, namely, the prestige of English relative to Spanish in the dominant language ideology of the United States (cf. Zentella 1994), and the prevailing discourse of disdain for immigrants who do not acquire English, even within Mexican-American or Latino communities (cf. García Bedolla 2003). In this way, the security guard's language choice could be viewed in the second order framework presented above as a simultaneous attack on Alicia's quality face and social identity face. In addition, it could be viewed as what Bousfield (this volume) calls an off record impoliteness tactic: the impoliteness is conveyed indirectly by way of an implicature.

Furthermore, while Alicia does not mention the element of power, it is clear that in the situation she describes, the security guard is at that moment the more powerful interactant, as he has power over (cf. Watts 1991: 61) her immediate physical environment and is able to force or coerce her to comply with his interests, and she is the less powerful one, as failing to comply could result in any number of outcomes contrary to her interests. Given this power over others, including Alicia, the security guard's assessments about the language proficiency of his interlocutors, which are seen to indicate where he sees them fitting in to the social structure of the latent network, may be evaluated as impolite, and this impoliteness may be seen as a tactic to secure or enhance his power over interactants. Alicia's resistance to this assignment of language proficiency by the security guard, despite the fact that she is fluent in Spanish, is an attempt to exercise her own power, thus renegotiating the power relationship.

In the second anecdote, very similar in nature to the first, Alicia is the 'speaker/performer' of the impoliteness:

(9)   I remember there was one time I was doing volunteer work for my church and basically it had been like a food drive they were basically distributing food to people who may not have had the resources (1.0) there was this lady- okay first of all the church catered mostly to a Hispanic community and there was this lady that came up she had you know dark hair darker skin and I addressed her in Spanish a lot of the people coming up were Spanish-speaking and they were very clearly more comfortable with Spanish and I addressed her in Spanish and she looked at me 'I DON'T SPEAK SPANISH' she yelled it at me in English and I think she was Native American and I think she just took offense at my having addressed her in Spanish I don't see why that would be offensive but then again if I put myself in the situation of somebody who wanted to see in my purse ((laughs)) I can kind of- I can relate but I couldn't exactly pinpoint why that wasn't (1.0) why that was offensive ((laughs)) (Alicia, 21)

Again, as in example (8), in example (9) Alicia contextualizes the language choice by emphasizing the ethnicity of participants and the language of the previous discourse. In contrast to the first anecdote, in the second situation, she also contextualizes the language choice by pointing out what might be called ethnically marked aspects of her addressee's appearance. Alicia attempts to sustain the argument that her language choice should not be interpreted as impolite while that of the security guard in example (8) should be, but she seems compelled to recognize the similarity of the two situations.[6] One difference, of course, that Alicia does not point out is her relative lack of power over her interactant as compared to the security guard's. Alicia, as someone distributing food, certainly had some degree of power over her interlocutor in example (9) in that she could have potentially refused to give her food, but not the same power as the security guard to force or coerce her. Another possible difference, although it is impossible to know for sure, is the ethnicity of the speaker of the impolite language choice. Alicia, of course, is Mexican-American, but the ethnicity of the security guard was not explicitly mentioned. As will be seen in examples (11) and (12) below, the ethnicity of the speaker can make a difference in the evaluation of a non-preferred language choice as impolite or non-politic.

When asked if he had ever been seen as impolite because of language choice, another interviewee explained:

(10)   Carlos: yeah there's definitely been times where I- I'll see like an elderly Hispanic person and I assume that they speak Spanish and I- and I'll start speaking

to them in Spanish and I can tell that it bothered them like like 'what? what I don't speak English or-?' I can- I can tell um and then- and then I also feel the other way like a lot of times people come to me and and uh I kind of hear them speaking like with an accent and so I feel like speaking to them in Spanish but then because they're trying to speak to me in English I think I might offend them if I if I don't speak to them back in English so so uh yeah

INT: But then if they find out later that you speak Spanish-?

Carlos: yeah and then sometimes they're like 'why didn't- why didn't you help me? didn't you see me struggling?' like so yeah I mean it's kind of like you know you're screwed either way ((laughs)) (Carlos, 27)

Here Carlos makes explicit the connection that Alicia alluded to in example (8) above: being addressed in Spanish can be interpreted as being judged incompetent in English, which in the context of the United States (cf. Bedolla García 2003) is negatively marked. At the same time, however, not choosing an interactant's preferred language – especially if that interactant is older or elderly – can also be interpreted as inappropriate and impolite. In a given situation, especially when interacting with an unknown person, these two possible interpretations of language choice can conflict leaving the bilingual speaker seemingly without an appropriate/politic, either unmarked or positively marked, option. This conflict indicates that, even without the possible cross-cultural misunderstanding that bilingual and bicultural speakers who are members of a language minority group may face in interactions with members of the dominant cultural/linguistic group, bilingual speakers face greater challenges and have additional resources in relational work. This is precisely because the language proficiency leaves their language choice open to stricter evaluation without the benefit or excuse of being judged incompetent and, therefore, not responsible for the effect of the language choice on the interactant.

When asked if he had ever viewed someone else as impolite because of the language she or he chose to use with him, the same interviewee, Carlos, said:

(11)   yeah ((laughs)) I have and- and- and I feel kind of bad about this but- but there's been times where- where somebody will- will come up to me and they just start speaking to me in Spanish and for some reason I mean I'm very like honest with myself but for some reason I'll get offended I'm like 'yeah why did you assume that I spoke Spanish?' or something I- I don't know what that's linked to I'm sure it's linked to like- like some kind of insecurities from having to experience all this and I don't know what it is you know and I don't think it's something good ((laughs)) (Carlos, 27)

A follow-up question clarified that in example (11) Carlos was talking about his evaluation of the choice of Spanish by an interactant who is Mexican or Latino. He said that he might also interpret an Anglophone person choosing to use Spanish with him as impolite, but he was surer of the reason that might motivate his assessment in that situation:

(12)   I would interpret it as like they're looking down on me ((laughs)) you know (Carlos, 27)

This interpretation seems similar to Alicia's in example (8) above. The ideological underpinnings for this interpretation are likely the same as those hypothesized above for Alicia: prestige of English relative to Spanish, disdain for immigrants who do not learn English, and, possibly, disparaging of physical attributes associated with Mexicans including dark hair and dark skin.

Finally, the three interviewees concurred that code-switching itself was not impolite, but it could be depending on the context. One interviewee, for example, said:

(13)   with an older person that is unknown to me even if they speak both (2.0) I'm either gonna address them in English or I'm gonna address them in Spanish but it's not- in my mind's eye it's not proper to throw in whichever one's handy (1.0) and I think it has to do back- it has to do again that whole idea of how you speak reflects your level of education your level of whatever (Alicia, 21)

A second interviewee agreed that context was important, commenting that she did not interpret her children's code-switching with her or amongst themselves as impolite, but she recognized that her monolingual, Spanish-speaking relatives might consider it impolite when her children code-switch in front of them. She described, however, even within that situation why code-switching might not be seen as impolite if it is related to the girls' proficiency:

(14)   but maybe sometimes there are some words they can't speak in Spanish some phrases they can't explain so maybe it's when they switch without tr- you know meaning it or anything so I don't know if that would be impolite (Noemi, 37)

A third interviewee agreed about the importance of context; in fact, he said that there are situations in which not code-switching could be viewed as impolite:

(15)   I mean yeah they might see it as you're not trying to be part of our group or you know you know you can do it so how come you don't- you're not doing it you know they would associate you with being like- like a gringo or you know yeah I mean yeah that's for sure I think (Carlos, 27)

Additionally, he described a situation in which he might use code-switching as a deliberate impoliteness strategy:

(16)   I know I- there's been times where if I- if I for some reason want to distance myself from a person like I'll speak in Spanish to my friend or whatever and- and deep down like it is kind of like to get back at somebody like yeah like you know you're not like uh you know like yeah I'm Mexican or whatever and I'm proud of it and you know you know I know that you don't like this but I don't care kind of a thing (Carlos, 27)

To sum up, it seems that the three Mexican-American, bilingual participants interviewed here viewed language choice and code-switching as a resource for *doing* (im)politeness as well as a cue for *interpreting* (im)politeness in inter- action. In some instances they were able to articulate quite easily why they interpret another person's language choice or code-switching as impolite, while other times they were not. Even when they were not able to articulate *why* they interpret another person's language choice as impolite, they were able to identify language choice or code-switching as the basis of their evaluation. Following or resisting the language choice expected by the norms of the community of practice seems to be one way that the bilingual speakers interviewed here ei- ther accept and reproduce or challenge and renegotiate the power relationships among participants.

4.2. *Performing impoliteness*

For a different, and it is hoped complementary, perspective on impoliteness and code-switching, we will now turn to examine an example from the corpus of role-plays described above. The following role-play was recorded by Marcos, a bilingual, Mexican-American graduate student in linguistics at Arizona State University from the greater metropolitan area of Phoenix, Arizona. The partic- ipant, whom I have called Bernardo here, is also a young, Mexican-American man. They are both in their early 20s and they know each other well, as they are both members of the same extended family. The set-up of the role-play, based on an item from Koike's (1994) oral questionnaire, is the following:

Imagine that a friend has gone with you to a family celebration for your grandfa- ther's birthday. Your friend sat down in the chair reserved for the guest of honor. You want him/her to move. You go to talk to him/her...

As this example was collected in the course of a completely unrelated research project, neither participant would have had any idea about the researcher's in- terest in impoliteness or the research questions set out in this chapter.

In example (17), Marcos is sitting in the chair of the guest of honour at the birthday party of his friend Bernardo's grandfather:[7]

(17)

1	Bernardo:	hey
2	Marcos:	hey qué pasó *(what's up)* (Benardo) what's going on man?
3	Bernardo:	what are you doing sitting in that chair?
4	Marcos:	pues *(well)* I was ((UNSURE)) to get comfortable you know [so but hey hey
5	Bernardo:	[you ain't in your home
6	Marcos:	can you tell somebody that we need some more chips and salsa man because there's- it's running out over here
7	Bernardo:	you've got some nerve get out of that- get out of that chair
8	Marcos:	why man?
9	Bernardo:	it is the chair for the guest of honor
10	Marcos:	oh okay
11	Bernardo:	and you're sitting in the chair muy conchudo *(very shameless)* thinking you're all bad
12	Marcos:	hey you- yo no sabía man por qué nadie me dijo nada? *(I didn't know man why didn't anyone tell me anything?)*
13	Bernardo:	hi can you read? there's a sticker that says (1.0)
14	Bernardo:	[guest of honor
15	Marcos:	[I didn't see that sticker
16	Bernardo:	that's because your back is planted to it
17	Marcos:	y [tú piensas que voy a p- que voy a poder a leer el inglés? *(and you think that I'm going to b- that I'm going to be able to read English?)*
18	Bernardo:	[you're not at home it's says it- it's bilingual
19	Marcos:	where's the bilingual part?

20	Bernardo:	flip [it over flip it over
21	Marcos:	[allí está atrás? está atrás?
		allí atrás? *(there it is on the back?*
		it's on the back? there behind?)
22	Bernardo:	it's- it's posted on the back
23	Marcos:	pues yo no sabía [y por qué tienes la
		parte de español atrás eh? why?
		(well I didn't know and why do you
		have the Spanish part on the back)
24	Bernardo:	[okay
25	Marcos:	what are- what are you trying to do
		here? what is- what is this? [this is
		discrimination
26	Bernardo:	[I don't
		want- I want you to [go into to the
		kitchen
27	Marcos:	[I'm out of here
		I'm gonna get over here I'm gonna sit
		over here that's what I'm gonna do
28	Bernardo:	please and grab a chip on the way out
		and stuff your mouth with it
29	Marcos:	I'm gonna give you something to stuff
		your mouth with
		[((laughter))
30	Bernardo:	[((laughter))

Even in the first few lines of this interaction, it is clear that the stance of the participant Bernardo in this role-play is markedly different from that of the other 29 participants in the role-plays. Generally, participants' stance in the role-plays seems self-conscious, even sometimes uncomfortably or awkwardly so. They interact in what one might call a 'doing a role-play' style. In contrast, Bernardo's approach to 'doing a role-play' in this example, while still self-conscious, is confident and comedic; in other words, his non-serious approach seems like a way of doing 'being cool'. Marcos, the fieldworker and interactant, responds to Bernardo in kind, and they engage in a competitive performance of constructing impoliteness: Bernardo constructs Marcos as being impolite for sitting in the guest of honour's chair and asking for more chips and salsa; Marcos constructs Bernardo as being impolite for speaking English to someone who is Spanish monolingual and, presumably, older if not elderly.

A closer look will demonstrate how code-switching is used in this example to perform impoliteness. Bernardo briefly switches to Spanish in line 11 in order to insult Marcos ('muy conchudo'), although he glosses the insult immediately in English ('thinking you're all bad'). Marcos switches to Spanish in the following turn (line 12) using the contrast between the languages to highlight the justification of what Bernardo has constructed as impolite (his sitting in the guest of honour's chair). Bernardo does not follow Marcos' shift to Spanish, and for a few turns they both use English while Bernardo accuses Marcos of being impolite and Marcos justifies his behaviour. Then, in line 17, Marcos switches back to Spanish and maintains this choice (with the exception of line 19) for several turns. This language choice, one might argue, can best be understood as a performance within the role-play because Marcos is 'doing' a character here – a monolingual, perhaps older or even elderly, perhaps Mexican gentleman. As highlighted in the analysis of the interviews above, all three participants agreed that speaking a language in front of others who do not speak it is generally interpreted as impolite and that Spanish is generally seen as the preferred (default) language choice for older people in the community. Therefore, by voicing this character, Marcos constructs Bernardo's talk as impolite, thus countering Bernardo's intentional face attack. Despite the fact that Marcos, who is claiming to be monolingual in Spanish, switches back to English, the role-play continues with each participant attempting to out-do the other in terms of (a) claiming impoliteness (e.g., Marcos' claim of discrimination in line 25 and Bernardo's reiteration of his request in line 26) and (b) being impolite (e.g., Bernardo's mock politeness in line 28 and Marcos' threat of physical violence in line 29).

Although this example is drawn from role-play data collected as part of a separate project and not from spontaneous interaction, it serves to demonstrate how bilingual participants might use code-switching and language choice as a resource for constructing or interpreting impoliteness and for negotiating power in interaction. Both Marcos and Bernardo use switches to highlight parts of their utterances that are either impolite face attacks ('muy conchudo') or are defensive reactions to accusations of impoliteness ('yo no sabía'). In addition, Marcos uses switches into Spanish in order to bring about a new situation with new norms for politeness in which he would in fact be the recipient rather than the perpetrator of impoliteness. Their use of offensive and defensive counters to impoliteness (Culpeper, Bousfield, and Wichmann 2003) result in a spiral of impoliteness through which both participants attempt to renegotiate the power relationship that obtains between them.[8]

4.3. Doing impoliteness in interaction

The third and final source of data, the corpus of spontaneous conversational interaction among bilingual, second grade students of approximately 7 to 8 years of age, will be analyzed in this section in order to discover if code-switching is used by participants as a resource for constructing and interpreting impoliteness. Code-switching would seem to be an ideal resource for carrying out many of the impoliteness strategies described by Culpeper (1996, 2005) and Culpeper, Bousfield and Wichmann (2003). Switching into a language that is not shared by all members of the group, for example, could accomplish the strategies *disassociate from the other* or *exclude the other* (Culpeper 1996: 357), both threats on a participant's association rights, to use terms from Spencer-Oatey's (2002, 2005) rapport management framework. Likewise, switching into a language in which some participants are more proficient than others could accomplish the strategy *impose on the other* (Cashman 2006: 231), and aid in the accomplishment of the strategy *hinder or block the other—physically or linguistically* (Culpeper, Bousfield, and Wichmann 2003). In addition, the use of code-switching as a contextualization cue (cf. Li Wei 2002) could serve to draw attention to and highlight any intentional face attack by setting it off from surrounding talk.

In the following example, three students are working in a group to construct a model of a bridge. Julia has negotiated her position as group leader, but her position of power over her interactants is tenuous and she must constantly work to defend it. Just prior to the interaction below, her two co-participants, Arturo and Jessica, have teamed up to carry out an idea proposed by Arturo and not sanctioned by Julia:

(18)
4	Jessica:	oh YEAH YEAH SAND ((adding sand))
5	Arturo:	yeah I told you I'm the good (guy)
		(1.0)
6	Arturo:	put sand in there and make it sa-
		it's [water
7	Julia:	[como: (ho:w)
8	Julia:	yeah yo sé cómo hacer la water (*I*
		know how to make the water)
		(0.5)
9	Julia:	yo sé- yo la hago solamente (*I know-*
		I'll do it alone)
10	Arturo:	NO porque YO- porque *(NO because I-*
		because) THAT WAS MY ide- [IDEA
11	Julia:	[no yo puse

esto primero *(no I put this first)*
12   Arturo: no porque *(no because)* that was my
idea

In lines 8 and 9 Julia attempts to assert her authority over her co-participants
after they have aligned with each other and attempts to exercise power in the
interaction by excluding Jessica and Arturo from the activity of creating water
under the bridge. She highlights this move by maintaining her use of Spanish
despite her co-participants' switch to English and by the redundant and repetitive use of the optional pronoun 'yo' ('I'). In line 10, Arturo constructs Julia's
talk (and behaviour) as impolite, an attack on his equity rights, using several
resources including increased volume, the use of the pronoun 'yo' and a switch
to English ('that was my idea'). He echoes this again in line 12, but his decreased
volume and dropping of the pronoun 'yo' may indicate a concession to Julia, at
least temporarily recognizing her as the more powerful interactant.

In example (19), taken from the same group bridge-building activity, Julia
tries to defend the group project, while Arturo disassociates himself from the
group:

(19)
1   Julia: ((student walks by group)) vas a
detruir our artwork *(you're going to
destroy our artwork)*
2   Arturo: yes I'm gonna DESTROY YOU
3   Jessica: ((gasp))
(1.0)
4   Arturo: ((laughs))
5   Julia: STOP IT ARTURO
6   Arturo: yes whatever

In line 1, Julia reprimands a student from another group for walking too close
to her group's model bridge. Arturo, in line 2, perhaps orienting to Jessica's
utterance as a reprimand of his behaviour, uses the strategy *frighten/threaten*
(Culpeper 1996; Culpeper, Bousfield, and Wichmann 2003) to attack the others'
association rights. The use of this impoliteness strategy is highlighted by a switch
into English as well as by the use of increased volume. Julia responds defensively,
matching his use of English, in line 5, and Arturo further employs the strategy
disassociate from the other using the word now ubiquitous in American English
'whatever'.

In a third example, during a different group activity involving the same three
participants, code-switching is again used to highlight a face attack:

(20)

196	Arturo:	tú agarra lo que quieras ya [(hice) todo *(you grab whatever you like I already did everything)*
197	Julia:	[(a tí te) falta agarrar- *(you have to get-*
198	Jessica:	yo no *(not me)*
199	Arturo:	yo no *(not me)*
200	Arturo:	tú vete *(you go)* [((inaudible))
201	Julia:	[((inaudible))
		(1.0)
202	Julia:	yo? *(me?)*
203	Arturo:	because I did it already (.) hazlo *(do it)*
204	Jessica:	(hice) los papeles mira *(I did the papers look)*
205	Arturo:	oh
206	Jessica:	((inaudible))
207	Arturo:	hurry up what you're making? nothing (3.0)
208	Arturo:	man that stinks

Here Arturo and Jessica, having been constructed as the less powerful interactants through Julia's negotiation of a leadership role, have aligned with each other to exercise power by resisting Julia's plan for the group activity, starting with her attempt to delegate them to collect materials while she plans. While Jessica in line 204 justifies her refusal to cooperate by pointing out that she already collected some of the necessary materials, Arturo in lines 207 and 208 attacks Julia's work. His switch to English highlights this attack of Julia's quality face using the strategy *attack the other's ability/work* (Cashman 2006).

5. Conclusions and directions for future research

What do these various data tell us about code-switching and impoliteness? Just as code-switching has been found to serve as a resource for doing politeness, code-switching, it is argued here, is a resource available to the bilingual interactants involved in the interviews, role-play and spontaneous interaction for constructing impoliteness. To revisit the research questions proposed at the outset, first, do bilingual speakers recognize code-switching as a resource for constructing/evaluating impoliteness? Based on the limited interview data examined here, I think it is fair to say as an answer to this research question that the three interviewees recognize code-switching as a possible resource for constructing impoliteness and interpreting impoliteness. More research is clearly needed. Second, do the bilingual participants in the role-play and spontaneous interaction data use code-switching as a resource for constructing/interpreting impoliteness in interaction? Although there is insufficient space here to explore more than a few examples, and although the analysis of interactional data is strictly qualitative, one could conclude from this analysis that the bilingual participants in these interactional data do in fact use code-switching as a resource for being impolite and for constructing others' talk as impolite. Once again, I would emphasize that more research into this question is needed. Third, (how) are code-switching and impoliteness involved in the emergence and alteration of power relationships and participants' identities in interaction? Analysis of data from all three areas in this chapter indicate that code-switching and impoliteness may serve as resources for more powerful interactants to maintain or recapture their position and for less powerful interactants to resist and renegotiate their position. Both language choice and code-switching were cited by interviewees as resources for relational work. The two participants in the role play, as well as the three participants in the spontaneous interactional data, contested existing power relationships using code-switching and verbal behaviour that may be interpreted as impolite.

Clearly, the analysis presented here has barely scratched the surface of a very complex issue, that is, the use of code-switching as a possible resource for co-constructing impoliteness and challenging, reaffirming or augmenting power. Compared to politeness, there is scarcity of studies on impoliteness in general (cf. Locher and Bousfield, this volume); within the research on impoliteness, there is little research on the phenomenon in bilingual contexts. This is a rich area for future research, given that in bilingual, bicultural communities the very norms of what is considered appropriate, already contested in monolingual contexts, are even more complicated. The present chapter, obviously exploratory in nature, can only point to the dire need for additional research in order to answer some of the most basic questions in the field.

Notes

1. The author gratefully acknowledges support from the Sociological Initiatives Foundation, which enabled the collection of the spontaneous conversation data in the Phoenix, AZ elementary school from January through June 2003, as well as a Faculty Grant in Aid from the College of Liberal Arts and Sciences at Arizona State University, which funded the collection of the role-play data in Summer 2005, and a competitive seed grant from the Institute for Humanities Research at Arizona State

University, which funded the author's participation in the Linguistic Impoliteness and Rudeness: Confrontation and Conflict in Discourse Conference (University of Huddersfield, 2006) at which an earlier version of this chapter was presented.

2. Note that this crucial aspect is not absent from Bousfield's (this volume) model of impoliteness.

3. See Gafaranga and Torras' (2002) argument for a more participant-centered approach to code-switching.

4. This and all other names mentioned in the interview, role-play and spontaneous conversation data are pseudonyms with the exception of Marcos Herrera, the field-worker who collected the role-play data, who is currently an M.A. student in Spanish specializing in Sociolinguistics at Arizona State University.

5. The use of the concept of community of practice in language politeness and impoliteness research is not unproblematic. Although it is not possible to fully explore this issue here, see Mills (2003), Culpeper (2005) and Cashman (2006) for discussions of the community of practice versus the activity type as ways of conceptualizing the context of impoliteness and politeness in interaction.

6. Alicia's reference in (9) to her interactant's physical attributes as a way of justifying her choice of Spanish may also indicate another meaning of being addressed in Spanish – that is, that she was comparatively darker in hair or skin colour than other interactants to whom he spoke English – that led Alicia to evaluate the guard's language choice as impolite in (8).

7. The transcription conventions used in both the role-play and spontaneous conversation data are the following:

plain	original talk
(italics)	translation of Spanish talk
bra[ckets	[overlapping talk
CAPS	comparatively louder talk
colon:::	lengthening of the preceding sound
hyphen-	self-interruption as determined by the analyst
(text)	analyst's best guess at inaudible talk
((text))	analyst's comments, usually about non-verbal information

8. It bears noting that this interaction might actually be considered banter, or mock impoliteness, which Bousfield (this volume) points out is the functional opposite of mock politeness, an impoliteness tactic.

Chapter 12
A manual for (im)politeness?: The impact of the FAQ in an electronic community of practice

Sage Lambert Graham

1. Introduction

Although linguists have been exploring the nuances of politeness for decades, beginning with the pioneering works of Lakoff (1973), Brown and Levinson ([1978] 1987) and Leech (1983), there has been significantly less research focusing on impoliteness in interaction. Most recently, Culpeper (1996, 2005), Culpeper, Bousfield and Wichmann (2003), Spencer-Oatey (2005), and Mills (2005) have explored the dynamics of impolite behaviour, proposing definitions of the term impoliteness and noting the need for more empirical research to test the parameters of this phenomenon. Spencer-Oatey (2005) proposes an approach that examines the impact of perceptions of politeness in rapport management, noting that additional research is needed in this area. The present case study begins to fill that gap by analyzing perceptions of appropriateness and politeness in messages sent to an email discussion list. This chapter takes an ethnographic discourse analytic approach in examining how members of the discussion list interpret and enact (im)polite and (non-)politic behaviour, and how their perceptions can lead to conflict.

In examining the notions of politeness in an electronic setting, it is important to acknowledge the parameters of the medium, since these can have an enormous impact on the interpretation and enactment of politeness. As Smith (1999) notes,

> [There are] a number of features of this [electronic] world that make conflict more likely and more difficult to manage than in real communities: wide cultural diversity; disparate interests, needs and expectations; the nature of electronic participation (anonymity, multiple avenues of entry, poor reliability of connections and so forth); text-based communication; and power asymmetry among them. (Smith 1999: 160)

While I would argue that electronic communities are "real communities," the wide diversity, disparate interests, needs and expectations and power asymmetry are all important elements in how e-community members craft their own politeness strategies and interpret the utterances of others with regard to politeness.

One influential element in navigating politeness in an email setting (given the diversity mentioned above) is the FAQ (frequently asked questions), which is sent to all members of the list I will be focusing on here upon subscribing. It provides both technical guidelines (e.g., how to unsubscribe) as well as guidelines for appropriate interaction within the community (e.g., don't "lurk"). Unlike face-to-face interactions, where there is not always a "manual" for appropriate behaviour, the FAQ, whether or not it *accurately* reflects communicative practice within the group, is respected by the community members as a guideline for appropriate behaviour. In fact, those who are perceived to have participated inappropriately are often told to "RTFM" (Read the Fucking Manual). This manual, the FAQ, therefore occupies a critical place within the email community as a baseline for determining what is politic (Watts 2003) or appropriate (Fraser 1990) behaviour (which, when deviations occur, can lead to breakdowns in rapport). It is unclear, however, how having an "e-politeness manual" affects interpretations of what counts as acceptable behaviour. It is the goal of this study to explore (1) how the FAQ represents norms and expectations of politic interaction in this Community of Practice (CofP), and (2) how the power relationships between individuals affect the ways that the rules of the FAQ are interpreted and enacted.

2.   Impolite and non-politic behaviour

While research on politeness has been ongoing since the 1970s, research addressing *im*politeness is much more recent. Much of this research has focused on how to define the term – a slippery concept at best. Culpeper (1996, 2005) and Culpeper, Bousfield and Wichmann (2003), note that intent and context play a critical role in identifying (im)politeness; they argue that, for impoliteness to occur, speakers must *intend* to attack or offend the hearer's face (for an alternative view see Terkourafi, this volume). Another factor consistently recognized as a critical element in impoliteness research is (subjective) perception. Culpeper (2005) argues that the hearer's perception of politeness is necessary for impoliteness to occur, stating that:

> Impoliteness comes about when: (1) the speaker communicates face-attack intentionally, or (2) the hearer *perceives and/or constructs* behaviour as intentionally face-attacking, or a combination of (1) and (2). (Culpeper 2005: 38, emphasis added)

Watts (2003) and Locher and Watts (2005) also note the importance of hearer interpretation in their discussion of polite and politic behaviours. Watts (2003) defines politic behaviour as "that behaviour, linguistic and non-linguistic, which *the participants construct* as being appropriate to the ongoing social interaction" (Watts 2003: 144, emphasis added). Watts (2003) also argues that "an integral part of a theory of (im)politeness₁ must be an account of the ability of individual participants to *recognize* the appropriate politic behaviour [within the situational context] in the first place." This raises the question of how interactants recognize the linguistic structures of politic behaviour:

> There is simply no objective means to measure our feel for politic behaviour, which of course makes it as open to discursive struggle as the term '(im)polite' itself. . . . *The evaluation remains individual and can at best become interpersonal and intersubjective, but can never be objectively verifiable.* (Watts 2003: 164, emphasis added)

Mills (2003: 79) notes that ". . . impoliteness only exists when it is classified as such by certain, usually dominant, community members, and/or when it leads to a breakdown in relations." Finally, Spencer-Oatey (2005), in her framework for rapport management, says

> I take (im)politeness to be the *subjective* judgments that people make about the *social appropriateness* of verbal and non-verbal behavior. In other words, it is not behavior per se that is polite, politic (Watts 2003) or impolite; rather (im)politeness is an evaluative label that people attach to behaviour, as a result of their subjective judgments about social appropriateness. (Spencer-Oatey 2005: 97, emphasis added)

As these researchers all argue convincingly, perceptions of (im)politeness and (non-)politic behaviour are varied and subjective. While I agree with this assessment, in an email context, I would argue that FAQs provide what is *perceived to be* an authoritative guideline for appropriate behaviour and therefore function to make interactants "consciously aware of appropriate politic behaviour" (Watts 2003: 164). While I agree with Watts that interpretations of what is politic "can never be objectively verifiable," I believe that (1) the FAQ reflects the intersubjective expectations for behaviour that are operational within a given Community of Practice, (2) these expectations are considered more-or-less stable by the members, and (3) the FAQ therefore occupies a place of prominence within the community as an important guideline for behaviour and it is therefore one goal of this study to test this idea.

In examining the role of the FAQ in influencing subjective assessments of (im)polite and (non-)politic behaviour, it is also important to recognize the power of the CofP in dictating the norms of interaction (for other examples of this phenomenon see Locher and Watts; Mullany; and Schnurr, Marra and Holmes, this volume). In the case of an email community, the FAQ is a representation of the community expectations; members must orient to both their individual face needs and also reconcile these with the norms and expectations of the group (which are reflected in the FAQ) in managing rapport. Spencer-Oatey (2002) proposes a framework of rapport management that explicitly addresses these two components: one's individual or personal identity and one's identity within a group. In this study, I will use Spencer-Oatey's (2002) framework of rapport management to examine the ways that e-community members use (or ignore) the FAQ as a guideline for behaviour, since this framework provides a means of teasing apart the influence of the individual's wants and needs from the group wants and needs in a given interaction. The 'rapport management' model involves two main components: the management of face (which is oriented to *value*) and the management of sociality rights (which is oriented to *entitlements*). Within the rapport management construct, face management is divided into two categories:

1. *Quality face*, which is individual and is similar to Brown & Levinson's notion of positive politeness – people have a desire to be liked/admired by others.
2. *Social Identity face*: which is group oriented and reflects the desire for people to acknowledge and uphold our social identities or roles, e.g. as group leader, valued customer, close friend. (Spencer-Oatey 2002: 540–541)

Similarly, sociality rights may also be divided into two categories: the personal (equity rights) and the social (association rights):

1. *Equity Rights*: We are entitled to personal consideration from others, so that we are treated fairly [and] are not unduly imposed upon (cf. Brown and Levinson's negative face).
2. *Association rights*: We are entitled to association with others that is in keeping with the type of relationship that we have with them. … we feel, for example, that we are entitled to an appropriate amount of conversational interaction and social chit-chat with others (e.g. not ignored on the one hand, but not overwhelmed on the other). (Spencer-Oatey 2002: 540–541)

By adopting a framework that allows us to account for both individual and group influences on behaviour we can gain a better understanding of the multi-faceted web of rapport management.

3.   Computer-mediated rapport management

As noted above, many researchers on politeness agree that, in determining which behaviours count as (im)polite, context and intent are crucial. In this study I will address the question of how behaviour in an email discussion group is perceived as (non-)politic and/or (im)polite using a Community of Practice framework

(Bucholtz 1999b; Eckert and McConnell-Ginet 1999; Holmes and Meyerhoff 1999; Lakoff 1973; Lave and Wenger 1991; Wenger 1998). Since a Community of Practice approach allows us to address the dynamic and emergent nature of a given community, it seems a particularly useful approach for analyzing constructs such as interpretations of (im)polite and (non-)politic behaviour which *are* interpersonal and intersubjective and will therefore be affected by the norms and expectations of the communities in which they occur. In this case, we can use context and an understanding of the communicative norms of the Community of Practice to examine the intersection between power relationships and interpretations of (im)polite and (non-)politic behaviour as they relate to establishing rapport within a community.

In examining (im)politeness and (non-)politic behaviour in a computer-mediated CofP, two (related) influences on politeness and politic behaviour emerge: (1) the limitations of the medium itself, and (2) the guidelines for Netiquette. I will now examine each of these in greater depth.

3.1. The computer medium

Speaker intent is difficult to determine under any circumstances, and in computer mediated communication (hereafter CMC) the resources for indicating intent are different than they are in face-to-face interactions. One example that illustrates this is prosody, which Culpeper et al. (2003) argue convincingly is an important element in interpreting different levels of impoliteness as well as speaker intent. In a computer context, however, prosody is unavailable. Guidelines for Netiquette offer alternative strategies for how to prevent misunderstanding – e.g., through the use of emoticons (smileys ☺), text-based approximations of interactional markers (e.g., <g> for grin, CAPITALS for shouting, etc.). As I noted in Graham (2003, 2005), however, these textual markers don't meet up to the complexities of conveying speaker intent. In many computer communities, for example, one would not use a "frowny" ☹ to indicate true sadness. Writing "I'm very upset today. A close family member of mine died last night ☺," for example, would likely be interpreted as inappropriate in most CofPs, since the smiley implies a joking (or "mock-sadness") register rather than a marker of true feelings. Smileys, therefore, are not adequate to approximate the range of paralinguistic markers that help clarify intent in a face-to-face setting. This doesn't mean that hearers can't and don't assign intent to speakers, but simply that the lack of adequate tools to approximate paralinguistic and non-verbal messages may complicate this process.

In addition to having limited paralinguistic cues and resources to help communicate intent, communication via email is also asynchronous. This asynchronicity can be problematic when participants post messages in which their intent is unclear. Even if a person doesn't *intend* to be impolite, if others interpret his/her message as impolite and respond in kind, the resulting conflict may have spiralled past the point where clarification by the original writer is sufficient to end the discussion. This differs from a face-to-face setting where paralinguistic cues are likely to make interpretations of (im)politeness clear fairly quickly and so allow for quicker resolution (positive or negative). In CMC, on the other hand, it is possible that by the time a writer becomes aware that others have interpreted his/her intent as being intentional impoliteness it will be too late for him/her to address or correct the misconception. In such a case, the discussion of the offensive action may have taken on a life of its own before the original sender realizes how his/her actions have been interpreted and makes a move to clarify them.

Computer-mediated interaction also has a participation structure that differs in some ways from face-to-face interaction. In the context of CMC, lurking (i.e., being subscribed to a list without posting/contributing) is an acknowledged fact. Although the norms of Netiquette discourage lurking, generally speaking, computer-users are aware that lurkers are present in email list communities. Because of this, one must be aware that there are multiple audiences to any given post. If you answer a question posed by one listmember, you are not only addressing the original questioner but also all of the other subscribers to the list (both the core group and the lurkers). The same is true when making "public" statements in response to an individual's posts; one must be aware that the individual will read the message in addition to the larger audience of subscribers. The presence of lurkers affects interpretations of politeness in two ways: (1) writers must frequently navigate rapport management to an audience which, since they are (partially) unknown, might have different notions of what constitutes polite behaviour, and (2) writers must take care to address *all* of the members of the "audience" or risk being accused of talking as if someone who is present is not there or intentionally excluding people.

3.2. Netiquette

A second factor that impacts interpretations of (im)politeness in CMC is Neti-quette, as set of guidelines which began early in the development of computer communication as a way to help codify the expectations of appropriate behaviour in an electronic arena. A prevailing assumption in the early days of Netiquette was that, in a setting where people couldn't see their interlocutors and had no investment in them as people, they would not feel a particular compulsion to work to protect others' face. There is, in fact, some research that suggests that, in the early development of computer-mediated communication there was perhaps more of a tendency to "flame"[1] people than would exist in face-to-face interactions. Dery (1994) posits that

> [T]he wraithlike nature of electronic communication – the flesh become word, the sender reincarnated as letter on a terminal screen – accelerates the escalation of hostilities once tempers flare; disembodied, sometimes pseudonymous combatants tend to feel that they can hurl insults with impunity (at least without fear of bodily harm). (Dery 1994: 1)

This idea that being in an online setting lessened the feeling of responsibility for one's words resulted in several guides for "Netiquette" or online etiquette. In addition to controlling for flaming behaviours, Netiquette also provides guidelines for less confrontational types of interaction. Shea (1994: 32–33) outlines the following Netiquette rules: Remember the human, lurk before you leap, respect other people's time and bandwidth,[2] don't post flame-bait, and "be forgiving of other people's mistakes (you were a newbie once too!)".

These guidelines for behaviour, therefore, while acknowledging that flame wars will and do happen, also make the argument that being polite online is important. In addition, they outline online behaviours that are, in some cases, related to the computer medium (e.g., don't waste bandwidth). Although these guidelines are given computer context labels, however, they are not, in fact, really different from face-to-face politeness expectations – don't cost other people money, don't waste their time, (both manifestations of Spencer-Oatey's equity rights) and don't be mean or call them names (both manifestations of Spencer-Oatey's quality face); in a computer-mediated context, however, breeches of these rules may manifest themselves in different ways (and/or elicit different responses) than occur in face-to-face interaction. In a face-to-face setting, for example, we are not told to RTFM (Read The Fucking Manual) when we breech the expectations for polite/politic interaction; the fact that there is a special acronym/flame for those who do not follow the tenets of Netiquette is a testament to the weight given to the FAQ document which lists guidelines based on Netiquette).

4. Data

In order to examine the relationship between the FAQ and notions/interpretations of email politeness, I examine two email threads where differences in expecatations for politeness resulted in conflict: one in which a new listmember posted an introduction questioning the community for not following its own rules (as outlined in the FAQ) and one in which a relative newcomer is accused of a breech of polite behaviour and then challenges the expectations and interpretations of politic and polite interaction that operate within the CofP. Both threads were taken from a corpus of over 80,000 email messages sent to ChurchList, an email discussion list which provides a forum for discussion of issues that affect the Anglican Church. All subscribers to this list receive a three part FAQ within 24 hours of subscribing;

> Part 1 – Technical instructions. This part addresses technical procedures (how to unsubscribe, receive messages in digest mode, etc.).
>
> Part 2 – Guidelines for how to tailor your postings to the expectations of the list community. This part addresses issues regarding what types of messages to post and how to format them and outlines expectations for appropriate behaviour (e.g., don't lurk, be respectful, etc.).
>
> Part 3 – Descriptions of the group of related lists. This part introduces the differences in the group of affiliated lists, each having its own specialized focus (one such affiliated list is specifically for church musicians, for example).

Here, I will focus on the second part of the FAQ, since it more specifically addresses the issues that are likely to cause misunderstandings regarding what is politic/polite, but it should be noted that technical procedures are also often linked to politeness in CMC. It is considered problematic, for example, to send "unsubscribe" messages to the whole list; the technical guidelines try to address this so that inexperienced computer users are not inadvertently non-politic.

I have chosen to look at "threads"[3] instead of individual messages because, as Culpeper, Bousfield and Wichmann (2003: 1560) note, through examining patterns of impoliteness and reactions to it *across exchanges* we can begin to understand "some of the richness of context necessary for identifying and analyzing impoliteness". In both of the threads I am examining here, the expectations for what counts as appropriate behaviour differ and these expectations shift during the course of each discussion. It also appears that power is an important element; both threads involve a newcomer who challenges the most experienced, "core" listmembers regarding what counts as politic behaviour. In Graham (2003 and 2005), I defined core members as those who had posted at least 100 messages over the course of one calendar year. Although this measure is accurate to indicate tenure within the community and active participation, numerical measures are not sufficient to delineate the complex power structures that exist in this

CofP. For my purposes, therefore, I define core members here to be those who (1) post over 100 messages in one calendar year, and (2) have the power (via their acceptance by the *other* "core" members) to influence norms of interaction within the CofP.

Before exploring the dynamics of impolite/non-politic interaction, some discussion of the FAQ guidelines themselves is in order, since the FAQ is an attempt to codify the expectations for politeness and politic behaviour that then emerge within the two threads.

5. The FAQ as a guideline for behaviour

As I stated above, many email discussion groups and bulletin board groups have FAQs that are designed to help newcomers address technical issues as well as determine what types of behaviours are (in)appropriate for the given community. Part two of the ChurchList FAQ includes the following 12 guidelines for interaction,[4] many of which are readily identifiable with relation to strategies of rapport management proposed by Spencer-Oatey (2002). Part 2 of the FAQ reads:

(1)   Subject: What should I put in my biography/introduction?
      If you are wondering what you should put in an introduction then have a look at the collection of those already submitted. [. . .]
      They are extremely varied, some being complete faith histories, other simple biographical details; some very short, others quite long; some very personal, some humorous.
(2)   It is . . . important for each poster to exercise restraint and to avoid unnecessary posts . . . These are, however, just guidelines, so don't let them stop you from contributing.
(3)   Please limit contributions to discussions of Anglican matters, and always be respectful to other subscribers; private discussions unrelated to the topic should not be sent to the list.
(4)   Don't send posts just saying "I agree," "Me too," or "Amen, Rev."
      Nobody will know what you're responding to, you'll be wasting some subscribers' money, and you will be adding nothing to the discussion.
      Explain yourself, think new thoughts, explore possibilities, challenge wrong beliefs, make lists of good books, go into detail.
(5)   . . . please limit the amount of included material.
(6)   Read all your mail before replying: someone else may already have answered a question or made the same point.
(7)   Include a signature with your name and e-mail address (preferably in Internet format) at the end of your article . . .

(8)   Be careful when using initials and other abbreviations: not everyone may know what you mean, especially as this is an international list; a good idea is to spell the subject out in full the first time.

(9)   Please use line lengths of no more than 72 characters.

(10)   Please remember that it does not help to throw insults around, whether they are aimed at a group or at individuals. A careful use of language is likely to help readers appreciate what you are trying to say, rather than to concentrate on the way you say it. In particular, there is very little call for bad language; for gratuitous insults; for messages attacking people rather than making contributions to a discussion.

(11)   Someone has posted blasphemy/A poster is clearly going to end up in Hell. What should I do?
        Keep calm. Do not reply immediately. [. . .]
        Read the previous section. Read it again. Consider whether any response will help the poster, yourself, or the rest of the list.

(12)   . . . The comments about careful use of language are not meant to discourage people from taking an active part in discussions.

Spencer-Oatey's (2002) framework for rapport management specifies that our interpretations of interactions are dependent on two components: face (which relates to personal and social value) and sociality rights (which relate to personal and social entitlements). In the FAQ, the feature of sociality rights most addressed is that of equity rights, which indicate that we should "expect consideration from others and not be taken advantage of or exploited" (Spencer-Oatey 2002: 540). In this context, the most common violation of equity rights involves wasting bandwidth. In the ChurchList FAQ above, the instances of wasting bandwidth described include:

–   posting messages with inaccurate subject lines (which may result in wasting time since participants don't want to read messages that are about something other than what they expect)
–   posting messages with high percentages of quoted material (since participants don't need to reread thirty lines of quoted material to get to a two line response)
–   posting messages that address issues that have been discussed before
–   posting messages that aren't related to "Anglican matters"
–   posting messages that only minimally contribute to the discussion (e.g., "Amen," "me, too," etc.)
–   failing to limit the lines of your messages to 72 characters (i.e., use text-wrap) so that recipients won't have to spend time scrolling through unformatted messages
–   failing to include a signature so that recipients can identify the writer

In a computer-mediated context, wasting bandwidth is associated with costing the recipient(s) both time and (in early modes of CMC) money. In the early development of internet and email access, computer users were often charged a fee not only for the amount of time they were online, but also for the amount of material they downloaded to their computers. The guideline that encourages writers to restrict the amount of quoted material in their messages, for example, is a direct result of this constraint, but among the membership of this community monetary cost is unlikely to be a concern due to technological advances and availability of high-speed monthly-flat-fee internet connections. I would further argue that, while no one wants to waste time, the stakes for wasting time on a voluntary email community are relatively low; wasting bandwidth in this context might elicit *irritation*, therefore, but is unlikely to elicit flaming.

Perhaps more importantly, not only are the guidelines of the FAQ outmoded (due to technological advances) in many cases, they are also frequently ignored by the core group of listmembers. This core group regularly posts messages that flout the guidelines of the FAQ, as in Examples (1) and (2) below:

Example (1)
You know how the FAQ says not to say "Me, too"? Well, me, too!!

Example (2)
Despite feeling just as Amy and Carrie do, I will avoid sending a message to the list just to say "me too!" (Please make a note of my good behavior.)

In these examples, long-time listmembers violate the dictate of the FAQ to avoid wasting bandwidth by posting messages that do not add significantly to the discussion. This violation, however, is in fact used to demonstrate their knowledge of the 'rules' while simultaneously flouting them in a humorous way (as in Example [2] above). Despite the fact that messages such as these directly violate the FAQ (and are acknowledged as doing so), occurrences such as this (as well as parallel but non-humorous 'me too' messages) do not ordinarily elicit flames in this CofP.

In addition to the guidelines that reflect the expectations of sociality rights, there are also rules in the FAQ that address issues of face, which, according to Spencer-Oatey's framework, includes the interrelated aspects of *quality face* (which is oriented toward the individual) and *social identity face* (which is oriented toward the group). In the FAQ, readers are admonished to be aware of others' quality face and, to use Shea's (1994) terminology, "remember the human":

– Don't use lots of specialized terminology (which excludes people).
– Don't throw insults around, use bad language or gratuitous insults.

– Don't say something that attacks a person rather than contributing to the general discussion.
– Keep calm and do not reply immediately if someone posts (1) something you disagree with or (2) something you consider blasphemous.

In 'remembering the human,' listmembers are told to avoid insulting/attacking one another and to avoid excluding people via the use of 'codes.' These guidelines that address quality face issues are far less specific than those that relate to equity concerns and elicit the most subjective interpretations. Moreover, as I will discuss in section 7, these are the rules that, when violated, elicit the most aggressive responses.

Finally, the FAQ also includes some direct discussion of politeness. It says that it is not *rude* to delete some of the messages without reading them (this is a way to manage the high volume of mail sent to the list). This act, however, in effect amounts to silencing others – if one does not read others' messages, then those others do not have a voice. Similarly, the FAQ advocates caution in responding to messages posted by others by noting that listmembers should check to see that no one else has already responded before replying to a message, exercise restraint to avoid unnecessary posts, etc. This, in effect, amounts to silencing as well. The discussion of what is rude with regard to silence here functions in two ways: (1) by delineating actions that are not *rude*, the FAQ acknowledges and reinforces its status as a guideline for polite/appropriate behaviour, and (2) by dictating when listmembers should not post (be silent), the FAQ changes the dynamics of silence in this computer-mediated context.

The guidelines in this FAQ seem common-sensical and clear enough, but it is noteworthy that the most seasoned (and perhaps accepted) listmembers regularly violate the tenets outlined in the FAQ. When a newcomer challenges that practice, moreover, they dismiss his or her concerns (albeit in a nice way) while simultaneously offering him or her inclusion if he or she will accommodate to *their* way of doing things (instead of the practices outlined in the FAQ). This sets up a potential conflict: newcomers are encouraged by the FAQ to post messages (i.e., not to lurk), yet they have no way of knowing what the expectations for behaviour are except through the FAQ, which is not an accurate reflection of the practices used in the community. As I will demonstrate below, one result of this paradox is that when a newcomer tries to use the FAQ as a guideline, he is corrected by the seasoned listmembers who are more versed in the communicative practices in this CofP. Moreover, on further examination, a number of contradictions emerge in the FAQ: (1) listmembers are encouraged to limit posts to "Anglican matters" but talk about books they have read, etc. (2) avoid unnecessary posts, but be active contributors, and (3) "lurk before they leap," but contribute and introduce themselves (rather than 'freeloading'). The fact that the FAQ is violated by the seasoned listmembers in conjunction with the fact that it is itself contradictory places the newcomer in a difficult situation as s/he must determine when and how to contribute amidst contradictory advice.

Next, I will examine how the guidelines of the FAQ are enacted within the CofP. Both cases address breeches of conduct that are outlined in the FAQ, but the interpretation of these rules clearly varies within the group. The first case involves an introduction that was posted when the "newbie" in question had been subscribed for three days – not long enough to get a feel for the list norms of interaction. The second involves a more-seasoned listmember whose actions were deemed inappropriate within the community.

6. The case of 'Donald Darwin'

There is likely a connection between the level of "experience/presence" a list-member has on the list and his/her ability to violate the rules outlined in the FAQ. Since the list is unmoderated, the relationships are, in terms of formalized hierarchical structures, equal. As Culpeper (1996) notes,

> the factors influencing the occurrence of impoliteness in equal relationships are complex. ... it is worth noting that a particular characteristic of impoliteness behavior in equal relationships is its tendency to escalate. Equal relationships – by definition – lack a default mechanism by which one participant achieves the upper hand. An insult can easily lead to a counter-insult and so on. (Culpeper 1996: 354)

Although ChurchList has a listowner and an elected vestry, the only real power disparity that exists is the listowner's ability to unsubscribe people (but to my knowledge this power is exercised extremely rarely and is unknown to most subscribers because in almost all cases it was executed without comment to the list). Despite the lack of hierarchical power, however, there is a social hierarchy. As in the type of family discourse explored by Blum-Kulka (1990), Watts (1991), and Locher (2004), there are power disparities that go beyond strict hierarchical relationships. On ChurchList, there is a "core" group of members who post the most frequently and have the most tenure on the list – and therefore have the most influence in establishing the list norms of practice. Although the FAQ encourages people to contribute, posting can be a dangerous game, since the reactions of the core group could either be welcoming or not.

One case where the actions of the core group were challenged in relation to appropriateness occurred when a new subscriber I call Donald introduced himself to the list. Introductions on ChurchList are marked as such in the subject line (e.g., "My Introduction," "Introducing myself (finally)," etc.) and frequently include faith histories ("I am a cradle Anglican", "I am a Roman Catholic who is shopping around for a new Church," etc.), as well as biographical information. In addition, these introductions frequently begin with a disclaimer about how long the poster has been subscribed, in many cases this is more than 4 weeks (e.g., "I subscribed in May and after 2 months I am finally getting around to introducing myself."). In posting his introduction, Donald satisfied one tenet of the FAQ, which encourages subscribers to introduce themselves and contribute to the community; since he had only been a member for three days, however, he simultaneously broke the FAQs admonishment to "lurk before you leap."

Example (3)

4   This post will surely get me in trouble; I have been here only 3 days.
5   But as in that short span there have been a dozen or more posts
6   concerning the list, its volume, make up and function, I
7   thought y'all might be interested in one man's
8   FIRST IMPRESSIONS OF churchlist

9   This list operates much differently than the other 3 lists I have ever
10   been on. Whether this list or those 3 are skewed remains to be
11   discovered, as I delve further into cyber-space. Note that in giving
12   my impressions below, I am not making judgments.

13   In the first place, I was surprised to see so many posts of a purely
14   personal nature being posted to the list at large. In my previous
15   experience, such notes are posted privately. (Such as the ones about going
16   to the zoo or whether there are walnuts in France or whatever. And please
17   don't hate me, whoever posted those notes – these just came to my mind
18   as examples.) It is probably the case that many use this list more as an
19   IRC type outlet than as a discussion of issues; I do not know – I'm new.

20   Second, related to the above is the so-called drivel, dribble, or whatever.[5]
21   A lot of people are talking in what almost seems like a secret code and that
22   turns new people off fast.

23   Third, the public posting of prayers creates volume. I am not being
24   judgmental but it may be the case that they could be posted privately to the
25   person(s) being prayed for. Something like going to one's prayer closet to
26   pray. And even if others are benefitted by reading the prayers, maybe
27   those who so desire can be CC'd.

28   Fourth, I estimate that fewer than 20% of the notes posted in 3 days have
29   been issue-oriented, which is what I expected from a mailing list. It is a
30   wonderful thing to have quasi-fellowship or cyber-fellowship or whatever,

31 but the list is not advertised as such and perhaps the list ought to be
32 changed to the friendship list or the drivel list or whatever. Or perhaps the
33 Anglican fellowship?

34 I do not make it a practice to criticize other people or their beloved lists, so
35 take all this with a grain of salt, as just one person's FIRST impressions..
36 but one which may in some modicum of a way throw insight into perhaps
37 why there is so much revolving door action (and unnecessary?) volume on
38 ChurchList.

39 I mean it is perfectly possible to discuss issues and ask for prayer requests
40 and ideas and stuff publicly and grow close together in lists posted
41 privately, when they are of the personal nature. But y'all have been here
42 much longer than I and you can do what you want!

43 Grace and peace,

44 Donald

45 Diocese of Texas [sic]

Donald's message might be classified by some readers as quite impolite. Although I would argue that there is nothing inherently impolite about criticizing others, and despite the fact that Donald's message does include some redressive action (lines 34–35), his linguistic choices in how he presents his criticisms are potentially problematic. He implies that ChurchList is *skewed* (lines 9–10), he accuses listmembers of posting trivial messages (lines 13–16, 18), and he accuses listmembers of wasting bandwidth by posting prayers (line 23), all of which, incidentally, are violations of the rules set forth in the FAQ. He also misuses the community's unique lexicon in line 20 with his reference to "so-called drivel, dribble, or whatever." "Drivel" is the ChurchList term for humorous or non-serious messages; the term is used on a regular basis by core listmembers and is granted a certain amount of credibility due to the fact that it is defined in a glossary of terms, acronyms and abbreviations on the ChurchList webpage. Donald's use of the phrase "or whatever" after his misuse of the term *drivel* dismisses the validity and/or importance of list terminology (which is one of the unique and defining features of this CofP). He also uses the phrase "or whatever" again in line 30, referring to the cyber-parish (this is the term used by the group to define itself) as a "quasi-fellowship or cyber-fellowship or whatever." By defining the group (which identifies itself as a place with a strong sense of community) as a *quasi*-fellowship, Donald trivializes this characteristic of the group; he compounds the insult by finishing his claim with "or whatever" which seems to imply that fellowship is not an important characteristic of an email list.

The (potentially) impolite content of the message aside, there is a larger issue here related to the contradictory advice given in the FAQ. At least some of Donald's impoliteness may be attributable to the fact that he has not been a member of the community long enough to understand the terminology and priorities of the list; he does not have a firm grasp on the list *identity*. Donald may have read the "don't lurk" clause of the FAQ as the priority, and therefore rushed into posting an introduction before he could get a sense of the norms of interaction in the CofP. The other listmembers, however, seem to expect newbies to "lurk before they leap."

Like the issues of bandwidth discussed above, however, lurking is an accepted part of CMC and is not usually treated with the same weight as, for example, breeches of quality face such as name-calling. With recent developments in technological resources, most people do not incur cost that is directly related to participating in email discussion groups. It is perhaps for this reason that lurking is much more likely to elicit friendly chastisement rather than an adversarial reaction. (This is not surprising, in fact, since the rules about lurking are designed to ensure the survival of the community – if people are attacked for lurking, they will be less likely to remain as community members and the community's survival will be threatened anyway). In this case, even though Donald has broken one rule outlined in the FAQ by posting a message before he got a feel for the community, he has also satisfied one of the guidelines by not lurking.

In the case of lurking described above, it is noteworthy that the "politeness stakes" are relatively low. As I have discussed above, although it is nice for people to contribute actively to the group, community members do not really incur cost if others lurk. I would therefore describe Donald's message as a breech of equity rights (in not lurking long enough to get a feel for the community, Donald has imposed on the other listmembers) and argue that his introduction is relatively unproblematic since his actions do not result in others' incurring (monetary) cost. It is also noteworthy that Donald's criticisms, for the most part, deal with breeches of sociality rights rather than face issues.

Donald's only criticism related to face issues (as Spencer-Oatey defines this term), in fact, is in criticizing the listmembers for using the 'secret code' term "drivel" discussed above. He also criticizes the listmembers for breaking their rules about limiting their messages to "Anglican matters" in lines 13–16, saying

Example (4)
In the first place, I was surprised to see so many posts of a purely
personal nature being posted to the list at large. In my previous
experience, such notes are posted privately. (Such as the ones about going
to the zoo or whether there are walnuts in France or whatever.

When the other listmembers respond to Donald, there is the potential that the conflictual responses will escalate (as Culpeper [1996] proposes), but this escalation does not occur in this case. The listmembers who respond to Donald do not waver in their commitment to the norms that are currently operational on the list. Instead, they acknowledge Donald's concerns and praise his skills in voicing them, but still let him know that he must accept the list "as is" if he would like to be a member of the group. One such response is seen in Example (5) below:

Example (5)
... thank you for your observations. They were well and gracefully put. I hope you stay with us ...
Welcome!

In Example (5), the writer protects Donald's quality face in acknowledging the quality of his writing, but does not indicate that Donald's criticisms will (or even should) bring change. Rather, by acknowledging Donald for contributing and then indicating that he hopes Donald stays with the community (a manifestation of *association rights*), the writer of this message instead underscores the fact that he is not proposing actual change. Other core listmembers who respond to Donald mitigate the disagreement while also either (1) explaining the rationale for the practice(s) and/or (2) reinforcing those practices without offering to change. This gives Donald the option of remaining in the community and accepting the norms of interaction or leaving.

In Example (5), as in the other responses to Donald, it is possible that the listmembers' reactions are non-confrontational because the stakes are low – since Donald has primarily accused the listmembers of violating equity rights (which, as I discussed earlier, has limited ramifications in CMC), there is relatively little face-threat and therefore a stronger response may not be necessary. It is also possible that, within a Christian group, threats to quality face are more marked and/or problematic than threats to equity rights, since it is perceived to be "non-Christian" to directly attack others' character (as opposed to imposing on them, which might not be so problematic and the 'cost' of infringement of equity rights in this computer-mediated context are relatively low. Whichever is the case, it seems clear that the FAQ is too open to varied interpretations to be a viable guideline for polite/politic interactional norms.

7. The case of 'Jane Dryden'

Just as the responses to Donald illuminate how association rights might be used as one possible response to differing expectations of behaviour, the case of Jane Dryden illustrates the way that potentially problematic interactions can evolve into all-out conflicts and then retreat back down the confrontational scale. It also highlights the power of the core listmembers to exclude one member due to behaviour that violates the tenets of rapport management. While core listmembers responded to Donald's message in a (more-or-less) welcoming (or at least neutral) way, there are other instances where this is not the case. Jane Dryden is a listmember who, while not described as a long-time subscriber (see Example (11) below) by the other community members, is someone who has contributed actively[6] to the ongoing interactions on the list prior to this conflict.

The conflict I am examining here occurred after Brad, a well-respected and long-term core listmember (who happens to also be homosexual) posted a request for support from the list community, stating that his job, his personal relationship with his partner, and his financial situation were all falling apart and he wished he were dead. Prayer requests are common in this community; listmembers frequently post requests for prayer – both for themselves and for others they know who are experiencing difficulties. After Brad posted his request, a less-established listmember I call Jane posted a response that the other listmembers interpreted as inappropriate. Her response is included below:

Example (6)
>[7] . . . I wish I were dead.

And people wonder at the gift of scripture's dictate to confine sexuality
to heterosexual marriage. Perhaps scripture goes this way as an
attempt to reduce the overwhelming confusion of boundaries listed here.

Perhaps scripture is not the arbitrary authoritarian abuse it is seen as
today, but an expression of understanding of what people have to go
through in their lives.

Jane

The other listmembers interpret Jane's post to Brad as an extreme and intentional threat to Brad's quality face and respond to her in kind. In their view, her post counts as invective (which is in direct violation of the FAQ). Jane, however, when she responds, claims that she intended to *help* Brad; moreover, she seems to classify her contribution as, to use the wording of the FAQ, *taking an active part in the discussion* of Anglican matters (which was plausible at this time since there was ongoing debate about same-sex marriage and ordination of homosexuals in the Anglican Church). In contributing to the discussion, Jane could also be said to satisfy the guidelines of the FAQ – don't lurk, take an active part in discussions, and "explain yourself, think new thoughts, explore possibilities, challenge wrong beliefs, make lists of good books, go into detail." Instead, however, Jane's message is assigned a whole range of negative assessments by the other listmembers. In their view, she has violated a firm list rule (which is unwritten but which is enacted often in regular list interactions) that prayer request messages should only elicit prayers. Since they view her message as non-supportive of Brad, they judge it inappropriate and, in fact, aggressive. In this case, if Jane had lurked longer before posting, she might have had a better sense of what other listmembers would view as an appropriate response to Brad's message.

While Jane later declares that her intent was not to attack Brad but to offer support, because of the asynchronous limitations of the medium, by the time she is able to make her declaration the conflict has snowballed to the point where she is unable to rectify or clarify her actions. An important note here is that Jane's message does not contain markers of bald on record impoliteness (e.g., taboo language) as outlined in Culpeper at al. (2003). Instead, she mitigates the strength of her initial statement with the word "perhaps" (although this might also be interpreted as mock politeness (this ambiguity might not exist if prosody were available to help clarify the intent here). If, as Jane explains in a later message, her intent was to help Brad, then "perhaps" could serve as a mitigator. The other listmembers, however, seem to interpret Jane's "perhaps" as judgmental – a violation of quality face, and repeat the lexical item in their own critical (and sarcastic) reprisals to Jane. One such response can be seen in Example (7):

Example (7)
And *perhaps*, Jane, you are a nasty piece of work so full
of your own agenda and looniness that you cannot see
anything at all.

Whatever Jane's intention, the other listmembers accuse Jane of being vindictive, calling her post cruel, labeling her as "looney" and, later in the conflict, "evil". They assault her vehemently with very direct quality face attacks such as the following:

Example (8)
... I see little in you other than anger and an insensitivity to people that
continues to amaze me.
...
Let me spell it out for you. When someone is in the kind of pain that Brad
revealed in his post – when someone talks about wanting to die – the response
of "nyah, nyah, God told you so" borders on the **demonic**. (emphasis added)

Example (9)
It is possible my dear, to add a prayer to the thread without being
sanctimonious and without **kicking the recipient in the balls** – especially
when he is down and has said he wished he were dead. (emphasis added)

Example (10)

Jane Dryden: **your posting was malicious, pointless, insane, cruel, unchristian, evil.**

Jane Dryden: talk to somebody competent soon. You are slashing out at strangers in inappropriate and loony ways. You are using your own pain, whether based on truth or **delusion** (for I cannot tell the truth of your words from here) as **a bludgeon to pummel those – anyone! – who are/[is] already in pain**. "Who when asked for bread would give a stone?" You, Jane! You gave a stone. Another stone. Enough. (emphasis added)

As one core listmember later notes: "As far as abusiveness goes, the language used regarding Jane is far worse than anything she said. As far as posts being filled with anger, the one's [sic] directed towards her are far more abusive... "

It is noteworthy that Jane received no messages of support in this conflict; although some core listmembers criticized other core listmembers for the vehemence of their *attacks* on Jane, Jane herself never receives messages supporting her actions or her viewpoint. In Examples (7) to (10) above, which are only a small sample of the 81 messages sent to the list that directly attacked Jane, the core group ignores the FAQ's rule to keep calm and avoid messages that attack people. In this case, as was the case with Donald's conflict, the attackers, who are primarily members of the powerful core group, break the rules of the FAQ (and get away with it while Jane does not). In part, this is the result of Jane's prior history on the list. If we use our assessments of others' actions as a tool for marking others as "in or out socially," then an individual's prior history within a community takes on special significance. Mills (2005) identifies the importance of prior interaction in interpreting an utterance as polite/impolite:

> ... if a person is not liked, practically any linguistic utterance or intonation can be classified as impolite ... impoliteness can be considered as any type of linguistic behavior which is assessed .. as transgressing the hypothesized Community of Practice's norms of appropriacy. (Mills 2005: 268)

In the case of Jane Dryden, her prior history is of critical importance in the interpretation of her postings as problematic. As one listmember observes,

Example (11)

Clearly Brad is a long time member and well-loved. Equally clearly Jane is fairly recent and not.

Another long-term and very well-respected listmember responds to the post above and says that this is the "straw that broke the camel's back," indicating that Jane's history resulted in the negative interpretation of her message and that it demanded an immediate and unambiguous response.

It is also noteworthy that both Jane and the respondents to Jane justify their actions, each claiming that their messages, while impolite, were necessary to achieve a higher purpose. Jane herself claims that she was justified in her message to Brad because her advice was intended to show him how to resolve his problems. This attempt, however, is unsuccessful; although there are several messages criticizing the vehemence of the attacks on Jane, there are no messages that support *her* actions. When Jane's attackers (who were all core listmembers) are criticized for name-calling (by other core listmembers), they justify their actions by saying that Jane's evil actions had to be addressed; that a "virtual slap" was necessary. A discussion results in which the listmembers debate what actions are acceptable. In this case, as in the case of Donald, then, the core listmembers are able to break the rules of the FAQ whereas newcomers do not seem to have this kind of power.

8.   Responses to impoliteness and the evolution of the FAQ

Culpeper, Bousfield and Wichmann (2003), in their call for more research on extended interactions pose the question of what happens after impolite exchanges. In the case of Donald described above, core listmembers divert the discussion to a topic which interests them – they essentially ignore Donald's complaints – but still welcome him into the group. In the larger conflict involving Jane (in which positive face is at stake), (1) the conflict arises and escalates to a peak of name-calling, (2) some listmembers threaten to leave because the list is no longer what they expect from a Christian mailing list, (3) there is a flurry of messages that say "Let's stop talking about this", (4) there are humorous exchanges/spin-off humorous threads, and finally (5) participation in the discussion trails off. This sequence seems consistent – it has occurred across multiple conflicts during my time as a subscriber. After the messages have tapered off, there is often a proposal made by a core listmember to revise and clarify the FAQ. This is what happens approximately one month after the conflict with Jane. Despite the attempt at refining the FAQ to provide more and better guidance, the root of the conflict between Jane and the community is about "what counts as support?" – a concept that may be quite difficult (if not impossible) to define in an FAQ for a mailing list with over 250 subscribers. Jane adamantly maintained throughout the conflict over her actions that her response was appropriate in this context and that she intended to be supportive of Brad. Clearly the majority of the other community members had different ideas about what constitutes support, but "support" cannot be codified. Nevertheless, the listmembers did revise the

FAQ approximately one month after the conflict with Jane occurred. It read, in part:

> Q: How do I post to the list?
> A: The first thing to say about this is: don't do it yet! Before you start posting a responding to posts, spend at least a week, and preferably a month or two getting to know the people on the list and their points of view (As you probably know, this is called "lurking".)
>
> **
>
> [. . .]
> We place a high value on civility: even in the heights (or depths) of passionate discussion, we mostly avoid invective and ad hominem arguments. We're not always as perfect in this area as we'd like to be but jumping in with both feet and cursing out the person you think just made an incredibly stupid statement is NOT the best introduction for a newbie.

While modifying the FAQ to meet the needs of the changing population seems like a positive move, in some ways it may cause more problems. After the revision of the FAQ above, one non-core listmember noted that, were she to receive the FAQ as a new subscriber, the admonition "Don't do it [introduce yourself] yet!" would be very off-putting and might even make her leave the list.

In truth, there cannot be an FAQ that will provide an accurate guideline for interaction because, (1) not only can "appropriateness" not be codified – it is too dependent on subjective or possibly intersubjective interpretations, but (2) despite the (ongoing) revision of the FAQ, the emergent nature of the community is likely to outpace any evolving guideline that the members produce. So, while the FAQ may provide an adequate starting point, it is still not adequate and ultimately does not override the "lurk before you leap" mantra in this community.

9.   Discussion and conclusions

What value does an FAQ have if it is doomed to inaccuracy? It seems clear that the FAQ is viewed by the community as a valuable guideline (why else would they revise it?) *despite* its inadequacies. One of the difficulties here is that, while the FAQ does its best to reflect the norms of the community, (1) the community norms are in a constant state of evolution and (2) the FAQ guidelines in many ways reflect a template of appropriate *computer* communication (i.e., Netiquette) without addressing the norms of communication within this CofP – this is the case with Donald, who criticizes the list for violating norms of computer-interaction like wasting bandwidth. While the FAQ brings guidelines to the table, the guidelines themselves are contradictory, placing the newbie in a difficult position – one where s/he must learn by trial and error what the norms of the community are. This is what Donald does – he jumps in with both feet and risks "getting into trouble" with the rest of the subscribers. The response he gets, however, is cordial while at the same time it reinforces the norms of the CofP. The respondents encourage Donald to stay, but also make it clear that the list is the way it is and he can take it or leave it.

Jane, on the other hand, gets a very different reception when she jumps into the discussion. Her postings are perceived as a direct attack on Brad which is a violation of his quality face. Several factors differentiate her from Donald; (1) she has participated more than Donald and therefore has a history on the list that causes the other subscribers to interpret her postings in a negative way; (2) while Donald's message criticized the list *community*, Jane was perceived as directly attacking a single individual; and (3) while most of Donald criticisms are based on violations of computer Netiquette (i.e., equity rights), Jane's message threatened an individual's quality face.

It seems that, based on this preliminary study, there is a high focus on equity rights in the FAQ, but the guidelines that help listmembers avoid truly problematic conflictual situations are much less prominent in the FAQ. In this community, then, the FAQ does not measure up, despite the fact that newcomers to the group uphold it as an authoritative guideline for behaviour. It is beyond the scope of this study to speculate about whether this pattern is present in email communities in general, but is an intriguing area for further study since FAQs are somewhat systematic in the guidelines (based on Netiquette) that they use.

A more explicit study on how core listmembers' perceptions of the FAQ as a guideline would also shed useful light on how this resource is regarded by the core listmembers and therefore illuminate their expectations for what counts as polite behaviour within this CofP. It could be that there is a "politic learning curve" where Jane has been subscribed long enough that the core listmembers expect her to have a better grasp of the list norms (in spite of what the FAQ may say). Once again, this is an area that would benefit from further study.

Finally, while this study indicates that power is related to perceptions of politeness that either conform to or challenge the guidelines presented in an FAQ within this CofP, an exploration of the consistency of this pattern in other electronic communities (either other email lists or other computer-mediated forums) is warranted.

Notes

1. "Flaming," as defined by Shea (1994: 43) is "what people do when they express a strongly held opinion without holding back any emotion. . . . Tact is not its objective." These messages may include taboo language and direct face-attacks and are often viewed as extremely face-threatening.
2. Bandwidth, as defined by Shea (1994:39), is the information-carrying capacity of the wires and channels that connect everyone in cyberspace; the word is also sometimes used to refer to the storage capacity of a host system. When you post the same note to the same newsgroup five times, you are wasting both time (of the people who check all five copies of the posting) and bandwidth (by sending repetitive information over the wires and requiring it to be stored somewhere).
3. For my purposes, I have defined an email thread as a set of messages with a common subject line. In an e-CofP, threads provide contextualization information for the content of a given email message; for this reason the FAQ on this list encourages writers to make sure that the subject line actually reflects the content of their messages.
4. Although the FAQ guidelines listed here have been numbered for ease of reference and edited due to space constraints, the contents are quoted directly from the document itself.
5. "Drivel" is the ChurchList term for humorous or non-serious messages.
6. Her name has appeared on the frequent-posters list for more than 3 months at the time of this conflict.
7. In email messages, a ">" symbol at the beginning of a line of text indicates material that is quoted from a previous message. In this case, the ">" indicates Brad's message, while the text that is not set of by ">" symbols is Jane's reply.

References

Achiba, Machiko
    2003   *Learning to Request in a Second Language: A Study of Child Interlanguage Pragmatics*. Clevedon/Buffalo, NY: Multilingual Matters.

Agha, Asif
    1997   Tropic aggression in the Clinton–Dole presidential debate. *Pragmatics* 7 (4), 461–497.

Ainsworth-Vaughn, Nancy
    1998   *Claiming Power in Doctor–Patient Talk*. Oxford: Oxford University Press.

Andersson, Lynne M. and Christine M. Pearson
    1999   Tit-for-tat? The spiraling effect of incivility in the workplace. *Academy of Management Review* 24 (3), 452–471.

Appelbaum, Steven, Lynda Audet and Joanne Miller
    2002   Gender and leadership? Leadership and gender? A journey through the landscape of theories. *Leadership and Organization Development* 24 (1), 43–51.

Archer, Dawn
    2002   Can innocent people be guilty? A sociopragmatic analysis of examination transcripts from the Salem Witchcraft Trials. *Journal of Historical Pragmatics* 3 (1), 1–30.
    2005   *Questions and Answers in the English Courtroom (1640–1760): A Sociopragmatic Analysis*. Amsterdam: John Benjamins.

Archer, Dawn and Jonathan Culpeper
    2003   Sociopragmatic annotation: New directions and possibilities in historical corpus linguistics. In Wilson, Andrew, Paul Rayson and Tony McEnery (eds.), *Corpus Linguistics by the Lune: A Festschrift for Geoffrey Leech, Peter Lang: Frankfurt/Main*. Frankfurt/Main: Peter Lang, 37–58.

Aristotle
    2007   *On Rhetoric: A Theory of Civic Discourse*. Translated with Introduction, Notes, and Appendices by George A. Kennedy (2nd Ed.). New York: Oxford University Press.

Arundale, Robert
    1999   An alternative model and ideology of communication for an alternative to politeness theory. *Pragmatics* 9 (1), 119–153.
    2004   Constituting face in conversation: An alternative to Brown and Levinson's politeness theory. Paper presented at the 90th Conference of the National Communication Association 2004, Chicago IL, USA.

2005   Face as relational and interactional: Alternative bases for research on face, facework, and politeness. Paper presented at the 9th International Pragmatics Conference, Riva del Garda, Italy.

2006   Face as relational and interactional: A communication framework for research on face, facework, and politeness. *Journal of Politeness Research* 2 (2), 193–217.

Arundale, Robert and Donna Ashton
1992   Is face ever ignored? The case of Brown and Levinson's "bald, on record" utterances. Paper presented at the Annual Conference of the International Communication Association 1992, Miami, USA.

Atkinson, J. Maxwell and John Heritage (eds.)
1984   *Structures of Social Action: Studies in Conversation Analysis.* Cambridge: Cambridge University Press.

Atkinson, John Maxwell and Paul Drew
1979   *Order in Court.* London: The Macmillan Press Limited.

Austin, Paddy
1990   Politeness revisited – the dark side. In Bell, Allan and Janet Holmes (eds.), *New Zealand Ways of Speaking English.* Philadelphia: Multilingual Matters, 277–293.

Barbe, Katharina
1995   *Irony in Context.* Amsterdam: Benjamins.

Bargiela-Chiappini, Francesca
2003   Face and politeness: New (insights) for old (concepts). *Journal of Pragmatics* 35 (10–11), 1453–1469.

Barron, Anne
2003   *Acquisition in Interlanguage Pragmatics: Learning How to Do Things with Words in a Study Abroad Context.* Amsterdam/Philadelphia, PA: John Benjamins.

Baxter, Judith
2003   *Positioning Gender in Discourse.* Basingstoke: Palgrave.

Baxter, Leslie A.
1984   An investigation of compliance-gaining as politeness. *Human Communication Research* 10 (3), 427–456.

Bayraktaroğlu, Arin
1991   Politeness and interactional imbalance. *International Journal of the Sociology of Language* 92, 5–34.

Bayraktaroğlu, Arin and Maria Sifianou (eds.)
2001   *Linguistic Politeness Across Boundaries: The Case of Greek and Turkish.* Amsterdam: John Benjamins.

Beattie, Geoffrey
  1982   Turn-taking and interruption in political interviews: Thatcher, Margaret and Callaghan, Jim, compared and contrasted. *Semiotica* 39 (1/2), 93–113.

Beebe, Leslie M.
  1995   Polite fictions: Instrumental rudeness as pragmatic competence. In Alatis, James E. et al. (eds.), *Linguistics and the Education of Language Teachers: Ethnolinguistic, Psycholinguistic and Sociolinguistic Aspects. Georgetown University Round Table on Languages and Linguistics (1995)*. Georgetown: Georgetown University Press, 154–168.

Beeching, Kate
  2002   *Gender, Politeness and Pragmatic Particles in French*. Amsterdam: John Benjamins.

Bem, Sandra
  1993   *The Lenses of Gender*. New Haven: Yale University Press.

Benoit, William and William T. Wells
  1996   *Candidates in Conflict: Persuasive Attack and Defense in the 1992 Presidential Debates*. Alabama: University of Alabama Press.

Berger, Charles
  1994   Power, dominance, and social interaction. In Knapp, Mark L. and Gerald R. Miller (eds.), *Handbook of Interpersonal Communication*. Thousand Oaks: Sage, 450–507.

Biber, Douglas, Susan Conrad and Randi Reppen
  1998   *Corpus Linguistics. Investigating Language Structure and Use*. Cambridge: Cambridge University Press.

Blas Arroyo, Jose Luís
  1998   Funciones y estructuras discursivas del moderador en el debate político. *Langues et Linguistique* 24, 3–45.
  2001   'No diga chorradas ...': La descortesía en el debate político cara a cara: Una aproximación pragma-variacionista. *Oralia: Análisis del Discurso Oral* 4, 9–45.
  2002   En los límites de la (des)cortesía: Formas atenuadas de la agresividad verbal en el debate político español. *International Review of Applied Linguistics* 137–138, 181–204.
  2003   'Perdóneme que se lo diga, pero vuelve usted a faltar a la verdad, señor González': Form and function of politic verbal behaviour in face-to-face Spanish political debates. *Discourse and Society* 14 (4), 395–423.

Blum-Kulka, Shoshana
  1990   You don't touch lettuce with your fingers: Parental politeness in family discourse. *Journal of Pragmatics* 14 (2), 259–288.

Bolívar, Adriana
  2005   The pragmatics of insults in political confrontation. Paper presented at the
          9th International Pragmatics Conference, Riva del Garda, Italy.

Bou Franch, Patricia
  2006   Solidarity and deference in Spanish computer-mediated communication: A
          discourse-pragmatic analysis of students' emails to lecturers. In Bou Franch,
          Patricia (ed.), *Ways into Discourse*. Granada: Comares, 74–94.

Bou Franch, Patricia and Pilar Garcés Conejos
  1994   La presentación de la imagen en conversaciones entre hablantes nativas y no
          nativas de inglés. *Pragmalingüística* 2, 37–61.

Bourdieu, Pierre
  1990   *The Logic of Practice*. Cambridge: Polity Press.
  1991   *Language and Symbolic Power* (Gino Raymond and Matthew Adamson,
          Trans.). Cambridge: Polity Press.

Bousfield, Derek
  2004   *Impoliteness in Interaction*. Unpublished PhD, Lancaster University, Lan-
          caster, UK.
  2006   The Grand Debate: Where next for politeness research? *Culture, Language
          and Representation* III, 9–16.
  2007a   Impoliteness, preference organization and conducivity. *Multilingua* 26 (1/2),
          1–33.
  2007b   Beginnings, middles and ends: A biopsy of the dynamics of impolite ex-
          changes. *Journal of Pragmatics* 39 (12): 2185–2216.

Brentano, Franz
  1981   *Psychology from an Empirical Standpoint* (Margarete Schattle and Linda L.
          McAlister, Trans.). London: Routledge and Kegan Paul.

Brewis, Joanna
  2001   Telling it like it is? Gender, language and organizational theory. In Westwood,
          Robert and Steven Linstead (eds.), *The Language of Organization*. London:
          Sage, 283–309.

Briggs, Charles
  1986   *Learning How to Ask: A Sociolinguistic Appraisal of the Role of the Interview
          in Social Science Research*. Cambridge: Cambridge University Press.

Brinck, Ingar
  2001   Attention and the evolution of intentional communication. *Pragmatics and
          Cognition* 9 (2), 259–277.

Brown, Penelope
  1980   How and why are women more polite: Some evidence from a Mayan com-
          munity. In McConnell-Ginet, Sally, Ruth Borker and Nellie Furman (eds.),
          Women and Language in Literature and Society. New York: Praeger, 111–136.

1995   Politeness strategies and the attribution of intentions: The case of Tzeltal irony.
         In Goody, Esther (ed.), *Social Intelligence and Interaction: Expressions and
         Implications of the Social Bias in Human Intelligence*. Cambridge: Cambridge
         University Press, 153–174.

Brown, Penelope and Stephen C. Levinson
1978   Universals in language usage: Politeness phenomena. In Goody, Esther N.
         (ed.), *Questions and Politeness*. Cambridge: Cambridge University Press,
         56–289.
1987   *Politeness. Some Universals in Language Usage*. Cambridge: Cambridge Uni-
         versity Press.

Brown, Roger and Albert Gilman
1989   Politeness theory and Shakespeare's four major tragedies. *Language in Society*
         18 (2), 159–213.
1960   The pronouns of power and solidarity. In Giglioli, Pier Paolo (ed.), *Language
         and Social Context*. Penguin: Harmondsworth, 252–282.

Bucholtz, Mary
1999a   Bad examples: Transgression and progress in language and gender studies.
         In Bucholtz, Mary, A. Liang and Laurel Sutton (eds.), *Reinventing Identities:
         The Gendered Self in Discourse*. Oxford: Oxford University Press, 3–24.
1999b   'Why be normal?' Language and identity practices in a community of nerd
         girls. *Language in Society* 18 (2), 203–223.

Butler, Judith
1990   *Gender Trouble: Feminism and the Subversion of Gender Identity*. New York:
         Routledge.

Cashman, Holly R.
2006   Impoliteness in children's interactions in a Spanish/English bilingual com-
         munity of practice. *Journal of Politeness Research* 2 (2), 217–246.
2008   Accomplishing marginalization in bilingual interaction: Relational work as a
         resource for the intersubjective construction of identity. *Multilingua* 27 (1–2).

Chen, Rong
2001   Self politeness: A proposal. *Journal of Pragmatics* 33 (1), 87–106.

Chilton, Paul
1990   Politeness, politics and diplomacy. *Discourse and Society* 1 (2), 201–224.
2002   Manipulation. In Verschueren, Jef, Jan-Ola Östman, Jan Blommaert and Chris
         Bulcaen (eds.), *Handbook of Pragmatics*. Amsterdam: John Benjamins, 1–16.

Chouliaraki, Lillie and Norman Fairclough
1999   *Discourse in Late Modernity: Rethinking Critical Discourse Analysis*. Edin-
         burgh: Edinburgh University Press.

Christie, Chris
   2002   Politeness and the linguistic construction of gender in parliament: An analysis
           of transgressions and apology behaviour. *Sheffield Hallam Working Papers* 3
           (1–27). Available at: http://www.shu.ac.uk/wpw/politeness/christie.htm
   2005   Editorial. *Journal of Politeness Research: Language, Behaviour, Culture* 1
           (1), 1–7.

Clark, Herbert
   1996   *Using Language*. Cambridge: Cambridge University Press.

Clayman, Steven and John Heritage
   2002   *The News Interview: Journalists and Public Figures on the Air*. Cambridge:
           Cambridge University Press.

Coleman, James S.
   1990   *Foundations of Social Theory*. Cambridge, MA: Harvard University Press.

Connolly, Ceci
   2000   October 2. "Gore: Methodical, skilled, aggressive." *The Washington Post,* pp.
           A1, A10.

Corsaro, William A. and Thomas A. Rizzo
   1990   Dispute in the peer culture of American and Italian nursery-school children.
           In Grimshaw, Allen D. (ed.), *Conflict Talk: Sociolinguistic Investigations of
           Arguments in Conversations*. Cambridge: Cambridge University Press, 21–
           66.

Craig, Robert T., Karen Tracy and Frances Spisak
   1986   The discourse of requests: Assessments of a politeness approach. *Human
           Communication Research* 12 (4), 437–468.

Critchmar, Julian
   2005   *President George Bush Junior's visit to the European Union. 21st February
           2005. 12:35 GMT*. Brussels: ITV News.

Cromdal, Jakob
   2004   Building bilingual oppositions: Code-switching in children's disputes. *Lan-
           guage in Society* 33 (1), 33–58.

Culpeper, Jonathan
   1996   Towards an anatomy of impoliteness. *Journal of Pragmatics* 25 (3), 349–367.
   1998   (Im)politeness in drama. In Verdonk, Peter, Mick Short and Jonathan Culpeper
           (eds.), *Exploring the Language of Drama: From Text to Context*. London:
           Routledge, 83–95.
   2001   *Language and Characterisation: People in Plays and other Texts*. London:
           Longman Pearson Education.
   2005   Impoliteness and *The Weakest Link*. Journal of Politeness Research 1 (1),
           35–72.

Culpeper, Jonathan, Derek Bousfield and Anne Wichmann
   2003   Impoliteness revisited: With special reference to dynamic and prosodic aspects. *Journal of Pragmatics* 35 (10–11), 1545–1579.

Culpeper, Jonathan, Robert Crawshaw and Julia Harrison
   2006   Activity types as a bridge for micro and macro politeness research: Contexts of culture in interactions between student foreign language assistants and their supervisors in schools in France and England. Paper presented at the 31st International LAUD Symposium, Landau, Germany.

Daly, Nicola, Janet Holmes, Jonathan Newton and Maria Stubbe
   2004   Expletives as solidarity signals in FTAs on the faculty floor. *Journal of Pragmatics* 36 (5), 945–964.

Damasio, Antonio
   1999   *The Feeling of What Happens: Body and Emotion in the Making of Consciousness*. London: Heinemann.

Danet, Brenda, Katherine B. Hoffman, N.C. Kermish, H.J. Rafn and D. G. Stayman
   1980   An ethnography of questioning in the courtroom. In Shuy, Roger W. and Anna Shnukal (eds.), *Language Use and Uses of Language*. Washington, DC: University of Georgetown Press, 222–234.

Davidson, Richard
   1992   Prolegomenon to the structure of emotion: Gleanings from neuropsychology. *Cognition and Emotion* 6 (3/4), 245–268.

Dery, Mark
   1994   *Flame Wars: The Discourse of Cyberculture*. Durham: Duke University Press.

Diamond, Julie
   1996   *Status and Power in Verbal Interaction. A Study of Discourse in a Close-knit Social Network*. Amsterdam: John Benjamins.

Dickey, Eleanor
   1997   Forms of address and terms of reference. *Journal of Linguistics* 33, 255–274.

Drew, Paul and John Heritage
   1992   Analyzing talk at work: An introduction. In Drew, Paul and John Heritage (eds.), *Talk at Work. Interaction in Institutional Settings*. Cambridge: Cambridge University Press, 3–65.

DuFon, Margaret A., Gabriele Kasper, Satomi Takahashi and Naoko Yoshinaga
   1994   Bibliography on linguistic politeness. *Journal of Pragmatics* 21 (5), 527–578.

Duranti, Alessandro and Charles Goodwin (eds.)
   1992   *Rethinking Context. Language as an Interactive Phenomenon*. Cambridge: Cambridge University Press.

Eakins, Barbara and Gene Eakins
  1979   Verbal turn-taking and exchanges in faculty dialogue. In Dubois, Betty-Lou
          and Isabel Crouch (eds.), *The Sociology of the Languages of American Women*.
          San Antonio, TX: Trinity University, 53–62.

Eckert, Penelope and Sally McConnell-Ginet
  1992   Think practically and act locally: Language and gender as community-based
          practice. *Annual Review of Anthropology* 21, 461–490.
  1995   Constructing meaning, constructing selves. Snapshots of language, gender,
          and class from Belten High. In Hall, Kira and Mary Bucholtz (eds.), *Gender
          Articulated*. New York: Routledge, 469–507.
  1999   New generalisations and explanations in language and gender research. *Lan-
          guage in Society* 28 (2), 185–203.
  2003   *Language and Gender*. Cambridge: Cambridge University Press.

Edelsky, Carol
  1981   Who's got the floor? *Language in Society* (10), 383–421.

Eelen, Gino
  1999   Politeness and ideology: A critical review. *Pragmatics* 9 (1), 163–173.
  2001   *A Critique of Politeness Theories*. Manchester: St. Jerome Publishing.

Ehlich, Konrad
  1992   On the historicity of politeness. In Watts, Richard J., Sachiko Ide and Kon-
          rad Ehlich (eds.), *Politeness in Language: Studies in its History, Theory and
          Practice*. Berlin: Mouton de Gruyter, 71–107.
  1993   HIAT: A transcription system for discourse data. In Edwards, Jane A. and Mar-
          tin D. Lampert (eds.), *Talking Data. Transcription and Coding in Discourse
          Research*. Hillsdale, NJ: Lawrence Erlbaum Associates, 123–148.

Emmet, Dorothy
  1953-4 The concept of power. *Proceedings of the Aristotelian Society, New Series*
          LIV: 1–26.

Ervin-Tripp, Susan, Kei Nakamura and Jiansheng Guo
  1995   Shifting face from Asia to Europe. In Shibatani, Masayoshi and Sandra Thomp-
          son (eds.), *Essays in Semantics and Pragmatics*. Amsterdam: John Benjamins,
          43–71.

Escandell-Vidal, Victoria
  1996   Towards a cognitive approach to politeness. *Language Sciences* 18 (3–4),
          629–650.

Eysenck, Michael W. and Mark T. Keane
  2000   *Cognitive Psychology: A Student's Handbook* (4th ed.). Hillsdale, N.Jersey:
          Lawrence Erlbaum.

Fairclough, Norman
  1989   *Language and Power*. London: Longman.
  1992   *Discourse and Social Change*. Cambridge: Polity Press.

Fernández García, Francisco
2000   *Estrategas del Diálogo: La Interacción Comunicativa en el Discurso Político-Electoral.* Granada: Método Ediciones.

Foucault, Michel
1972   *The Archeology of Knowledge.* London: Routledge.
1980   *Power/Knowledge: Selected Interviews and Other Writings 1972–77.* Brighton: Harvester.

Fraser, Bruce
1975   Warning and threatening. *Centrum* 3 (2), 169–180.
1990   Perspectives on politeness. *Journal of Pragmatics* 14 (2), 219–236.
1998   Threatening revisited. *Forensic Linguistic* 5 (2), 159–173.
1999   Whither politeness? Paper presented at The International Symposium on Linguistic Politeness, Chulalongkhorn University, Bangkok, Thailand.
2006   Whither politeness? In Lakoff, Robin and Sachiko Ide (eds.), *Broadening the Horizon of Linguistic Politeness.* Amsterdam/Philadelphia: John Benjamins, 65–83.

Fraser, Bruce and William Nolen
1981   The association of deference with linguistic form. *International Journal of the Sociology of Language* 27 (2), 93–109.

Freed, Alice
1996   Language and gender in an experimental setting. In Bergvall, Victoria, Janet Bing and Alice Freed (eds.), *Rethinking Language and Gender Research: Theory and Practice.* New York: Longman, 54–76.

French, John R. P. and Bertram Raven
1959   The bases of social power. In Cartwright, Dorwin (ed.), *Studies in Social Power.* Ann Arbor: University of Michigan Press, 150–167.

Fukushima, Saeko
2000   *Requests and Culture: Politeness in British English and Japanese.* Bern: Peter Lang.

Gafaranga, Joseph and Maria-Carme Torras
2002   Interactional otherness: Towards a redefinition of code-switching. *International Journal of Bilingualism* 6 (1), 1–22.

Galasinski, Dariusz
1998   Strategies of talking to each other: Rule breaking in Polish presidential debates. *Journal of Language and Social Psychology* 17 (2), 165–182.

García Bedolla, Lisa
2003   The identity paradox: Latino language, politics and selective dissociation. *Latino Studies* 1 (2), 264–283.

García-Pastor, Maria D.
2002   Face aggravation, mitigation, and unofficial power in a political campaign debate. In Walton, David and Dagmar Scheu (eds.), *Culture and Power*. Bern: Peter Lang, 347–367.
2006   *A Socio-Cognitive Approach to Political Interaction: An Analysis of Candidates' Discourses in U.S. Political Campaign Debates.* Unpublished PhD, University of Valencia, Valencia, Spain.

García-Pastor, Maria D. and Vicente Sanjosé
in prep. Latent semantic analysis and the semantic representation of politeness in political interaction.

Gardner-Chloros, Penelope and Katerina Finnis
2003   How code-switching mediates politeness: Gender-related speech among London Greek-Cypriots. *Estudios de Sociolinguistica* 4 (2), 505–532.

Gibbs, Raymond W.
1999   *Intentions in the Experience of Meaning.* Cambridge: Cambridge University Press.

Gibson, James
1982   Notes on affordances. In Reed, Edward and Rebecca Jones (eds.), *Reasons for Realism*. Hillsdale, NJ: Lawrence Erlbaum, 403–406.

Goffman, Erving
1955   On face work: An analysis of ritual elements in social interaction. *Psychiatry* 18, 213–231.
1967   *Interaction Ritual: Essays on Face-to-face Behavior.* Garden City, NY: Anchor Books.
1971   *Relations in Public. Microstudies of the Public Order.* London: Penguin.
1981   *Forms of Talk.* Philadelphia: University of Pennsylvania Press.

Goodwin, Charles and Marjorie Harness Goodwin
1990   Interstitial argument. In Grimshaw, Allen D. (ed.), *Conflict Talk. Sociolinguistic Investigations of Arguments in Conversations*. Cambridge: Cambridge University Press, 85–117.

Gottman, John M.
1994   *What Predicts Divorce? The Relationship between Marital Processes and Marital Outcomes.* Hillsdale, NJ: Lawrence Erlbaum Associates.

Graham, Sage
2003   *Cooperation, Conflict and Community in Computer-Mediated Communication.* Unpublished PhD, Georgetown University, Washington, D.C., USA.
2005   A cyber-parish: Gendered identity construction in an online episcopal community. In Jule, Allyson (ed.), *Gender and the Language of Religion*. Basingstoke, U.K.: Palgrave Macmillan, 133–150.

Greatbatch, David
1986   Aspects of topical organization in news interviews: The use of agenda-shifting procedures by interviewees. *Media, Culture and Society* 8 (4), 441–455.

Gregori-Signes, Carmen
1998   *Telling It All: A Genre-based Approach to the Analysis of the American Tabloid Talkshow.* Unpublished PhD, University of Valencia, Spain, Valencia.
2000a   *A Genre Based Approach to Daytime Talk on Television, SELL Monographs 1.* Valencia: Universitat de València.
2000b   The tabloid talkshow as a quasi-conversational type of face-to-face interaction. *Pragmatics* 10 (2), 195–213.
2005   Descortesía en el discurso televisivo de los dibujos animados: La serie South Park. In Carrió-Pastor, María L. (ed.), *Perspectivas Interdisciplinares de la Lingüística Aplicada. Vol. 2.* Valencia: Universitat Politècnica de València, 117–126.

Grice, Herbert Paul
1969   Utterer's meaning and intentions. *The Philosophical Review* 78, 147–177.
1975   Logic and conversation. In Cole, Peter and Jerry Morgan (eds.), *Syntax and Semantics. Vol. III: Speech Acts.* New York: Academic Press, 41–58.
1989a   Reprint. Logic and conversation. In H. P. Grice, *Studies in the Way of Words.* Cambridge, MA: Harvard University Press, 22–40.
1989b   Reprint. Utterer's meaning and intentions. In H. P. Grice, *Studies in the Way of Words.* Cambridge, MA: Harvard University Press, 86–116.

Grimshaw, Allen D. (ed.)
1990   *Conflict Talk. Sociolinguistic Investigations of Arguments in Conversations.* Cambridge: Cambridge University Press.

Gruber, Helmut
1998   Disagreeing: Sequential placement and internal structure of disagreements in conflict episodes. *Text* 18 (4), 467–503.

Gu, Yuego
1990   Politeness phenomena in Modern Chinese. *Journal of Pragmatics* 14 (2), 237–257.

Halford, Sue and Pauline Leonard
2001   *Gender, Power and Organisations: An Introduction.* Basingstoke: Palgrave.

Halliday, M. A. K
1978   *Language as a Social Semiotic: The Social Interpretation of Language and Meaning.* London: Edward Arnold.

Harris, Sandra
1984a   The form and function of threats in court. *Language and Communication* 4 (4), 247–271.
1984b   Questions as a mode of control in magistrates' courts. *International Journal of Sociology of Language* 49, 5–27.

1995   Pragmatics and power. *Journal of Pragmatics* 23 (2), 117–135.
2001   Being politically impolite: Extending politeness theory to adversarial political discourse. *Discourse and Society* 12 (4), 451–472.
2003   Politeness and power: Making and responding to "requests" in institutional settings. *Text* 23 (1), 27–52.
2005   Review of *Power and Politeness in Action: Disagreements in Oral Communication. Journal of Politeness Research* 1 (1), 165–169.
2007   Politeness and power. In Llamas, Carmen, Louise Mullany and Peter Stockwell (eds.), *The Routledge Companion to Sociolinguistics*. London: Routledge, 122–129.

Harris, Sandra, Karen Grainger and Louise Mullany
2006   The pragmatics of political apologies. *Discourse and Society* 17 (6), 715–737.

Haugh, Michael
2003   Anticipated versus inferred politeness. *Multilingua* 22 (4), 397–413.

Heritage, John and David Greatbatch
1991   On the institutional character of institutional talk: The case of news interviews. In Boden, Deirdre and Don H. Zimmerman (eds.), *Talk and Social Structure. Studies in Ethnomethodology and Conversation Analysis*. Berkeley: University of California Press, 93–137.

Hickey, Leo
1991   Surprise, surprise, but do so politely. *Journal of Pragmatics* 15 (4), 367–372.

Hickey, Leo and Miranda Stewart (eds.)
2005   *Politeness in Europe*. Clevedon, Buffalo: Multilingual Matters.

Holmes, Janet
1984   Modifying illocutionary force. *Journal of Pragmatics* 8 (3), 345–365.
1995   *Women, Men and Politeness*. New York: Longman.
2000   Women at work: Analysing women's talk in New Zealand. *Australian Review of Applied Linguistics* 22 (2), 1–17.
2006   *Gendered Talk at Work*. Oxford: Blackwell.

Holmes, Janet and Meredith Marra
2002a   Having a laugh at work: How humour contributes to workplace culture. *Journal of Pragmatics* 34 (12), 1683–1710.
2002b   Over the edge? Subversive humour between colleagues and friends. *Humor* 15 (1), 65–87.
2004   Relational practice in the workplace: Women's talk or gendered discourse? *Language in Society* 33, 377–398.

Holmes, Janet and Stephanie Schnurr
2005   Politeness, humor and gender in the workplace: Negotiating norms and identifying contestation. *Journal of Politeness Research* 1 (1), 121–149.

Holmes, Janet and Maria Stubbe
2003a   "Feminine" workplaces: Stereotype and reality. In Holmes, Janet and Miriam Meyerhoff (eds.), *The Handbook of Language and Gender*. London: Blackwell, 573–599.
2003b   *Power and Politeness in the Workplace. A Sociolinguistic Analysis of Talk at Work*. London: Longman.

Holtgraves, Thomas
1986   Language structure in social interaction: Perceptions of direct and indirect speech acts and interactants who use them. *Journal of Personality and Social Psychology* 51 (2), 305–314.

Holtgraves, Thomas and Joong-Nam Yang
1990   Politeness as universal: Cross-cultural perceptions of request strategies and inferences based on their use. *Journal of Personality and Social Psychology* 59 (4), 719–729.

Hunter, John E. and Franklin J. Boster
1987   A model of compliance-gaining message selection. *Communication Monographs* 54 (1), 63–84.

Husserl, Edmund
1900   *Logical Investigations. Reprint.* 1970. (J. N. Findlay, Trans.). London: Routledge and Kegan Paul.

Hutchby, Ian
1997   Building alignments in public TV debate: A case study from British TV. *Text* 17 (2), 161–179.

Ide, Sachiko
1989   Formal forms and discernment: Two neglected aspects of universals of linguistic politeness. *Multilingua* 8 (2/3), 223–248.

Jacob, Pierre
2003   *Intentionality*, [Stanford Encyclopedia of Philosophy]. Available at: http://plato.stanford.edu/entries/intentionality/ [2006, 14 November].

Jaworski, Adam and Dariusz Galasinski
2000   Unilateral norm breaking in a presidential debate: Lech Walêsa versus Aleksander Kwaœniewski. *Research on Language and Social Interaction* 33 (3), 321–345.

Jørgensen, J. Normann
1998   Children's acquisition of code-switching for power wielding. In Auer, Peter (ed.), *Code-switching in Conversation: Linguistic Perspectives on Bilingualism*. London: Routledge, 237–258.

Jucker, Andreas H.
1986   *News Interviews: A Pragmalinguistic Analysis*. Amsterdam: Benjamins.
2005   Mass media. In Östman, Jan-Ola, Jef Verschueren and Eline Versluys (eds.), *Handbook of Pragmatics 2003–2005*. Amsterdam: Benjamins, 1–18.

Kasper, Gabriele
1990   Linguistic politeness: Current research issues. *Journal of Pragmatics* 14 (2), 193–218.

Kasper, Gabriele and Merete Dahl
1991   Research methods in interlanguage pragmatics. *Studies in Second Language Acquisition* 13 (2), 215–247.

Kasper, Gabriele and Kenneth R. Rose
2002   *Pragmatic Development in a Second Language.* Oxford: Blackwell.

Kellermann, Kathy and B. Christine Shea
1996   Threats, suggestions, hints, and promises: Gaining compliance efficiently and politely. *Communication Quarterly* 44 (2), 145–165.

Kienpointner, Manfred
1997   Varieties of rudeness: Types and functions of impolite utterances. *Functions of Language* 4 (2), 251–287.

Kochman, Thomas
1984   The politics of politeness: Social warrants in mainstream American public etiquette. In Schiffrin, Deborah (ed.), *Georgetown University Round Table on Languages and Linguistics 1984.* Washington, D.C.: Georgetown University Press, 200–209.

Koike, Dale April
1994   Negation in Spanish and English suggestions and requests: Mitigating effects? *Journal of Pragmatics* 21 (5), 513–526.

Kotthoff, Helga
1993   Disagreement and concession in disputes: On the context sensitivity of preference structures. *Language in Society* 22 (2), 193–216.

Kryk-Kastovsky, Barbara
2006   Impoliteness in Early Modern English courtroom discourse. Special issues of historical courtroom discourse. *Journal of Historical Pragmatics* 7 (2), 213–243.

Kulick, Don
2003   No. *Language and Communication* 23 (2), 139–151.

Kumar, Ibha
2001   *Expressions of Politeness and Gratitude: A General Theory.* New Delhi: Munshirm Manoharlal.

Kytö, Merja and Terry Walker
2003   The linguistic study of Early Modern English speech-related texts: How "bad" can "bad" data be? *Journal of English Linguistics* 31 (3), 221–248.

Labov, William
1966   *The Social Stratification of English in New York City.* Washington, D.C.: Center for Applied Linguistics.

1972   *Language in the Inner City. Studies in the Black English Vernacular.* Oxford: Blackwill.

1984   Field methods of the project on linguistic change and variation. In Baugh, John and Joel Sherzer (eds.), *Language in Use: Readings in Sociolinguistics.* Englewood Cliffs, NJ: Prentice-Hall, 28–66.

Labov, William and David Fanshel

1977   *Therapeutic Discourse.* New York: Academic Press.

Lachenicht, Lance G.

1980   Aggravating language. A study of abusive and insulting language. *Papers in Linguistics: International Journal in Human Communication* 13 (4), 607–687.

Lakoff, Robin Tolmach

1973   The logic of politeness, or minding your p's and q's. *Chicago Linguistics Society* 9, 292–305.

1975   *Language and Woman's Place.* New York: Harper and Row.

1989   The limits of politeness: Therapeutic and courtroom discourse. *Multilingua* 8 (2–3), 101–129.

1990   *Talking Power: The Politics of Language.* New York: Basic Books.

2003   Language, gender and politics: Putting "women" and "power" in the same sentence. In Holmes, Janet and Miriam Meyerhoff (eds.), *The Handbook of Language and Gender.* Oxford: Blackwell, 161–178.

2006   Civility and its discontents: Or, getting in your face. In Lakoff, Robin and Sachiko Ide (eds.), *Broadening the Horizon of Linguistic Politeness.* Amsterdam/Philadel-phia: John Benjamins, 23–43.

Landsman, Stephen

1990   The rise of the contentious spirit: Adversary procedure in eighteenth-century England. *Cornell Law Review* 75, 498–609.

Langbein, John H.

1978   The criminal trial before the lawyers. *University of Chicago Law Review* 45, 263–316.

2003   *The Origins of the Adversary Criminal Trial.* Oxford: Oxford University Press.

Lave, Jean and Etienne Wenger

1991   *Situated Learning: Legitimate Peripheral Participation.* Cambridge: Cambridge University Press.

LeDoux, Joseph

1998   *The Emotional Brain: The Mysterious Underpinnings of Emotional Life.* New York: Simon and Schuster.

Leech, Geoffrey N.

1983   *Principles of Pragmatics.* New York: Longman.

2003   Towards an anatomy of politeness in communication. *International Journal of Pragmatics* 14, 101–123.

Lee-Wong, Song Mei
  2000   *Politeness and Face in Chinese Culture.* Bern: Peter Lang.

Leezenberg, Michiel
  2002   Power in communication: Implications for the semantics-pragmatics inter-
          face. *Journal of Pragmatics* 34 (7), 893–908.

Leichty, G. and J. L. Applegate
  1991   Social-cognitive and situational influences on the use of face-saving persua-
          sive strategies. *Human Communication Research* 17 (3), 451–484.

Levinson, Stephen C.
  1992   Activity types and language. In Drew, Paul and John Heritage (eds.), *Talk at
          Work. Interaction in Institutional Settings.* Cambridge: Cambridge University
          Press, 66–100.
  2000   *Presumptive Meanings: The Theory of Generalised Conversational Implica-
          ture.* Cambridge, MA: MIT Press.

Lim, Tae-Seop and John Waite Bowers
  1991   Facework. Solidarity, approbation and tact. *Human Communication Research*
          17 (3), 415–450.

Liu, Runquing
  1986   *A Dream of Red Mansions.* Unpublished MPhil dissertation, Lancaster Uni-
          versity.

Llamas, Carmen, Louise Mullany and Peter Stockwell (eds.)
  2007   *The Routledge Companion to Sociolinguistics.* London: Routledge.

Locher, Miriam A.
  2004   *Power and Politeness in Action: Disagreements in Oral Communication.*
          Berlin: Mouton de Gruyter.
  2006a   Polite behavior within relational work: The discursive approach to politeness.
          Multilingua 25 (3), 249–267.
  2006b   *Advice Online. Advice-giving in an American Internet Health Column.* Ams-
          terdam: John Benjamins.

Locher, Miriam A. and Richard J. Watts
  2005   Politeness theory and relational work. *Journal of Politeness Research* 1 (1),
          9–33.

Luchjenbroers, June
  1997   In your own words: Questions and answers in a Supreme Court trial. *Journal
          of Pragmatics* 27 (4), 477–503.

Mao, LuMing Robert
  1994   Beyond politeness theory: "Face" revisited and renewed. *Journal of Pragmat-
          ics* 21 (5), 451–486.

Marquez-Reiter, Rosina
2000   *Linguistic Politeness in Britain and Uruguay: A Contrastive Study of Requests and Apologies.* Amsterdam: John Benjamins.

Marra, Meredith
2007   Humour in workplace meetings: Challenging hierarchies. In Westwood, Robert and Carl Rhodes (eds.), *Humour, Organisation and Work.* Oxford and New York: Routledge, 139–157.

Marra, Meredith, Stephanie Schnurr and Janet Holmes
2006   Effective leadership in New Zealand workplaces. In Baxter, Judith (ed.), *Speaking Out: The Female Voice in Public Contexts.* Basingstoke: Palgrave, 240–260.

Martel, Myles
1983   *Political Campaign Debates: Images, Strategies and Tactics.* London: Longman.

Matsumoto, Yoshiko
1988   Reexamination of the universality of face: Politeness phenomena in Japanese. *Journal of Pragmatics* 12 (4), 403–426.

McElhinny, Bonnie
2003   Theorizing gender in sociolinguistics and linguistic anthropology. In Holmes, Janet and Miriam Meyerhoff (eds.), *The Handbook of Language and Gender.* Oxford: Blackwell, 21–42.

Mehan, Hugh
1990   Rules versus relationships in small claims disputes. In Grimshaw, Allen D. (ed.), *Conflict Talk: Sociolinguistic Investigations of Arguments and Conversations.* Cambridge: Cambridge University Press, 160–177.

Meier, Ardith J.
1995   Passages of politeness. *Journal of Pragmatics* 24 (4), 381–392.

Meyerhoff, Miriam
2002   Communities of practice. In Chambers, J. K., Peter Trudgill and Natalie Schilling-Estes (eds.), *Handbook of Language Variation and Change.* Oxford: Blackwell, 526–548.

Mills, Sara
1997   *Discourse.* London: Routledge.
2002   Rethinking politeness, impoliteness and gender identity. In Litosseliti, Lia and Jane Sunderland (eds.), *Gender Identity and Discourse Analysis.* Amsterdam: John Benjamins, 69–89.
2003   *Gender and Politeness.* Cambridge: Cambridge University Press.
2005   Gender and impoliteness. *Journal of Politeness Research* 1 (2), 263–280.

Milroy, Lesley and Matthew Gordon
2003   *Sociolinguistics: Method and Interpretation.* Oxford/Malden, MA: Blackwell.

Mühleisen, Susanne and Bettina Migge (eds.)
  2005   *Politeness and Face in Caribbean Creoles*. Amsterdam: John Benjamins.

Mullany, Louise
  2002   "I don't think you want me to get a word in edgeways do you John?" Re-
          assessing (im)politeness, language and gender in political broadcast inter-
          views. *Sheffield Hallam Working Papers* 3, 1–20. Available at: http://www.shu.
          ac.uk/wpw/politeness/mullany.htm
  2004   Gender, politeness and institutional power roles: Humour as a tactic to gain
          compliance in workplace business meetings. *Multilingua* 23 (1–2), 13–37.
  2006   "Girls on tour": Politeness, small talk and gender in managerial business
          meetings. *Journal of Politeness Research* 2 (1), 55–77.
  2007   *Gendered Discourse in the Professional Workplace*. Basingstoke: Palgrave.

Mumby, Dennis
  1988   *Communication and Power in Organizations: Discourse, Ideology and Dom-
          ination*. Norwood, NJ: Ablex.

Muntigl, Peter and William Turnbull
  1998   Conversational structure and facework in arguing. *Journal of Pragmatics* 29
          (3), 225–256.

Newton, Jonathan
  2004   Face-threatening talk on the factory floor: Using authentic workplace inter-
          actions in language teaching. *Prospect* 19 (1), 47–64.

Nicoloff, Franck
  1989   Threats and illocutions. *Journal of Pragmatics* 13 (4), 501–522.

Nwoye, Onuigbo G.
  1992   Linguistic politeness and socio-cultural variations of the notion of face. *Jour-
          nal of Pragmatics* 18 (4), 309–328.

O'Barr, William
  1982   *Linguistic Evidence: Language, Power, and Strategy in the Courtroom*. New
          York: Academic Press.

O'Driscoll, Jim
  1996   About face: A defence and elaboration of universal dualism. *Journal of Prag-
          matics* 25 (1), 1–32.

Olsson, Sue
  2000   Acknowledging the female archetype: Women managers' narratives of gender.
          Women in Management Review 5 (6), 396–302.

Olsson, Sue and Robin Walker
  2003   Through a gendered lens? Male and female executives' representations of one
          another. *Leadership and Organization Development* 24 (7), 387–396.

Ortony, Andrew, Donald Norman and William Revelle
2005   Affect and proto-affect in effective functioning. In Fellous, J. M. and Michael Arbib (eds.), *Who Needs Emotions: The Brain Meets the Machine.* New York: Oxford University Press, 173–202.

Oxford English Dictionary
1989   Online Second Edition. www.oed.com

Pan, Yuling
2000   *Politeness in Chinese Face-to-face Interaction. Advances in Discourse Processes.* Stamford, CT: Ablex.

Pearson, Christine M., Lynne M. Andersson and Judith W. Wegner
2001   When workers flout convention: A study of workplace incivility. *Human Relations* 54 (11), 1387–1419.

Penman, Robyn
1990   Facework and politeness: Multiple goals in courtroom discourse. In Tracy, Karen and Nikolas Coupland (eds.), *Multiple Goals in Discourse.* Clevedon: Multilingual Matters, 15–37.

Pérez de Ayala, Soledad
2001   FTA and Erskine May: Conflicting needs? Politeness in question time. *Journal of Pragmatics* 33 (2), 143–169.

Preston, Stephanie and Frans de Waal
2002   Empathy: Its ultimate and proximate bases. *Behavioral and Brain Sciences* 25 (1), 1–72.

Quinn, Naomi
2005   How to reconstruct schemas people share, from what they say. In Quinn, Naomi (ed.), *Finding Culture in Talk: A Collection of Methods.* New York: Palgrave Macmillan, 35–81.

Rhodes, Richard
1989   "We are going to go there": Positive politeness in Ojibwa. *Multilingua* 8 (2/3), 249–258.

Rudanko, Juhani
1995   The Bill of Rights in the balance: The debate of June 8, 1789. *Multilingua* 14 (4), 391–409.
2006   Aggravated impoliteness and two types of speaker intention in an episode in Shakespeare's Timon of Athens. *Journal of Pragmatics* 38 (6), 829–841.

Schiffrin, Deborah
1984   Jewish argument as sociability. *Language in Society* 13 (3), 311–335.

Schnurr, Stephanie, Meredith Marra and Janet Holmes
2007   Being (im)polite in New Zealand workplaces: Maori and Pakeha leaders. *Journal of Pragmatics* 39 (4), 712–729.

Schore, Allan
1994   *Affect Regulation and the Origin of the Self*. Hillsdale NJ: Lawrence Erlbaum Associates.

Searle, John
1969   *Speech Acts. An Essay in the Philosophy of Language*. Cambridge: Cambridge University Press.
1995   *The Construction of Social Reality*. New York: Free Press.
1996   Reprint. Indirect speech acts. In Martinich, A. P. (ed.), *The Philosophy of Language*. Oxford: Oxford University Press, 168–183. [originally appeared in Cole, Peter and Jerry Morgan (eds.), *Syntax and Semantics. Vol. III: Speech Acts*. New York: Academic Press, 59–82. [1975].]

Seckman, Mark and Carl Couch
1989   Jocularity, sarcasm, and relationships. *Journal of Contemporary Ethnography* 18 (3), 327–344.

Sell, Roger D.
1992   Literary texts and diachronic aspects of politeness. In Watts, Richard J., Sachiko Ide and Konrad Ehlich (eds.), *Politeness in Language: Studies in its History, Theory and Practice*. Berlin: Mouton de Gruyter, 109–129.

Semino, Elena and Jonathan Culpeper (eds.)
2002   *Cognitive Stylistics: Language and Cognition in Text Analysis*. Amsterdam: John Benjamins.

Shea, Virginia
1994   *Netiquette*. San Francisco, CA: Albion Books.

Shon, Phillip Chong Ho
1998   "Now you got a dead baby on your hands": Discursive tyranny in "Cop Talk". *International Journal for the Semiotics of Law* 11 (33), 275–301.
2003   Bringing the spoken words back in: Conversationalizing (postmodernizing) police-citizen encounter research. *Critical Criminology* 11 (2), 151–172.
2005   "I'd grab the S-O-B by his hair and yank him out the window": The fraternal order of warnings and threats in police-citizen encounters. *Discourse and Society* 16 (6), 829–845.

Sifianou, Maria
1992a   *Politeness Phenomena in England and Greece*. Oxford: Clarendon Press.
1992b   The use of diminutives in expressing politeness: Modern Greek versus English. *Journal of Pragmatics* 17 (2), 155–173.

Silverman, David
2000   *Doing Qualitative Research: A Practical Guide*. London: Sage.

Sinclair, John
1987   *Collins Cobuild English Language Dictionary*. London: Harper Collins Publishers.

2004   *Trust the Text: Language, Corpus, Discourse.* (Edited and selected by Ronald Carter). London: Routledge.

Smith, Anna DuVal
1999   Problems of conflict management in virtual communities. In Smith, Marc and Peter Kollock (eds.), *Communities in Cyberspace.* New York: Routledge, 134–166.

Spencer-Oatey, Helen
1992   *Cross-Cultural Politeness: British and Chinese Conceptions of the Tutor-Student Relationship.* Unpublished PhD, Lancaster University, Lancaster, UK.
1996   Reconsidering power and distance. *Journal of Pragmatics* 26 (1), 1–24.
2000a   *Culturally Speaking: Managing Rapport through Talk across Cultures.* London: Continuum.
2000b   Rapport management: A framework for analysis. In Spencer-Oatey, Helen (ed.), *Culturally Speaking: Managing Rapport through Talk across Cultures.* London: Continuum, 11–46.
2002   Managing rapport in talk: Using rapport sensitive incidents to explore the motivational concerns underlying the management of relations. *Journal of Pragmatics* 34 (5), 529–545.
2005   (Im)Politeness, face and perceptions of rapport: Unpackaging their bases and interrelationships. *Journal of Politeness Research* 1 (1), 95–119.

Sperber, Dan and Deirdre Wilson
1995   *Relevance. Communication and Cognition* (Second ed.). Oxford: Blackwell.

Stewart, Devin
1997   Impoliteness formulae: The cognate curse in Egyptian Arabic. *Journal of Semitic Studies* XLII (2), 327–360.

Storey, Kate
1995   The language of threats. *Forensic Linguistics* 2 (1), 74–80.

Sunderland, Jane
2004   *Gendered Discourses.* Basingstoke: Palgrave Macmillan.

Talbot, Mary
2003   Gender stereotypes: Reproduction and challenge. In Holmes, Janet and Miriam Meyerhoff (eds.), *The Handbook of Language and Gender.* Oxford: Blackwell, 468–486.

Tannen, Deborah
1981   New York Jewish conversational style. *International Journal of the Sociology of Language* 30, 133–149.
1987   Remarks on discourse and power. In Kedar, Leah (ed.), *Power through Discourse.* Norwood, NJ: Ablex Publishing Corporation, 3–10.

1990   Silence as conflict management in fiction and drama: Pinter's *Betrayal* and a short story "Great Wits". In Grimshaw, Allen D. (ed.), *Conflict Talk: Sociolinguistic Investigations of Arguments and Conversations*. Cambridge: Cambridge University Press, 260–279.

1993   What's in a frame?: Surface evidence for underlying expectations. In Tannen, Deborah (ed.), *Framing in Discourse*. Oxford: Oxford University Press, 14–56.

Terkourafi, Marina

2001   *Politeness in Cypriot Greek: A Frame-based Approach.* Unpublished PhD, University of Cambridge, Cambridge, UK.

2002   Politeness and formulaicity: Evidence from Cypriot Greek. *Journal of Greek Linguistics* 3, 179–201.

2003   Generalised and particularised implicatures of politeness. In Kühnlein, Peter, Hannes Rieser and Henk Zeevat (eds.), *Perspectives on Dialogue in the New Millennium*. Amsterdam: John Benjamins, 151–166.

2005a   Beyond the micro-level in politeness research. *Journal of Politeness Research* 1 (2), 237–262.

2005b   Identity and semantic change: Aspects of T/V usage in Cyprus. *Journal of Historical Pragmatics* 6 (2), 283–306.

2005c   Pragmatic correlates of frequency of use: The case for a notion of 'minimal context'. In Marmaridou, Sophia, Kiki Nikiforidou and Eleni Antonopoulou (eds.), *Reviewing Linguistic Thought: Converging Trends for the 21st Century*. Berlin: Mouton de Gruyter, 209–233.

2007a   Toward a universal notion of face for a universal notion of co-operation. In Kecskes, Istvan and Laurence Horn (eds.), *Explorations in Pragmatics: Linguistic, Cognitive and Intercultural Aspects*. Berlin: Mouton de Gruyter, 307–338.

2007b   On the interactional motivation for formulaicity. Paper presented at the Linguistics Symposium on Formulaic Language, University of Wisconsin at Milwaukee, USA.

        i.p.. On de-limiting context. In Bergs, Alexander and Gabriele Diewald (eds.), *Context in Construction Grammar,* Amsterdam: John Benjamins.

Theodoropoulou, Maria

2004   *On the Linguistic Path to Fear: Psyche and Language* [in Greek]. Athens: Nisos.

Thimm, Caja, Sabine Koch and Sabine Schey

2003   Communicating gendered professional identity: Competence, cooperation, and conflict in the workplace. In Holmes, Janet and Miriam Meyerhoff (eds.), *The Handbook of Language and Gender*. Oxford: Blackwell, 528–549.

Thomas, Jenny

1985   The language of power: Towards a dynamic pragmatics. *Journal of Pragmatics* 9 (6), 765–783.

1986   *The Dynamics of Discourse: A Pragmatic Approach to the Analysis of Confrontational Interaction.* Unpublished PhD, Lancaster University, Lancaster, UK.

1995   *Meaning in Interaction: An Introduction to Pragmatics.* London: Longman.

Thompson, John
1991   Editor's introduction. In *Bourdieu, Pierre. Language and Symbolic Power.* Cambridge: Polity Press, 1–34.

Thornborrow, Joanna
2002   *Power Talk: Language and Interaction in Institutional Discourse.* Harlow: Longman.

Tiisala, Seija
2004   Power and politeness: Languages and salutation formulas in correspondence between Sweden and the German Hanse. *Journal of Historical Pragmatics* 5 (2), 193–206.

Tomasello, Michael
1999   *The Cultural Origins of Human Cognition.* Cambridge, MA: Harvard University Press.

Tracy, Karen
1990   The many faces of facework. In Giles, Howard and Peter Robinson (eds.), *Handbook of Language and Social Psychology.* Chichester: Wiley, 209–226.

Tracy, Karen and Sarah J. Tracy
1998   Rudeness at 911: Reconceptualizing face and face attack. *Human Communication Research* 25 (2), 225–251.

Truss, Lynne
2005   *Talk to the Hand: The Utter Bloody Rudeness of Everyday Life (or Six Good Reasons to Stay Home and Bolt the Door).* London: Profile Books.

Turner, Ken
2003   Wx = D(S, H) + P(H, S) + Rx : (Notes towards an investigation). *Revue de Sémantique et Pragmatique* 13, 47–67.

UK Department of Health
2002   *Withholding Treatment from Violent and Abusive Patients in NHS Trusts.* Resource Guide. NHS, Department of Health: Crown Copyright.

Usami, Mayumi
2002   *Discourse Politeness in Japanese Conversation: Some Implications for a Universal Theory of Politeness.* Tokyo: Hituzi Syobo.

Valdés, Guadalupe
1981   Codeswitching as deliberate verbal strategy: a microanalysis of direct and indirect requests among bilingual speakers. In Durán, Richard (ed.), *Latino Language and Communicative Behavior.* Norwood, NJ: Ablex, 95–107.

van Dijk, Teun A.
1989   Structures of discourse and structures of power. *Communication Yearbook* 12, 18–59.
1996   Discourse, power and access. In Caldas-Coulthard, Carmen Rosa and Malcolm Coulthard (eds.), *Texts and Practices. Readings in Critical Discourse Analysis*. London: Routledge, 84–104.
1997   Discourse as interaction in society. In van Dijk, Teun A. (ed.), *Discourse as Social Interaction*. (Vol. 2). Thousand Oaks, CA: Sage Publications, 1–37.
2006   Discourse and manipulation. *Discourse and Society* 17 (3), 359–383.

Vinnicombe, Sue and Val Singh
2003   Locks and keys to the boardroom. *Women in Management Review* 18 (6), 325–333.

Vuchinich, Samuel
1990   The sequential organization of closing in verbal family conflict. In Grimshaw, Allen D. (ed.), *Conflict Talk. Sociolinguistic Investigations of Arguments in Conversations*. Cambridge: Cambridge University Press, 118–138.

Wajcman, Judy
1998   *Managing like a Man.* London: Sage.

Walker, Anne Graffam
1987   Linguistic manipulation, power, and the legal setting. In Kedar, Leah (ed.), *Power through Discourse*. Norwood, NJ: Ablex Publishing Corporation, 57–82.

Wartenberg, Thomas E.
1990   *The Forms of Power. From Domination to Transformation.* Philadelphia: Temple University Press.

Watts, Richard J.
1989   Relevance and relational work: Linguistic politeness as politic behavior. *Multilingua* 8 (2–3), 131–166.
1991   *Power in Family Discourse.* Berlin: Mouton de Gruyter.
1992   Linguistic politeness and politic verbal behaviour: Reconsidering claims for universality. In Watts, Richard J., Sachiko Ide and Konrad Ehlich (eds.), *Politeness in Language: Studies in its History, Theory and Practice*. Berlin: Mouton de Gruyter, 43–69.
2003   *Politeness.* Cambridge: Cambridge University Press.
2005   Linguistic politeness research. *Quo vadis?* In Watts, Richard J., Sachiko Ide and Konrad Ehlich (eds.), *Politeness in Language: Studies in its History, Theory and Practice.* (2nd revised and expanded edition). Berlin: Mouton, xi–xlvii.
2006   Impoliteness as an aspect of relational work. Paper presented at the Linguistic impoliteness and rudeness: Confrontation and conflict in discourse, University of Huddersfield, UK.

Watts, Richard J. and Tony Bex (eds.)
1999   *Standard English: The Widening Debate*. London: Routledge.

Watts, Richard J., Sachiko Ide and Konrad Ehlich (eds.)
1992   *Politeness in Language: Studies in its History, Theory and Practice*. Berlin: Mouton de Gruyter.
2005   *Politeness in Language: Studies in its History, Theory and Practice* (2nd revised and expanded edition). Berlin: Mouton.

Watts, Richard J., Sachiko Ide and Konrad Ehlich
1992   Introduction. In Watts, Richard J., Sachiko Ide and Konrad Ehlich (eds.), *Politeness in Language: Studies in its History, Theory and Practice*. Berlin: Mouton de Gruyter, 1–17.

Watts, Richard J. and Peter Trudgill (eds.)
2002   *Alternative Histories of English*. London and New York: Routledge.

Watzlawick, Paul, Janet Helmick Beavin and Don D. Jackson
1967   *Pragmatics of Human Communication. A Study of Interactional Patterns, Pathologies and Paradoxes*. New York: Norton.

Wei, Li
1995   Code-switching, preference marking and politeness in bilingual cross-generational talk: Examples from a Chinese community in Britain. *Journal of Multilingual and Multicultural Development* 16 (3), 197–214.
2002   'What do you want me to say?': On the conversation analysis approach to bilingual interaction. *Language in Society* 31, 159–180.

Wenger, Etienne
1998   *Communities of Practice: Learning, Meaning, and Identity*. Cambridge: Cambridge University Press.

Werkhofer, Konrad T.
1992   Traditional and modern views: The social constitution and the power of politeness. In Watts, Richard J., Sachiko Ide and Konrad Ehlich (eds.), *Politeness in Language: Studies in its History, Theory and Practice*. Berlin: Mouton de Gruyter, 155–197.

Whitaker, Gordon P.
1982   What is patrol work? *Police Studies* 4 (4), 13–22.

Wichmann, Anne
2004   The intonation of please-requests: a corpus-based study. *Journal of Pragmatics* 36 (9), 1521–1549.

Wolfson, Nessa
1976   Speech events and natural speech: Some implications for sociolinguistic methodology. *Language in Society* 5 (2), 188–209.

Woodbury, Hanni
1984   The strategic use of questions in court. *Semiotica* 48 (2/4), 197–228.

Wray, Alison
    2002   Dual processing in protolanguage: Performance without competence. In Wray, Alison (ed.), *The Transition to Language*. Oxford: Oxford University Press, 113–137.

Xie, Chaoqun
    2003   A critique of politeness theories: Review of Gino Eelen. *Journal of Pragmatics* 35 (5), 811–818.

Youmans, Madeleine
    2006   *Chicano-Anglo Conversations: Truth, Honesty, and Politeness*. Mahwah, NJ: Lawrence Erlbaum Associates.

Younge, Gary, John Henley
    2003   Wimps, weasels and monkeys – the US media view of 'perfidious France'. *The Guardian*. Available at: http://www.guardian.co.uk/france/story/ 0,,893202,00.html, 11th February.

Zentella, Ana Celia
    1994   The 'chiquitafication' of U.S. Latinos and their languages, or why we need an anthropolitical linguistics. In Ide, Risako, Rebecca Parker and Yukako Sunaoshi (eds.), *Proceedings of the Third Annual Symposium About Language and Society-Austin, Texas Linguistic Forum 36*. Austin, Texas: Texas Linguistic Forum, 1–18.

Zupnik, Yael-Janette
    1994   A pragmatic analysis of the use of person deixis in political discourse. *Journal of Pragmatics* 21 (4), 339–383.

Contributors

DAWN ARCHER is Head of English language and linguistics at the University of Central Lancashire, UK. Her historical courtroom research seeks to bring together historical linguistics, corpus linguistics, (socio-)pragmatics and legal history. An executive board member of the Association of Literary and Linguistic Computing (ALLC), she is especially interested in developing manual and automatic annotation systems to help researchers exploit historical texts using corpus linguistic techniques. Her recent monograph, *Questions and Answers in the English Courtroom (1640–1760)*, made use of two such annotation schemes (see Archer and Culpeper 2003 and Archer 2005 for further detail).

DEREK BOUSFIELD is a lecturer in English Language and Linguistics at the University of Central Lancashire, UK. His main research interests are in pragmatics, stylistics, context, and linguistic approaches to conflict and conflict resolution. He has recently completed a monograph entitled *Impoliteness in Interaction*, published by John Benjamins in the Pragmatics and Beyond (New) Series. He is a member of the International Pragmatics Association (IPrA), the Linguistic Politeness Research Group (LPRG) and the Poetics and Linguistics Association (PALA). He co-founded (with Lesley Jeffries and Dan McIntyre) the Stylistics Research Centre at The University of Huddersfield in 2006.

HOLLY CASHMAN is an Assistant Professor of Spanish Linguistics at Arizona State University, USA. Her research examines the language practices of bilingual Chicanas/Chicanos and Latinas/Latinos in Phoenix, Arizona communities of practice, including code-switching, relational work, and the construction and negotiation of social and interactional identities in conversation. She has published articles recently in the *Journal of Pragmatics,* the *Journal of Multilingual and Multicultural Development*, and the *Journal of Politeness Research*, as well as contributed chapters to *Research on Politeness in the Spanish Speaking World* (María Elena Placencia and Carmen García, eds.) and *Blackwell Guide to Research Methods in Bilingualism* (Li Wei and Melissa Moyer, eds.). She received her Ph.D. from the University of Michigan in 2001.

JONATHAN CULPEPER is a senior lecturer in the Department of Linguistics and English Language at Lancaster University, UK. His work spans pragmatics, stylistics and the history of English, and his major publications include *History of English* (2nd edition, 2005), *Cognitive Stylistics* (2002, edited with Elena Semino), *Exploring the Language of Drama* (1998, co-edited with Mick Short and Peter Verdonk) and *Language and Characterisation in Plays and Other*

Texts (2001). He is currently working on a three-year research project on the topic of impoliteness.

MARÍA DOLORES GARCÍA-PASTOR has a PhD and M.A. in English Linguistics (University of Valencia), and an M.A. in Communication Studies (University of Iowa, USA). She is a lecturer in the Department of Language and Literature Teaching at the School of Education 'Ausiàs March' in the University of Valencia, Spain. Her main research interests are within politeness theory, political communication, ethnography of speaking, and applied linguistics. She is currently working on a monograph on political campaign debates.

SAGE LAMBERT GRAHAM, PhD, is an Assistant Professor of Linguistics in the Department of English at the University of Memphis in Memphis, Tennessee, USA. Using language as an analytical lens, her research explores causes of misunderstanding and conflict in computer-mediated communication, patterns of identity construction through language choices, and discourse analysis of professional communicative practices in medical and social work settings. She has published articles on the topic of gendered language use in religious contexts and politeness in computer-mediated communities of practice.

JANET HOLMES is Director of the Language in the Workplace Project and holds a personal Chair in Linguistics at Victoria University of Wellington, New Zealand, where she teaches a variety of sociolinguistics courses. She has published on a wide range of topics including New Zealand English, language and gender, and various aspects of workplace discourse. Her recent books include *Power and Politeness in the Workplace* co-authored with Maria Stubbe, and *Gendered Talk at Work*.

HOLGER LIMBERG is a Research Associate and Assistant Lecturer for English Linguistics at the Carl von Ossietzky University in Oldenburg, Germany. He has been working in Oldenburg since 2004 after graduating from the University of Münster. His research interests include spoken academic discourse as well as aspects of linguistic politeness and impoliteness in social interaction. He is currently working on his PhD thesis about Office Hour Interactions at University.

MIRIAM LOCHER's work has been in the field of linguistic politeness and the exercise of power in oral communication ('Power and Politeness in Action: Disagreements in Oral Communication', Mouton de Gruyter, 2004) and advice-giving in an American Internet advice column (2006, John Benjamins). She holds a Lizentiat ('MA') from the University of Zurich and a PhD and Habilitation from the University of Berne. Currently, she is working in the English Department of the University of Berne, Switzerland.

MEREDITH MARRA is Research Fellow for Victoria University's Language in the Workplace Project and a lecturer in sociolinguistics within the School of Linguistics and Applied Language Studies, Victoria University of Wellington, New Zealand. Meredith's primary research interest is the language of meetings (including her PhD research which investigated the language of decision making in business meetings), but she has also published in the areas of humour and gender in workplace interactions.

LOUISE MULLANY is Lecturer in Applied Linguistics in the School of English Studies at the University of Nottingham, UK. Her research interests are in the fields of sociolinguistics and pragmatics, primarily focusing on language and gender in business, media and medical settings. Her most recent publications include the monograph *Gendered Discourse in the Professional Workplace* (2007) and the *Routledge Companion to Sociolinguistics* (2007), co-edited with Carmen Llamas and Peter Stockwell. She has also published in a range of international journals and edited collections on the topics of language and gender, professional discourse and politeness.

STEPHANIE SCHNURR has completed her PhD at Victoria University of Wellington, New Zealand. She now works as Assistant Professor at the University of Hong Kong. As a member of the Language in the Workplace Project, her main research interests are the sociolinguistic performance of leadership and gender at work, and in particular the multiple functions and strategic uses of humour in workplace discourse.

MARINA TERKOURAFI is Assistant Professor of Linguistics at the University of Illinois, Urbana-Champaign, USA. She has held post-doctoral positions at the British School at Athens and at the Computer Laboratory, University of Cambridge, and taught at the Universities of Cambridge, Cyprus, and Athens. Her research interests include pragmatic theory, sociolinguistics, cognitive linguistics, and the history and use of the Cypriot dialect. In her PhD thesis (Cambridge, 2002), she proposed a frame-based approach to politeness drawing on a large corpus of spontaneous Cypriot Greek conversations. Currently, she is developing that approach investigating the theoretical underpinnings of face and their ramifications for linguistic behaviour, as well as the implications of this approach for grammar.

RICHARD J. WATTS is Professor of English Linguistics at the University of Berne in multilingual Switzerland. His work has been in the field of linguistic politeness, pragmatics and the sociolinguistics of English. His previous publications include *Power in Family Discourse* (Mouton de Gruyter, 1991), *Standard English: The Widening Debate* (with Tony Bex, Routledge, 1999), *Alternative His-*

tories of English (with Peter Trudgill, Routledge, 2002), *Politeness in Language* (with Sachiko Ide and Konrad Ehlich, Mouton de Gruyter, 1992, 2005), and *Politeness* (Cambridge University Press, 2003).

Contact information

Dawn Elizabeth Archer
Head of English Language and Linguistics, Department of Humanities,
University of Central Lancashire, Preston, Lancashire, PR1 2HE, UK,
Email: dearcher@uclan.ac.uk

Derek Bousfield
Department of Humanities, University of Central Lancashire, Preston,
Lancashire, PR1 2HE, United Kingdom, Email: debousfield@uclan.ac.uk

Holly Cashman
Dept. of Languages & Literatures, PO Box 870202, Arizona State University,
Tempe, AZ 85287–0202, USA, Email: holly.cashman@asu.edu

Jonathan Culpeper
Department of Linguistics and English Language, Bowland College, Lancaster
University, Lancaster LA1 4YT, U.K., Email: j.culpeper@lancaster.ac.uk

María Dolores García-Pastor
Dept. of Language and Literature Teaching (English section), School of
Education 'Ausiàs March', University of Valencia, C/Alcalde Reig 8, 46006
Valencia, Spain, Email: maria.d.garcia@uv.es

Sage Lambert Graham
Assistant Professor of Linguistics, Department of English, University of
Memphis, Memphis, TN 38152, Email: sgraham2@memphis.edu

Janet Holmes
School of Linguistics and Applied Language Studies, Victoria University of
Wellington, P.O. Box 600, Wellington, New Zealand,
Email: Janet.Holmes@vuw.ac.nz

Holger Limberg
Carl von Ossietzky University Oldenburg, Fak. III, Seminar für Anglistik,
Ammerländer Heerstr. 114–118, D-26129 Oldenburg, Germany,
Email: h.limberg@uni-oldenburg.de

Miriam Locher
Department of English Languages and Literatures, University of Berne,
Länggass Str. 49, 3000 Bern 9, Switzerland, Email: locher@ens.unibe.ch

Meredith Marra
School of Linguistics and Applied Language Studies, Victoria University of
Wellington, New Zealand, Email: meredith.marra@vuw.ac.nz

Louise Mullany
Lecturer in Applied Linguistics, School of English Studies, University of
Nottingham, Nottingham, NG7 2RD, UK,
Email: louise.mullany@nottingham.ac.uk

Stephanie Schnurr
School of English, The University of Hong Kong, Pokfulam Road, Hong
Kong, China, Email: sschnurr@hkucc.hku.hk

Marina Terkourafi
Department of Linguistics, University of Illinois at Urbana-Champaign, 4080
Foreign Language Building, 707 S Mathews Avenue, MC-168, Urbana, IL
61801, Email: mt217@uiuc.edu

Richard J. Watts
Department of English Languages and Literatures, University of Berne,
Länggass Str. 49, 3000 Bern 9, Switzerland, Email: watts@ens.unibe.ch

Author index

Subject index